BA

SCHOOL OF ORIENTAL AND AFRICAN STUDIES
UNIVERSITY OF LONDON

Jordan Lectures in Comparative Religion

IX

The Louis H. Jordan Bequest

The will of the Rev. Louis H. Jordan provided that the greater part of his estate should be paid over to the School of Oriental and African Studies to be employed for the furtherance of studies in Comparative Religion, to which his life had been devoted. Part of the funds which thus became available was to be used for the endowment of a Louis H. Jordan Lectureship in Comparative Religion. The lecturer is required to deliver a course of six or eight lectures for subsequent publication. The first series of lectures was delivered in 1951.

JORDAN LECTURES 1969

Viṣṇuism and Śivaism

A Comparison

by

J. GONDA

Professor of Sanskrit, University of Utrecht

UNIVERSITY OF LONDON
THE ATHLONE PRESS
1970

Published by
THE ATHLONE PRESS
UNIVERSITY OF LONDON
at 2 Gower Street London WC1

Distributed by Tiptree Book Services Ltd
Tiptree Essex

Australia and New Zealand
Melbourne University Press

U.S.A.
Oxford University Press Inc
New York

0 485 17409 x

Printed in Great Britain by
WILLIAM CLOWES AND SONS LTD
LONDON AND BECCLES

PREFACE

THESE LECTURES were written in 1967 and 1968 and delivered, in an abridged form, in June 1969. My intention was to collect, in a small compass, some material illustrating the characters and interrelations of the great Hindu gods Viṣṇu and Śiva and to establish a comparison between their religions. The field surveyed is, however, so vast and our sources are so copious and manifold that inevitably many aspects are only briefly treated or even completely omitted.

It gives me great pleasure to express my gratitude to the Governing Body of the School of Oriental and African Studies who invited me to write this book for publication in this series and to Mr L. A. van Daalen and Miss Y. B. W. Van Reck for supplying it with an index.

April 1970 J. G.

CONTENTS

I

The Character of Viṣṇu and Rudra-Śiva in the Veda and the Mahābhārata

ONE OF THE ARGUMENTS which could be adduced in favour of the usual division of Indian culture into an older period, Vedism, and a later period, called Hinduism, would be that the former, at least at first sight, presents itself as a unity, whereas the latter is a varied and, already in the Mahābhārata, a confused spectacle of beliefs and practices. On closer inspection it becomes clear however, first that many features of Hinduism have their roots in the Vedic past, and in the second place that it has been a few main currents which, from the very beginning up to the present day, have come into prominence and have largely determined the character of that many-sided and all-enfolding culture which we in the West have chosen to call Hinduism. There can be no doubt whatever that these currents must, when viewed from their doctrinal and philosophical aspects be considered first and foremost soteriologies, and that they also present many aspects which make them worth studying from the angles of philosophy and sociology. This does not however prevent us from calling Viṣṇuism and Śivaism as they presented, and still present, themselves to their adherents, religions. It will, in this series of lectures, be my endeavour to institute a comparison between these two Indian religions, Śivaism and Viṣṇuism. That is not to say that I shall overlook the fact that neither current is in itself a unity. There is, within Viṣṇuism, a considerable difference between, for instance, the theories and the ritualism of the Vaikhānasas in the South and the devotionalism of the followers of Caitanya in Bengal, and Vīraśaivism, flourishing in Karṇāṭaka, has rejected the traditional brahmanical rites which the Śaiva-Siddhānta has, in many respects, retained. Nevertheless, there is a Śivaism and there is a Viṣṇuism and it will be part of my task—while comparing these religions and drawing attention to parallel or divergent developments, to the common heritage and interrelations—to bring out what is common to all forms of each of the two great religious currents.

Considering myself absolved from the obligation to give a regular account of the main relevant facts such as those relating to the history of Viṣṇu and Śiva worship from the earliest times, the mythological concepts to which their figures have given rise, their iconography in plastic arts and the philosophical and theological doctrines developed in the communities of their worshippers,[1] I would like to make an attempt at instituting, in a series of more or less condensed studies, a somewhat detailed comparison between those aspects of both religious currents which in the last years have attracted my special attention. Since it cannot even be my purpose to treat all important questions or to deal adequately with all periods of the religious history of India, I intend to dwell especially upon some significant points which have perhaps not been sufficiently stressed in the publications of my predecessors. I hope that a certain personal preference for definite problems and definite periods or phases in the development of Śaivism and Vaiṣṇavism will not be beyond forgiveness.

It may be true that in our oldest document, the Ṛgveda, Viṣṇu occupies but a subordinate position, his personality—to use this term in this connection—is at the same time not only more important there than would appear from the number of the occurrences of his name in this text, but is also in its striking features sufficiently clean-cut and, moreover, in remarkable harmony with the god's image as given by the later sources.[2] Rudra also has from the very beginning a character and even a position of his own[3] and some important features in the later Śiva can likewise be said to emerge from the Vedic texts with all clearness desirable.

It is therefore interesting to compare the most important traits of character of both gods as far as they appear from the Vedic *saṃhitās*.[4] It has long ago been observed[5] that the only anthropomorphic traits of Viṣṇu are his often-mentioned three strides and his being a youth (ṚV. 1, 155, 6). These essential features of his character, to which he owes epithets such as 'swift' and 'wide-striding', make him known to us as the immense (ṚV. 7, 99, 1; 2) god of far-extending motion who—for man in distress, to make his existence possible[6]—penetrates and traverses the spaces, whereas his highest step or abode is beyond mortal ken, in his dear and highest resort, the bright realm of heaven. While all beings dwell in these three strides or footsteps (ṚV. 1, 154, 2), the highest is the place of a well of honey, where rejoice the gods and those men who turn to the gods. Of Rudra, the terrible, dreadful one, on the other hand, quite a number of physical features are recorded: arms, hand, limbs, lip, eyes, mouth, tongue, etc.; he wears braided hair (1, 114, 1; 5), his colour is brown (e.g. 2, 33, 5), his belly black and his back red.[7] Frequent mention is made of his weapons, and these are weapons of offence. On Viṣṇu's disk and club the oldest texts are, however, silent. Rudra is clothed in a skin[8] and haunts and dwells in mountains, an abode also attributed to Viṣṇu. But while the passage *VS.* 16, 2–4 in which this feature is emphasized tries to induce Śiva to show his auspicious aspect and to prevent him from injuring men, and while forests, mountains and wilderness are the sphere of his destructive activities, Viṣṇu's association with the mountains, where he is said to have been born and of which he is the ruler, impresses us as beneficial to human interests:[9] the defeat of Vṛta is, for instance, repeatedly said to have taken place in the mountains, which, however, seem to be an element of the scenery of the 'Urzeit'.

Viṣṇu is benevolent, never inimical (ṚV. 1, 186, 10), and a friend and ally of Indra whom he assists in slaying the great fiend and antagonist Vṛtra, the representative of chaos, and in spreading out the spaces between heaven and earth (ṚV. 6, 69, 5). Both gods are sometimes so intimately associated as to form a sort of dual deity, Indrāviṣṇū, and to participate in each other's qualities and activities. Rudra, on the other hand, has no special friend among the gods. Only once he appears associated with Soma (ṚV. 6, 74), not directly because of his formidable nature[10] but because he is supposed to be able to avert illness, destruction and other manifestations of evil. And he enjoys this reputation owing to his dreadful power of sending and causing fever, evil and disaster, to his fierceness, malevolence and destructiveness. However much the poets try to deprecate his wrath—impending also when there is no offence—they do not hesitate to mention his bad points: he is a cheat, deceiver and lord of robbers, and most statements of his power occur in appeals for mercy.

Their relation to the demoniac powers and the Maruts is in this connection of special interest. Wheras Viṣṇu is engaged in vanquishing the demons, Rudra does not come into conflict with them. As to the not-individualized group of the Maruts, as Indra's brilliant allies and attendants they enter into association with Viṣṇu, but Rudra, who is repeatedly said to be their father, is never drawn into the warlike activities of these deities who, though occasionally showing the malevolent traits of their father, are on the whole benefactors of man and world. Rudra is, on the contrary, the chief of an indefinite host of partial manifestations of his own nature which, like this god (in the singular) himself may make their numinous presence felt everywhere and at any time. He moreover maintains intimate relations with the great mass of demoniac beings. In this connection it is interesting to notice also that, whereas Viṣṇu—although he may assume various forms[11]—is so to say one single individual, Rudra has in these ancient texts some doubles, which are sometimes identical with him—thus Śarva and Bhava in *VS.* 16, 18; 28—sometimes are described as distinct from him.

There is one god with whom both Rudra (e.g. AV. 7, 87, 1) and Viṣṇu (e.g. ṚV. 2, 1, 3) are identified. But here also the difference is obvious. Rudra is said to be, i.e. to manifest himself in, or as, fire:[12] 'Agni is Rudra; just as a tiger stands in anger, so he also (stands)' (*TS.* 5, 5, 7, 4)—Viṣṇu's relations with the god of fire are co-operative and complementary in nature: they are for instance invoked conjointly and both of them are, in a brāhmaṇa, it is true (*AiB.* 1, 4, 10), lords and guardians of the consecration, which they confer on man. Besides, Agni is the sacrificial fire and Viṣṇu the sacrifice (*TS.* 2, 29, 1), and both gods rejoice in the sacrificial butter (AV. 7, 29).

Extending our inquiries to the later parts of Vedic literature we see that Rudra's malevolence is still more prominent. He houses in forests and jungles, in places where man falls a victim to fright and terror. He is the lord of the wild animals, which are said to be a manifestation of his cruel nature (*ŚB.* 12, 7, 3, 20), and the patron of those who hold aloof from the Aryan society and its way of living. In contradistinction to the other gods who are believed to live in the East, Rudra dwells in the North, the region of dangerous mountains. His isolated position is emphasized by the myth according to which he remained behind when the other gods succeeded in attaining heaven by ritual means (*ŚB.* 1, 7, 3, 1). He is indeed excluded from the normal soma cult, but receives informal balis (offerings of food thrown on the ground), often also the remainders of oblations, or what is injured in the sacrifice (*ŚB.* 1, 7, 4, 9); besides, he has some sacrificial rites of his own. His cult requires precaution and he is appeased (ṚV. 2, 33, 5, etc.), that is to say one gives him offerings in order to get rid of him. The benevolent or rather merciful aspects of his ambivalent nature find on the other hand expression in some epithets such as Śambhu 'the beneficent or kind one' and Śiva: (*VS.* 3, 59; 63) 'Śiva is thy name; thou art a healing medicine, forbear to do me harm'. This epithet—which is already given to him at ṚV. 10, 92, 9—is however also applied to other gods, without being peculiar to any particular figure.

With regard to Viṣṇu it is important to notice that in the brāhmaṇas his relations with the sacrifice are evident and of special practical consequence for the Vedic worshipper: he is the sacrifice itself (e.g. *ŚB.* 14, 1, 1, 6) and the sacrificer who imitates his great cosmic act, by which he obtained for the gods the ability to manifest their power everywhere, viz. his three strides, gains, whilst identifying himself with the god, the three provinces of the universe to attain heaven (*ŚB.* 1, 9, 3, 9 f.; 15).

I shall not repeat here what has in many books and articles been said on the so-called original character of these gods, or rather what has a bearing on the kernel of the Rudra and Viṣṇu conceptions. Let it suffice to say that in my opinion the essence of the former was, in the minds of Vedic men, the power of the uncultivated and unconquered, dangerous, unreliable, unpredictable, hence much to be feared nature, experienced as a divinity. His very character lent itself admirably to splitting up into partial manifestations as well as to assimilation of divine or demoniac powers of cognate nature, were they Aryan or non-Aryan. It hardly needs saying that the class poetry of the Ṛgveda does not show us the whole Rudra and that the later Veda has recorded more popular traits; the conclusion that those features which are foreign to the earliest corpus did not exist at the time of its compilation is, I am convinced, inadmissible.[13]

The solution of the much debated and often wrongly posed question as to the so-called origin of the Viṣṇu conception—we had better inquire after the core and essence of the god's nature as understood by Vedic man—has very often on too onesidedly naturalistic lines of argument been supposed to lie in an interpretation as a solar deity. Yāska (*Nir.* 12, 19) cited already an authority who identified the god's striding with the diurnal course of the sun. I must confess that in the course of time my own ideas of this question have considerably evolved. Although I am still inclined to assume that there is much truth in the time-honoured interpretation of the god's character as representing pervasiveness and spatial extensiveness, and especially that pervasiveness which is essential to the establishment and maintenance of our cosmos and beneficial to the interests of men and gods, I would now hesitate to add that 'the general idea originally underlying this central mythical act seems to have been the eternal phenomenon of the pervading and omnipresent, mighty and blessing stream of celestial light, warmth, and energy'.[14] At the moment I would lay greater emphasis upon the pervasiveness as such which was believed to manifest itself in a great variety of phenomena and on the god's relations to the *axis mundi*.[15]

This is not to say that I am convinced by that interpretation of the function and significance of the god which was some years ago proposed by my esteemed colleague and compatriot Kuiper,[16] who, focussing his readers' attention almost exclusively on the Ṛgveda there to find the truest image of the god's character and on his supposedly principal cosmogonic significance, regards him as the ambiguous mythological figure which, occuping the central place in the cosmic classificatory system and thus standing between the two parties of the Vṛtra-fight, nevertheless turned the scale in favour of Indra. It is true that Viṣṇu is closely associated with the *dhruvā dik*—which is not the nadir, but the fixed or central quarter, that is the central place on the earth under the zenith[17]—but one does not see in the texts that the relation between Indra in the South (AV. 3, 27, 2),[18] Varuṇa, the great asura—who however plays no part in the Vṛtra combat—in the West and Viṣṇu in the centre[19] is developed into a coherent system or has any significance in Indra's great cosmogonic achievement and the ensuing organisation of our cosmos. I am rather inclined to suppose that Viṣṇu's undeniable relations with the centre may be interpreted otherwise. Although I am[20] disposed to admit that the centre represents 'the totality of the parts distributed over the four quarters', I do not think that this is its full import. We now know that from the point of view of archaic religions this centre or navel (ὀμφαλός)[21] is the place in which the *axis mundi*, the central pillar or frame of creation,[22] reaches the earth, putting the cosmic levels into communication and constituting a means of 'travelling to' heaven as well as a canal through which the heavenly blessings may penetrate into the abode of men. Viṣṇu may even be considered as representing this cosmic pillar[23] itself: he is for instance (ṚV. 7, 99, 2) explicitly said to sustain the upper component of the universe, a well-known function of that pillar. His vertical pervasiveness is moreover illustrated by the fact that the *yūpa*—the sacrificial post which in definite rites is mounted by the sacrificer to reach heaven[24] and which may be considered a representative of this axis[25]—belongs to him and that he lives in the mountains,[26] another manifestation of the axis[27] and a place where heaven and earth meet.[28]

Nor is it clear to me why Viṣṇu should be the 'unity of the two antagonistic parties, upper world and nether world',[29] standing in, and being of each of these two worlds, and belonging consequently also to the gods of the nether world,[30] whom he could not fight, as Indra did, 'because'—I quote Kuiper—'these two were part of his essence'. But even the Ṛgveda describes him as destroying demons (7, 99, 4 f.)[31] and states (1, 155, 6) that Viṣṇu goes to war, that accompanied by Indra he forces open the cattle-shed of Vala, the mythological duplicate of Vṛtra[32] (1, 156, 4).[33] As far as I am able to see there is no textual evidence of Viṣṇu's arising from the nether world and subsequent standing on the mountain or mountains.[34] I would rather say that Vedic man considered him to be present in any part of the cosmic axis: his is, at the lower end, the *yūpa*, and the brahmans constantly identify him with the sacrifice which is located in the navel of the earth;[35] at the upper end is his high domain or 'protectorate';[36] as the god of three seats (*triṣadhastha*: 1, 156, 5) he manifests himself also in the middle.[37] Hence also, I would suppose, Viṣṇu's relations—sometimes even matrimonial relations—with Aditi,[38] whose womb he protects;[39] this womb, which is explicitly identified with the navel of the earth (*VS.* 1, 11), but which is more than that, namely the 'place of universal creation', because Aditi—whose name in all probability means 'Freedom'—manifests her nature not only in the earth but in any broad and wide expanse in the generative and life-sustaining nature, in any expansion of phenomenal life. Viṣṇu on the other hand, far from being a static representative of the axis, creates, while striding widely and traversing the universe, the room, which is indispensable to that expansion.[40]

If it be permitted to prolong this digression for a moment, I would repeat that I am unable to read in the texts that Viṣṇu rose up from the nether world to which he originally belonged at the very moment when the dual world was, by Indra's great achievement, created.[41] It is Indra who called on his companion and associate[42] for co-operation, asking him to stride, for him, Indra, over a great distance,[43] or as the Bṛhaddevatā (6, 122 f.) has it: 'Going to Viṣṇu Indra said: "I wish to slay Vṛtra. Stride forth to-day and stand at my side. Heaven must make room for my outstretched bolt." Saying "Yes", Viṣṇu did so....' So Viṣṇu's activity[44] preceded Indra's fight with Vṛtra[45] which in its turn made the organization of our world possible.

It is also in this connection that mention is (ṚV. 8, 12, 27) made of *three* strides, the well-known and obviously most important feature in Viṣṇu's traversing movement. From the Ṛgvedic references to this activity it does not however emerge that the first step, or only the first step, was taken in the nether world or corresponds to it. On the contrary, the poets do not omit stating that Viṣṇu has taken his strides from the same place as the Maruts who exert their influence in the higher atmosphere (ṚV. 5, 87, 4) and from that place from which the gods are expected to promote man's interests (1, 22, 16)[46]. Although the poets do not indeed lay much stress on the exact places where the steps were taken, they are quite explicit in describing them as establishing the broad dimensional actuality of the earthly space,[47] or in stating that the god strode out on the earth (AV. 12, 1, 10). There is no doubt much truth in the explication of the number three as expressing the idea of totality and therefore referring to the expansion of the whole earth or even of the whole universe,[48] but it is very doubtful whether the relevant texts may be supposed to point to an ascending movement of the god.[49] Yet one of the poets (ṚV. 7, 99, 1) makes a distinction between 'both terrestrial spaces' of the god known to men—which has been rightly explained as earth and atmosphere[50]—and the highest, of which Viṣṇu himself has knowledge. The texts do not say that the third step represents all three movements,[51] they state that there is a highest step, station or abode of Viṣṇu—the term *padam* admits of all these translations—which[52] may be seen for ever by the successful sacrificers (ṚV. 1, 22, 20), and is also called his dear domain or protectorate; there is a spring of honey, i.e. the draught of immortality (1, 154, 5) and there is the god's *bandhu*, which means that the god who is active in the universe is closely and mysteriously connected with that 'place', which is practically 'heaven'.[53] There is nothing to prevent us from assuming that there is the 'place beyond space' (7, 100, 5),[54] where the god is said to reside.

As is well known there has been a tendency, even since the oldest Yajurvedic texts and the pre-Yāska interpreters of the Ṛgveda, to connect Viṣṇu's strides with the triple division of the universe (sky or heaven, earth and what is between them). It is however doubtful whether this interpretation can be called a merely naturalistic one. And it may, on the other hand, be true that the poets of the Ṛgveda, in connection with these strides, never refer to this triple division,[55] it is dangerous to rely on the *argumentum e silentio* and to isolate the Ṛgveda too much from the other Vedic literature. We should moreover always be aware of the fact that the Ṛgveda is first and foremost a religious document[56] and that the cosmographic and cosmogonic details contained in it are not represented with a view to describe the universe or to explain its origin in a scientific or philosophical way.[57] What was relevant was to know if the Great Pervader has really pervaded the *whole* universe in which he is worshipped and if men also were safe in these three steps (*VS*. 23, 49 f.; cf. ṚV. 1, 154, 2), that is, in this world, as it was relevant to know for certain that out of the primordial chaos Indra—I do not mention other gods whose names are sometimes recorded in this connection—with Viṣṇu's help produced and organized this cosmos.[58] This fact must always be commemorated and celebrated because thus man substantially contributes to the maintenance, renewal and reproduction of the creation of this god[59] who always remains, *hic et nunc*, an active promoter of positive values and beneficial processes in this world.[60]

In a similar way Viṣṇu's activity for the welfare of gods and men is celebrated in the hope that he will continue to create safety and room to live in for the latter[61] and to win *vikrānti*,[62] i.e. the power to display their beneficent activities for the former. Moreover, as the traversing and pervading god *par excellence* Viṣṇu does not only make room for man's sacrifice to reach the powers of heaven (ṚV. 7, 99, 4),[63] but also helps the sacrificer (1, 156, 5), brings him wealth and other valuables[64] and conducts him along undangerous paths to a state of safety (6, 69, 1; 8, 77, 10).[65] He is also often allied with that important power of life which circulates in the universe, is the main element of the sacrifice and imparts divine life, that is to say, with the soma.[66] He is therefore on the one hand implored to fill his hands from the sky, the earth and the vast wide atmosphere, and to bestow objects of value from the right and from the left (AV. 7, 26, 8)[67]—his traversing movement was no doubt supposed to expand also on the horizontal plane[68]—and on the other expected to lead, as the sacrifice—or simply as the traverser—, man upwards so as to rescue him from all evil.[69] For last but not least Viṣṇu is the god who acquired for the sacrificer that all-pervading power which is characteristic of his own nature: by ritually imitating the god's strides the sacrificer gains the earth, the aerial expanse, and heaven, to reach 'the goal, the safe foundation (*pratiṣṭhā*), the highest light'.[70] The sacrificer, duly consecrated and taking these strides, *is* Viṣṇu[71] and the strides lead him to the highest goal.[72] Although in this connection these three strides may impress us as symbolizing an analysis for ritual purposes of the totality expressed by the three strides,[73] they are in my opinion not exactly coordinated with the three parts of the visible universe, because the third stride does not lead to the firmament, but into heaven.[74] That that highest step or place is also described as being extended like the eye in heaven (ṚV. 1, 22, 20)[75] is of course no counter-argument.[76]

As far as I can see now, the power complex experienced by Vedic man as the presence and the activity of a divine personality called Viṣṇu may, to sum up, best be described as the 'idea' of universal penetration or pervasiveness, as the axis mundi and otherwise, of the omnipresence of a mighty and beneficent energy, in which all beings abide and which essentially contributes to the maintenance of those conditions and those processes in the universe on which man's life and subsistence depend. Among these are also the processes connected with fertility and procreation which I have not stressed in the foregoing.[77]

Let us continue our exposition of the main facts relating to the development of both divine figures in the following centuries.

As to Rudra the tendency to adopt this outsider by emphasizing his benevolent aspects and putting him on a par with other gods continues. Already in the Ṛgveda a deprecation, a request not to send disease but to approach kindly, may combine with the expression of his sovereign might, which enables him to come into contact with the race of the celestial powers (ṚV. 7, 46, 2). Whilst, in the Pravargya ritual, the formula 'Hail to Rudra' is, even without offering, pronounced, 'lest the god should do harm' (*ŚB*. 14, 2, 2, 38), in the ritual of the royal consecration Rudra Paśupati is beside Agni Gṛhapati, Soma Vanaspati, Bṛhaspati Vāk, Mitra Satya, etc., one of the recipients of oblations (*ŚB*. 5, 3, 3, 1 ff.).[78] The frequent appeal to him for help in case of disease —of which he may be the originator[79]—may have contributed much to his gaining access, as the god who grants remedies, to a circle of honourable deities who preside over other spheres of human interest: one must, for instance, sacrifice to Agni, the despoiler, if one finds a forest-fire in one's way; to Pūṣan, the pathmaker, if one is to undertake a journey; to Rudra, if there is a multitude of diseases, etc.[80] In the morning litany he should (according to the Śāṅkhāyana-Śrautasūtra, 6, 3, 4) be addressed, together with Soma, as the regent of the North, on an equal footing with Mitra and Varuṇa, the regents of the West, Indra and Bṛhaspati and other powers who are besought to grant their protection in the other regions of the universe. Moreover, as the leader of a host of minor deities Rudra is, according to the

Śatapatha-Brāhmaṇa, to be considered a chief, *kṣatraḥ*.[81] In some important brāhmaṇas[82] his figure indeed appears to have acquired special importance and a reality different from that of many other members of the pantheon. Later on, the author of the Bṛhadāraṇyaka-Upaniṣad (1, 4, 11) regards him as one of the *kṣatrāḥ* among the gods, his colleagues being Indra, Varuṇa, Soma, Parjanya, Yama, Mṛtyu and Iśāna.[83] These gods, it is said, represent *kṣatram*, ruling power, which is called "an excellent manifestation'. Elsewhere in the same text Parjanya, Āditya and Indra admit him as a partner (2, 2, 2).[84] An important factor in the process of Rudra's growth—which should not however be one-sidedly emphasized[85]—is his identification with the mighty god of fire, Agni,[86] and which may, in a sense, point to a process analogous to Viṣṇu's appropriating part of the greatness of Indra.[87] In a later upaniṣad (*PrU.* 2, 9) the god is together with Indra, Sūrya and other gods said to be an aspect of the universal life or vital power,[88] the most essential of all powers, on which everything is firmly established (2, 6), whereas another upaniṣadic author, discussing the nature of the Ātman—that is the Supreme universal Soul, identical with Brahman, of which every intelligent being is a partial individuation—equates him with a considerable number of divine powers, among whom are not only Indra and Savitar, but also Īśāna, Bhava and Śambhu—aspects or partial manifestations of Rudra's nature—Prajāpati, Viṣṇu and Nārāyaṇa (*MaiU.* 6, 8; 7, 7). Meanwhile this development had culminated in those particular circles which produced the Śvetāśvatara-Upaniṣad. This work will claim our special attention in the next lecture.

At the same period, in which Rudra-Śiva was gradually reaching the supreme rank, the Viṣṇu of our texts had likewise been advanced to a higher position. His relations, or community of interests, with Prajāpati,[89] which date already from Ṛgvedic times, are intensified. Whereas the oldest upaniṣads added nothing important to his history, those of the second period which possibly were, roughly speaking, compiled about the same time as the Bhagavadgītā[90] or somewhat later, begin to recognize him as a supreme monotheistic God. In the Maitrāyaṇīya-Upaniṣad he is not only one of the chief 'bodies' of Prajāpati or a manifestation of that one overlord who is the totality (*sarvaḥ kaścit prabhuḥ*), but is also called the Supreme Light, which is unmoving, free from death, unwavering and stable, pure griefless bliss.[91] One place is of special interest, because it contains a stanza which with slight variation occurs also in the Bṛhadāraṇyaka:[92]: 'The face of the True-and-Real is covered with a golden vessel; uncover it, O Pūṣan, in order to see him whose (that of which the) normal behaviour-and-observance is the True-and-Real.' Instead of the last words (*satyadharmāya dṛṣṭaye*) the Maitrāyaṇīya reads *satyadharmāya viṣṇave* which must mean 'in order to (establish contact with) Viṣṇu whose normal and fundamental conduct consists in being the True-and-Real'. Satyadharman, in the Ṛgveda an epithet of Agni, Varuṇa, Savitar, is, in the Mahābhārata, among the thousand names of Viṣṇu.[93] Nevertheless it is quite true that many phases in the long process of Viṣṇu's rise to the highest position have completely disappeared from our sight.[94] That his ancient functions, known to us from a regrettably limited number of references in the saṃhitās, have, in their totality and as a whole, contributed much to this process seems indisputable.

There would be little sense in repeating what may be read in every History of Hinduism on these gods as they present themselves to us in the epic period. Suffice it to say that both Viṣṇu and Śiva are, in the epics, ambiguous figures, being on the one hand deities with heroic traits of character and, on the other, rising to supramundane dignity, representing or tending to represent the Supreme Being. Not rarely it is not at all clear whether they are to be regarded as devas or as the supreme God,[95] whether, for instance, Śiva's protection is to be sought because he is the boon-giving Lord, the omnipresent soul and creator of the universe and the embodiment of its three divisions or because he is the great *deva* of frightful aspects who has now also become a conqueror of demoniac power.[96] Both gods are now endowed with all divine qualities imaginable and have become the central characters in mythical tales which will enthral the minds of many generations to come. Both are adored by other gods, Viṣṇu also by his fellow Ādityas of whom he is the youngest and in accordance with the well-known 'youngest-smartest' motif of mythical tales also the greatest.[97] Neither of them had however, in the last centuries before and the first centuries after the beginning of our era, ascended to the zenith of his power and dignity. Leaving Kṛṣṇa and the other doubles of his personality out of consideration Viṣṇu plays, in his own name, a less important part in the epics than his rival who—although mention is still, but rarely, made of a distinct deity Rudra—is now almost generally known as Śiva, notwithstanding, it is true, his 'doubles' or partial manifestations continue to be distinguished: 'To Paśupati, to Śiva, to Śaṃkara.'[98]

Both of them retain striking features which they possessed already in the Vedic past,[99] but absorb, as supramundane figures, other divine beings. Those who adore the Sun are for instance said actually to worship Śiva[100] and Viṣṇu has now taken over Indra's task[101] to fight demons and perform heroic deeds. Becoming the typical fighter for the gods it is he who after recovering the *amṛta* from the *asuras* defeated them with his discus.[102] The idea of *avatāras*—incarnations in order to rehabilitate the world—is in course of development,[103] but his benevolence is rarely in doubt and he essentially remains actively interested in the welfare and prosperity of man and the world. Śiva, uncanny, wrathful and incalculable,[104] not rarely terrible, fierce and impetuous, famous for his preponderantly destructive energy,[105] is still a much-feared author of mischief. That certain circles continued to regard him as an outsider standing apart from the other gods may appear from the popular story of Dakṣa's sacrifice.[106] But he is an ambivalent god: the early epic recognizes him as an ascetic, rapt in the contemplation of his own unfathomable being, who, though performing terrific austerities, is also often willing to grant boons and to confer favours upon his worshippers.[107] His phallic aspect, attesting to his ability for unlimited production, which archaeological finds show us to have existed already in the Ist century B.C.,[108] is not unknown to the Mahābhārata.[109] In the Rāmāyaṇa references to his divine power and greatness are not wanting, but most of these occur in similes referring to his destructive activities in battle, etc.; in any case they do not indicate that he was regarded as supreme. In short Viṣṇu is, generally speaking, a friend nearer to man, Śiva a lord and master, ambivalent and many-sided.[110]

The Indians were always inclined to father religious, philosophical or sociological doctrine upon superhuman authorities. In the great epic it is not only Kṛṣṇa who himself preaches his religion and soteriology, but also Viṣṇu who, appearing, after a sacrifice, in the form of Indra, expounded the *dharma* of the kṣatriyas,[111] resolving the doubts of the kings about the application of the *daṇḍanīti*. Śivaite parallels are not wanting: Śiva is described as promulgating the Pāśupata doctrine and the science of *daṇḍanīti*, the administration of justice.[112]

Part of the events narrated in connection with these gods is to explain epithets or traits of their character and these tales are of special interest because—though as a rule etymologically or historically wrong—they are a welcome source of information on the beliefs and convictions of those who invented and divulged them. Thus Śiva is also called Nīlakaṇṭha because he swallowed the poison *kālakūṭa*, or, according to a variant tale explaining the colour of his neck, Śitikaṇṭha because Nārāyaṇa seized him by the throat which became dark.[113] Part of these explanations actually are reinterpretations: thus his name Sthāṇu—which characterizes him as the motionless one and is often connected with his ascetic performances[114]—is also attributed to his ithyphallic character,[115] and his name Tryambaka to his love for three goddesses, viz. the sky, the waters and the earth.[116]

The names and epithets attributed to these two figures are indeed especially instructive. We may, to begin with, distinguish between those names which are of more or less frequent occurrence and those which are only rarely given to them. As to the former category it strikes us that only a few names of a very general character and applicable to any divine being of rank are given to both figures: Aja 'the unborn One, i.e. the Eternal'; Ananta 'the infinite One'; the untranslatable[117] Bhagavat; Devaśreṣṭha 'the best of the gods'; Īśāna 'the Lord' (mostly, it is true, of Śiva); Maheśvara 'the great Lord'; Yogeśvara; Satya, i.e. he who is and acts in conformity with the true and real.[118] To those other names which are really distinctive belong in the first place some that are old and traditional: Bhava, Paśupati, Rudra, Śaṅkara, Śarva in the case of Śiva, Hari, and Vaikuṇṭha[119] in the case of Viṣṇu, and for the most part these originally belonged to doubles or *Teilwesenheiten* of the gods or to manifestations of divine power[120] which in the course of time came to fuse with them. In Śiva's case some pre-epic (originally adjectival) names reveal to us[121] various aspects of his nature; Ugra 'the Powerful'; Bhīma 'the Formidable'; Hara 'the Seizer', but also Mīḍhvas 'the Bountiful'. Interestingly enough, authorities observe that names such as Brahman, Paramātman and Bhagavan, when applied to Viṣṇu, do not refer to three persons but to one divine person in different aspects.[122] Other names are indicative of their relations with other gods: thus Viṣṇu is Indrānuja 'Indra's younger brother', Śiva Bhūtapati 'the lord of divine and demoniac beings of lower rank'; of their outward appearance: Śiva, the ascetic, wears matted locks, braided or tufted hair and is therefore called Jaṭila, Kapardin, Śikhin; is naked: Digvāsas or clad in skins: Kṛttivāsas; he has three eyes: Tryakṣa. Viṣṇu has four arms: Caturbhuja; is lotus-eyed: Padmalocana and from his navel he produces the lotus from which arose the creator Brahmā:[123] Padmanābha. The names may be related to their weapons or attributes: Śiva is armed with the trident or his peculiar weapon called *pināka*, hence his being Śūlabhṛt, Śūlapāṇi, etc., Pinākin, etc. (also Dhanvin 'the one with the bow'), Viṣṇu with the discus: Cakrapāṇi, etc. Śiva is also, and frequently, Vṛṣabhadhvaja 'the one who has a bull on his banner' or Vṛṣabhavāhana 'the one who has a bull as his vehicle', or Nandīśvara 'the master of the bull Nandin', Viṣṇu however is only once called Garuḍadhvaja. Part of their names are connected with their deeds or achievements, thus Śiva is the destroyer of Tripura, the triple city of the *asuras*, and hence called Tripuraghna etc., and Viṣṇu is known as Janārdana, because, an epic poet says (*Mbh.* 5, 68, 6), he strikes terror into the demons, or as the killer of Madhu: Madhuhan. Śiva is also called after the divine woman with whom he now has entered into a regular alliance: Umāpati, Gaurīśa, and Viṣṇu is in his epithets variously associated with Śrī. Interestingly enough Viṣṇu, not Śiva is, in the great epic, known as Acintya 'the Inconceivable', Anādi 'the Eternal', Vibhu 'the one whose might and sovereignty extend far and pervade all', a term applied in the Muṇḍaka-Upaniṣad (1, 1, 6) to the imperishable source of all existence, the substantive *vibhūti* coming into use for Viṣṇu's divine and universal power and dignity, and as Acyuta which characterizes him as the Inmovable and Unwavering One.[124] Śiva is on the other hand often known as the great god or lord: Mahādeva, Maheśvara, and, incidentally, Mahāghora, Mahākarman, etc., etc., although epic authors give these names sometimes also to Viṣṇu-Kṛṣṇa.

A well-known literary and liturgical form of praise, adoration and magnification of a god consists in pronouncing his names and epithets. This is at the same time a device for meditatively identifying oneself with aspects of the god's nature; Viṣṇu is even supposed to grant final emancipation to him who mentally recites his names.[125] Shorter or longer enumerations are found already in the Veda. The names may, as in the Vedic Śatarudrīya hymn,[126] be embedded in prayers, homage and references to the god's might, or consist, like the largely stereotyped *sahasranāmastotras* of Hinduism,[127] of a sort of general description of the god's character or of a mere enumeration of names and epithets.[128] In many circles this 'prayer of names' came to be one of the most characteristic expressions of devotion, its mental recitation being an excellent protective against evil which however easily degenerated into verbal magic.[129] What strikes us in these enumerations of 'a thousand[130] names' is that both gods have only a comparatively small number—about eighty[131]—of epithets and surnames in common. Some of these belong to well-known ancient deities who are equated to the two representatives of the Highest (Vāyu, Yama, Dhātar), or are ancient epithets of other exalted beings (Sahasrākṣa 'with a thousand eyes'), some are divine titles of a more general character expressing aspects of divinity or superiority (Ananta, Ugra, Bhānu, Bhāvana, Śānta, Śreṣṭha, Kāla, Daṇḍa, Dhruva, Guru, Gopati, Guha, Gambhīra, Sarva, Sthira, Sthavira, Varada, Bhū, Bhūtātman, Mārga, Kṣobhaṇa, and of course Deva, Prabhu, Īśāna, Īśvara); there is a honorific epithet such as Sumukha 'fair-faced' or a philosophical term such as Karaṇa 'the one who causes'; both gods are sometimes equated with brahman, and elsewhere Viṣṇu bears the names Rudra, Śarva and Śiva, which traditionally belong to his colleague, a point worth investigating in full detail. The other names, those which are exclusively given to one god, help us again to understand the ideas fostered by the worshippers and the qualities attributed by them to the object of their adoration. Thus the number of negated nouns assigned in the great epic to Viṣṇu exceeds that used in connection with Śiva; as the privative prefix often serves to emphasize the idea opposite to that expressed by the second member of the compound[132] the former god was obviously believed to be firm and reliable (Acala 'immovable'), happy and one who causes happiness (Aśoka 'free from sorrow' and so a resort for those who are unhappy), humble and modest (Amānin). Other names do not fail to inspire trust and confidence: he is a physician (Bhiṣaj), and medicine (Bheṣaja).[133]

Thus it is not surprising that Aśvatthāman in order to obtain Śiva's aid in entering the camp of the enemy does not find difficulty in combining, in his prayer, a series of typically Śivaite names and epithets with a selected variety of appropriate references to the god's readiness to grant boons, to his protective and destructive power and irresistibility as well as to his ability to assume many forms—the god will indeed manifest himself—and his being the chief of large hosts of minor deities who in fact are not long in appearing.[134] Yudhiṣṭhira, on the other hand, whilst extolling in a hymn of adoration Viṣṇu-Kṛṣṇa as the author of his success, the recovery of his kingdom—which he ascribes to the god's grace, prudence and force, intelligence and pervasive energy—addresses him not only appositely as 'destroyer of enemies' or Jiṣṇu 'the victorious one', but also as Puruṣa, the True-and-Real (Satya), the universal sovereign (Vibhu Samrāj), and he does not forget to add a considerable number of the god's traditional epithets and to identify him with powerful deities and important concepts with whom he, the origin and dissolution of the universe, in the course of time has become intimately allied.[135]

We must confine ourselves to these instances and to the remark that this nomenclature could suggest the headings under which to arrange the data relative to the gods' nature and deeds. Not only the epics but, to mention only these, also the works of the great classical authors admit of the conclusion that the names and attributes which are preferentially assigned to these gods bring out the main aspects of their powerful and venerable character.[136] The great diversity of names and epithets was a welcome means of throwing light, in a particular context, on some one or other side of a god's activity or of voicing the feelings or conceptions of the authors with regard to his character. The preference of particular Śaiva or Vaiṣṇava schools or communities for one of the many names of their god—for instance, of the Paśupati-Śaivas for Paśupati, reinterpreted as 'Lord of the (cattle-like) souls', and of many Vaiṣṇavas for Hari,—is as illustrative of important trends of Indian religious life as the aversion of, for instance, exclusive Vaiṣṇavas to using the most representative name, Śiva, of their God's rival.

II

The Gods' Rise to Superiority

LET US NOW return to the Śvetāśvatara-Upaniṣad and consider it more closely. Coming chronologically after the Bṛhadāraṇyaka and Chāndogya, but preceding the Bhagavadgītā this important work—which is generally thought to have been compiled by the Vth or IVth centuries B.C.—represents, in my opinion,[1] a stage of development in Indian thought, in which the germs which had lain in the preceding centuries and from which the various philosophical views or metaphysical doctrines of the future generations were to develop, had already reached the first stage of growth without differentiating in any considerable degree. That is to say, the differentiation between the doctrines about the essence and foundation of the universe, the soul and the material world had not yet made so great progress as five or six centuries later when the streams of Sāṃkhya and Vedānta thought had found their own beds. Leaving, however, the philosophical aspects of the Śvetāśvatara undiscussed we see, on the one hand, that for the compiler—as also for those authors who lived before and after him—the ultimate goal of all speculation was to show a way of escape from the saṃsāra, that is victory over death, and, further, that the desire to identify and to know the Real, the foundation of all existence—which is almost from the beginning a consistent and conspicuous characteristic of Indian thought—has continued unaltered. It is, on the other hand, evident that the relations between microcosmos and macrocosmos, between individual and universe, between ātman and brahman are now more complicated and problematic than they were considered to be in the preceding period.

This appears already from the opening stanza which, quoting those who discourse on brahman, inquires after the ultimate cause or origin of our existence: 'Is brahma the cause?[2] What is our origin? By what do we live, and on what are we firmly established?' (It may be remembered that the search for a *pratiṣṭhā*, a firm foundation, on which for instance our own existence is established, was among those important problems which engaged the attention of the authors of the brāhmaṇas).[3] 'Presided over by whom', the stanza continues, 'do we live our different condition in pleasures and pains . . .?' The author obviously belonged to those circles of meditative ascetics (6, 21) to whom he owed the insight that the ultimate foundation of all existence and the origin and ruler or governor of all life is the sole eternal (4, 21; 5, 13) Lord who bears both the perishable and the imperishable, the manifest and unmanifest (1, 8; 1, 10). It is in this connection worth noticing that the text significantly uses the verb *īśate* 'he rules' and the noun *īśaḥ* 'the Lord' to express the supreme ruling of a Lord who is characterized as immortal and imperishable, as the One, the Supreme Being emanating and withdrawing the world, the goal of that identificatory 'meditation' which leads to complete cessation from all phenomenal existence and Who therefore is the last cause of bondage and liberation (1, 10 f.). That means that here some of the most salient features in the character of the post-Vedic Īśvara are indicated with all distinctness desirable.

It is the author's main endeavour to establish the existence of this Highest Being. Quoting, integrating, and reinterpreting in what we might call a monotheistic sense numerous passages from Vedic texts[4] he suggests that Agni,[5] Savitar,[6] the universal instigator and originator of all movement, and other gods, including the great lord of (biological) creation Prajāpati (4, 2), the divine architect Viśvakarman[7] as well as the impersonal brahman (3, 7) actually are the Great Lord, who also created Hiraṇyagarbha,[8] the Golden Germ of Ṛgveda 10, 121: according to this text the One, in the beginning, became the Golden Germ, which supporting heaven and earth was to be the sole Lord (*patiḥ*) of creation. These divine figures attested, already in the later parts of the Ṛgvedic corpus, to the growing tendency to extol one god as the greatest and highest of all, in short as the Supreme Lord and Originator. Time-honoured images, metaphors[9] and terminology are quoted, not only to illustrate this identification but especially to corroborate the thesis that Rudra-Śiva is this Supreme Being, that it is He, who is meant by the Vedic texts when they describe the creator whose eyes and faces, arms and feet are everywhere.[10] Being beyond day and night, beyond being and 'non-being',[11] Rudra-Śiva is the 'imperishable' (*akṣaram*)[12] and 'the desirable (splendour) of Savitar' mentioned in the Sāvitrī stanza ṚV. 3, 62, 10.[13] This Sole Being stands like a tree firmly fixed in heaven (3, 9),[14] penetrates the All, that is the totality of existence (3, 11), and the author does not hesitate to compare his God to a fire with fuel burnt[15] and to consider him the best bridge to immortality (6, 19).[16]

It is therefore not surprising that he also adopts that principle which is coextensive with the universe while penetrating it completely, to wit the Puruṣa of the famous Ṛgvedic hymn 10, 90, to which we shall have to revert in connection with the development of Viṣṇuite theology (3, 14 f.), and that he introduces the relative quotation by a positive answer to a question raised in the beginning of the upaniṣad (1, 2): 'Is perhaps the Puruṣa to be considered the ultimate cause?': 'I know this great Primeval Person, by whom this All is filled, who is a mighty universal ruler, who is omnipresent, Śiva' (3, 8 ff.). One should remember that the equation Rudra = the All = the Puruṣa occurs for instance in the Taittirīya-Āraṇyaka (10, 16, 1; 17, 1). This conception of the Supreme as a Primeval and omnipresent Person who is the All, whatever has come into existence and what is to be,[17] is, however, at the same time elaborated with reference to the microcosmos, to animate nature: He dwells in the hidden interior (i.e. the 'heart') of all beings and is their *antarātman*, their inner Self (3, 11; 6, 11). With regard to men this God, who 'has been born and will be born' (2, 16), shows three aspects of his nature: He has created all beings, protects them, and at the end of time, He absorbs them completely (3, 2). To denote this Supreme Being, the sovereign position and absolute character of which are described in the last chapter of his exposition, the author resorts to a great variety of epithets and characterizations: 'Him who is the Supreme Lord of lords, and who is the supreme deity of deities and the supreme master of masters, transcendent, him let us know as God, the lord of the world, the adorable' (6, 7). But, I already had the opportunity to say that one term, *īśāna*, and its relatives *īśa* and *maheśvara* 'the one who has power, who rules or is the Master', come decidedly to the fore.[18]

Yet this important attempt at harmonizing in a great synthesis the main themes and theories connected with the divine essence underlying the phenomenal world—Puruṣa, Brahman, Prajāpati, etc.[19]—this teaching of a personal god who is the creator, preserver and destroyer of all phenomenal existence does not preach a God who is above the world of myth. This Īśvara might be an abstract idea or figure hardly accessible to the hearts and the minds of the masses, the author could ill afford to do without the imagery, popular belief[20] and mythical thought of his Śivaite tradition, and his God plays a part in mythology, though on a more exalted level.[21] God is not only the Lord, but—despite his being the origin of the devas (3, 4)—also a deva himself (4, 13; 16; 6, 7; 11) and, moreover, that particular god who in the popular worship was traditionally known as Hara, Rudra, Śiva,[22] that is to say, though higher,[23] He is at the same time a god who bears a proper name and is characterized by functions and attributes of his own,[24] a deity whose wrath is feared and averted by a prayer borrowed from Vedic texts: 'Do not injure us in life and offspring, do not slay our men in anger!'[25]

It is time now to institute a summary comparison between this oldest document of rising Śivaism and that famous ancient Gospel of Viṣṇuism, the Bhagavadgītā.[26] I need not, to begin with, dwell on the well-known fact that both poems must have been compiled in those circles which, finding no satisfaction in Vedic ritualism,[27] sought after bliss and salvation through the help of a personal God. Both poems also agree in their ideas of the Highest Being[28] and in the conviction that God's help can only be obtained by him who knows Him truly, that is who mentally and spiritually realizes his identity with Him: says the Śvetāśvatara (1, 11): 'By knowing God there is a falling off of all fetters' (1, 11):[29] 'only by knowing him one passes over death' (6, 15) and the Gītā: 'as a knower of Brahman established in Brahman' (5, 20) and 'having come to know Me (Kṛṣṇa) in truth, one forthwith enters into Me' (18, 55), that means: 'one is not born again' (4, 9).[30] Both works are also agreed that in this world nobody, or hardly anyone, knows God, who himself knows what is to be known.[31]

Mere knowledge, however, does not suffice.[32] In a stanza which Śvetāśvatara's discourse has in common with two other ancient works it is expressly stated that only through the grace (*prasāda*) of the creator one sees the Lord and His majesty and becomes free from sorrow.[33] The views of the Gītā are clearly expressed in its last chapter: 'In Him alone seek refuge with all your being; by His grace you will win peace supreme, the eternal "abode"'.[34] But there are some conditions for receiving Śvetāśvatara's doctrine, and one of these is that the adept must be a man of extreme love-and-devotion[35] for God and for his spiritual teacher as for God (6, 23). The term *bhakti* itself,[36] denoting an affective 'participation' of the soul in the divine, occurs, probably,[37] here for the first time, and it is certainly not permissible to view its context through the spectacles of the adherents of the *bhakti* movements of later times, when the idea had been widely propagated and had come to manifest itself in various aspects. Nor can we, relying on the *argumentum e silentio*, be sure that the idea and the religious attitude for which the term stands are non-Vedic in origin.[38] We should rather consider the probability of the existence of *bhakti*[39]-like currents of religiosity within the fold of Aryan antiquity and of their failing, for a long time, to receive the recognition of those leading brahmans who preferred to perfect and to systematize the ritual aspects of ancient Aryan religion.[40] It cannot be denied that every cult of a personal god may involve some form of *bhakti* and we are certainly justified in searching[41] Vedic literature for anticipations of post-Vedic devotionalism.

Dismissing, however, this question of origin it must be emphasized that the *bhakti* idea, though emerging in Śvetāśvatara's poem, occupies a much more important place in the Bhagavadgītā. *Bhakti* is, in the Gītā, one of the three ways to salvation and it is, moreover, the way for which the author feels a growing sympathy. By undivided devotion God can be known, seen and 'entered into',[42] but here also a prospect of variant ways to the goal is held out: the emergence of the identificatory knowledge of God's nature may also precede the devotion and make it possible.[43] Or *jñāna* and *bhakti* may have the same effect, viz. the annihilation of all *karman*[44] and the obtainment of eternal peace.[45] Anyhow it is clear that then already—that is, about the IIIrd or IInd century B.C.—*bhakti* was better adapted to a Viṣṇuite background, of which it was to remain a very distinctive feature, no doubt because in the Gītā the central position of Kṛṣṇa himself as the teacher and his continual references to his divinity and to his willingness to help and save those who approach him devotedly were much more fitted to appeal to the hearer's emotions and to sustain the bhakti conceptions than the more abstract and impersonal teaching of Śvetāśvatara.

For whereas Rudra-Śiva is esoterically preached and his nature explained by an author who in a learned and elaborate argument tries to show that that god—whose figure remains invisible (*ŚvU.* 4, 20)—is the Supreme Being meant by the Vedic authorities,[46] Kṛṣṇa, declaring that the Veda is no longer necessary for him who has attained the wisdom of the Supreme[47] and revealing that by his pervasive power he is the most prominent representative of all concrete objects and phenomena,[48] the light of the sun, the vital power of animate nature, appears—notwithstanding his identity with the impersonal Brahman[49]

—in the flesh and shows, in the famous epiphany of canto XI, his supreme form as Lord. Whereas, moreover, Śvetāśvatara's ascetic audience are supposed to have in their relations with God almost no personal interests outside the victory over death, or the final release of all fetters, Kṛṣṇa, professing the wide catholicity of his religion which is open to everybody,[50] teaches several ways toward salvation adapted to various types of men,[51] but emphasizes that the most preferable way consists in a combination of disinterested performance of one's personal, social and religious duties[52] in this world and faithful devotion to God: 'He who does his work for Me (as a sacrifice to Me), who looks upon Me as his goal, who devotedly worships Me, free from attachment and from enmity to all creatures, he comes to Me.'[53] This very phrase,[54] which is repeated, suggests the possibility of communion with a loving personal God, to whom, according to Kṛṣṇa's own words (7, 17; 12, 20), his devotee is dear, and who, though beyond definition, unborn and eternal,[55] supreme and all-pervading,[56] though the incomprehensible transcendent origin and supporter of the universe as well as its dissolution,[57] is easy of access; an object of reverence, impartial and ready to grant even the desires of those who worship other divine beings;[58] a God who, while pre-eminently exalted, resides in the hearts of men and is willing to appear in an adorable human form which may even be the object of *pūjā*.[59] A god, who, far from being inactive like Śvetāśvatara's Īśvara (*ŚvU.* 6, 19), to destroy the wicked and to protect the good assumes—through his own incomprehensible divine creative power, *māyā*, an exhibition of this faculty, foreign to the Śvetāśvatara[60]—a visible body from age to age, whenever there is a decline of *dharma* and rise of *adharma*:[61] the first formulation of the *avatāra* doctrine which has been an important source of Viṣṇuite power and influence, enabling the faithful to combine a firm belief in Viṣṇu, the personal aspect of Brahman, and worship of a saviour, and putting by its historical or supposedly historical occurrences God's love of the world and of mankind beyond doubt.[62]

By demanding that his worshippers fulfil their duties and observe the general rules of moral conduct disinterestedly Lord Kṛṣṇa successfully bridged over the chasm between that ascetic morality, which for instance was propagated by the Buddhists, and Śvetāśvatara's one-sided accentuation of the ideal of final emancipation on the one hand and the exigencies of daily life[63] on the other. To those who wished, or were obliged, to lead a socially and religiously normal life and who had, for the sake of the maintenance of our human society (3, 20), to be active in this world, he gave a moral, a philosophy of life, and a prospect of final liberation. He also founded on the basis of Vaiṣṇava religion what may be called social ethics, a subject foreign to the Śvetāśvatara: since God is, as their physical and psychical substratum, in all beings, sages see no difference between them; like God himself, one should be impartial and the same to friends and foes.[64] Significantly enough, the devotee who, friendly and compassionate, and without ill will to any being, lives up to this ideal while fixing his mind on God is said to be most perfect in yoga.[65] In contradistinction to the almost classic type of yoga proclaimed by Śvetāśvatara[66] who emphasizes its technical aspects and automatic effects, Kṛṣṇa, while stressing continuous vigilance over body and mind and concentration on God or the Self as essential elements,[67] preaches the *karmayoga*, which is a performance of duty characterized by self-control, balance of mind, and the abandonment of all attachment and desire of results.[68]

Thus the Bhagavadgītā, while continuing and developing the doctrine of an Īśvara who is the goal of those seeking final emancipation,[69] at the same time met the wishes of the masses which demanded a personal God to worship. Unfortunately we possess no ancient records showing us in a pure form the development of popular religion, which the Gītā presupposes and which was distinct from the more abstract and speculative thought of the early upaniṣads. This lacuna is the more regrettable as in the centuries preceding this document various cults and beliefs, presumably tending towards some more or less distinct form of monotheism, must have contributed to the rise of Viṣṇuism. For whereas in the Śvetāśvatara-Upaniṣad God, the Lord, is Rudra, also called Śiva, who as such attracts a considerable part of the compiler's attention, in comparable ancient works belonging to the Viṣṇuite tradition—the MahāNārāyaṇa Upaniṣad and the Bhagavadgītā—Viṣṇu himself is only passingly mentioned, the divine persons occupying, especially in the latter text, a central position being Nārāyaṇa and Kṛṣṇa, who only in the course of time came to fuse with the Vedic Viṣṇu.[70] How these cults of Nārāyaṇa and that of the in all probability tribal hero and deity Kṛṣṇa-Vāsudeva came to combine with that religious current which succeeded in raising Vedic Viṣṇu to the rank of the supreme deity is for lack of textual evidence not clear.[71] Recently the opinion was expressed in connection with this insoluble problem[72] that the three great figures were, due to fortuitous circumstances, raised to that high position and that 'thus as a matter of course they were equalized by a mysterious process of religious syncretism'. This however leaves us where we were.

Yet it would appear to me that a few factors in this process may, by way of hypothesis, be recovered, if only we would consider more closely some characteristics of early Viṣṇuism which have not yet attracted the attention they deserve. These are in the first place the tendency to identify the various ideas of the Highest, which I propose to illustrate with the part played by the Puruṣa concept and, further, the functions of the god and the use and signification of some names and epithets attributed to him in pre-epic texts. As to the former, it is well known that in Ṛgveda 10, 90[73] the phenomenally evolved universe is described as having issued from a primeval Person, Man (*Puruṣa*), whose origin is left unexplained and who, being co-extensive with the earth and even larger than that, is this All; one fourth of his is all beings and three quarters are what is immortal in heaven.[74] From this Person, the ultimate reality,—in whom God and matter are one, and who is the universe and transcends it—Virāj—grammatically feminine and literally the idea of 'extending and ruling far and wide'—was born, and from Virāj, being the hypostatization of the conception of the universe as a whole,[75] as evolving, expanding and creative, and as such the intermediate between the primeval Puruṣa and the evolved Puruṣa—arose again the Puruṣa. This is no doubt a variant of the well-known idea of the bisexual primeval being. Then this Person became the victim or oblation in a primeval—and hence exemplary—sacrifice, performed by the gods. From his dissected body arose the particular elements of the phenomenal creation. The closing stanza[76] underlines, by way of résumé, the fundamental ideas of the poem: the rite and the victim on the one hand and the one worshipped on the other are identical; this sacrifice is an *opus operans* and an *opus operatum*;[76] the powers which were generated in this way reach heaven.

We must now dwell for a moment upon the use made in the course of time by teachers and other authorities of this Puruṣasūkta, which is the first expression of the idea that creation is the self-limitation of the transcendent Person manifesting himself in the realm of our experience. It is, to begin with, incorporated in those Vedic texts which deal with the Puruṣamedha or human sacrifice.[77] In contradistinction to other texts, which give this rite the character of a real human sacrifice, by which the sacrificer can reach that which is not reached by the horse sacrifice (*ŚŚS.* 16, 10, 1), the White Yajurveda, enjoining that the victims be released, describes it as a so-called symbolic rite (*ŚB.* 13, 6, 2, 13).[78] The author of the Śatapatha-Brāhmaṇa extends the idea of the *sūkta* (13, 6, 1, 1). Puruṣa, then already called Nārāyaṇa—who according to the ancient tradition[79] is the inspired poet of the *sūkta*—desired: 'Would that I surpassed all beings! would that I alone were this All (*idaṃ sarvam*: the totality)' 'He beheld', the text continues, 'this five-days' (*pāñcarātram*) sacrificial rite, the Puruṣamedha, and after having performed it, he surpassed all beings and became the Totality. The man who knowing this performs the Puruṣamedha, or who just knows this, surpasses all beings and becomes, i.e. realizes his identity with, the Totality of existence (*idaṃ sarvam*)'. These ideas were not however completely new: the Puruṣa-Nārāyaṇa litany (as it is called *ŚB.* 13, 6, 2, 12) was also in other rites recited during the performance of acts intended to make the sacrificer attain a higher state of existence or to bring about his reintegration.[80] Thus it is recited over the sacrificer of the Aśvamedha[81]—which may have been the model of the Puruṣamedha[82]—at the moment of his unction, a ritual act intended to disintegrate and reintegrate the sacrificer and to mark his 'rebirth' out of the sacrifice and his identification with the Cosmic Man.[83] The sheet of gold which as part of this rite is placed on his head helps to make him surpass the normal human condition.[84] The number of the stanzas of the *sūkta*, sixteen, is essential, because Totality is, like Puruṣa himself, (*ŚŚS.* 16, 14, 16), sixteenfold (*ŚB.* 13, 6, 2, 12).[85] For our subject the closing paragraph of this chapter of the Śatapatha-Brāhmaṇa is not devoid of interest: the sacrificer should, after having placed his sacrificial fires into his own self—an act to be performed when one desired to embrace the career of an ascetic who no longer needs his fires—worship the sun with the Uttara-Nārāyaṇa litany, which in the Vājasaneyī-Saṃhitā follows immediately on the Puruṣasūkta,[86] and then go to the forest not to return home. In this connection the commentary on the Kātyāyana-Śrautasūtra (21, 1, 17) speaks of an entrance into another stage of life: that means that the sacrificer now becomes a *saṃnyāsin*. The author of the Śatapatha-Brāhmaṇa ends by saying that one should not impart the knowledge of this obviously esoteric 'symbolical' sacrifice to anyone, but only to one who is known and dear to the teacher and who is versed in the Veda. A much later document, the Mudgala-Upaniṣad, after explaining the Puruṣasūkta, goes into more details: one should teach this secret knowledge only under auspicious circumstances and to him who is a pupil. When one does so, the student as well as the teacher realize already in this existence their identity with the Puruṣa.

A cosmogony is, in archaic thought, the exemplary model for creation of every kind.[87] The Puruṣasūkta was for instance prescribed in a rite for obtaining a son,[88] in bathing practices for that renewal which is called purification, and in the ceremonies performed in founding a temple which is constructed in the likeness of the Puruṣa.[89] The text was intelligibly enough also repeated at *śrāddhas*, rites for the benefit of the deceased. Part of our sources assert that after death the soul assumes what is called an *ātivāhika śarīra* consisting of only three of the five elements (viz. fire, wind and space) which enabled it, if the relative rites were duly performed, to bridge over the space between death and the formation of a new gross body in the following incarnation, which as appears from the use of this sūkta was considered a renewal. The same virtue and potency of the text explains why it was deemed to purify a person of sins and why it was—and often still is—to be pronounced at the time of bathing: in both cases it was likewise to renew the person concerned, a fact in the latter case also underlined by the obligatory change of clothes. It is therefore perfectly clear that already at an early date and throughout the ages this text was, in religious practice not only an account of the creation but also an instrument of rising above one's present state of existence. By identifying oneself with the mythical Puruṣa[90] and by ritually repeating the mythical event and so reactivating its inherent power for the benefit of oneself and with a view to one's own reintegration one believed oneself to achieve one's own 'rebirth'.[91] The Puruṣa is, moreover, immolated and the *sūkta* embraces also the institution of sacrifice, which in the view of the Vedic ritualists is the counterpart and re-enactment of the great cosmic drama of integration and disintegration.[92] In performing the sacrifice—which in the myth is the power or technique starting the process of creation—the priests set in motion the cosmic processes for the benefit of the sacrificer; and this benefit may even consist in a rebirth.

There is much truth in Renou's remark[93] that this theme of the Puruṣa constitutes the principal link between the subject-matter of the Ṛgveda and that of the Atharvaveda in that most cosmological poems of the latter corpus contain some allusion to it. Not only was the Puruṣasūkta, as 19, 6,[94] incorporated in the Atharvaveda-Saṃhitā, there is another hymn, likewise traditionally ascribed to Nārāyaṇa,[95] viz. 10, 2, which, while describing the wonderful structure of the human body, actually deals also with the Puruṣa,[96] with the important addition that this 'body' is the stronghold of Brahman (neuter) which has established heaven, earth and atmosphere. This same Brahman, 'which governs both what is and what is to be, and the All and whose alone is heaven' (*AVŚ.* 10, 8, 1) and which is also said to be in man (10, 7, 17) impresses us here as being another name or aspect of the frame of creation, the *skambha* or *axis mundi*,[97] in which everything is contained. This frame, in which the creator god (10, 7, 8) Prajāpati fixed and sustained all the worlds and which with part of its being has entered creation (10, 7, 7 f.), is in its turn identical with the Puruṣa (10, 7, 15), and tends, in this same context, to fuse with that creator god,[98] who is moreover said to be the lord of immortality (ṚV. 10, 9, 2; AV. 19, 6, 4: *īśvara*) so that here the way is paved for that synthesis which was to be of fundamental importance for later Indian philosophical and theological thought.[99]

Viṣṇu does not appear on the scene here, but it is worth recalling that the Śatapatha-Brāhmaṇa is quite explicit in stating that Prajāpati in order to create offspring and the world imitated, that is identified himself with, Viṣṇu, making this god's three strides which we know to be a variant of the all-pervading idea expressed by the *skambha*.[100] It is further, in the same brāhmaṇa, asserted that it is the Puruṣa who became Prajāpati,[101] who is therefore with reference to Ṛgveda 10, 90, substituted for the former as the primeval victim offered by the gods (10, 2, 2, 1 f.). And we should, finally, remember that the same work —probably through the well-known process of identification of an historical or legendary founder of a religious movement with the god he preaches—gives the Puruṣa the name Nārāyaṇa.[102]

This process is repeated. When, toward the close of the period represented by the brāhmaṇas, thinkers and teachers were no longer satisfied with these speculations and attempted to formulate theories of their own with regard to the ulterior source of mundane life and existence, they were likewise inclined to defend the thesis that the personal God whom they wanted to regard as the Supreme Being or the idea they chose to be the world ground,[103] was identical with the Puruṣa,[104] the primeval Person, the adumbration of whose nature found in the Puruṣasūkta is now expanded and developed.[105] An interesting example is furnished by Śvetāśvatara. It may be repeated here.[106] After making (1, 2) the enquiry whether for instance time, nature, destiny, chance or Puruṣa should be the cause of the universe[107] and implying a negative answer in the following stanzas which intimate that the sole cause and power is a personal God, who is one and who appears to be identical with the Highest Brahman, the author declares that he knows that great Puruṣa who turns out to be the same as his god Rudra-Śiva (3, 8 ff.). The same identification occurs—in a striking minority of cases, it is true—in the Mahābhārata:[108] 'Thou art the Puruṣa, and Thou residest in the heart of everything.'

Turning now to those currents of thought which are collectively known as Viṣṇuite the first document to arrest our attention is the Mahā-Nārāyaṇa-Upaniṣad,[109] a breviary for saṃnyāsins incorporating a considerable number of quotations from older works. This āraṇyaka-like manual, which may have been compiled approximately in the IIIrd century B.C.,[110] can be considered an attempt at harmonizing the ascetic and the ritual way of religious life and a device for receiving the anchorites into the fold of the brahmanical, so-called orthodox community. In its central section (st. 201–269) it praises Nārāyaṇa as the Absolute. The origin of this figure, whose name we have already had occasion to mention several times, is shrouded in mystery.[111] It would be an attractive, but unwarranted supposition to regard the picture of his asceticism and his hermitage on the Ganges[112] as reminiscent of historical facts.[113] Be that as it may, the upaniṣad under consideration[114] glorifies him as the Supreme Lord of the Universe, Brahman, the Eternal, Prajāpati, the Highest Light, which on the other hand is also Viṣṇu. He is also the Puruṣa,[115] who fills the whole universe, is in the brilliant light of the sun, is identical with Order (*ṛtam*), Reality-and-truth (*satyam*), the highest Brahman and may assume every form. From this Puruṣa[116] have arisen all divisions of time, seconds, minutes, hours, days and nights, seasons and year, and it is He, who produces water, space and the heavens. It is not possible to see, grasp or control him.[117] Besides, the Puruṣa is not different from the Ātman and is compared to a tree which is fixed in heaven, that is, no doubt, again, the *skambha*.[118] This Puruṣa is also addressed as if he were a divine person, given epithets elsewhere applied to deities, and implored to deliver those speaking from every impurity, pride and latent conditions or affections of the soul.[119] Those who, like the author himself, know him become immortal,[120] and the only way leading to this knowledge of the Highest, which is the only mode of access to immortality, is that of vision and introspection. The highest goal is specified as the intimate union with Brahman and co-existence in its world,[121] but it is also known to the author as the world of Viṣṇu on 'the surface of the firmament', that is this god's famous highest place.[122] In short, the world ground, the so-called absolute, which sometimes is indicated by a grammatically neuter form, is Prajāpati, also called Puruṣa and Nārāyaṇa, whom we know to represent another version of the One becoming phenomenal plurality; in its, or his, identity merge that of gods such as Agni, Vāyu and the Sun;[123] he is also called Hari and Viṣṇu, and he has entered light, plants and men,[124] supports the universe of which he is the navel—i.e. the centre and place of creation—,[125] rules men and animals and is all-seeing and omniscient.[126]

I mentioned the name of the god Agni, and he seems, in this connection, worth a short digression, not only because he is also among the deities merging in the Kṛṣṇa of the Bhagavadgītā,[127] but also, and especially, because this upaniṣad[128] represents him as the supreme Ātman (249 ff.).[129] While describing him as one of the manifestations of the universal divinity the essence of which is Puruṣa-Nārāyaṇa[130] that statements of this manual run parallel with other upaniṣads in which the One god is said to be or to manifest himself in Agni, Vāyu and other deities fulfilling great cosmic functions.[131] This representation of Agni as a form, or as the energy, of Śiva or Viṣṇu, which is not foreign to the epos,[132] cannot be dissociated[133] from those brāhmaṇa speculations according to which the god of fire and, like Viṣṇu, sacrifice (*ŚB.* 5, 2, 3, 6), is in the rite of the construction of the great fire-place the Puruṣa and Prajāpati.[134] The performance of the rite itself constituted for the sacrificer a development of his personality culminating in a transformation or 'new birth'.

It is in the same character that Nārāyaṇa, expounding his own nature, appears, in the Mahābhārata, as the founder of a religion of devotion, and at the same time as the exalted Being, the Universal Spirit, the ultimate source of the world and all its inhabitants.[135] And here he is again the Puruṣa[136] a glorification of whom even constitutes the last chapter of the Nārāyaṇīya section of the XIIth book which is devoted to this figure and his religion. The first words of this eulogy 'He is eternal, undecaying, imperishable, immeasurable, omnipresent' are explained by the commentator Nīlakaṇṭha as follows: 'He is the Puruṣa, because of the attribute of fulness; eternal, because he has neither beginning nor end; undecaying, because there is no change in him; imperishable, because he has no body which may be subject to decay; immeasurable, because mind and speech cannot conceive of him in his fulness; omnipresent, because he is the material cause of all.'[137]

Dismissing for a moment Nārāyaṇa we now come to Kṛṣṇa. The most seminal of all Viṣṇuite scriptures, the Bhagavadgītā—in harmony with its central doctrine, viz. the identity of Kṛṣṇa-Vāsudeva with the All (*sarvam*, i.e. Totality: 7, 19) implying that he is Brahman—does not omit to emphasize that Kṛṣṇa is the Īśvara[138] and one with the Puruṣa.[139] The man who seeks final emancipation must meditatively know Kṛṣṇa to be the supreme celestial Person and through this knowledge and exclusive bhakti realize his identity with that Person, by which the All is pervaded and supported and in which all beings abide.[140] This is another soteriological application of the ancient idea: spiritual identification with the Primeval Being which is the ultimate reality means the attainment of a new 'birth' *in casu* final liberation. The identification of ideas and aspects of the indescribable continues. Although in no place does Kṛṣṇa himself explicitly claim to be Viṣṇu, all the ṛṣis are quoted as declaring him to be 'the Highest Brahman, the supreme manifestation of divine essence, the purifying power *par excellence*, the eternal celestial Puruṣa, the unborn universal ruler . . .',[141] and for all practical purposes that Puruṣa is one with Kṛṣṇa's highest *dhāman*, i.e. with God's very Presence to which the devout worshipper may go without returning.[142] Other places in the Mahābhārata agree with the Gītā in considering Kṛṣṇa the eternal Puruṣa, the ungenerated self-existent One (*Svayaṃbhū*).[143]

Interestingly enough the same identification takes place with regard to Viṣṇu, and the same phrases which, in expressing the identity, are used in connection with Kṛṣṇa may apply to him: the (high) Puruṣa of olden times,[144] *purāṇaḥ Puruṣaḥ*, etc. Thus Viṣṇu is the primeval Puruṣa,[145] and as such he is also the eternal and omnipresent Brahman, *sat* and *asat*, and above *sat* and *asat*. And now the conclusion is drawn that Kṛṣṇa is the unborn primal god Viṣṇu Puruṣa.[146] Viṣṇu with the thousand heads (the initial epithet of the Puruṣasūkta) is incarnate as Kṛṣṇa,[147] who is described as bearing the conch-shell, the discus and the club.[148]

It is indeed not surprising that this representative of the All was already at a much earlier date associated with the pervader of the universe, that other representative of the Totality, Viṣṇu. At a given moment of the Aśvamedha rites some of the priests engage in a conversation of the brahmodya type, that is they propound to each other, as part of the rite, riddles on cosmogonic, cosmologic, metaphysical and ritualistic subjects, a well-known device to penetrate the mysteries of the unknown and thus to generate and liberate power and to get a hold on the potencies which are the subject of the riddles.[149] Among the questions posed are, in close succession: 'Has Viṣṇu entered the whole universe?'[150] and 'Into what has the Puruṣa entered—the same verb (*āviveśa*) is used—and what is established in the Puruṣa?' This very idea of 'entering the All', that is of being the Totality, shared by both Viṣṇu and the Puruṣa, and the strong appeal made by the idea of reintegration and hence emancipation through sacrifice[151] has no doubt largely contributed to the fact that in the course of time the Viṣṇuites came to emphasize that which their god and the Puruṣa had in common and to transfer to the former what the Veda ascribed to the latter: according to a purāṇic account of the creation of the universe[152] it was Viṣṇu who emanated Virāj, and Virāj who produced the Puruṣa.

Thus this summary study of the Puruṣa concept[153]—which could be followed up by investigations into the history of other ideas, names and epithets which eventually came to merge in the great figure of Viṣṇu[154]—reveals to us part of the gradual and intricate processes by which Kṛṣṇa, Nārāyaṇa and other representatives of the Supreme Being came to draw near to each other and to Viṣṇu. The Mahābhārata does not show us the last stage of this development. Though pervading this epic as a general attitude in an ever-shifting manner, Viṣṇuism is not yet a well-defined religious doctrine; the term Vaiṣṇava is not employed, but Viṣṇu himself is becoming the powerful, yet benevolent loving and lovable deity, the centre of personal worship and devotion, the externalization of religious and philosophical ideas also contained in myths and legends. The Rāmāyaṇa, while giving us important information, not on the growth of Viṣṇuism as a whole, but rather on that aspect of it which may be called Rāmaism,[155] likewise insists on declaring the Puruṣa one with Viṣṇu. Thus queen Kausalyā is stated to have meditated on the Puruṣa who was Janārdana,[156] a name already in the other epic very often given to Kṛṣṇa (Viṣṇu-Janārdana).

It may be added that the content of the Puruṣasūkta which, in the course of time, was, so to say, made the foundation stone of Viṣṇuite philosophy, continued to engage the attention of its exponents,[157] although it must—to avoid misunderstanding—be added that the Śivaite tradition continued quoting this text also.[158] Thus—to mention some random examples[159]—when in the Xth century, Yāmuna made an attempt to prove the supremacy of Viṣṇu he also asserted his identity with the Mahāpuruṣa of the Puruṣasūkta, the essence of the Vedas.[160] Quotations from this hymn are regularly found in arguments to explain the nature of the Supreme Being and to assure adherents of the possibility of attaining the Supreme Place, the firmament where are the gods, of ṚV. 10, 90, 16, and which is regarded as identical with Viṣṇu's highest place.[161]

In their sūtra text—a late document, dating perhaps from the IVth century A.D.—the Viṣṇuite Vaikhānasas—according to whom Nārāyaṇa is the Highest Brahman to be reached by meditation and concentration[162]—prescribe the use of the sūkta in a bali offering to that deity who is explicitly called the god with a thousand heads, the highest Puruṣa, the highest Brahman (*paraṃ brahma*), etc. and the cause of all, whose soul (*ātman*) is the sacrifice (10, 10). The other text to be used in performing that rite—the successful performer of which will reach Viṣṇu's 'world' there to be magnified—is, characteristically enough the well-known verse 'I shall proclaim the mighty deeds of Viṣṇu', that is ṚV. 1, 154, 1, the famous Viṣṇu-sūkta. Here the fusion of the Ṛgvedic Puruṣa and Viṣṇu-Nārāyaṇa is complete.[163]

III

Theology

I NOW PROPOSE to deal with what briefly may be called the structure of the idea of God, the Sole Reality which underlies, as its innermost and true Self, not only every experiencing being but also everything else in the universe, as well as the universe itself as a totality. It may be quite true that Viṣṇuites as well as Śivaites claim for their God identity with Brahman, which is the All—'the primeval Puruṣa, the Lord, Brahman, the eternal One, who is Viṣṇu';[1] 'Śiva, the blue-necked one, (is) Brahman'—and it may be also true that the well-known Vedantic formula 'Brahman, being beyond qualification, is the Universal One which is the All; the Īśvara is on the empirical level Brahman endowed with qualifications', sounds quite simple, the determination of the relations between the One and the phenomenal many, between God and the world, between the Lord and his individual devotees, confronted philosophers as well as theologians with an immense complex of intricate problems. There were religious practices and the ideas of God fostered by the masses and by the learned; there were the peculiar traditions and convictions with regard to the Highest Being of Śivaites and Viṣṇuites; there were, already in the beginning of the Christian era, the composite figures of Viṣṇu and Śiva themselves with their aspects and manifestations, their relations and attendants, there were cults and religions which came to fuse with the two great currents; there were the philosophical schools, which, tending to differentiate and growing in importance, explained the relation between the One and the many or the structure and evolution of the world and taught a way of salvation; there also was the innate Indian desire for systematization. Both communities shouldered the task and faced its risks and difficulties, both undertook to establish a system, a theology, an explanation of the world and a coherent and acceptable account of man's relations with God. Both, however, proceeded on their own lines, clinging to their own traditions and emphasizing their own particular beliefs and doctrines. It will be relevant to survey here some of their theories to compare the outcome of their endeavour as it was incorporated in the purāṇas.

Purāṇic Śivaism[2] is, to begin with, characterized by the doctrines of God's five manifestations or so-called faces (*pañcavaktra*) and that of his eight forms or embodiments (*aṣṭamūrti*). The five manifestations are Īśāna, Tatpuruṣa, Aghora, Vāmadeva, Sadyojāta. His eight embodiments are the five elements, sun, moon and sacrificer, to each of which corresponds one of his traditional names, Śarva, Bhava, and so on.

Now there is one point which is too obvious to be left out of further consideration. It concerns the name Īśāna which is the only one which occurs among the eight *mūrtis* as well as the five 'faces'. This is not all. Īśāna is also one of the eight *lokapālas* or *dikpālas*, the regents or guardians of the quarters of the sky or, rather, regions of the universe. It may be remembered that the participle *īśāna* 'the ruling one, the master' was already in early times, in the Ṛgveda, often used to denote the one who has authority,[3] who is mighty or wields power[4] over, for instance, wealth, the world, 'immortality'. At first this word was as a characterization applied to various gods (Indra, Varuṇa, Mitra, Dhātar, etc.), but from the Atharvaveda-Saṃhitā (15, 5, 2) and the Taittirīya-Brāhmaṇa (1, 5, 5, 2) it regularly appears also without a genitive to qualify as a substantive an individual god: 'the Lord, the Master'.[5] The compiler of the Bṛhadāraṇyaka-Upaniṣad[6] interestingly enough uses it, on the one hand, to indicate the supreme Lord of what has come into existence and what is to be, by knowing whom one becomes immortal, who is the maker and the creator, whose is the world and who is the world, and on the other hand, as the last of a group of eight to which belong also Indra, Varuṇa, Soma, Rudra, Parjanya, Yama and Mṛtyu. In the Buddhist canon[7] Īśāna is, together with Indra, Soma, Varuṇa, Prajāpati, Brahmā, Mahiddhi[8] and Yama, mentioned again as one of the chief *devas*. The name was adopted by the author of the Śvetāśvatara-Upaniṣad to characterize the Supreme God,[9] that is Rudra-Śiva, as the Lord, the universal authority (*prabhu*), and the firm refuge (*śaraṇam bṛhat*) of all, the goal of those who seek final emancipation. Although the name was, for instance in the Mahābhārata,[10] given to Viṣṇu or to the Supreme Being in general, it became especially favourite in Śivaite circles to designate their God.[11] It may parenthetically be recalled that the title *bhagavān*, i.e. 'the one who is rich in *bhaga* "dignity, excellence, majesty, loveliness, etc."', translated by 'the Holy or Adorable One, the Blessed Lord', though sometimes used in connection with Śiva,[12] was very often preferred by the Viṣṇuites—in the Viṣṇu-Purāṇa, for instance, Bhagavān is always Kṛṣṇa-Viṣṇu—to be constantly employed in later days by the adherents of the school of *bhakti* to describe the Supreme God of their devotion.[13] Īśāna—whose name may often have been used for reasons of taboo or euphemism—must, in the Śivaite sphere it is true, have led also a semi-independent existence, because he was, as we shall see further on, with two other figures of Śivaite affiliation, regarded as his wife and, probably, his son, the object of a popular rite described in the Āpastambīya-Gṛhyasūtra.[14] Judging from the infrequency of his iconic representations[15] he does not however seem to have played in Hinduism an important part as an individual god.

It is not clear whether, or how far, the above groups of eight gods were, or could be, associated with the regions of the universe. There is on the other hand no doubt whatever that these regions were in pre-purāṇic times also believed to be under the protection of a group of eight (or ten) gods which did not include Īśāna; in a description of the Vedic rites connected with the building of a house (*vāstuśamana*) mention is, for instance, made of 'ten *bali*-offerings to be given to the regents of the ten regions (*diśaḥ*), namely Indra (in the East), Vāyu, Yama, the Pitaraḥ, Varuṇa, Mahārāja, Soma, Mahendra (North-East), Vāsuki (the nadir) and Brahmā (in the zenith)'.[16] In Manu 5, 96 these gods are[17] Indra, the Wind, Yama, the Sun, Agni, Varuṇa, the Moon, Kubera.[18] Anyhow, the group of these great devas of the early epic literature was open to variation[19] and in the well-developed puraṇic mythology Nirṛti or Virūpākṣa and Īśāna are substituted for Sūrya and Candra. However, the name Īśāna may also be replaced by Śiva's other names Rudra or Śaṅkara.[20] The increasing popularity of this god has no doubt enabled his aspect Īśāna to oust one of the old devas from that quarter of the universe which is next to his traditional region, the North.

The lokapāla Īśāna, the regent of the North-East, is an ambiguous figure. Sometimes he is with his colleagues represented as a worshipper of Śiva: 'Thou that, in every quarter of the sky, art worshipped by Yama, Agni, Rudra (=Īśāna) and so on'[21] and in various rites he is, like the other ritually very important[22] guardians of the regions, invoked and adored with flowers and incense.[23] Ritualists, iconographers and theologians did not on the other hand lose sight of his identity with the Great God himself and so they gave him Śiva's bull as a mount,[24] endowed him with such iconographic features as the three eyes, the matted hair, the tiger-skin garment, the trident[25] and the alms-bowl,[26] or described his image as Gaurī-Śarva, that is Śiva Ardhanārīśvara.[27] His identity with Śiva is also apparent from the occasional presence of Viṣṇu on the left and Brahmā on the right side of his image,[28] or, as already observed, from the occasional interchangeability of his name and other names of the god, Śambhu, Rudra, Īśvara, etc.[29] It is interesting to recall that the younger version of the mantras pronounced in adoring the *lokapālas* is modelled upon the ancient[30] so-called Rudragāyatrī (*tatpuruṣāya vidmahe, madādevāya dhīmahi, tan no rudraḥ pracodayāt*). The mantra addressed to Īśāna, to mention only this, runs as follows: *sarveśvarāya vidmahe, śūlahastāya dhīmahi, tan no rudraḥ pracodayāt*,[31] which may approximately be translated 'We know the Great Lord, we meditate on him who has the trident in hand, that Rudra (will) inspire (stimulate) us!'[32]

It remained however always possible to group these deities—usually in the same order, beginning with Indra (in the East)—together without express mention of the fact that they are regarded as *lokapālas*.[33] Īśāna might, moreover, also in later times belong to other groups of gods. He probably owed this honour to a certain continuing popularity[34] which may also account for his occurrence in a number of myths in which—being distinct from Śiva—he is said to join other gods, for instance in praising new-born Nandin, Śiva's bull, in accompanying Śiva marching against Tripura, in being Vīrabhadra's victim on the occasion of Dakṣa's sacrifice.[35] That he plays, in these tales, a subordinate part does not prove that he was in religious practice a pale and insignificant figure.[36] The other gods (Yama, Agni, Kubera, etc.) do not play, in these narratives, a more prominent part.[37]

Hence, no doubt, also the possibility of substituting in certain rites part of the lokapālas by other manifestations of Śiva. Thus the Liṅga-Purāṇa describing the *jayābhiṣeka* or 'unction for victory'[38] mentions a series of oblations, successively destined, not for Indra, Yama, Varuṇa, Kubera, but for Śiva's five manifestations.

Now, Īśāna belonged already in the Atharvaveda to a group of obviously popular divinities which may be regarded as embodiments,[39] or rather doubles,[40] of Rudra, or as partial manifestations of his essence.[41] In any case the statement (15, 5, 1, etc.) that neither Śarva, nor Bhava, nor Īśāna injures the man, his cattle or his fellows, who has acquired a certain knowledge impresses us as a reference to a distribution of identical or similar divine power over three manifestations:[42] as is well known, many ancient texts are, according to the views prevailing in a definite context, to the predominant religious convictions or to the exigences of some ritual argumentation, inclined to what might be called either synthetic or analytic representation of the same divine reality or power complex. Interestingly enough the same Atharvaṇic text does not only mention more aspects of this divine concept, but also correlates them with the regions of the universe: Bhava with the East, Śarva with the South—notice that the sequence of the regions is in the *pradakṣiṇa*-order[43]—Paśupati with the West, Ugra[44] with the North, Rudra with the *dhruvā dik*, i.e. the fixed central region,[45] Mahādeva with the upward quarter, and Īśāna with all the quarters. Here already, Īśāna is the last and obviously the most important of the group because representing all the regions he seems to unite in himself the functions of his 'colleagues'.[46] The text under consideration exhibits one of those well-known sequences of the quarters of the sky which—whether or not in connection with deities[47]—play a very important part in religious practice.[48] The man who duly pronounces a sequence of stanzas addressed to the quarters while performing a *pradakṣiṇa* ensures their protection either for himself or for some object.[49] An invocation of the quarters—which in their totality represent the whole of the universe—may also induce them to co-operate in propitiation, homage or reverential salutation:[50] they are in a way made submissive to the person speaking or the officiant and willing to guarantee him, so to say, an unlimited 'horizon' or expanse. The sacrificer may also win them in order to master the whole of the universe with respect to space.[51]

There is no point in entering into more particulars. The importance of the regions and their relevance to our theme are immediately apparent.[52] I for me am inclined to consider the tetradic organization of the universe to have been, in the Indian classificatory systems under consideration, of fundamental significance, in any case more fundamental than a system of principal colours to which Willibald Kirfel was inclined to attach, in this connection, greater importance.[53]

However, there are in the Veda groupings of divine names in which the points of the compass play no part whatever. An interesting passage in the Kauṣītaki-Brāhmaṇa (6, 1 ff.), dealing with the creative activity of Prajāpati, a new-born divine being—of a thousand eyes and a thousand feet, and arisen from the seed of Prajāpati's children Agni,

Vāyu, Āditya and Candramas—is eight times—notice this number!—in succession given a name and these names are every time correlated with one of the provinces of nature or other important entities. The first name given is Bhava, and the waters are said to be Bhava, the second Śarva and the fire is Śarva; in a similar way are paired Paśupati—again another name of Rudra-Śiva—and the wind (Vāyu), Ugra and the vegetable kingdom,[54] Mahān Deva ('the Great God') and the sun (Āditya), Rudra and the moon, Īśāna and food, Aśani (the Flash of lightning) and Indra. The closing words of the pericope are especially interesting: This is the great god of eight names, distributed eightfold.[55] And as this system of correlations and identifications pursues a practical purpose, the author assures his audience that the offspring of the man who knows and understands what has been said will up to the eighth generation be secure from lack of food. A similar statement was contained in each of the preceding paragraphs: Bhava, Śarva, etc., will not do harm. The coincidence of the possession of food in the last paragraph and the identity of Īśāna and food are anyway remarkable. This passage puts the belief, of definite ritualistic circles of about 400 B.C. or perhaps earlier,[56] in the eightfold character and eightfold distribution of the divine complex called Rudra-Śiva beyond question. I cannot suppress the occurrence of a parallel version in the Śatapatha[57] in which not only the order of the names, but also all identifications are different.[58] Here Īśāna, being the sun, 'who rules over this All', is the last of the group.[59] Besides, the text speaks of the eight forms of Agni, who obviously is identified with Rudra.[60]

This is not the only enumeration of the god's eight aspects.[61] In a description of the Śūlagava a series of invocations is addressed to Bhava, Rudra, Śarva, Īśāna, Paśupati, Ugra, Bhīma and the Mahān Deva (*sic*), 'the Great God'.[62] Another gṛhyasūtra[63] however furnishes us in this connection with twelve names, adding that six formulas, or even one, viz. *rudrāya svāhā*, may suffice. The names, followed by the exclamation *svāhā* are: Hara, Mṛḍa, Śarva, Śiva, Bhava, Mahādeva, Ugra, Bhīma, Paśupati, Rudra, Śaṅkara, Īśāna. Six names (Bhava, Śarva, Īśāna, Īśvara, Paśupati, Adhipati) are mentioned in the sūtra of the Kāṭhakas.[64] Another authority, Pāraskara,[65] however enjoins those who perform this so-called spit-ox sacrifice to offer to nine manifestations of Rudra-Śiva, the first of which is Agni,[66] the last again Īśāna; Bhīma of the list of eight names is now—as in the Śatapatha-Brāhmaṇa—replaced by Aśani.[67] As Pāraskara's list differs from that occurring in the Śatapatha only in having Agni at the beginning,[68] this sequence may have enjoyed a certain popularity in those circles which followed the White Yajurveda.[69]

Three points are worth noticing. First, the name of Īśāna is in these invocations never omitted. In the second place: the different version of the rite handed down by the Āpastambins[70] comprises an oblation to Īśāna and Kṣetrapati 'the lord of the field, i.e. the tutelary deity of the soil' and special acts of worship of these two gods.[71] Lastly, the name Īśāna[72] is more than other names of the god connected with this rite because it is also called Īśānabali,[73] that means an offering or propitiatory oblation of portions of food of a popular character in honour of Īśāna.[74] These facts corroborate us in our view that Īśāna must have been a figure of no mean importance in popular religion. He was already at an early date the object of a cult which then already was characterized by some 'Hinduist' features,[75] but succeeded in gaining admittance to the ritual handbooks of the brahmans. The *śūlagava* is even described in the Śāṅkhāyana-Śrautasūtra,[76] where the series of divine names accompanying the oblations is interestingly enough identical with the name given, according to the allied brāhmaṇa, by Prajāpati to the young god who had arisen from the seed of Agni, etc.[77] Whereas we may[78] to a certain extent explain the occurrence of the rite in this sūtra from the incorporation of the names in the brāhmaṇa, it seems on the other hand warranted to suppose that the author of the brāhmaṇa had borrowed these names and the order in which they occur from an eightfold rite.

The eight names of Śiva and their correlations with some elements, sun, moon, etc.[79] moreover, recur—not without some variation, it is true—in the epic and purāṇic systems of Śiva *aṣṭamūrti* to which we shall turn now.[80] In the Liṅga-Purāna the order of the god's embodiments usually is: earth, water, fire, wind (i.e. the air), space, sun, moon and sacrificer, the last being also called *dīkṣita* ('the consecrated one'), *ātman*, or otherwise.[81] When his eight names are correlated with these manifestations, the earth usually[82] goes with Śarva, water with Bhava, fire with Rudra, the air with Ugra, space with Bhīma, the sun with Īśāna, the moon with Mahādeva, the *yajamāna* with Paśupati; that means that this puraṇic system has only one identification (Bhava = water) in common with the Kauṣītaki-Brāhmaṇa, but four with the Śatapatha: Rudra is fire, Ugra is air or wind, Mahādeva is the moon, Īśāna the sun.

I cannot discuss the other identifications and systematizations added to and grafted upon these names and embodiments by Śivaite speculation. Let it suffice to say that the five elements as names and embodiments of the god are also held to compose the different coverings of the huge egg (*brahmāṇḍa*) which is our universe[83] and that these five are completed with three other concepts which according to the Sāṃkhya theory have not only a share in the evolution[84] of the universe but also in its constitution: *ahaṃkāra*, i.e. Maheśvara, *buddhi*, i.e. Īśa (Īśāna), and Parameśvara who, taking Paśupati's place, obviously represents the *prakṛti* (also *ananta* or *mahad avyakta*) which constitutes the outermost sheath.[85] As Aṣṭamūrti—the occurrence in the Mahābhārata 3, 46, 26 is only a variant of slight importance—Śiva fulfils all functions which belong to these eight realities or constituents. The world is a product of his eight forms, it consists of them, and can only exist and fulfil its task because these forms co-operate.[86] Since also the microcosmos of our own body is composed of the same five elements and the three other realities the god Śiva is believed to make up, in eightfold manifestation, the corporeal frame and the psychical organism of every living being.[87] Any being is identical with God,[88] who as Śarva is his bones, etc., as Rudra is the light of his eyes which is connected with the sun, as Mahādeva his *manas* ('mind' or, rather, the co-ordinating and directive central organ) which is related to the moon: no doubt a reminiscence of the Puruṣa myth: the moon arose from his manas, the sun from his eye.[89] The eighth constituent is the *ātman* which, being the sacrificer, is as indispensable an element as the seven other constituents:[90] the cosmic processes are indeed performed by the gods who really are Śiva's faculties (his *vibhūtis* or divine powers), and these gods are sustained by the divine rites as plants by regular watering.[91]

It is, to conclude with, sufficiently clear that Śivaite speculation, utilizing elements of an ancient cosmogonical myth and guided by the influential Sāṃkhya theory of the evolution of the world and the cosmic processes, had remodelled the ancient idea of God's eight aspects distributed over the whole universe into a system of His eightfold manifestation, presence and activity which at the same time expressed the fundamental truth that God and the world are one. In mythological imagery the purāṇic tale[92] of the divine boy who being born to Prajāpati's successor Brahmā, cries[93] because he wants to have a name and then after having been called Rudra receives seven other names in addition may be regarded as the parallel continuation of this theory.

Brahmā gave him also stations[94] for these eight aspects of his being, viz. sun, water, earth, etc., and, in addition to these, wives and sons.[95]

The quarters of the universe are no element of this purāṇic system of correlations. Nor does the *aṣṭamūrti* play a prominent part in the cult. These two facts may be put in relation with each other.[96] In a little known rite, the 'Gift of the eight Rudras',[97] these manifestations of Śiva are, in order to receive the oblations accruing to them, placed in a square to the East, South-East, South, etc., of Brahmā who occupies the central place. That there also was a tendency to amplify the correlative system may appear from the adaptation to which the ancient mantras handed down in Hiraṇyakeśin's Gṛhyasūtra[98] were subjected: to the Vedic formulas *bhavāya devāya svāhā* correspond in the Liṅga-Purāṇa:[99] *Oṃ bhava jalaṃ me gopāya jihvāyāṃ rasam, bhavāya devāya bhuvo namaḥ* 'Oṃ, Bhava, protect for me the water, the taste in my tongue; adoration to the god Bhava, *bhuvaḥ* adoration'.[100] (As is well known, water is supposed to convey the flavour of things.[101]

Śiva's five 'faces'[102] are, unlike the eight embodiments, of great ritual significance. Attention should first be paid to the names of these five aspects: Sadyojāta, Vāmadeva, Aghora, Tatpuruṣa and, again as the last, Īśāna whose special importance is notable in this assemblage of divine figures also. It is true that their origin is wrapped in darkness, that they do not occur in the Mahābhārata and that their oldest occurrence in the tenth book of the Taittirīya-Āraṇyaka, that is the Mahā-Nārāyaṇa-Upaniṣad,[103] is of uncertain date (IIIrd century B.C.).[104] Yet it is sufficiently clear that this oldest occurrence constitutes a series of formulas addressed, in a fixed order, to Śiva. In later times these were called the *pañca suvaktramantrāḥ* 'the formulas of (Śiva's) five auspicious faces'.[105] They are to be pronounced in a low voice in order to promote a devotee's meditation and to produce (higher) knowledge.[106]

In the first formula the devotee takes refuge with Sadyojāta 'the New-born',[107] paying homage to him who is the origin of all existence.[108] This Sadyojāta[109] mantra occurs[110] also in Atharvaveda-Pariśiṣṭa 20, 6, 1 as a part of a collection of formulas to accompany a ceremony in honour of Skanda. It is immediately followed by a stanza mentioning the names Skanda and Kumāra.[111] According to the Liṅga-Purāṇa Śiva (also called Vāmadeva) was as a boy (Kumāra) in each world-age born from Brahmā.[112] Is it too bold an assumption that the Sadyojāta originally was a boy god, or even the boy god

Skanda Kumāra who is already mentioned in the Chāndogya-Upaniṣad (7, 26, 2),[113] and who is the embodiment of one of the characteristic traits of Śiva himself, accordingly to become, in the course of time, the great god's son?

It is difficult to decide whether the second person is historically related to the *ṛṣi* Vāmadeva who is credited with the authorship of the fourth maṇḍala of the Ṛgveda.[114] It seems in any case worth recalling that the name of this seer is in the Vedic tradition not only connected with Vedic stanzas[115] or with the origin of definite elements of the ritual,[116] but also with the supernormal vision of so-called worlds (*loka*).[117] He is moreover related to have possessed knowledge before birth:[118] 'Being yet in embryo, I knew well all the births (origins, races) of these gods',[119] and to have become awakened to the insight that he was Brahman and, hence, the All,[120] and so to have started a poem: 'I was Manu and the Sun'.[121] Of greater interest is that he is associated with the southern region from which he is invited to protect a definite sacrifice;[122] that he was believed to be able to protect 'all this' from evil,[123] the gods calling him who is life-breath Vāmadeva, and further that he is explicitly identified with Prajāpati.[124] If these facts might suffice to found the hypothesis that this figure was, under circumstances hidden from us, śivaized or adopted by Śivaite circles, the in itself not insurmountable difficulty remains that the Mahābhārata knows him as a *ṛṣi* who has wonderful swift steeds and appears in Indra's palace,[125] and that in the Rāmāyaṇa he functions at Rāma's court.[126] In the Matsya-Purāṇa Vāmadeva appears as Brahmā's son and as the author of the four classes of society, taking the place of the Puruṣa of Ṛgveda 10, 90,[127] but here he is doubtless identical with Śiva.[128] Generally speaking the purāṇas continue to distinguish one or several ancient sages of this name from Vāmadeva who is Śiva.[129]

Of the five figures composing the Pañcavaktra Aghora is the most distinct and independent.[130] His character manifests the uncanny traits of Śiva's nature: evil, diseases, death, punishment of sinful behaviour, and magical practices, but also their opposites, viz. fertility, recovery from illness, and deliverance of sins and evil are his main fields of activity.[131] His figure also—though left unmentioned by the poets of the Mahābhārata—may have arisen at a rather early date, probably as a hypostatization of that side of the god's character which led the Indians also to prefer his name Śiva. The adjective *aghora* indeed denotes the absence of, and restraint in, awful, terrific and violent action and attitude and, hence, friendliness.[132] In the Veda the god is, in the beginning of the Śatarudriya litany, requested to look auspiciously on those praying with his kindly (*śivā*), friendly or reassuring (*aghorā*) body (*tanū*) which is most potent to heal.[133] As is well known the noun *tanū* was used to denote a manifestation of a divinity, the self or idea of a divine person or sacred object conceived of as corporeal,[134] and not rarely, in the plural, a god's more or less hypostatized powers, faculties or qualities; a god may have a friendly and a terrific a *śivā* and a *ghorā*, *tanū*.[135] The Vedic stanza referred to occurs also in the Śvetāśvatara-Upaniṣad (3, 5) and may therefore be considered to have held the continuous attention of Śivaite communities.[136] It is worth observing that the third formula of the *pañca suvaktramantrāḥ* is properly speaking not addressed to the divine personality Aghora but to the reassuring and awful forms or manifestations of the god.[137]

The curious name of Śiva's fourth face Tatpuruṣa seems to owe its existence to a reinterpretation of a Śivaite[138] variant of the Gāyatrī, viz. *tat puruṣāya vidmahe mahādevāya dhīmahi / tan no rudraḥ pracodayāt*[139] which, amalgamating a reminiscence of the Puruṣa with the sacredness of that stanza and stating the devotee's knowledge of the Puruṣa, expresses the intention to meditate on the Great God and the hope of divine inspiration and instigation. Apprehended as a compound the term may be translated by 'Soul of the Universe'.[140]

Now God's five 'faces' were in the course of time made the central element of a comprehensive classificatory system. The five manifestations were identified with parts of His body,[141] with ontological principles, organs of sense and action, the subtle and gross elements,[142] etc. Thus this system is an attempt at explaining Śiva's being the All, the universe, and the universe's being exclusively composed of sides and manifestations of Śiva. That means that each of Śiva's five faces corresponds to, or is identical with, one of the components of the five groups which, in the Saṃkhyā school of thought, constitute the twenty-five *tattvas* (principles or basic categories).[143] In his fivefold nature Śiva is therefore identical with the five times five elements of reality.[144]

However, the idea underlying this system was not new. A brāhmaṇa already spoke of the five forms (*tanū*) of Prajāpati which are the hair on his face, the skin, the flesh, the bone, and the marrow; and the five which are mind (*manas*), voice, vital air, eye and ear; elsewhere it is observed that Prajāpati's *tanūs* constitute the whole of this god,[145] who elsewhere is explicitly styled 'fivefold'.[146] This view of the creator god's nature was also of great ritual significance. It provided the Vedic ritualists with a theoretical basis for the important and complicated Agnicayana rite, the so-called construction of the fire-place,[147] which, consisting of the construction of five layers, is periodically to re-integrate Prajāpati, so that he will be able to continue his creative activity. It is expressly stated[148] that the five *tanūs* of the god are these five layers, and that, when the five layers are built up, the god himself is built up by those bodily parts. Moreover, Prajāpati being the All, and hence Totality with respect to time, is at the same time, as the year, built up with the five seasons, and these are in their turn identical with the five regions of the universe, so that the god is also built up with the regions. The system of correlations and identifications is extended by the incorporation of the five provinces of the universe (earth, atmosphere, heaven and the two 'intermediate regions'[149] and the different parts of the body.

Here the question arises why such a prominent place should, not only in this connection,[150] have been given to the number five. A survey of the relevant Vedic texts cannot, in my opinion, fail to show, as already observed, the fundamental importance of the regions of the universe. The five directions—which in archaic thought means: the totality of the fourfold division of the universe[151]—are explicitly said to be distributed over all the gods,[152] that is to say over the representatives of the provinces and forces of the cosmos. It is the five directions[153] which are invoked to make a man king and an essential element in the ritual of the royal consecration is articulated on this number: the royal sacrificer has to step in each of the five directions in order to appropriate the whole universe,[154] and these directions are here again co-ordinated with other fivefold systems (the Vedic metres, the seasons, etc.). In short, the five regions, which constitute the world,[155] may be supposed to have induced the ancient Indians to speak of the five parts of the earth and the 'five peoples'[156] to indicate the totality of the human communities distributed over the earth. Basing themselves on a principle of so-called numerical 'symbolism' the authors of these texts grouped and articulated not only the divisions of space[157] and time (the quarters of the seasons,[158] but also divine[159] and ritual powers (metres, victims,[160] gifts, arts, utensils or functionaries[161] and the forces constituting the 'social cosmos'[162] on the number five.[163] Part of these groups[164] were already at an early date associated[165] or even co-ordinated with each other.[166] Such a co-ordination was explicitly regarded as a union,[167] or as an identity;[166] or the identity in number implied transference of the characteristic nature of one of the groups of five[169] to another. Very often a basic group of five[170] in nature (regions, seasons) was to motivate or explain a ritual act or element characterized by the same number.[171]

A complete survey of all relevant places would fill many pages; let it suffice to add that Vedic and upaniṣadic authors refer to a fivefold ritual address,[172] to five prayers for prosperity,[173] to five questions posed in succession[174] and to an esoteric doctrine expounded under five heads;[175] that they make mention of five openings for the gods in the heart correlating to sun, moon, fire, rain, space and functioning as the doorkeepers of the world of heaven.[176] They assumed that Prajāpati entered in the creatures which he had produced as five in number, viz. as the five vital breaths.[177] They prescribed rites of a fivefold character and ritual acts to be executed five times in succession,[178] consisting of five parallel acts accompanied by five similar mantras. And so they arrived, on the strength of the considerations that man's completeness consists in his being fivefold—for man is composed of mind, speech, breath, eye and ear—and that sacrifice and cattle and the 'person' (*puruṣa*) are likewise fivefold, at the conclusion that 'this All, whatever there is, is fivefold'.[179] They also established a parallelism between the fivefold nature of the macrocosmos and the corresponding fivefold nature of the microcosmos: 'Earth, atmosphere, heaven, the (main) quarters and the intermediate quarters; fire, air, sun, moon and stars; water, plants, trees, space and the body, thus with regard to material existence; and with regard to the individual: the five vital breaths;[180] sight, hearing, 'mind', speech, touch; skin, flesh, muscle, bone, marrow. Fivefold indeed, is this All, with the (individual) fivefold does one win the (cosmic) fivefold (i.e. the All).'[181] We should indeed be always aware of the fact that the ultimate aim of all these speculations was practical: 'The paṅkti (a Vedic metre) is five-fold, the sacrifice consists of five; so one reaches thereby (i.e. by the five-day's rite) all what is fivefold, with regard to the deity and with regard to one's self';[182] 'He who knows (this doctrine of) these five fires thus is not stained with evil, even though consorting with those (wicked) people; he who knows this becomes pure, clean, possessor of a pure sphere of safety or state of bliss (*loka*)'.[183] One might feel fortified in this view of the significance of the number five by the fact that some important categories in nature and in the human body—for instance, the 'elements', the sensory organs—are, or may be taken as, fivefold.[184]

It is therefore easily intelligible that the author of the Śvetāśvatara-Upaniṣad, whose influence upon the development of Śivaite ideas is unmistakable, describes the Highest Being as a river of five streams, from five sources, whose waves are the five vital breaths, whose original source is fivefold perception-and-intelligence (*buddhi*), which has five whirlpools, an impetuous flood of fivefold misery, divided into five distresses and five joints. According to the traditional explanation the streams are the five senses; the sources, the five elements; the waves, the five organs of action (or the five *prāṇas*?); the whirlpools, the objects of sense; the fivefold misery, the successive painful stages of development: embryo, birth, old age, illness, death; the five distresses, the so-called *kleśas*, i.e. ignorance, egotism, desire, aversion, tenacity of mundane existences, the five joints being left unexplained. The simile speaks for itself: it is highly illustrative of a view of God and the world which considers *prakṛti* (undifferentiated primordial material) to be the very nature of God and ascribes the categories and processes which characterize psycho-physical reality to Him who is at the same time believed to have brought forth the world substance out of His own being (6, 10).

It is therefore not surprising that pentads play also an important part in Śivaism[185] and—as we shall see instantly—Viṣṇuism.[186] Thus Śiva's body consists, in a way which is beyond human intelligence, of the five mantras, the so-called *pañca brahmāṇi* of Taittirīya-Āraṇyaka 10, 43 ff.[187] These mantras are in a variety of ritual ceremonies used to accompany fivefold ritual acts. They may correspond to parts of God's body which they by the very invocation create or evoke.[188] Thus the Īśānamantra, in Hindu practice *Hoṃ īśānamūrdhne namaḥ*, correlates to His head, the Tatpuruṣamantra *Heṃ Tatpuruṣavaktrāya namaḥ* to his face, etc.[189] They may correspond to the five directions or also accompany a sequence of acts which do not seem to be related to God's body or to the quarters of the universe.[190] The five faces are moreover put in relation with five colours, Īśāna being white or colourless,[19] and, what is especially interesting, with God's five functions.[192] With his creative function, by which he provokes the evolution of the possibilities of the causa materialis of the universe, is in this system associated Sadyojāta; he maintains the world as Vāmadeva, he re-absorbs it as Aghora; his power of obscuration—by which the souls are concealed in the phenomena of the *saṃsāra*—is associated with Tatpuruṣa and he bestows his grace which leads to final emancipation as Īśāna.[193]

These five functions[194] are an emanation from the Niṣkala, i.e. the formless or unmanifesting Śiva who is the Highest Brahman of the Vedāntins. The identifications and co-ordinations do not indeed end here. The five faces are also known individually as Mahādeva (in the East), Bhairava (in the South), Nandivaktra (in the West), Umāvaktra (in the North) and Sadāśiva[195] (also Īśāna, the fifth who is 'on the top').[196] With the 'five faces', the first of which is Īśāna (*īśānādayaḥ*) and which are collectively also known as the Pañcabrahmas[197] are, moreover, associated the five so-called Sādākhyas[198] which have evolved from God's fivefold *śakti*.[199] In these Sādākhyas 'dwells' God in his aspect called Sadāśiva. I cannot dwell upon other pentads,[200] for instance upon God's attributes in the five right and five left hands of his Pañcavaktra figure[201] and upon the fivefold origin, in five different colours—Īśāna is omni-coloured—of the highly important Gāyatrī mantra from this form of the god. I must also refrain from surveying those texts in which this doctrine is elaborated and, for instance, Īśāna is described as urging on all divine powers and as the Lord of past and future and of all gods.[202]

This doctrine of the five manifestations of Śiva, who according to his worshippers is first and foremost the Great Lord,[203] expresses the belief that he is the All (in German, das Allwesen), the Highest and the Unique who embraces and comprises the universe and all beings and of whom they are composed. Like the *aṣṭamūrti* concept, to which it, so to say, forms a complement, it emphasizes—now clearly in its static aspect—God's identity with the Universe and the universe's identity with God who is omnipresent and manifests Himself and His activity always and everywhere.[204] Both doctrines are ingenious attempts at explaining the omnipotence and omnipresence of God, the Force which rules, absorbs and reproduces the universe and in performing one of these acts necessarily performs the others. They give no picture of the ideal to which saints may aspire nor of heroic and selfless acts for the benefit of mankind.

It is time now to turn to the Viṣṇuists and to focus our attention on their attempts to explain the relation between God, who is Brahman, and the universe and to assign to the manifestations of God's essence a place in a harmonious theological and philosophical system. Unlike the eightfold and fivefold Śivaite systems the Viṣṇuite doctrine of the *vyūhas*—successive emanations from God and at the same time part of His essential nature—emphasizes the evolutional aspect of the relation between the One and the many. Unlike these doctrines it did not, in a developed form, gain access to the traditional orthodoxy of the purāṇas.[205] It is true that in the comparatively late Bhāgavata-Purāṇa God is often spoken of as having the four forms of Vāsudeva, Saṃkarṣaṇa, Pradyumna and Aniruddha, but what this means, what God is or does in or with these four forms is hardly elaborated. Only once[206] homage is paid 'to the Universal Soul from whose navel springs a lotus, who is Vāsudeva (and as such) is tranquil, unchangeable, luminous with his own light, (who is) Saṃkarṣaṇa (and as such) subtle, the infinite, the end-maker, (who is) Pradyumna (and as such) the all-wakening, the internal 'soul', (who is) Aniruddha, (and as such) Hṛṣīkeśa[207] whose *ātman* consists of the organs of sense'. The text however continues: '(who is) the Paramahaṃsa (and as such is) the abundant, the one of passionless nature', and so on, showing that the former four figures do not here constitute a separate group.

Scholars are, it is true, agreed that the Vyūha doctrine is one of the foremost tenets of the earlier Pāñcarātra school of thought, but are at a loss to explain its origin and the exact historical relations between the Kṛṣṇaism or Bhāgavatism of the Bhagavadgītā and the fully developed Pāñcarātra religion.[208] It does not however seem too bold an assumption that the Pāñcarātrins,[209] whose monotheistic doctrines, sometimes attributed to the reputed Sāṃkhya-Yoga authority Pañcaśikha,[210] are referred to in the Nārāyaṇīya[211] section of the Great Epic and who adored Vāsudeva as the Highest Being, were only secondarily absorbed by the broad current of Viṣṇuism.[212] Although this process involved the replacement of Vāsudeva by Viṣṇu, they were, because of their attachment to the non-Vedic tenets of their scriptures, the Saṃhitās, and in spite of their own insistence upon their orthodoxy,[213] stamped as deviating from Vedic truth and tradition.

Being philosophically allied with the Sāṃkhya schools of thought[214] by the doctrine of the eternity of *prakṛti* and the three *guṇas*, their theory of the fourfold form of the Highest Being constitutes a modification of theism peculiar to themselves. This Vyūha doctrine may indeed be considered another attempt at maintaining the fundamental monotheistic starting-point whilst incorporating a number of adorable manifestations and doubles of God, and at assigning to them positions and functions in a systematic explanation of the universe and its origin, an attempt at conceiving God as the unaffected and unchanging One who nevertheless is the cause of all change[215]—for God and his *vyūhas* are identical[216]—an attempt also at harmonizing theology with mythology and elements of evolutionist philosophy.[217]

The term *vyūha* has not always been adequately translated. It is not exactly an 'expansion',[218] or 'emanation',[219] still less a 'form'[220] or a 'conglomeration'.[221] In the technical vocabulary of the Vedic ritualists the verb *vy-ūh-* and the noun *vyūha* are often used to express the idea of an effective arranging, taking or pushing asunder the parts of a coherent whole.[222] Thus a twelve days' sacrifice can be performed according to the normal schema; then it is called *samūḍhachandas*, that means: its metres (or rather its stotras and śastras) are 'regularly arranged, settled, or restored to their normal order'. When however the proper order of the ritual acts is changed and the cups of soma are disarranged (*vy-ūh-*) the different arrangements of the hymns and recitations involved characterizes the performance as *vyūḍhachandas*.[223] The dislocation of the soma pressings is afterwards rectified by disposing the various cups in their normal order. The author of the Aitareya-Brāhmaṇa says[224] that this transposition (*vyūha*) of the ritual acts[225] was instituted by Prajāpati and that by doing so one also avoids exhaustion or impairment of the inherent force, or rather one makes the rite efficient[226] so that one will attain all desires and will be successful.[227] One indeed 'pushes away' evil which is imminent on all sides.[228] The division of a definite chant of fifteen stanzas—which are identified with a thunderbolt (*vajra*)—is in a similar way considered as resulting in appeasement of evil (*śāntyai*), for then the stanzas are no longer a thunderbolt.[229] By pushing asunder the *gāyatrī* 'five syllables in front and three behind', the gods protected the sacrifice and the sacrificer.[230]

That by pushing asunder parts of a coherent whole one may also obtain a central place which is a position of safety appears from another brāhmaṇa passage:[231] Indra after having pushed twenty-four syllables of the *anuṣṭubh* stanza (which ordinarily consists of thirty-two syllables) entered the eight syllables in the middle which were left as his home. By imitating this act one enters Indra's home and defeats one's rivals.

The verb *vy-ūh*—which is also applied to the sun spreading its rays[232]—is not infrequently used in connection with a sacrificial cake which is broken from west to east or transversely; thereupon both parts are pushed asunder with the thumb and ringfinger.[233] The cake may also be separated into four quarters and it is expressly stated[234] that in doing so one finds support in the regions of the universe. There is another unmistakable relation to these four regions in the ritual separation[235] of the Āhavanīya fire which in the Rājasūya rite is divided into four parts in the directions of the points of the compass, another piece of fire-wood being placed in the middle. The accompanying formulas are addressed to Agni and other gods residing in the East, to Yama and others residing in the South and so on, the last one being directed to the gods in the centre, namely those who dwell above and Bṛhaspati. By pushing the pieces of fire-wood together towards the central one one destroys, with the collaboration of these gods, the demoniac power. To a similar process the primeval waters were subjected by Agni who shoved them asunder, upwards and downwards.[236] By ritually pushing asunder the sacrificial grass a central place is formed which is regarded as the navel of the earth.[237] The terms under discussion are however also applicable to a division of brahman which is identical with the gāyatrī into eight parts[238] and to one of the twenty-four 'arrangements'[239] into which Prajāpati, after having divided his 'body' into two, three, four, etc., separated himself.[240]

So the conclusion may—as already intimated—be that already in Vedic ritualism the idea of *vyūha* implied an effective arrangement of the parts of a coherent whole. In this connection the number four again appears to have been of cosmic significance.

It seems on the other hand fairly certain that the reference to the five worshipful heroes, *pañcavīras*, of the Vṛṣṇis in the fragmentary Morā inscription[241] combined with the piece of information furnished by the Brahmāṇḍa- and Vāyu-Purāṇas[242] which, in connection with the avatāras of Viṣṇu, make mention of five gods of human origin, well known as the great men of their race (family),[243] proves the existence, in the Mathurā region about the beginning of the Christian era, of a cult of deified 'heroes' bearing the title *bhagavat* and belonging to the Vṛṣṇis, that is the famous epic tribe of the Yādava people, whose most prominent scion was Kṛṣṇa. Their names were Saṃkarṣaṇa, Vāsudeva, Pradyumna, Aniruddha and Sāmba.[244] The last-mentioned soon fell in the estimation of the worshippers,[245] but the others were deified,[246] the first of them being identical with Kṛṣṇa Vāsudeva's elder brother Bālarāma, the others being his elder son[247] and grandson. Their relationship was transformed into the metaphysical system of Vāsudeva—who now was given precedence—and the three other *vyūhas* of the one great God, Vāsudeva, who is the fountain head of the others and may therefore be addressed by all four names.[248]

It is quite clear that the human element and especially the hero cult played a prominent part in the development of this religious current. Kṛṣṇa himself and his relations are indeed well-known central figures of many epic and purāṇic narratives.[249] We have no sufficient information definitely to answer the question as to whether, or how far, the three other *vyūhas* ever were independent, more or less divine figures and the object of cults of their own. Nor should we draw unfounded conclusions from the connections, relations and functions attributed to them in the Mahābhārata and the purāṇas, which are no doubt largely due to a tendency to harmonization, systematization and the desire to express religious truths in the form of mythological imagery. Saṃkarṣaṇa[250] evinces, not only in his name which may be explained as 'the ploughing one', but also in his characteristic emblems, a ploughshare and sometimes a pestle used in pounding corn, traits of character which are usually proper to a bucolic or harvest deity.[251] If so, are we right in supposing that his personality became indistinguishably united with that of a legendary figure, well-known to the epic poets, Balarāma or Baladeva, called Halāyudha, 'the one who has a plough for his weapon'?[252] That this Baladeva was, with Vāsudeva, among many deities and other beings who were the object of a comparatively early cult appears from a passage in a Buddhist text,[253] the Niddesa. Pradyumna, whose name does not appear in the older literature, is in the epos, which generally knows him as a hero, regarded as identical with or an incarnation of Brahmā's son, the ṛṣi Sanatkumāra,[254] the one who is 'always a youth', and elsewhere is identified with Skanda[255] or also with Varuṇa.[256] These facts neither corroborate nor contradict the hypothesis that he once was not Kṛṣṇa's son.

As to Aniruddha,[257] this name often given to Viṣṇu does not appear in the older Vedic literature either and it is not known when, where and by whom it was first applied to this High God. So much seems however clear that the name Aniruddha in itself could have been preferred to characterize Viṣṇu as the divine power which can function freely, whose activities, influence and movements are unobstructed and unhampered and who can manifest itself at will.[258] Śrī-Lakṣmī's irresistible immanent power which pervades everything is indeed said to be known under this name.[259] Anyhow, Aniruddha is in the epos not only a royal person but also a manifestation of the Supreme God,[260] the Lord (Īśāna) himself,[261] or a high figure of independently creative power who, known as being the eternal Viṣṇu, even produced Brahmā-Prajāpati and the five elements.[262] Is there sufficient room for the supposition that the name before being associated with Viṣṇu was borne by a more or less distinct individual, a more or less deified person who was believed to have creative power and to be immune and safe from any form of restraint or frustration? Or was a legendary person of this name in the course of time identified with creative divine figures and important cosmogonic and philosophical principles and thanks to his relations with Kṛṣṇa introduced into Viṣṇuism?[263]

It is, further, part of the doctrines of the Pāñcarātrins—and of the Śrī-Vaiṣṇavas—that each *vyūha* has two activities, a creative and preservative one and an ethical one, by which they lend assistance to those devotees who seek to attain the ultimate emancipation.[264] Saṃkarṣaṇa is responsible for the evolution of the universe and teaches the true monotheistic religion; Pradyumna is concerned with the appearance of the duality of *puruṣa* and *prakṛti* and the translation of the religious precepts into practice, i.e. the teaching of the *dharma*; Aniruddha with the creation of souls, the maintenance and government of the world and the promulgation of the good results of the observance of the *dharma*, i.e. the way to liberation; he proclaims the Pāñcarātra religion.[265] This doctrine again seems to be an elaboration and systematization of ancient tendencies. Prajāpati. from whom, when he was alone, are the three worlds,[266] gives advice to the gods,[267] exhorts Puruṣa Nārāyaṇa to sacrifice,[268] inspires devotion[269] and assigns the conditions of life, etc., to the creatures.[270] Considering that all existing things are in the threefold Vedic lore he made himself that lore[271] I need not recall the famous figure of Kṛṣṇa who reveals and preaches his religion while proclaiming himself Brahman and the Īśvara.[272]

There is no reference to the *vyūhas* in the monotheistic (*ekānta*) doctrine of the Bhagavadgītā but it may be observed that its introduction was in a way facilitated by the theory of God's 'natures' (*prakṛti*).[273] God's lower nature is eightfold divided into the five elements and the three principles of Sāṃkhya psychology *manas, buddhi* and *ahaṃkāra*,[274] but distinct from this is his higher nature, which is the very life by which the universe is upheld.[275] Although eternal, He moreover comes into existence by an act of his will with regard to his own *prakṛti* and by means of his marvellous creative power (*māyā*),[276] and resting on his own nature he sends forth (or 'creates') again and again all beings.[277]

Besides, the hero element played an important part in the evolution of the *bhakti* cult which is so prominent in the Gītā.[278]

The *vyūha* doctrine must indeed have taken a long time to attain its fully developed form.[279] The earliest sources mentioning it give neither a consistent account nor all the 'biographical' particulars which we find in some purāṇas. It appears however that it was traditionally connected with Kṛṣṇa's revelation communicated in the Gītā,[280] that Nārāyaṇa explains the Sātvata religion of Vāsudeva and his three other forms whilst identifying himself with him; that there were different forms or even schools teaching one, two, three or four *vyūhas*,[281] a way to beatitude by passing through the sun entering into the Aniruddha form and, becoming *manas*, into the Pradyumna form and the Saṃkarṣaṇa form (i.e. *jīva*, the individual soul) finally to attain to Vāsudeva, the omnipresent Supreme Soul;[282] or also the possibility of reaching the goal, i.e. of attaining to Hari, who is the final and absolute reality, without passing through the three stages of Aniruddha, Pradyumna and Saṃkarṣaṇa.[283]

We would go too far afield if we tried to examine also the variant forms of the *vyūha* doctrine and the successive emanation in three stages of the universe which is another characteristic of the Pāñcarātrins.[284] One example may suffice. The Mārkaṇḍeya-Purāṇa,[285] describing the lord of the gods, the universal soul (*puruṣa*), the eternal and changeless as existing in four forms (*caturvyūhātman*), that is (as) the adorable Nārāyaṇa who, pervading all things, lives in a quadruple form, argues that his first form (*mūrti*) is inscrutable, transcendent, the acme of perfection to devotees; when called Vāsudeva his shape, etc., can only be conceived mentally. His second form is Śeṣa, who supports the earth and is characterized by the *tamoguṇa*. His third form is active, devoted to the preservation of the creatures and characterized by the predominance of the *sattvaguṇa*; it creates itself in *avatāras* and is called Pradyumna. His fourth form, characterized by the *rajoguṇa*, abides on a serpent as its bed in the waters, and is always creative.[286]

Nor can I enter here into a discussion of the sub-*vyūhas*[287] and *vibhavas* (manifestations) or *avatāras* (descents or incarnations)[288] of God or His *vyūhas*. Among the thirty-nine *vibhavas* or 'special existencies' assumed by the Ahirbudhnya Saṃhitā[289] are beside Kapila, Dharma, Nara, Nārāyaṇa and others some of the well-known 'classical' avatāras: Varāha, Kṛṣṇa, both Rāmas and Kalkin.[290] The belief in the existence of Kṛṣṇa Vāsudeva, who as Para Vāsudeva is the Highest

Being, as an *avatāra* led to the conclusion that in his latter aspect he was only a partial incarnation of the Supreme Kṛṣṇa.[291] The distinction between these different forms of the divine essence is however not without practical interest. In accordance with the different degrees of His grace God qualifies those who have fully realized the truth to understand His highest self; those who are incompletely successful are allowed to approach the *vyūha* forms; the unsuccessful may adore the *vibhavas*.[292]

Although Pāñcarātra ideas were largely absorbed by post-epic Viṣṇuism, the doctrine of the essentially cosmic and emanative *vyūhas* receded into the background when the intramundane incarnatory saviours, the *avatāras*, came to enjoy general popularity.[293] In contradistinction to the Ālvārs, whose passionate belief in and love of God prevented them from showing any interest in cosmology, Rāmānuja and the Śrī-Vaiṣṇavas were however prepared to accept it;[294] 'out of affection for those who resort to Him, the Highest Brahman called Vāsudeva out of his own free will exists in fourfold form in order to become (more easily) accessible to them'.[295] For them Vāsudeva, like Sadāśiva of the Śivaites, was the Para-Brahman of the Vedantic schools of thought, which assumed the forms called *vyūhas* out of tenderness to its devotees and for purposes of worship.[296] By the successive worship of the manifestations (*avatāras*) and the *vyūhas* one attains to the 'Subtle' called Vāsudeva, that is the Highest Brahman.[297]

One of the tenets of Pāñcarātra Viṣṇuism concerns the six ideal *guṇas* (component attributes) which, being *aprākṛta* ('not belonging to nature', because nature does in this phase not exist as yet)[298] make up, in their totality, the 'body' of the highest personal God as well as that of Lakṣmī. In this form God is usually called Vāsudeva.[299] These six *guṇas* are the instruments or material of pure creation, but their evolution does not affect God's being or essence. It is merely concerned with His 'becoming', that is, with His Śakti, His efficacious power by which He is able to produce something which cannot be accounted for by empirical methods,[300] and with which a god could, already in Ṛgvedic times, fill the universe[301] and perform creative deeds.[302] The process of emanation which therefore leaves the source of the product unchanged is enacted by the six *guṇas* in their totality and by pairs, and the very appearance of these pairs denotes the beginning of the process. The first beings which come into existence as a result of the chain of emanations which is started in this way are the *vyūhas*. The pair of *guṇas* which becomes manifest in Saṃkarṣaṇa is *jñāna* ('omniscience') and *bala* ('force')—it may be remembered that this figure is also called Baladeva 'god of force'—, that becoming manifest in Pradyumna *aiśvarya* ('activity based on independent lordship') and *vīrya* ('virility, unaffectedness'), that relating to Aniruddha *śakti* ('potency, ability') and *tejas* ('brilliant energy, self-sufficiency').[303]

Now, although this theory is proper to this school of religious thought it makes use of some well-known older ideas. The coupling in pairs, self-evident as it is when there is a question of creation, cannot in my opinion be disconnected from the Vedic maxim that a pair (*dvandvam*) means strength and a productive copulation.[304] The greater part of the six *guṇas* are moreover power concepts of considerable occurrence in earlier literature so as to enter into combinations with other entities of the same class.[305] Thus *bala* 'strength'—defined by the Pāñcarātrins as 'indefatigability in connection with the production of the world' or 'power to sustain all things'—combines, in brāhmaṇa contexts, with *vīrya*[306]—explained by the Pāñcarātrins as 'being free from alteration'—, with *ojas* 'creative and inaugurative power',[307] or with *varcas* 'lustrous energy'.[308] Just as, moreover, the six *guṇas* compose the 'body' of Vāsudeva, the goddess Śrī is in a brāhmaṇa[309] said, by implication and in a more mythological sphere, to consist of ten power substances among which are *bala*, *brahmavarcasa* (tentatively translatable by 'holiness' or 'sanctity'), *bhaga* ('good fortune; distinction'), *puṣṭi* ('prosperity'),[310] and Indra is stated to be his own special energy.[311] The conception that nothing exists or happens without the great god who is (a) firm ground and in whom all energies unite is expressed already in the Ṛgveda.[312] Elsewhere[313] Prajāpati, one of the 'predecessors' of the Viṣṇuite Lord, is said to have strengthened himself with the two energies, *tejas* and *indriyaṃ vīryam*, which are Agni and Indra. One of the combinations assumed by the Pāñcarātrins, viz. *jñāna* and *bala*, occurs as a compound in a stanza of the Śvetāśvatara-Upaniṣad,[314] describing God as being without work to be done (effect to be reached) and without organ: 'His highest power (*śakti*) is described as manifold, the activity of his knowledge and strength belongs to his nature'. It is interesting to add that in later times an authority such as Rāmānuja[315] was inclined to interpret the occurrence of one of those terms as referring, by implication, to all six *guṇas*; for instance, *vīrya* ascribed, in the Bhagavadgītā, to the Lord, as really meaning that He is a treasure of boundless knowledge, power, force and so on.

It would carry us too far to give an exposition of variant forms of this theory which is subscribed to by definite Viṣṇuite circles, for instance of the belief that Nārāyaṇa, the Highest God and Supreme Brahman, being *caturātman* (that is comprising four divine persons) takes, for the sake of creation, two *guṇas* and appears as the trinity, Brahmā, Viṣṇu and Hara.[316]

The theory of the six ideal *guṇas* and the *vyūhas* proceeding from them may impress us as an elaboration of what Schrader[317] tentatively considered the Pāñcarātra solution of the old Indian problem of God becoming the world without sharing its imperfections. Whether or not this scholar was right in taking what he considers 'the original worship, proved by archaeology and the Buddhist[318] scripture', of only Vāsudeva and Baladeva-Saṃkarṣaṇa to signify nothing else than that by 'the original Pāñcarātrins' Kṛṣṇa-Vāsudeva was revered and adored as the transcendent High God and His brother as His immanent aspect, the addition of two more, probably less popular, it is true,[319] 'members of Kṛṣṇa's family' may safely be regarded as an attempt to harmonize their non-orthodox views with the Vedic doctrine of the fourfold Puruṣa.

One of the documents attesting to this process of penetration of Vedic and originally unorthodox 'Viṣṇuite' doctrines, the Mudgala-Upaniṣad,[320] enunciates the rather uncomplicated theory that one fourth of the full Brahman, the Infinite One, Puruṣa Nārāyaṇa, viz. Aniruddha Nārāyaṇa,[321] orders Brahmā to create the universe by means of self-immolation and emanation. A more complicated explanation of the first five stanzas of the Puruṣa-sūkta is found in the Ahirbudhnya-Saṃhitā of the Pāñcarātrins.[322] It is taught that the first half of the initial stanza refers to Vāsudeva whose connection with Śrī-Lakṣmī, the *puruṣas*, and *prakṛti* respectively is expressed by the epithets 'with a thousand heads, a thousand eyes, a thousand feet'. The third quarter of the stanza 'having covered the earth (*bhūmim*) on all sides', is interpreted as a reference to the Matter aspect of Lakṣmī as the material cause of the universe,[323] the fourth, 'he extended beyond it the length of ten fingers', as indicating the infinity of the cause[324] as compared with its products. Whereas according to the Mudgala-Upaniṣad the second stanza ('The Puruṣa is this All, What has been and is to be; and he is the lord of immortality, which he grows beyond through food') expresses God's universal pervasion with respect to time, the Ahirbudhnya-Saṃhitā takes it as a reference to Saṃkarṣaṇa who is the lord of immortality with whose help the soul through the material universe reaches liberation. The third stanza is said to state that Pradyumna's service is still greater because he is the creator of *puruṣa* and *prakṛti*. The Mudgalopaniṣad on the other hand considers it to express Hari's high-power-and-greatness (*vaibhavam*) and, alternatively, his being the One of four *vyūhas*: 'Such is his greatness and more than that is Puruṣa. A fourth of him is all beings, three-fourths of him the immortal in heaven'.

Both explanations agree in identifying the fourth quarter mentioned in the next stanza ('With three quarters Puruṣa rose upward; one quarter of him here came into being again . . . '[325] with Aniruddha, the Inner Ruler (*antaryāmin*[326] of all beings, who pervades the animate and inanimate nature. The fifth stanza ('From him Virāj was born, from Virāj Puruṣa . . .') refers, according to the Saṃhitā, to the first Puruṣa, who is Aniruddha[327] and the second Puruṣa, i.e. Brahmā, the Virāj being the Highest *prakṛti*, the matter in the form of an egg out of which the demiurge produced the world. The upaniṣad is however of the opinion that the poet deals with the origin of prakṛti and puruṣa from Pāda Nārāyaṇa, who really is Hari.[328]

It may in this connection be remembered that a belief in a fourfold division of the Supreme Reality[329] is also apparent in other Viṣṇuite contexts.[330] 'In the epoch of Manu Svayambhū the eternal Nārāyaṇa was'—according to an epic passage[331]—'born as the son of Dharma in a quadruple form, namely, Nara, Nārāyaṇa, Hari and Kṛṣṇa.' According to the well-known account of the Rāmāyaṇa[332] Rāma and his three brothers were incarnations of Viṣṇu. Fourfoldness is in a way also characteristic of the epic Viṣṇu, among whose thousand names is Caturvyūha.[333] The author of the Viṣṇu-Purāṇa asserts that the Highest Being, Viṣṇu-Vāsudeva, is in four forms, viz. *pradhāna* (indiscrete primal matter), *puruṣa* (spirit), *vyakta* (the manifested) and *kāla* (time) the cause of production, preservation and absorption.[334] It is therefore not surprising to find, also in Pāñcarātric and other Viṣṇuite texts, many correlations of God and his *śakti* with the four regions of the universe.[335]

It may be worth while to dwell for a moment on the elaboration of the concept of the composite God in which the *vyūhas* were merged into One.[336] The idea of 'One in Four' is for instance illustrated by the four-faced early medieval Viṣṇu images from Northern India, mostly Kashmir.[337] Laying much emphasis on the ideology behind the images of the gods, which they regard as the consecrated symbols of these divine powers, iconographical texts inform us that Viṣṇu's eight arms stand for the four cardinal and intermediate points of the compass, that his four faces, illustrating the concept of the unified *vyūhas*, typify the ideal *guṇas bala*, *jñāna*, *aiśvarya* and *śakti* which, being associated with the four *vyūhas*, are in this connection, interestingly enough, reduced to four.[338] The four faces are allocated as follows: the front or eastern (human) face is that of Vāsudeva, the southern (lion) face belongs to Saṃkarṣaṇa, the northern (boar) face to Pradyumna and the back or western one, the fierce (*raudra*), to Aniruddha.[339] It may be asked[340] whether the last figure is here the representative of destruction,[341] a function elsewhere[342] attributed to Saṃkarṣaṇa.[343]

It remains briefly to revert to the important part played by Lakṣmī, God's *śakti*. Whereas in his supreme state Viṣṇu and his *śakti* are said to be always associated with one another[344] and to constitute one Paramātman, the Supreme Brahman[345] without distinction,[346]—hence the use of the compound Lakṣmī-Nārāyaṇa[347]—in the first stage of primary creation the latter 'awakes' in her two aspects *kriyā* and *bhūti*, 'action' and 'becoming'. That means that she is the *causa instrumentalis* and the *causa materialis* of the universe.[348] Then she manifests the six ideal guṇas which together constitute Vāsudeva and Lakṣmī. Here again it is of some interest to remember that *bhūti* 'becoming, thriving, development'[349] is an old term which already in the Ṛgveda conveyed the meaning 'coming into being, genesis'.[350] Vṛtra, the fiend, who does not wish the constitution of an inhabitable world is said to keep us from *bhūti*.[351] The term[352] sometimes occurs in the same context as *śrī*, which as the name of the goddess is in the course of time to fuse with Lakṣmī, God's Śakti: thus the Earth is[353] requested 'to set the person praying in well-being and development (prosperity)'. In the ideal condition of humanity sketched in the closing stanza of the Bhagavadgītā[354] *śrī*, triumph, *bhūti* and morality will be sure. Bhūti is also adored as a divine person,[355] and then is one of the goddesses who are invoked together with Śrī to promote the welfare of the creatures.[356] In the Great Epic this figure is not only identified with Śrī[357] but also with Viṣṇu himself.[358] The idea that a divine being starts creating with an aspect of itself—as is asserted by the Viṣṇuites in Lakṣmī's case—had already been expressed in connection with Prajāpati who in order to develop and to become manifold[359] differentiated himself into sixteen aspects.[360] After that he started creating. As to

Śrī-Lakṣmī's relation to Viṣṇu both components of this goddess' essence were in the Vedic period considered the consorts of Puruṣa, who is Prajāpati,[361] from whom, according to another place,[362] she came forth, high in rank and possessed of royal power, universal sovereignty, prosperity and pre-eminence in holiness.

Lakṣmī's other aspect, *kriyā*, is indicated by a term which though expressing the general idea of 'performance, action, activity', was often especially applied to ritual acts and performances,[363] that is to acts which, though performed in the mundane sphere, result in cosmic and superhuman effects.

How extremely important the place occupied by Lakṣmī is in this system appears from the fact that the so-called 'pure creation', that is the stage in which God's ideal guṇas become distinct, is said to be the consequence of the first phase of her manifestation.[364] That means that she, the ultimate eternal power of Viṣṇu, manifests herself as the *vyūhas*. In the second stage of primary creation it is her *bhūti* aspect which is manifested in the grosser forms of the aggregate of the individual souls[365] and the *māyā śakti*, the energy which is the immaterial source of the universe. Hence the belief that this metaphysical complement of the Lord assumes also, not only the forms of the *śaktis* of the *vyūhas* and of His manifestations, but also the functions ordinarily ascribed to the great gods who supervise all origin, maintenance and reabsorption in the universe. It is therefore Lakṣmī, the ultimate supreme power into which all other powers resolve themselves and mythologically, the queen of the Highest Heaven,[366] who is also called Brahmā, Viṣṇu and Śiva. It is Lakṣmī who is creatively active,[367] while taking into consideration the accumulated *karman* of the living beings[368] and who manifests her nature in other goddesses such as Durgā, Kālī and so on, who is Mahālakṣmī because she stamps (*lakṣayati*) mundane existence as merit and demerit; who is Bhadrā in her beneficial form and Kālī as the destroyer of the wicked.[369] It is Lakṣmī, mythologically God's wife,[370] and always intent on delivering, by her favour and compassion (*anugraha*), the incarnated souls out of the misery of mundane existence,[371] who, identified with Viṣṇu's highest location or manifestation (*paraṃ dhāma* or *paramaṃ padam*[372]) is the highest goal of the devotees—whose souls are parts or rather 'contractions'[373] of the Goddess; it is she into whom enter the emancipated. The belief that the liberated soul 'becomes one' (*ekībhavati*) with the Lord, that is with Viṣṇu as Para Vāsudeva, should therefore be qualified as follows:

as having entered Lakṣmī he takes part in the perfect embrace of the divine couple.

In studying the great significance of the Śakti concept in general we may moreover do well to remember that this term also could at an early date convey the idea of an energy by which man might, in the ritual sphere, come into contact with the divine. It is the *śakti* of the sacrificer which is believed to induce Indra to approach, but also the latter's *śakti* which is gracious and salutary (*bhadrā*) for the former.[374] Indra is requested to intercede for men and Agni said to fill heaven and earth with their *śaktis*.[375] It may be recalled that the epithet *śacīpati* 'lord of energy' is in the Veda often given to Indra in passages mentioning his heroic deeds which made the world an inhabitable cosmos and his readiness to help and assist man.[376] The possession of *śakti* was also an essential requirement of those who wanted to reach heaven.[377] In the Pāñcarātric view of God's Śakti Śrī-Lakṣmī has spontaneously and by virtue of her own power differentiated herself from God for the sake of the liberation of all souls.[378]

These few remarks may help to explain why the goddess—whether she is conceived as Viṣṇu's spouse or as a really metaphysical principle—should have been become the central figure in the expositions of some Pāñcarātra authorities.

IV

Ritual

BEFORE EMBARKING upon a study of the ritual and ceremonial aspects of Śaivism and Vaiṣṇavism we should be aware of the fact that despite their enormous and long-established significance in literature, both gods and the typical rites of their religions do not nowadays, and in all probability did not for many centuries, play the same prominent role in the daily religious practice of the masses. Worshipped by part of the population as the Supreme Being, Śiva and Viṣṇu belong in the first place also to a group of major and remote divine figures, who appear prominently in literature and in the religion of the higher classes which are concerned with the acquisition of good fortune or religious merit which is expected to determine the devotee's fate after death. These higher deities are objects of a cult practised in temples or in shrines in private houses, where their images are installed. They are also generally iconographically represented and, as they are presumed to be the purest and most respectable group of higher beings, they are worshipped only after the devotee has ritually purified himself. Their worship is performed regularly and at least once a year they are honoured with special celebrations. Although their devotees sometimes invoke their aid and favour, they are above manipulation and cannot be forced to comply with man's requests. They are generally not supposed to cause, like the lower deities, misfortune, but rather to withhold their favour in case some evil should befall the worshipper. They are on the other hand concerned with the weal and woe of the universe and with the ultimate fate of the individual's soul.[1]

A discussion of the cult of Viṣṇu[2] and Śiva[3] must in the second place be prefaced by the remark that, although generally speaking all Hindus know of these gods,[4] and have a notion of their main functions, their daily concern in the workaday world is rather with a host of minor deities whose special business it is to regulate matters of immediate personal interest.[5] This fact is, on the side of Viṣṇu and Śiva, in harmony with a certain lack of prominence in ancient and traditional popular belief, for instance in astronomical and cosmological systems[6] where they are put on a par with many colleagues, and in works dealing with portents and prognostication, in which these two gods do it is true occur, but mainly act like Indra, Vāyu, Yama and other parochial deities.[7] Their increasing significance as high gods[8] led, on the other hand, to their introduction into ever new situations and provinces of religious life.[9]

A closely connected preliminary observation concerns the relations between these two gods of the so-called Great, that is Sanskritic and philosophical, tradition[10] on the one hand and the powers and deities of the Little, that is the popular, on the whole regional, tradition including innumerable religious observances not described in Sanskrit literature—a distinction which is largely similar to that between transcendental and pragmatic complexes. The relations between general Hindu religious and philosophical doctrines on one hand and village practice on the other is a subtle and complicated topic which we cannot tackle here. The centuries-old, ever continuing process of mutual 'osmosis' and penetration of these two traditions involves also the adoption of popular and local deities into the pantheon recognized by the Sanskrit-writing authorities and their occasional identification with Hindu gods.[11] Thus Viṣṇu—whose worshippers were already at an early date inclined to include other gods in their faith—, after identifying himself with Kṛṣṇa and Nārāyaṇa, absorbed local divinities into himself, such as Veṅkateśa and Tirupati in the South and Viṭhoba of Mahārāṣṭra. Viṣṇuite authors also adopted, to mention another instance, Vindhyavāsinī, the most prominent among the female deities of the Vindhya mountains, and connected her with Viṣṇu by taking her to be an incarnation of his Yoganīdrā or Yogamāyā. The question however arises why the goddesses of the villages,[12] when they make their appearance also in the big temples of the Hindu gods should, in the South and elsewhere, be more often regarded as consorts of Śiva than as allied with Viṣṇu, and how we are to account for the fact that 'the differentiation between Śaivas and Vaiṣṇavas is maintained a long way out among the so-called village gods'.[13] The explanation that the strong trend to connect the village deities with Śiva was because he was the more popular is unlikely.[14] We should rather think of his special character and his special affinity with the popular deities. The god who in Vedic times was the ruler of a host of Rudras and whose spouse, Durgā, maintains close relations with the uncivilized part of the Indian world, may on the contrary have won the sympathy of many uneducated countrymen because his ambivalent and incalculable character could strongly appeal to their feelings and easily chime in with their conceptions of divinity.

As soon as a religious community tends to split up into a number of members who are inclined to 'leave the world' and a group of devotees which are not, or not yet, able or willing to take this step, the former group may assume the character of an 'inner circle' or 'order' which seeking a life of devotion, retains, adopts, or develops a common cult, particular vows and observances and a form of initiation. Whereas Hindus, generally speaking, are free, mainly from individual motives, to join such an inner circle, once they have joined they have to submit to its rites and way of living. I first select for a short discussion the *dīkṣā*,[15] initiation or consecration, which, involving a transformation of the aspirant's personality, bears a greater resemblance to the traditional *upanayana*—the pupilage and 'second birth' of a twice-born boy—[16] than to the Vedic *dīkṣā* of the sacrificer—with which it however is functionally related[17]—and which in milieux aspiring to a more permanent state of sanctity was regarded as a complement to, or even a valuable substitute for, a previous *upanayana*. Ancient and widespread ideas and customs in connection with initiation were gradually put into practice in the framework of Hindu ritual and embedded in Viṣṇuite or Śivaite patterns of Hinduism. Both religions feeling the need of this institution very strongly, Viṣṇuism emphasized its character as an initiation to a life of devotion, as an entrance into closer contact with God,[18] although freedom from *karma* and *saṃsāra* are, besides happiness, prosperity, knowledge, a long life and other ambitions, among the ideals to be realized through this rite.[19] Śivaism,[20] on the other hand, urges the absolute necessity of *śaivī dīkṣā*, initiation into a Śaiva 'order', performed in accordance with the Śaiva ritual, for anyone who wishes to attain to final liberation. All religious schools are agreed[21] that the one who has the authority to initiate others is the qualified *guru*,[22] as a rule a brahman[23]—but among the Śaivas[24] and in some Vaiṣṇava communities also members of the other ranks—who has received the special *gurudīkṣā*, and whom Śaivas as well as Vaiṣṇavas often regard as representing God himself.[25] The Śrī-Vaiṣṇavas even believe him to be a visible partial incarnation of God; for them, as for all Vaiṣṇavas, the *guru* is indeed more than a teacher, and even more than a mediator between God and men; in the Śaiva conviction every initiate is considered a manifestation of Śiva himself, several schools emphasizing that guru and aspirant are brought into contact through divine grace.[26]

It is the opinion of both religions that the main object of *dīkṣā* is purification.[27] Whereas the Viṣṇuites assert that this is a prerequisite to admission to a religious order or community because the soul needs purification before it can become God-conscious, the Śaivas hold that the *dīkṣā* imparted by a *guru*, who represents God himself and who after the initiation continues to assist the initiate, destroys the original impurity (*āṇava-mala*)[28] and paves the way for removing 'animality' (*paśutva*) and for attaining the state of being Śiva (*śivatva*). Pāñcarātra Viṣṇuites commit the postulant to a confession—a well-known sort of purification—and a probationary period;[29] the Vīraśaivas combine it with ethical preachings and yoga mysticism.[30] It would carry us too far to survey all *dīkṣā* ceremonies recognized as duty and custom by the various communities. Mention may only be made here of the *samaya-dīkṣā*,[31] by which a person is admitted into the fold of Śaivism and becomes entitled[32] to perform rites (with the exception of the fire ritual).[33] It may be said to correspond to the *pañcasaṃskāra* ceremony, 'the fivefold sacraments', of the Śrī-Vaiṣṇavas. The latter consists of the distinct sacral acts of branding the symbols of God on the postulant's shoulders (*tāpa*, a custom known also to the Śaivas[34]), the application of the distinctive mark on the forehead (*puṇḍra*), the reception, by the initiate, of a devotional name (*nāman*) and of the distinctive holy formulas of the community (*mantra*) and, finally, the presenting of an image of God for worshipping (*yāga*, *yajana*).[35]

The *mantra* is of special importance. The Sudarśana *mantra* imparted to a Pāñcarātra novice should, to mention only this, on no account be used for trifling objects or mundane purposes, only for welfare, never for destruction. The Śivaites are likewise convinced that the *mantra* is a form or representative of God himself,[36] the phenomenal world being the materialization of the mantras, without which no cult is possible. After the ceremony of branding the Vaiṣṇava postulant often requests to be initiated into one of the sacred scriptures of Viṣṇuism, to catch the real spirit of which he now becomes prepared. In Vaiṣṇava practice, moreover, *dīkṣā* for admission into the 'inner circle' is, in accordance with the four classes of men, fourfold. If the candidate is a *kṣatriya* or a *vaiśya* he must renounce his customary way of life.[37] The Śaivas on the other hand, convinced that God does not manifest Himself to all souls in the same way, recognize different methods of initiation varying with the recipients. Some of them need oral instruction, others an introduction into asceticism and *yoga*, or instruction through religious symbols, etc. In this they agree with the Tantrists who are of the opinion that the mode of initiation has to vary according to the disciple's disposition and competency.[38] A certain propensity to Tantrist practices[39] is however not foreign to definite Viṣṇuite communities either. Admitting no less than four procedures, one of which[40] follows the directions of the Pāñcarātra authorities, they may also initiate a candidate in accordance with the *nyāsa* practice, i.e. the imposition of so-called mystic syllables on his body in order to unite him with spiritual qualities,[41] and with the penetrating (*vedhamayī*) procedure[42] consisting in teaching how to penetrate into the six circles assumed by the Yoga doctrine to exist in the human body.

The ascetic (*sādhu*) usually wears some distinctive mark (*puṇḍra*) on his forehead and often carries some symbol of his religion. If he recognizes Viṣṇu as the Supreme Being he may possess a discus and a conch shell (*śaṅkha*), replicas of God's invincible flaming weapon, through which its owner is superior to men, gods and demons, and of His instrument of beneficent power and protection against evil which, penetrating the universe, symbolizes his omnipresent power.[43] In addition to these he has a *śālagrāma* stone[44] or a *tulasī* plant[45] which are representatives of Viṣṇu's own essence and of that of his consort Lakṣmī. If he is a Śaiva he will, impersonating his God himself, carry a trident[46] which denotes empire and the irresistible force of transcendental reality, wear a small liṅga[47] and possess a human skull[48] which shows his being above the terror inspired by worldly transitoriness of which it is reminiscent, and a ḍamaru drum,[49] which symbolizes God's creative power, and a tiger skin, his well-known garment. In imitation of his god he may have his body smeared with white ashes and he will set up the *liṅga*—from which all life in the universe has issued—for worship[50] wherever he settles. All communities agree that the sacredness of these emblems—like that of images—is due to the fact that the presence of God, when invoked by *mantras*, is felt to be in them so that they enable the devotee to worship the Invisible through the visible.

That the opposition between the two great religious currents related to their socio-ritual differences rather than the theoretic sides of their religion, theology and philosophical foundations, is only a special case of the general Hindu conviction that it is the *dharma*—an untranslatable term[51] implying *inter alia* the whole of the socio-religious norms and duties, the being in harmony with the right order, the traditional Hindu way of life implying morality as well as right and virtuous conduct—that really matters and not the *mata*, i.e. the opinions, beliefs and doctrines, regarding which one may to a considerable extent use one's own discretion,[52] because, while freedom of opinion obtains to an exceptional degree, the *dharma*, maintained and observed, supports the structure of society, upholds the regular and harmonious progress of the cosmic processes and is essential to the continuity of all phenomena in the universe.[53] It becomes, then, intelligible that also in matters of cults and rites right and correct behaviour is viewed as an important personal duty and responsibility: Viṣṇuites are averse to taking part in Śivaite ritual performances, to observing Śivaite practices, to pronounce Śivaite mantras. A *mantra* containing the name of a god—for instance *namaḥ śivāya*—is indeed regarded as embodying the energy of the god which is activated by pronouncing the formula. The knowledge of, and meditation on, a mantra enables the adept to exert influence upon the god, to exercise power over the potencies manifesting in it, to establish connections between the divinity and himself, or to realize his identity with that divinity. The idea expressed by means of a *mantra* which is characteristic of, and handed down in, a definite religious community, and by being informed of which one is received into membership, is described as 'the sum of all spiritual truth', as the concentrated essence of divine reality, etc. Such a formula becomes so to say the 'watch-word'[54] of a community or the 'hallmark' of the correct ritual behaviour of the one who pronounces it. Using strange mantras means following strange gods and dissociating oneself from the traditions of one's group, and this implies a serious infraction of the *dharma*.[55] In this connection it is interesting to notice that not only the most important *Gāyatrī mantra* (ṚV. 3, 62, 10) was in various religious communities subjected to variation so as to make it more adapted to their particular purposes, but even the ancient syllable *Oṃ* was differently interpreted, Śaivas regarding it as an equivalent to the five syllables of their mantra *namaḥ śivāya* and Pāñcarātrins believing it to represent the three *vyūhas* of Aniruddha, Pradyumna and Saṃkarṣaṇa.[56]

The masses being bound up with external observances and the main form of their religious activity being ritual and ceremonial, the traditional Hindu is convinced that, in view of the fundamental oneness of the universe, an harmonious co-operation of men in ceremonial activities[57] is necessary for the harmonious functioning of the world. All must co-operate if the crops are to be good, and if the life of the village is to be happy. Constituting, in the sphere of the *hic et nunc*, a repetition and representation of timeless mythological events of universal significance and expressing at selected or critical moments—which may be dangerous or beneficent—man's feeling of oneness with higher power, their celebration carries him beyond the critical moment. In practice, they serve multiple ends: the collective experience of the nearness and the stimulation of power on high-days, purification, protection, honouring of deities. They are a source of pleasure and recreation, nourish spiritual life and, moreover, provide the principal occasion on which most villages may engage in concerted symbolic activities.[58] Although the great gods play, in many festivities, no important part, it would carry us too far to enter into a detailed survey of the main Viṣṇuite and Śivaite high-days.[59] Let it suffice to recall that, speaking quite generally, the Śivaite festivals are less strictly vegetarian and non-alcoholic[60] than the Viṣṇuite; that one and the same festival may comprise the worship of either god; that there is no hesitation in partaking of the food offered to Viṣṇu, but much aversion to eating that which even nominally remains of an oblation, presented to Śiva; that particular elements of the rites and festivities are traditionally associated with the characters of these divine figures or find their motivation in Viṣṇuite or Śivaite mythology;[61] that the same ceremonies may be known to both communities but be practised differently; that Viṣṇu is not only often represented by one of his *avatāras*[62] but also associated with other gods, who then are also adored by Śaivas, whereas the festivals for Durgā cannot be disconnected from her matrimonial relations with Śiva; that in this point also, the gods may, to a certain extent, be said to complement each other, the fifth month of Hindu year being, for instance, sacred to Viṣṇu, the tenth to Śiva.

I must however pay some attention to the matutinal ritual. This very important part of the duties of the traditional Indian householder, which—in spite of some insertions and modifications—is mainly Vedic in character[63] and is elaborately described in the dharma literature,[64] is in Śaiva and Vaiṣṇava circles much the same.[65] The principal topics mentioned under the head 'daily duties and ceremonies' (*āhnika*) are the following: getting up from bed, care of the bodily purity (*śauca*), brushing the teeth (*dantadhāvana*),[66] bath (*snāna*), worship in the morning and evening twilight (*saṃdhyā*), offering water to gods, sages and deceased ancestors (*tarpaṇa*),[67] the five so-called *mahāyajñas* (i.e. offering, in fire, to the gods; offering to the Fathers; presenting a *bali*-oblation to demons and spirits; giving food to brahmans or honouring guests; study of the Veda),[68] attending the fire, the midday meal, professional duties, gifts, performing sacrifices at certain times, going to bed.[69] The rules of ritual conduct and routine and the objectives recognized in both religions—which in this respect also do not conform exactly to the same principles—are different only in details. The ritual leads to *bhukti* (mundane results) and *mukti* (final liberation), but the Vaiṣṇavas[70] attach much value to what is called the *sāttvika tyāga*, which, being regarded as the climax of their observances, consists in renouncing any kind of fruit or benefit and in performing them only to please Lord Viṣṇu.[71] Emphasizing that it is the end and aim of man's life to attain final liberation (*mokṣa*) and that this end is best gained by the continual service of God, they perform the daily rites in order to preserve the state of corporeal and mental purity which is an absolute requirement and to adore God while realizing their entire dependence on Him.[72] It may further be recalled that the Viṣṇuites, who are also known as Bhāgavatas, Sāttvikas, etc., adore their god in many manifestations and under different names.[73]

The preparatory acts executed in purification and sanctification of the worshipper himself give no occasion for many remarks.[74] Those Śivaite manuals which are to a considerable extent influenced by Tantrist practices pay attention to the dedication of the worshipper's daily inhalations and exhalations to the deities residing in the seven *cakras*, i.e. power centres, in his body,[75] and the subsequent *prāṇapratiṣṭhā*, i.e. the establishment of God's life-breath into the person of the worshipper.[76] That other Śivaite manuals insert, after the teeth-cleaning,[77] a prayer to Bhairava at bathing time is not surprising. The complex of rites connected with bathing[78] comprises, inter alia, the recitation of the *mūlamantra*, that is the basic or principal mantra of a religious community, viz. *namaḥ śivāya* for the Śaivas, *Oṃ namo nārāyaṇāya*[79] for a Śrī-Vaiṣṇava, etc. In addition to this other mantras and formularized prayers are muttered, the Viṣṇuites being enjoined exclusively to think of the service of God, urging Him to be pleased with the most auspicious materials for worship.[80] While under water the devotee should imagine that his head is below the feet of God and he should repeat the eight-syllabled *mantra* as many times as he possibly can. Having come out of the water he repeats stanzas about God and the hierarchy of his *ācāryas* (spiritual teachers) and he proceeds to pronounce some Vedic *mantras*, taking two cloths for drying and cleaning his body with: 'At the impulse of god Savitar I take thee with the arms of the Aśvins, with the hands of Pūṣan'[81] and showing them to the sun with ṚV. 1, 50, 1, etc. 'The rays support that well-known god Jātavedas (here the Sun is meant), that the whole (world) may see him',[82] which is followed by *VS.* 1, 14, etc. 'Shaken off are the evil spirits, shaken off the (envious) enemies',[83] pronounced while the cloths are shaken. Wrapping them round his head he prays with *TĀ.* 7, 4, 1 f.[84] for prosperity, clothes, cows, food, drink and good fortune. Finally[85] he concentrates his thoughts on God as effulgent with innumerable suns and carrying conch, disk, club and lotus in his four hands.

Instead of these acts and formulas Śivaite texts enjoin the worshipper to pronounce the non-Vedic *astra-mantra* (*astrāya namaḥ* or *Oṃ haḥ astrāya huṃ phaṭ*)[86] which is a protection against evil influences, to consecrate the mud with which his body is to be rubbed[87] with the three likewise non-Vedic *tattva-mantras* honouring the representatives of the three groups of principles *ātman*, *vidyā* ('wisdom') and Śiva,[88] to practise a definite ritual finger position (*mudrā*)[89] and to perform the elaborate *astra-śānti*. This is a rite of appeasement and propitiation[90] consisting of, *inter alia*, a meditation on God's *astradevatā*, i.e. his deified trident,[91] which may be followed[92] by a Tantric rite to control the vital forces of the body (*prāṇāyāma*),[93] a technique which paves the way for mental stability, concentration and 'unification' of consciousness.[94] Finally the worshipper has to bathe while pronouncing several mantras and performing various acts for fortifying himself against evil,[95] and sip—of course also in the prescribed ritual way—water. The latter act (*ācamana*)[96] is to wipe out all traces of preceding acts[97] so that the worshipper is, 'as a new man', able to pass on to another stage of his (ritual) performances. An additional Śivaite rite to be mentioned in this connection is the purification and powdering of the body by means of sacred ashes, remaining after burning cow-dung[98] which being intrinsically pure needs only a consecration, no purification.[99]

One of the other elements of the ritual, the offering to the gods, *ṛṣis* and Fathers (*tarpaṇa*),[100] is performed by the Śrī-Vaiṣṇavas in the consciousness of their being integral parts (*aṃśa*) of God's nature.[101] In contradistinction to the Vedic gṛhyasūtras,[102] which recognize the rite as an appendage[103] of the early morning bath, Śrī-Vaiṣṇava authorities do not insist on the names of the gods, etc. being mentioned individually,[104] but prescribe a comprehensive formula of the type allowed by later authorities on *dharma* if the worshipper has no time for the lengthy enumeration of names.[105] The Vaikhānasas,[106] according a place of honour to Nārāyaṇa, steer a middle course, enumerating the names of many gods, but limiting those of the ṛṣis to the most prominent. The Śaivas, besides the use of other mantras introduced by the Vedic vyāhṛtis (*Oṃ bhūr bhuvaḥ svaḥ*),[107] recognize additional ritual acts which are partly Tantric in character.[108]

The next act, if the devotee is a Śaiva,[109] is the application of the sacred ashes in the *tripuṇḍra* form (three horizontal lines),[110] if he is a Vaiṣṇava, the putting on of the *ūrdhvapuṇḍra*, that is of the perpendicular mark on the forehead, characteristic of the adherents of his religion. Both worshippers put the consecrated material—the Vaiṣṇava uses a kind of white clay and turmeric powder—in their left[111] hand, pronounce mantras and proceed to apply them, not only to the forehead but also to other parts of the body.[112] The Śrī-Vaiṣṇava has, here again, ancient mantras, e.g. stanza of the Śrīsūkta *ṚVKh.* 5, 87[113] 'I invoke here that Śrī, who is perceptible through her odour, who is irresistible, always well supplied (with nourishment), abounding in dung, the ruler of all creatures'. It may be remembered[114] that Śrī, the goddess of welfare and prosperity, and Viṣṇu's spouse, makes her presence felt also in dung, abundant food and in the fertile soil, hence also in the clay applied by the Viṣṇuite to his body.[115] The function of both substances, clay and ashes, is indeed lustral and fortifying; the marks themselves, though in daily practice largely serving as means of identifying the bearer's caste or religious group, are considered to express or 'symbolize' his living in connection with divine power.[116] Other *mantras* to be pronounced—in addition to the *mūla-mantra*, etc.—by a Śrī-Vaiṣṇava are ṚV. 1, 154, 1 the first stanza of the Viṣṇusūkta: 'I will now proclaim the heroic deeds of Viṣṇu, who has measured out the terrestrial regions; who established the upper abode having, wide-paced, strode out triply'[117] and a series of short formulas which, being identical with a series of Vedic *mantras* used, in another ritual context, together with ṚV. 1, 154, 1 and other formulas, are to consecrate the dedication of some parts of the worshipper's body to God.[118] This stanza is immediately followed by two stanzas and a half (five lines) which would be almost completely identical with a passage in the Tattirīya-Āraṇyaka, 10, that is the Mahā-Nārāyaṇa-Upaniṣad, but that the order of the *pādas* is different.[119] In the upaniṣad these formulas are to consecrate a lump of clay with which an ascetic who has renounced all earthly concerns has to smear his body before taking a bath:[120] an indication of historical connections between these Viṣṇuites and ancient ascetic circles.[121]

Then the worshipper puts the marks on the forehead and eleven other places of the body while repeating in definite order twelve names of Viṣṇu: *Oṃ keśavāya namaḥ*, etc. This act is followed by the likewise twelvefold application, with a mixture of Śrī-Lakṣmī's turmeric, of marks of *ścrīcūrṇa* (i.e. 'sacred powder') in the middle of the other marks;[122] while doing so twelve similar *mantras* are addressed to Śrī: *śriyai namaḥ, amṛtodbhavāya namaḥ*, etc. Thereupon the marks are touched while repeating twelve longer mantras in which the same names of Viṣṇu return in the same order.[123] These expressions of homage and humility[124] are non-Vedic but the order of the names,[125] occurring already in Baudhāyana's dharmaśāstra,[126] is traditional.[127] While pronouncing these formulas one presses the hands together and moves them in the correct order to the respective marks.[128] Nowadays most Śrī-Vaiṣṇavas perform the complete ceremony only on festival days, limiting themselves usually to two *puṇḍras* (and the relative mantras), one in the face and the other at the back of the neck.[129] Finally a number of Sanskrit (and in the South also Tamil) formulas and verses are quoted in praise of the *ācāryas*, the highly honoured 'fathers of the church'.

The Śaivas have of course mantras of their own,[130] one consecratory formula in which the elements and everything, including the organs of sense, etc., is stated to be equivalent to the sacred ashes and the water with which they are mixed with light, life-juice, *amṛta*, Brahmā, the three divisions of the universe and the mystic syllable *Oṃ*, and another to worship Śiva, the giver of strength and final emancipation. The identification of the ashes with *amṛta*, the draught of immortality,[131] is especially interesting because one of the Śaiva rites of a Tantric character performed in this connection and frequently also in other ritual contexts is the *amṛtīkaraṇa*,[132] the making of *amṛta*, transmutation of water into the draught of life and immortality.[133] In performing the rites connected with the sacred ashes Śaivas appear to attach much value to a meditation (*dhyāna*) consisting in picturing mentally the iconographic representation of their God in order to achieve the realization of their identity with Him.

An element of the daily rites performed after the application of the *puṇḍra* and, though Tantric in character, adopted by members of both communities is *nyāsa*, the assignment, by means of mantras and the simultaneous imposition of fingers, of various divine powers to parts of the body.[134] According to Śaiva authorities the divinities in different parts of the body represent the five aspects or faces of Śiva, Īśāna residing in the head, Tatpuruṣa in the mouth, etc.[135] The accompanying formulas which occur already in the Mahā-Nārāyaṇa-Upaniṣad, are traditional.[136] At the end of this part of the rites the worshipper has realized his identity with God.

Now he is fully qualified to perform the ritual acts of worship and meditative concentration for the morning (and, if he should perform these also,[137] midday and evening) *samdhyās*.[138] The *saṃdhyā*, an important complex ritual act without which one is impure and unfit for further rites, mainly consists, with variations in detail, in an adoration of, and presentation of offerings (water, sesame, flowers, etc.) to, the sun.[139] Here is room for the observation that the Śaiva, after a complex ritual of breath control, *mudrās*, *mantras*, etc., proceeds to meditate, first on the aspects of the *saṃdhi*—morning-twilight, noon, evening-twilight, considered to be goddesses and the *śaktis* of the three great gods[140]—and after the indispensable *mārjana*, a kind of self-baptism,[141] performed by Śiva—the worshipper *is* Śiva—on himself, continues to meditate on the sun and on Sadāśiva in the centre of the sun's orb, praising him with a long formula. After another *tarpaṇa* ceremony and some other acts he reduces the holy water, called *Śivatīrtha*, to its original elements and makes Śiva return to his sun-form. Finally he goes to a sacred spot to repeat the *mūlamantra*.

Now we should remember that *saṃdhyā* (crepuscular) adorations were already prescribed by ancient authorities on Vedic ritual[142] and *dharma*,[143] some of whom being of the opinion that the first oblation in the morning should be made to Sūrya, or to Sūrya and Prajāpati,[144] and most of them stating that the recitation of the Sāvitrī-stanza addressed to the Sun: We hope to obtain that desirable brightness of Savitar who is expected to stimulate our visions'[145] is the principal element in this rite.[146] This rite, including praise and confirmation of his glory and power,[147] was on the one hand to fortify Sūrya against the powers of darkness[148] and on the other to secure inspiration and, in general, the stimulant and salutary contact with the source of all light.[149] Add to this that the ritual comprised also bathing and the use of other mantras and practices,[150] and that the belief obtained that the god called Āditya represented by, or present in, the orb of the sun was identical with Brahman,[151] it became clear that Śaiva and Vaiṣṇava communities, whose God was no other than Prajāpati or Brahman,[152] could easily adopt the ancient rites while changing some details[153] and incorporating other suitable acts and formulas.[154]

I say Śaivas and Vaiṣṇavas, because the Vaiṣṇava variant of the crepuscular ceremonies is in substance similar, the insertions and innovations tending, of course, to be Viṣṇuite in character. Thus it is nowadays the practice in the Deccan to repeat Viṣṇu's twenty-four names at the very beginning of the complex of rites.[155] What strikes us, here again, is the considerable number of Vedic mantras in use in their communities. Thus the formula *amṛtopastaraṇam asi*[156] 'you are the layer for *amṛta*', which in Vedic rites is to accompany the preparation of a layer for the cup containing the *madhuparka*, i.e. the mixture of honey and milk to be offered to an honoured guest,[157] or the sipping, by that guest, of water,[158]—whereas the Gopatha-Brāhmaṇa mentions it in the section on the *ācamana*, the ritual act of rinsing the mouth[159]—is in Vaiṣṇava practice pronounced to consecrate the drinking of a little of the *tīrtha*, i.e. sacred water. Thereupon the worshipper eats some *prasāda*, that is food that had been offered to God and hence is sacred and believed to bring salvation.[160] Another formula which is to accompany the preceding act, the repeated sprinkling of water, is *satyaṃ tvartena pariṣiñcāmi* 'With ṛta (Order and Truth) I sprinkle round Thee, the true'. Here we have a reminiscence of the Vedic Agnihotra rite, the morning and evening attendance on, and oblation of milk to, Agni,[161] which the important Hinduist *saṃdhyā* rites, while borrowing from it, have replaced. Whereas in the Vedic rite these consecrating words are to accompany the sprinkling, in the morning, round the sacrificial fires,[162] they are now pronounced while water is sprinkled round the plate on which *prasāda* is served.

There is no need to quote further examples of ancient *mantras*[163] or to dwell on the typically Viṣṇuite formulation of the intention (*saṃkalpa*). Let it suffice to add that a Śrī-Vaiṣṇava should not see, while performing these rites, wicked people, *śūdras* and those who worship other deities. If he cannot avoid seeing these spreaders of ritual impurity who would nullify his efforts he should see the sun after them.[164] As to the *upasthāna*, the prayer to that luminary—that is, according to Vaiṣṇava belief, to God being in its disk[165]—, this is performed with the hand in the position of prayer, a *pradakṣiṇa* (a clockwise circumambulation) and three successive stanzas addressed to Mitra, which go back to the Yajurveda, and are in Vedic ritual used in connection with the worship of the ritual fire.[166]

It is time now to pass on to temple worship[167] which reveals a religious life considerably different from that recommended in the Veda.[168]

From the point of view of construction there is no more difference between Śaiva and Vaiṣṇava temples than there has always been in the purposes of those erecting and visiting them.[169] Temple worship obviously originated when the main religious communities had not yet considerably differentiated and it continued to develop along similar lines: while the sanctuaries are dedicated to different deities, the structure of the buildings as well as the daily practices performed in them follow a common pattern.[170] There are, it is true, differences in the symbols or image in the centre,[171] the images on the walls, the symbol fixed on the finial of the top[172] and, likewise, in the *vāhanas* before the entrance, etc., as well as in the mythical motivation of the sacredness of a place. Śiva temples have not rarely been built in consequence of the miraculous appearance or ancient worship of the *liṅga*.[173] Sacred to Durgā are fifty-one places on which parts of her body fell on the earth after she had been cut to pieces by Viṣṇu when Śiva carried her dead body through the world,[174] to Viṣṇu localities of special prominence in the hagiography of his *avatāras*.[175] For, although the gods may manifest themselves wherever they please they have certain favourite abodes on earth and these have acquired sanctity through the permanence of their presence.[176]

Among the many factors to be considered in erecting the temple is its place in relation to the dwellings of men. According to the most comprehensive manual on architecture, etc., the Mānasāra Śilpaśāstra (9, 255 ff.), sanctuaries of Viṣṇu and Lakṣmī in their benevolent aspects should face the village, no doubt in order to allow these deities to radiate their beneficial power throughout its houses. A temple of Narasiṃha, Viṣṇu's fierce lion-man aspect, should however face away from a village; then it will ward off demons and disease. Other authorities are of the opinion that Śiva's temple should be situated in the region sacred to him, that is in the North-East[177]—according to Viṣṇuites,[178] with the god's back towards the village, because 'Hara's (Śiva's) back brings fortune'—Viṣṇu's shrine in the West, facing the village, because 'Hari's (Viṣṇu's) look brings fortune'; but Kauṭilya, while describing the layout of a town, speaks of temples of Śiva, Śrī and other deities in the centre.[179] According to Śaiva authorities, the *liṅga* may be placed anywhere, but the blessings radiated by it vary with every point of the compass: in the East it will confer royal dignity, in the South a long term of life, etc.[180]

On entering a temple, one passes in the precincts, when the sacred complex is dedicated to Śiva, his bull Nandin, when it is Viṣṇuite, the bird Garuḍa.[181] Mythologically the gods' *vāhanas*, vehicles and attendants, these animals are, in the eyes of a student of religion, theriomorph duplicate manifestations or representations of Śiva's and Viṣṇu's nature and energy.[182] Nandin represents the fertility and procreation aspect of the god who already in the Ṛgveda (2, 33, 8) was described as a bull. Whatever the much debated 'original nature' of Garuḍa,[183] if it is true that Viṣṇu was the god who pervades the sphere surrounding the earth in order to maintain the communication with the celestial regions, a mighty bird, an eagle with outstretched wings, poised motionless in mid-heaven, was a felicitous expression of his columnar nature as the pillar of the universe and of his sustaining, pervasive power.[184]

Proceeding now to the temple ritual,[185] I may, to begin with, repeat a statement made by several authors: the daily pursuits of an officiant[186] in one temple is on the whole similar to that in others; the rites and ceremonies take place on much the same lines, but with certain differences due to for instance the fact that Śiva is very often adored in an aniconic form,[187] this *liṅga* worship being however also a pure ritualistic temple cult. The *devapūjā* as performed in public for the 'well-being of the world'[188] is moreover, though somewhat more elaborate, largely identical with that executed, for his personal interest, by an initiated and otherwise qualified Hindu. On closer investigation there however appear to exist many differences in details, not only between Śaivas and Vaiṣṇavas and, to mention these also, worshippers of other gods, but also between the various Śaiva and Vaiṣṇava persuasions among themselves.[189] Thus the ritual of the Vaikhānasas is essentially based on the domestic worship as described in their late Vedic gṛhyasūtra (which may date back to the IIIrd century A.D.),[190] a fact which is in perfect accordance with the conservative character of this community which, in contradistinction to the Pāñcarātrins, only reluctantly incorporated non-Vedic elements.[191] We must even go further; there are, within the same community, interesting regional differences[192] and we can be sure that the rites and ceremonies have, everywhere and in almost all communities, been subject, in the course of time, to omissions and additions, to change and transformation.[193] The study of these rituals has, moreover, up to recent time been much neglected and the relative texts,[194] of which there exists, in India, an abundance, hardly attracted the attention of Sanskrit scholars[195] before the last decades. Hence it is clear that the following observations on this point will—like those made on the domestic rites—be eclectic and far from definitive.

The Hindu *devapūjā* originally and essentially is an invocation, reception and entertainment of God as a royal guest. It normally consists of sixteen 'attendances' (*upacāra*).[196] Despite an unmistakable similarity due to the tendency to conform to this traditional schema there are, as already intimated, interesting differences, even between co-religionists.[197] Generally speaking the Śivaite communities were at an earlier date and on a larger scale open to foreign elements and inclined to adopt yoga techniques and Tantrist elements and among the Viṣṇuites it was the Pāñcarātrins who in this respect put into practice rather advanced ideas.[198] That Viṣṇuite tradition which, accepting the Pāñcarātra views, was between about 900 and 1130 inaugurated by Nāthamuni, Yāmuna and especially by Rāmānuja,[199] and which is known as the Śrī-Vaiṣṇavas,[200] introduced the songs of the Dravidian poets, the Ālvārs,[201] in their temple ceremonies, holding, up to the present day, these poets and the *ācaryas*, the great thinkers and teachers, in special veneration. Considering them to be *aṃśas* of God they often worship their images in their temples.[202] It was also Rāmānuja (± 1050–1137) who, being convinced that the Viṣṇuite religion and the traditional ritual of the 'aristocratic orthodoxy' should be united in perfect harmony, emphasized the preparatory and purificatory significance of the ritual in addition to meritorious works, devotion (*bhakti*) and a cheerful disinterested discharge of duties.[203] The Southern Śivaites on the other hand consider the collection of the works of their Dravidian poets[204] equivalent to the Veda, singing them at home, in the temples and during processions. It was they who in their cult admitted to a much larger scale the dances executed, in honour and support of their dancing god, by the *devadāsīs*.[205]

As to the language used during the rites, that is the language of the mantras, there have been, in both religions, communities which cling to the traditional Sanskrit and others who use also other languages.[206] Generally speaking, the origin and nature of the mantras is either Vedic with or without modifications or Hindu and in the latter case often of unknown origin and very frequently of the Tantric type. An instance of the latter is the Śaiva *Īśānamantra*: *Hoṃ īśāna-mūrdhne namaḥ*. In the course of time the *bhakti* movements changed over to the use of vernaculars in their preaching and congregational services. The South-Indian Śaiva-Siddhānta, on the other hand, presents a case of extreme Tamilization.[207]

Although numerous acts performed by the *arcakas* (those qualified for temple worship) are common to many religious groups,[208] their motivation does not seem to be the same in every particular tradition.[209] Whereas the first phase of the cult, the reverential opening of the temple door and the adoration of the powers presiding over it,[210] is, according to Śaivas, to secure the building's protection, the Vaikhānasas take up the keys to destroy thwarting demoniac power and emphasize that the opening of the door[211] is equivalent to the opening of heaven, because the temple is God's abode.[212] Man cannot indeed enter into the presence of the Supreme which is established in the cella (*garbhagṛha*); he has to undergo a transmutation or regeneration, and this process is promoted by the divine powers carved in the door-jambs, for instance river goddesses, or (often in Viṣṇuite buildings) serpents.[213] Several descriptions published so far make mention of the sounding of a bell and of clasping the hands after entering[214] the temple in order to chase away the evil powers[215] and to draw the god's attention to his worship.[216] After that the *arcaka* should express his intention to worship and ask God for His consent.[217] At this ceremony and all those which are to follow no congregation is present, but devotees may desire to have a *darśana*, that is to experience, as spectators, the fortifying and benedictive influence radiating from the sacred acts.

Turning now to the central ritual acts I begin with the Vaikhānasas, whose sūtra text already comprised a form of regular worship of Viṣṇu to take place after an obligatory fire sacrifice.[218] In accordance with their doctrine of Viṣṇu's two forms, the *niṣkala* one, i.e. the primeval and indivisible form which is unperceivable even by Brahmā, and the *sakala* one, the divisible, emanated and movable,[219] they distinguish, *inter alia*, two cult images, the large immovable[220] one which representing God's *niṣkala* form is ritually placed in a sanctuary and elaborately consecrated, and a movable one[221] which represents God's movable form underlying his manifestations. Worship can be performed with either image.[222] A person who has temporal and eternal results in view should worship with both; if he exclusively strives after eternal results, with an immovable only.[223] Before the worship proper he should, moreover, abandon his normal human consciousness and identify himself, in the *brahmanyāsa*—a combination of meditation and *nyāsa* practice[224]—with Viṣṇu. Having prepared (that is also, purified) himself and surrendered himself to God and his five manifestations,[225] he places the movable image on the bathing pedestal[226] and proceeds to bathe it elaborately. Then it is considered prepared for receiving, by immediate contact by means of a connecting string, the presence of God.[227] The accompanying mantra states that now the imperishable origin of All is connected with the perishable and that the Self, knowing God, is released from all evils. All deities who are believed to be present are honoured with flowers.[228]

The invocation[229] comprises also the recitation, by the worshipper, of the Ātmasūkta, a special Vaikhānasa hymn of nine stanzas[230] in which the identity of his body with the cosmos is emphasized, and the meditation on the analysable Highest Self (*sakalaparamātmā*),[231] the indispensable complement of the concentration on Viṣṇu's unanalysable (*niṣkala*) aspect as Brahman which has preceded. These elements of the rite are to request God to take, in His analysable aspect, His abode in the movable image, so that the world, represented by the worshipper (officiant), will be able to converse with Him. Thereupon the worshipper invokes God to enter without leaving the immovable image, first the *praṇidhi* vessel containing ritually prepared water[232] and then, leaving this, the movable image, from which He will, at the end of the ceremony, be dismissed again into the immovable image.[233] This act should be performed with special devotion; then God will descend out of compassion for His devotees.[234] The worship proper consists of a *pūjā* ceremony, during which God is honoured as a royal guest, followed by a fire offering (*homa*) and a *bali* offering. The object presented may be visible, touchable, audible or eatable.[235] An important element of the observances is the preparation and offering of cooked food (*havis*), God's principal meal. The purpose of this burnt offering appears from one of the *mantras*: 'May I attain that beloved protectorate of His, where men who strive for the divine are exulting . . ., the source of honey in His highest step (place)'.[236] The *homa* (offering into the fire) which, being of Vedic origin, has, curiously enough, been retained in nearly all extended *pūjā* ceremonies,[237] is strictly speaking an interruption.[238] After that the offered food is taken away to be eaten by the worshipper and distributed among those who might be present (*prasāda*), the site is cleaned, a *bali* consisting of cooked rice sprinkled with butter is offered to God himself[239] and a circumambulation[240] executed round the temple. At the end of the ceremonies the officiant and his assistants bow to Viṣṇu's image while pronouncing the Viṣṇusūkta, i.e. ṚV. 1, 154.[241] After the *dakṣiṇā* has been given Viṣṇu is, according to the Vaikhānasa-Smārtasūtra (4, 12) to be meditated upon as the personal manifestation of the sacrifice—a piece of Vedic belief not repeated in the later treatises of this community—, and to be praised with the Puruṣasūkta.[242] Finally a handful of flowers (*puṣpāñjali*) is offered to God's image[243] and the temple-door is closed.

Turning now to some characteristics of the *devapūjā* as performed by the Śrī-Vaiṣṇavas, I draw attention to the elaborate purificatory rites to be observed by the *arcaka*,[244] the numerous mantras of the Hinduist (Tantric) type accompanying its many elements and the so-called *sātvikatyāga*, a sort of confession in which God is said to be the master of all, the creator, who induces man to perform *pūjā* and to offer Him objects created by Him so as to satisfy Him.[245] In the course of time this community also adopted the Tantric belief, to which the Vaikhānasas have always been averse, that God comes, during the *pūjā* ceremonies, also out of the worshipper's heart.[246] The latter's soul (*jīva*) is moreover held to leave his body—which as it were has been burnt—and to reach God's feet in heaven, to descend from there into a new, pure body which is meditatively created. Then he must by a similar procedure mentally put Viṣṇu's attributes, the club, etc., into his hands. Now[247] the *arcaka* has identified himself with Viṣṇu-Nārāyaṇa and is fit to worship. Concentrating himself exclusively on God, he mentally invites Him to occupy the seat on which He is to be bathed and likewise mentally receives and honours Him as a respected guest, and after other *nyāsa* gestures praises Him, thereupon to purify and so to say to re-create the utensils for the *pūjā* service. Next, after worshipping the vessels, etc., he proceeds to perform, while concentrating on the ritual acts and pronouncing *mantras*,[248] the *pūjā* proper. He invokes God to approach (*āvāhana*),[249] who is supposed to enter a definite vessel (here called *āvāhanapātra*), and is requested to be present till the end of the worship (here known as *ārādhana*).[250] Then he makes the image of Viṣṇu and those of other deities (Śrī, Bhūdevī) the object of that worship and meditation afterwards elaborately to attend upon the first, to pray to Him and to bring the *pūjā* to a close.[251]

The temple worship of Viṣṇu-Viṭhobā in Paṇḍharpūr, Mahārāṣṭra,[252] though essentially similar, has some characteristics of its own: the rites are performed by a number of specialized ministrants; the daily ceremonies are divided into five services, beginning at three before noon and ending at ten in the evening, each service consisting of a certain *pūjā* and of several *āratīs*, that is the devotional waving of various lamps in front of the image. It is the task of one of the ministrants, the *haridāsa*, to sing suitable hymns. The many pilgrims attracted by the holiness of the temple throw flowers at the image and receive the *tīrtha* (holy water) and *prasāda* (holy food) as well as the flowers of the faded garlands and the water used for washing God's feet.[253]

The temple cult of the Mādhvas, Viṣṇuite in character but much influenced by Śivaite elements,[254] likewise deserves a passing notice. Regarding Śiva and Viṣṇu as identical they recite the thousand names of the former as well as those of the latter, but show a certain preference for Viṣṇu in that they follow the doctrines of the Bhāgavata-Purāṇa, mark their foreheads with the same symbol as the Bhāgavatas, and attach much value to fasting on the eleventh of every fortnight, the holiest days of the month.[255] Their temple ceremonies are characterized by special cleanness and accuracy. The ritual removal of any impurity is the first of the nine elements constituting the daily worship. Viṣṇu shares the homage paid to him with other gods who are regarded as subordinate to him and as pervaded by his divine being. Hence the presence of Śiva, Durgā, Skanda, Gaṇeśa and others, embodied in their idols, in Viṣṇu's temples. The true devotee however forgets that it is but an idol to which every honour and every homage conceivable is paid, day after day, with tireless patience and obeisance.[256] He rises above all trivialities of daily life and feels himself admitted to the divine Presence and enabled to come, through the image, into spiritual contact with God himself.

In order to give an impression of the observances prevailing among other Viṣṇuite communities I may recall that the ritual of the very numerous Kṛṣṇaites has likewise developed from Pāñcarātra origins,[257] which in its turn, though adopting many non-Vedic[258] elements, had not severed its connections with the Vedic rites.[259] No adorer of Śrī-Kṛṣṇa can begin his daily worship of God in his image[260] without a previous application of a *tilaka* (a distinctive mark) on twelve places of his body.[261] The material used is *gopīcandana*, that is a sort of white clay to be brought from Kṛṣṇa's residence Dvāraka.[262] The twelve *mantras* to be pronounced meanwhile combine with a meditation on the same number of God's aspects.[263] The two perpendicular lines on both sides of a point on the forehead are considered to be Kṛṣṇa's temple, housing Brahmā and Śiva at either side of God who occupies the middle.[264] Before and after[265] entering the temple the worshipper has to adore God's associates or attendants (*pārṣada*) among whom are Lakṣmī, Garuḍa, and again the lord of the site. Authorities disagree with regard to the material of which the sacrificial vessels are made, some of them rejecting all metals and others holding out prospects of very desirable results if gold or silver is used.[266] In any case water poured from a conch is generally preferred.[267] The water, mixed in the usual way with sesame seed,[268] flowers, rice, etc., which is used in washing God's feet, in making Him drink, rinse out His mouth, etc., is protected by a special imposition of hands, known as *cakramudrā*.[269]

The theory and practice of the *nyāsas* has under the influence of yoga been much elaborated. There is a *mātṛkanyāsa* consisting in the introduction of the six parts of God's body[270] into those of the worshipper by means of fifty nasalized sounds corresponding to the petals of lotus flowers believed to be present in these parts of the image. There is, further, a Keśavanyāsa performed to invoke and introduce the fifty-one aspects of God and the corresponding aspects of His Śakti.[271] The very important and indispensable *tattvanyāsa*,[272] to be executed with mantras beginning with the nasalized sounds of the language and letters of the alphabet in inverse order,[273] is to assign soul, life, intelligence, the senses, the elements, etc. and lastly, Vāsudeva, Saṃkarṣaṇa, Pradyumna, Aniruddha and Nārāyaṇa to one's body.

According to some authorities[274] the adoration of the conch is an essential element of the worship. It is, in a triangular place to the left of the devotee, put on a support, purified with the *mantra astrāya phaṭ*[275] which destroys all thwarting influences, filled with water, covered with flowers and sandal and consecrated with *mantras*. Then fire is adored on the support and sun and moon in the conch. After having invited the holy water (Gaṅgā, Yamunā, etc.) to leave the orb of the sun and Kṛṣṇa to cease to reside in the heart, the water in the conch is through gazing, imposition of hands and *mantras* transformed into *amṛta*. This holy liquid is then utilized in adoring Kṛṣṇa and washing his image.[276] After the ablution sandal, flowers, incense and food are offered to Him.[277] Other remarkable observances are a meditation on the light which shining forth from God's face enters the food, a *nīrājana* ceremony (lustration[278]) consisting in making circles of light before the image, a repeated circumambulation (*pradakṣiṇa*), a prostration (*praṇāma*) before the image. Finally the holy water is distributed among the devotees who drink of it and sprinkle a few drops on their heads.

At this point a Śivaite variety of *devapūjā* calls for closer attention.[279] The temple worship in the Tamil speaking South consists of four *sandhyā* celebrations—the last at midnight—and two intermediary services. The ritual for Śiva is repeated for his spouse. In each celebration one may distinguish between the image worship which is mainly Tantric in character (the *pūjā* proper), fire cult (*homa*), and 'festivals' (*nityotsava*). It would take too long even to mention the numerous elements of the *pūjā* and the different stages of its performance. After entering the sanctuary the temple priest (*ācārya*)[280] performs a long series of purificatory and otherwise preparatory[281] ritual acts, at the end of which he has transformed himself into Śiva,[282] because the scriptures say that 'One should become Śiva in order to be able to worship Śiva'.[283] Some authorities now enjoin a mental worship[284] and a sacrifice into the interior fire[285] without which the 'exterior' rites are senseless. Thereupon the officiant prepares and consecrates the water which is to be offered to God,[286] smears the floor in front of God with cow-dung and consecrates a mixture of the five products of the cow (milk, sour milk, butter and the liquid and solid excreta). He also makes *amṛta*[287]—I have already referred to this curious rite—, invokes Śiva to be present in the middle one of five pots (*āvāhana*) filled with a mixture of milk, fruit, honey, etc., invites other gods, worships the *liṅga* in the central part of the sanctuary[288] with the five products of the cow, the five 'nectars' contained in the other pots and the sacred bathing water. When everything is ready for the daily worship to begin the sun (Sūrya), whose orb is permeated by Sadāśiva,[289] is, according to many authorities to be adored first,[290] the relative *nyāsa* rites and mantras transforming the *ācārya* into that luminary, which is, moreover, invoked to be present and to accept offerings and prayers. 'The Sun indeed is God's *sakala* aspect, Śiva being *niṣkala*; therefore the wise adore first the corporeal one, then God (that is, His *liṅga*)'.[291]

Passing over the following items of ritual (worship of Gaṇeśa,[292] cleaning the *liṅga*, etc.[293]) I only mention the special *pūjā* to the *ādhāraśakti*,[294] the power supporting the universe residing in the primeval tortoise,[295] here represented by the tortoise-like stone bottom of the pedestal on which the *liṅga*, 'God's crystalline form',[296] is fixed;[297] and the worship of Śiva's lion-seat[298] or throne,[299] on which the worshipper must, in his mind, install[300] God pure like crystal, that is in His highest crystalline, that is formless, aspect of Sadāśiva, after having, in a complicated rite, invocated Him. Commentators[301] observe that the process is not inconsistent with God's omnipresence: God is not absent, and the *āvāhana* is only to make Him direct His special attention to the worshipper.[302] Then the worshipper, declaring that he belongs to God makes—again by a *mudrā*—sure of God's uninterrupted presence,[303] which is nothing else but God's accepting of this act of self-surrender.[304] Thereupon the *ācārya* executes the rite of *sakalī-karaṇa*[305] with regard to God's manifestation, that is, he assigns by means of *mantras*—which are divine—and imposition of hands divinity to it. Śiva, being meditated upon as a form of light, is then as Sadāśiva to appear[306] above the *liṅga*. He is given water for washing his feet, etc., and made the object of a very elaborate ablution (*abhiṣeka*) with the five products of the cow, the five 'nectars' and the water mixed with *bael* flowers (which are sacred to him), etc.[307] Among the other rites which must, or may, be performed are the adoration of God's limbs in four directions;[308] offering of food (*naivedya*)[309]—which is not considered fit to be eaten by the worshippers—and drinking-water (*toya*) to God and His retinue; the fivefold worship of the gods housed in the precincts surrounding the central shrine; the worship of the twenty-five 'realities' or 'real principles' (*tattvārcanā*),[310] followed by the muttering or recitation of the *mūlamantra*, which is to be repeated one hundred and eight times and to be accompanied by offerings and prayers for the attainment of the objects desired by the performer of the rite.[311]

The fire ritual (*nityahoma*) which is to follow is a very detailed ceremony of distinct character held to be obligatory for those who wish to attain to final emancipation.[312] Carrying the vessel with *arghya* water[313] the worshipper makes for the fireplace,[314] which is carefully—and of course ritually—prepared to receive Agni. The *kuṇḍa* is sprinkled with *arghya*. The five spheres of action of Śiva (*kalā*)—one for each direction including the centre—are worshipped, the goddess and god of Speech (Vāgīśvarī and Vāgīśvara) invoked[315] and meditated upon. Fire is procured in accordance with the prescripts,[316] worshipped with the *mūlamantra* and 'united' with the fire of the *mūlādhāra*, i.e. the lowermost power centre (*cakra*)[317] and with that of the *bindu* in the forehead.[318] Thus the worshipper enacts his unification with the fire in which now Agni's spirit (*caitanya*) is introduced. The fire is thereupon transformed into *amṛta*,[319] worshipped and regarded as Śiva's seed, and then emitted by Vāgīśvara into Vāgīśvarī's womb.

After the fire-in-the-womb has been adored and various measures have been taken to protect it the so-called sacraments (*saṃskāras*)[320] to be performed for the unborn and young child in order to fortify it and to make it fit to enter the next stage in its development,[321] are executed through symbolic actions. When the fire child, which is thus completely treated as an embryo, is in the tenth month considered to have been born, and the defilements of birth have been removed[322] it is, after several other ritual acts,[323] meditated upon. Now the worshipper, soul and mind, shares in the process which is taking place. While considering himself identical with Brahmā, Viṣṇu and Rudra successively, and simultaneously performing the three ceremonies of establishing the fire, putting on the vessel and dismissal, he purifies and consecrates sacrificial butter[324] and sprinkles with it the faces of young Agni, who then receives the name of Śivāgni. His parents, Vāgīśvarī and Vāgīśvara, are honourably dismissed, and Śiva is invoked to be present in the heart of the fire, seated on his throne, brilliant and supreme, worshipped and offered food. After that the worshipper must unite the arteries of his (yogic) body (*nāḍī*)[325] with those of Śiva-of-the-temple and of Śiva-of-the-fire, creating a sort of luminous circuit between these and proceed to perform the fire sacrifice (*homa*), consisting of oblations of ghee, and accompanied by offerings of fried rice grain, sugar-cane, flowers, etc. Finally he installs Śiva-of-the-fire[326] in his own heart and after some other observances returns to the temple to implore God to accept the *pūjā*, the homa and the merit produced by these.[327]

Although the ritual manuals are not quite explicit on this point,[328] the meaning of the performance is clear. It is, by means of techniques partly Vedic, partly purāṇic and partly Tantric, the enactment,[329] in a gradual process of development, of the realization of the unity of the worshipper's soul,[330] the place and material for worship and God, who is the only recipient of worship, who can be worshipped only by those who realize their identity with Him, and to whom therefore accrue not only the homage and the oblations, but also the merit earned by them, which is, as a deposit entrusted to His keeping for the sake of His worshipper.[331] For bliss and heaven, if not emancipation,[332] is the ultimate aim of those who perform the ritual.[333]

V

The Mutual Relations of the Two Religions

IN INSTITUTING a comparison between Viṣṇuism and Śivaism which since the beginning of our era are, in India, the two most prominent religious currents and communities,[1] it does not seem to be out of place briefly to recall also their interrelations, the interchange of ideas, their friendly and unfriendly contacts, the opinions they fostered of each other.

It is, to begin with, interesting to notice that in the Ṛgveda Rudra and Viṣṇu, excepting two cases one of which is insignificant, maintained no direct relations with each other. No mention is made of Viṣṇu in the hymns addressed to Rudra, no reference to Rudra found in the texts dedicated to Viṣṇu.[2] Only once the outsider god, 'conscious of his greatness as Rudra', seems, as also on other occasions, to be sent away with an oblation, after or during an offering presented to Viṣṇu,[3] but this coincidence does not point to intimate relations. In other celebrations of the Viśve Devāḥ the two gods, sharing the eulogies with several other divinities are not mentioned in the same stanza,[4] or their mere names occur in collective invocations of a number of gods.[5] In a hymn dedicated to the Maruts, the sons of Rudra[6] (5, 87),[7] these deities are, it is true, described as being the satellites of Viṣṇu—like this deity these storm gods dwell in the mountains[8] and traverse the spaces—but more important is Ṛgveda 4, 3, 7, expressing an opposition between Viṣṇu, the god of the seed (*retaḥ*), that is of generation, and the firm missile weapon of Rudra, who, being here identical with Agni, represents destruction.[9]

About the other Vedic saṃhitās there is in this connection nothing to be said.[10] Nor do I remember any passage in the brāhmaṇas worth mentioning unless we would discuss also the insertion of a stanza addressed to Rudra after the recitation of a hymn containing the names of Viṣṇu and other gods.[11] Let us not be misled by this practice which is continued in later times, when in definite milieus one god has risen to prominence. The adoration of Nārāyaṇa as the Highest Being, the conviction that only through the grace of this god it is possible to realize one's oneness with Brahman and to gain immortality does not exclude the invocation of deities considered to be of minor rank and position, for instance Rudra, whose assistance and co-operation may be deemed necessary.[12] Another point which is perhaps not always sufficiently stressed is this: a preacher or a visionary who has gone into ecstasies over the indescribable glory of the Highest Being, feeling himself unable to choose between several divine names, designates the source and creator of All as Viṣṇu, Śiva, Brahmā, etc.:[13] the Highest Being is more than each individual god who is no more than one of the manifestations of His omnipotence. This does not mean that the author wavers between Śaivism, Vaiṣṇavism or other religions.

It is not before the beginning of the Christian era, or what may broadly speaking be called epic times, that Śivaism—which as a definite religious group with its own tenets and theology can hardly be shown to have existed before that period[14]—and Viṣṇuism—some components of which must have adopted the character of religious communities in at least the IInd century B.C.[15]—definitely became, at least in our sources, more prominent than other cults and might be said to have entered into more or less distinct and definite relations which led to more or less regular forms of co-existence. In studying these relations it should always be borne in mind that, however prominently these two religions were to figure in the so-called epic and early purāṇic periods, they were not alone in satisfying the religious needs, interests and aspirations of the Indian people at large. The Vedic gods were not forgotten within the space of a few centuries[16] and Vedic rituals continued to be performed by a section of the people. The propagation of Viṣṇuite and Śivaite beliefs did not prevent the mass of smārta Hindus[17] from worshipping, or meditating on, other deities regarded as their equals, together with the two great gods.[18] In addition to this form of Hinduism there existed some other cults,[19] whether or not allied with Vedic gods or derived from Vedic forms of worship, the whole constituting an interesting medley of cults and beliefs which defies any systematic classification.[20] It is also worth noticing that even the names of Śiva and Viṣṇu are far from being regularly included in epic lists of divine names, invocations or references to gods.[21] One should not rashly explain[22] such facts integrally from a tendency intentionally to exclude the god worshipped by another religious group, resulting—after a Viṣṇuite and a Śivaite recast of the same text—in the absence of both deities. There always were real social and regional differences[23] and changes in religious conditions, and the spread of Viṣṇuism and Śivaism, though steady and constant, must have been slow and gradual.

In view of my present purpose another point is, however, of special relevance. Although the Bombay edition of the Rāmāyaṇa contains many references to Śiva and Viṣṇu, these gods are not invoked together. This may, to a certain extent, be a reflection of reality: however many gods were worshipped conjointly, there is, in this work also, unmistakable evidence of trends in religious practice which at a later date were to culminate in the existence of distinct and fully developed Viṣṇuite and Śivaite communities and religions.

As to the world of the great epic—I intentionally refrain from saying: epic times—Hopkins'[24] recapitulation of the relevant facts may, in general, be subscribed to. Both Śiva and Viṣṇu are, alternatively and within the discretion of the authors, recognized as chief gods;[25] both eventually represent God. As such, as the All, Viṣṇu may also act as the destroyer. Śiva's character remains essentially true to that of the ancient Rudra, but he receives new fame and features which are illustrated by various narrative episodes. His appearances are, it is true, rare, but when he does, in the Mahābhārata, appear on the scene, Kṛṣṇa, when present, invariably seems to recede from the first place: together with Arjuna he visits and praises Śiva who gives Arjuna the *pāśupata* weapon; Kṛṣṇa gratifies him at the *tīrtha* Badarī and declares him to be the creator of all.[26] After having practised, in the Himālayas, severe austerities Nārāyaṇa, realizing his identity with Brahman, obtained a vision of Śiva, the master and origin of the universe, the supreme deity, smaller than the smallest and larger than the largest, Rudra, Hara, Śambhu, the infuser of life in every form and the all-destroyer, the source of immortality, whose body is the universe, who can only be seen, with their mind's eye, by brahmans of pure conduct and cleansed from sins. Nārāyaṇa, after having obtained this vision, became filled with delight and proceeded to praise and worship that divine Lord.[27] Elsewhere in the same epic (13, a. 14) it is Kṛṣṇa, who after going through a *dīkṣā* ceremony and severe austerities, succeeds in the sixth month in obtaining a vision of Śiva surrounded by all the gods, among whom were Indra and Viṣṇu. Kṛṣṇa praises him as the supreme deity and receives eight boons of the god and eight more of Umā.[28] One of these boons is, curiously enough, the close proximity of Śiva. Nevertheless, the compilers of the great epic have been largely instrumental in propagating Viṣṇuism and Kṛṣṇaism. In the Rāmāyaṇa Śiva, designated by several names and, here also, the performer of some well-known feats, is as a rule not regarded as higher than the devas.[29]

Yet there does not seem to exist some special antagonism between the two religions. 'Theological animus, lacking political aims, appears to be in abeyance.' For, although Kaurava adherents of Śivaism scorn the claims of Kṛṣṇa to be regarded as God,[30] the eternal Viṣṇu himself, this attitude seems to be dictated by what may, broadly speaking, be called political reasons.[31] Draupadī, while eulogizing Kṛṣṇa as the Highest Principle and complaining of the contumely offered to her by the Kauravas, expresses the opinion that Kṛṣṇa plays with Śiva and other gods as with a toy: an obvious comparison of might and influence of both gods (*Mbh.* 3, a. 13). Even when Sudyumna, as a result of the wrath of Lord Śiva, was transformed into a woman, the ṛṣis wishing to restore him to his sex, prayed to Viṣṇu, who granted their request.[32] The king of the Yavanas, who according to the purāṇic legend, advanced with many barbarians against Kṛṣṇa and Mathurā, was born after his father had succeeded in propitiating Śiva.[33]

In a similar way, the epic combatants, generally speaking, appear to have different faiths.[34] It is certainly not due to mere chance that in the Uttarakāṇḍa of the Rāmāyaṇa—which in its enlarged form has been called[35] 'the first of all Viṣṇuite scriptures'—Rāvaṇa is depicted as a devotee of Śiva,[36] taking with him a golden *liṅga* which he worshipped with flowers and incense. 'Thus the *rākṣasa* paid homage to it which was the highest, the giver of boons, and the destroyer of the sufferings of people of correct behaviour.'[37] That, on the other hand, Kausalyā paid also homage to Śiva and that Rāma's brahmin are said to have worshipped this god[38] on the occasion of the performance of the Aśvamedha rite, may be a reflection of the reality known to the author of these passages.[39]

The same form of antagonism is apparent from legends about supporters and opponents of the two religions. In these Śiva, living up to his reputation, sometimes sides with the demons, whereas Viṣṇu acts as the champion of the gods.[40] Already in the Mahābhārata reference is made to the *asura* Bāṇa, the son of Bali, a follower of Rudra and an enemy of Viṣṇu who eventually killed him in battle.[41] In the Viṣṇu-Purāṇa—which in any case is one of the oldest compositions of this genre, dating back to, perhaps, the IVth century A.D.—the story is told in full detail, that is, probably, enriched with Viṣṇuite material.[42] Through the agency of the goddess Pārvatī[43] Bāṇa's daughter Ūṣā fell in love with Aniruddha, the grandson of Kṛṣṇa, and had him conveyed to her by magic art. In the meantime Bāṇa solicited Śiva for war, because he felt depressed by having a thousand arms in a prolonged state of peace. His wish was fulfilled, because prince Aniruddha, whose presence in the palace was discovered, slew Bāṇa's servants, sent to arrest him. As he was unable to subdue him by prowess, Bāṇa succeeded in capturing the youth with his *māyā*, that is his supernormal deceptive faculty. Being informed of these events Kṛṣṇa, his brother Baladeva and his son Pradyumna set off for Bāṇa's city, but on their approach they were opposed by a mighty Maheśvara, i.e. an emanation from Śiva, called Fever, who however was defeated by a Counter-Fever engendered by Kṛṣṇa himself. After some other heroic feats Bāṇa appears to have received the assistance of Śiva and his son Skanda, the general of the gods. A fierce combat ensued between Hari-Viṣṇu and Śaṅkara-Śiva; the denizens of heaven felt that the end of the universe was drawing near. Of the vicissitudes of the battle pictured in absorbing particulars I only mention Kṛṣṇa's use of the weapon of yawning with which he disabled Śiva, overcome with incessant gaping. When, after several other feats of heroism, Kṛṣṇa was about to put Bāṇa to death with his discus Sudarśana and had already lopped off his arms, Śiva approached him to solicit a suspension of hostilities, addressing him as the lord of the world and highest Puruṣa, and asking him to be propitious because he, Śiva, had given Bāṇa, his old devotee, assurance of safety. Thereupon Kṛṣṇa, dismissing his resentment against the asura, looked graciously on his antagonist and said: 'Since you, Śaṅkara, have given a boon to Bāṇa, let him live; from respect to your promises my discus is arrested. The assurance of safety granted by you is granted also by me. You are fit to apprehend that you are not distinct from me. We are identical with each other as is the whole world with us. Only because they are stupified by ignorance men contemplate distinctions.' Having spoken thus, Kṛṣṇa freed his grandson from his fetters and returned home, together with his brother, son, grandson and Ūṣā.

There can be little doubt that Wilson[44] was in the main right in surmising that this narrative—which in various degrees of detail is also found in several other purāṇas[45]—reflects, as far as its general tendency is concerned, historical reality. I would not however say that it describes a definite serious struggle between both persuasions, but rather that it attests to the existence of antagonism and animosity in those circles which invented and reproduced the story.[46] We can indeed be sure that historical reality did not always answer to the mild catholicity often prevailing in epic literature or to the eulogistic descriptions of royal impartiality which, being a favourite topic of *kāvya* authors, is not infrequently attested to by epigraphic and iconographic sources.[47]

Hinduism has often been described as very tolerant, and there is from certain points of view and in comparison with other civilizations, for instance European history, a considerable element of truth in this judgement. Yet there is some room for reserve. We should admit that there have been exceptions; we should not mistake the theories of the *dharma* books and their doctrine that the king should be impartial and well-disposed towards all denominations, even to the heretics,[48] with the daily practice of the population in general.[49] We should also distinguish between doctrinal and practical tolerance. As to the latter an answer to the question as to how far Indians of different creeds were, in different times and regions, inclined to tolerate, and show forbearance to, opinions and forms of worship which they did not share themselves, can be given only with reserve and many delicate distinctions.[50] It is for instance worth noticing that the rules of ritual purity to be observed with respect to contact with those who repudiate the authority of the Veda were sometimes also applied to the Śivaite Pāśupatas, who seem to have been the oldest form of Śivaism prevalent in North India. If, for instance, a man touched Buddhists, Jainas, materialists, *śūdras*, and Pāśupatas he should, in order to purify himself, bathe with his clothes on.[51] This discrimination against the Pāśupatas[52] shows that they were suspect because of their ritual practices, and, in general, of their particular manners and customs. In an interpolated epic passage[53] they are described as defying[54] the dharma of the *varṇas* and *āśramas* (the social classes and the stages in life), although in a very few cases they agree with it; their way of living and some of their ritual customs obviously gave offence to people of other persuasions.[55] Some authorities went so far as to prescribe purificatory rites after touching Śaivas in general and after entering Buddhist or Śivaite sanctuaries.[56] Others even included other Śaiva groups—Bhairavas, Kāpālikas, Vāmas—among the censurable and blameworthy, their books being meant for deluding the world.[57] The outbursts of aversion[58] were especially borne towards the Kāpālikas[59] whose dress and manners were, in the eyes of the differently minded, very repulsive. Purāṇic stories were invented to warn people against violating the rules of the *varṇāśramadharma*:[60] 'Kāpālikas and various others holding themselves followers of some *deva* or other will', according to descriptions of the Kali age,[61] 'corrupt the dharma',[62] and work the ruin of man and world. The Viṣṇuite Pāñcarātras, of whom the Pāśupatas—for a certain period probably their most formidable rivals—are assumed to be the Śivaite counterpart,[63] are likewise added to the list of those who falsely pretend to be traditional Hindus (*pāṣaṇḍas*).[64] Even casteless Viṣṇuites rank in the view of these exponents of pure Hinduism higher than non-Viṣṇuite brahmans.[65]

With regard to their attitude towards the other great religious community we find, generally speaking, a characteristic trend on both sides. In social intercourse Viṣṇuism tends to be passively intolerant,[66] that means: a Vaiṣṇava should avoid direct contact with the Śaivas but not injure them or prejudice their rights. An adherent of Viṣṇu should consider the others unworthy to perform rites; he should not ritually behave like a Śaiva; he should purify himself and subject himself to an atonement for receiving a non-Vaiṣṇava priest as a guest, eating with him, honouring him, or employing him, because such a man is contemptible everywhere. A true Vaiṣṇava should be *ekāntin*, i.e. 'devoted to only one goal or god'[67] and disinclined to permit the cult of another god beside Viṣṇu. This attitude of 'exclusivism' (*ekāntibhāva*) is strongly opposed by the Śaivas[68] who sometimes go so far as to hold out a prospect of hell to those who exclude Śiva from divine honours. But the Vaiṣṇava who recites a mantra received from a non-Vaiṣṇava guru will likewise for millions of years be cooked in the fire of hell.[69] In daily practice this attitude often entails attempts to consider Śiva a great deity of secondary importance and to subordinate him to Viṣṇu. This explains why in an avowedly Viṣṇuite book[70] an exposition is made also of the worship of Śiva, Durgā and other deities, although they rank below Viṣṇu: they are represented as his attendants.

One should indeed have no scruples about the divine personality of Śiva, but one should avoid adoring him as a greaty deity in his own right. Attaching an obvious meaning to name-giving exclusive Viṣṇuites of higher rank and station do not like to call the god who competes with Viṣṇu for the highest position by his principal name Śiva, but prefer Rudra, Śaṅkara, or one of his other names.[71] This aversion is not rarely mutual: brahmans belonging to some Śaiva or Vaiṣṇava communities would not even mutter the names of each other's gods.[72] It would not however be warranted to assume that also on the Viṣṇuite side there has never been malice and hard-handedness. The lower in the social scale did not miss the opportunity from time to time to come to fisticuffs. In an XVIIIth-century Tamil work describing an altercation of the wives of a low caste man, one being a Vaiṣṇava and the other a Śaiva, both gods are dragged into the quarrel in a most unseemly way.[73] The French priest Dubois,[74] who in the first quarter of the XIXth century lived for over thirty years in Pondicherry, even speaks of numerous troops of religious mendicants and vagabonds always ready to provoke each other and to hurl gross and obscene abuse[75] at each other's heads. But at the end of his vivid description he adds that their field of battle only rarely is sprinkled with blood.

It is, indeed, no wonder that legend and history inform us of various forms of unfriendly contact,[76] such as controversial discussion and struggle for superiority, not only between Hindus and outsiders but also between Śaivas and Vaiṣṇavas. Both communities, indeed, though largely worshipping their god in the general Hindu way, claimed to revere the true or supreme manifestation of the Highest. Thus Viṣṇuite tradition has it that the poet (*ālvār*[77]) Tirumaṅgai—the same who was miraculously converted[78] to Viṣṇuism after hearing a mantra from a man whom he, as a waylayer, had robbed[79]—was invited by the great Śaiva saint Jñānasambandha for a religious discussion, which he accepted with the result that he vanquished his Śaiva adversary without difficulty.[80] It is on the other hand interesting to see that among the stereotyped features of the Kaliyuga is, in purāṇic treatises, the defamation of the own god by the rival community.[81] This was, obviously, not regarded as good behaviour.

Nor is it however surprising that we must except the Pāñcarātrins, who in many other circles had a doubtful reputation. They showed a sort of tolerance which, with Professor Hacker of Münster, may be called inclusive:[82] the worship of other gods is, in their view, to be regarded as an indirect way ultimately leading to their own God. There are, according to their manuals, five recognized systems, namely that of the Veda, the Sāṃkhya, the Yoga, the Pāśupata—i.e. the younger so-called form of āgamic Śaivism—and the Sāttvata or Pāñcarātra, the remaining doctrines of Jainas, Buddhists, etc., being fallacious and founded by gods or *brahmarṣis* in order to spread confusion among the wicked.[83]

In this the Pāñcarātrins resemble the Śaivas who have very often taken, with regard to those who follow other gods, the standpoint which has been characterized as an inclusivism admitting that dissentient views are to a greater or lesser extent true. Thus, according to a Śivaite authority,[84] Viṣṇu-Kṛṣṇa is the eternal highest *ātman*, endowed with the incomprehensible and divine creative power called *māyā*, enjoying everything; nevertheless he worships Śiva, believing that the essence of this god is completely contained in his *liṅga*. To Śiva he owes his invincibility in the universe.

Something more must therefore be said now on this point which is among the most characteristic features of Hinduism. I mean the tendency to what has been called inclusivism, a term which should be distinguished from adaptation and syncretism. The Indian adherent of a definite view of life does not as a rule explicitly combat and integrally reject the opinions and institutions of other religious communities. His philosophers may often feel inclined to polemize and to argue against different opinions, the Hindu generally respects these to a certain extent, because they represent a view of, or at least some aspects of, truth and reality, or just because they exist and belong to the traditions of definite groups of people. But he denies that they are as excellent and efficacious as his own doctrine. They may, it is true, suffice for people of a lower social, moral or intellectual standard, but they do not lead himself and his co-religionists to their goal, or not far enough on their way to the goal.[85] Thus one does not easily reject a definite unfamiliar form of devotion, or argue that a strange doctrine is fundamentally incorrect; one rather regards them as inadequate and insufficient. When one finds oneself confronted with spiritual currents of prestige one may go further. Since Hindu thinkers often find little difficulty in absorbing almost anything extraneous into their own system and in assimilating ideas that seem to be of value or to have affinity with their own trains of thought, they are even inclined to include and completely to incorporate a foreign system into their own, declaring it to represent the next best doctrine,[86] reinterpreting its mythology, symbolism and metaphysics, and accepting its god as a servant or manifestation of their Highest Being.[87] On the mythological plane the Śivaite purāṇas, which were generally speaking inclined to what has been called 'a tendency to compromise',[88] could in this way regard Viṣṇu and Brahmā as Śiva's servants and allow their cults.[89]

This remarkable tendency has no doubt been promoted by the essentially kindred and congenial doctrine of the Trimūrti, the triune unity of Brahmā, Viṣṇu and Śiva as aspects and manifestations of the Highest Being[90] which, of course, in Viṣṇuite eyes was Viṣṇu, in Śivaite opinion Śiva.[91] Thus dominant Śaivism was already at an early date able to cover,[92] include and adopt, not to reconcile and syncretize, Vaiṣṇavism by accepting Viṣṇu as one of the components of the Trinity and putting him on a par with the other members Brahmā and Rudra-Śiva.[93]

In illustration of this tendency to adopt foreign gods and cults and to display what might impress us as a conciliatory attitude towards the other great religion attention may be drawn to an interesting sample of purāṇic theology. The Kūrma-Purāṇa—of uncertain date, but before 1000 A.D.—is, despite its title, a Śaiva work, in which Viṣṇu, it is true, is occasionally eulogized, but, like Brahmā, only as a form of the unique supreme god Śiva. One of the most interesting sections of this purāṇa is the Īśvaragītā (II, 1–11),[94] a Śivaite imitation of the Bhagavadgītā,[95] which must have been very popular, not only among Śivaites but also among adepts of the Yoga and Sāṃkhya schools.[96] Here it is the Highest Lord, Śiva, himself who in the famous hermitage at Badarikā[97] expounds his doctrine of salvation to twelve *ṛṣis*. This doctrine is a clever attempt at harmonizing, in a spirit of conciliation, Śaiva theism, the *bhakti* theory, yoga, epic Sāṃkhya philosophy[98] and the main tenets of the upaniṣadic tradition. This spirit of conciliation is especially apparent in the author's attitude towards the Supreme Being: he adores Śiva, but venerates also Viṣṇu. The narrator of the episode, Vyāsa, is requested to expound the doctrine which, dealing exclusively with Brahman, leads to final emancipation as taught previously by Viṣṇu the tortoise, but it is Rudra-Śiva to whom he pays obeisance before beginning his expositions. He tells his audience that in the days of yore a party of *ṛṣis*, after severe austerities, received the favour of a vision of Viṣṇu-Nārāyaṇa, the best knower of yoga, the soul of the universe, the eternal; they asked him, the only knower of the highest secret, to inform them about the origin of the universe, that which is subject to *saṃsāra*, the nature of the *ātman* and final emancipation, the cause of transmigration and who is the lord who watches everything (I, 26 f.). But before Nārāyaṇa could answer Śiva-Mahādeva appears who is immediately praised by the *ṛṣis* and addressed as the soul of the universe (1, 34). Śiva embraces Viṣṇu[99] and asks him why the *ṛṣis* have assembled and what he might do for them. Viṣṇu informs him and invites him to expound the divine knowledge, adding that he, Śiva, is the only one who is qualified for that task, that is for explaining his own nature and essence. Then a celestial throne comes down on which both gods sit down and Śiva, while looking at Viṣṇu,[100] begins to speak. It strikes us that also in the episode of Śiva's dance, in which he as the Highest Being displays his divine energies (ch. 5), and which is the counterpart of the famous epiphany of the Bhagavadgītā, Viṣṇu is near to him (5, 2). Further on (5, 15) Indra and Viṣṇu are said to pay homage to him, and in a moment the spectators see Nārāyaṇa, the origin of the world, become one with the Lord (5, 16) who then is described as being Brahmā, Viṣṇu and the most excellent Supreme Being and Highest Lord (Parameṣṭhin, 5, 30; 35).[101] That all divine personages are in reality Śiva is not left unmentioned: (5, 33) 'The sages say that Thou art the unique Rudra, Hari, Agni, the Lord, the eternal Rudra, Air, Āditya . . .', but the identity of Śiva and Viṣṇu is especially emphasized: at the end of his expositions the former, while committing the promulgation of his doctrine to the care of his colleague,[102] explicitly declares the latter, Nārāyaṇa, identical with himself,[103] adding that the doctrine should be taught (exclusively) to those who are convinced of this identity. 'My highest embodiment, which, being gentle and imperishable, resides in all beings and is their *ātman*, is called Nārāyaṇa. Those who regard both gods as different will never obtain final emancipation, but those who believe them to be identical will never be reborn. That is why the eternal Viṣṇu should be honoured and regarded as Śiva himself. For emancipation will be given to those who take refuge with Śiva without disregarding Viṣṇu.' And elsewhere (4, 25): 'Those who are devout worshippers of Hari while propitiating me, they also come to me and do not come back to this world'. And so it is not surprising to read in another chapter (9, 9) that that highest divine presence is identical with Viṣṇu's highest 'step' or 'abode' (*viṣṇoḥ paramaṃ padam*).

Strange though it at first sight might seem, these great gods did not hesitate to praise and adore each other, or to try to win the other's favour.[104] Thus Viṣṇu is in Śivaite circles related to have offered, every day, a thousand lotus flowers to Śiva's feet; when, one day, he was short by one he extracted one of his lotus-like eyes.[105] A Pāśupata tradition has it that Viṣṇu-Kṛṣṇa worshipped Śiva for a son,[106] but the

Pāñcarātras say[107] that Śiva first adored Nārāyaṇa who, at the former's prayer, granted the boon that he would worship Śiva for a favour. Many passages of this character are indeed obvious attempts at raising one's own god over the other or at baffling similar attempts of the adversaries rather than attempts at conciliation.[108]

It may therefore, broadly speaking, be observed that—in spite of the tension and competition between the two gods and their worshippers which in the post-epic period there is throughout—the authors of the purāṇas, whether they were Śaivas or Vaiṣṇavas, assigned the rival god a particular and privileged place in the pantheon. Not rarely the order in which statements about a plurality of gods are made, precedence accorded to one of them,[109] or numerical relations occurring in this connection provide good ground for ascertaining the author's estimation of their relative importance.[110] Thus in the Agni-Purāṇa (38, 8) it reads: 'By erecting one sanctuary one goes to heaven; by making three one goes to the world of Brahmā; by making five one goes to the world of Śambu (Śiva); by making eight one will abide in the region of Hari.'[111] An interesting passage[112] occurs in the Śivaite Saura-Purāṇa—which may have been compiled between about 1000 and 1200 A.D.:[113] Śiva is on the authority of *śruti* and other scriptures[114] the highest god. The man who truly knows the Lord Who is to be known through the Vedānta, the husband of Pārvatī, is Viṣṇu-Vaikuṇṭha; the man who duly believes Vaikuṇṭha to be the lord is Indra-Puraṃdara; the man who considers Indra to be the lord of all, is a *ṛṣi*.[115] However, without recognizing Śiva as the supreme Lord emancipation is impossible. In a similar passage the same purāṇa adds, in answer to the question as to why so many people have fallen away from Śaivism to become adorers of Viṣṇu, that Śiva himself, pleased with Viṣṇu's devotion for him, had conceded him the privilege of being the highest god of a minority of men.[116] Or we might learn something from the story narrated in the same book (a. 41): the gods resort to Viṣṇu for help, Viṣṇu praises Śiva who, after putting him to the test, grants him the discus and invincibility. Or the relative rank assigned to divine persons may be understood from their successive appearances in a narrative, the success of their activities, etc. In a Śivaite context a monster which is eventually slain by Durgā will, for instance, be given occasion to conquer, among other gods, Viṣṇu.[117]

The higher position or greater power of either god[118] or their temporary friendly or unfriendly relations are often illustrated by more or less casual remarks or references, explanations added by an author to an episode of his work, etc. According to an interpolated stanza in the Mahābhārata[119] Viṣṇu is the only one who is able to see Śiva when the latter, blazing like the fire which at the end of a yuga destroys the universe, sports, as Puruṣa, with Prakṛti and nobody, no other god, not even the lotus-born Brahmā or Śiva, is able to fathom the depth of Viṣṇu's *māyā*, his inscrutable creative power.[120] Elsewhere Rudra is said to appear on Kṛṣṇa's breast and Brahmā on his forehead, when he, after having burst out into a loud laughter, produced from his body, which resembled a blazing fire, myriads of gods, not bigger than his thumb (*Mbh.* 5, 129, 4).[121]

One should not however treat all Viṣṇuites and all Śivaites alike. There are nuances and variations in the opinions of, and attitudes towards, the rival persuasions. The Vaiṣṇava school founded by Madhva (probably 1199–1298)[122] is on the one hand of the opinion that the whole Veda is not only Viṣṇu's revelation but also an explanation of his nature. The undeniable facts that that corpus contains also innumerable references to other gods and that *smṛti* texts often proclaim Śiva the Highest Being are explained away, either by the application of the principle that all passages which are inconsistent with the doctrine of Viṣṇu's uniqueness and omnipotence are to be regarded as lacking the sanction of authority, or by an interpretative method based on the axiom that all authoritative scriptures teach Viṣṇu's absolute supremacy. The first category of texts has, it is held, been composed, at Viṣṇu's command, by Śiva in order to confuse the minds of men and to draw a distinction between the truly faithful and the adherents of false doctrines.[123] Śiva is even Viṣṇu's creature and endowed by him with special destructive power because he has to bring about the periodical reabsorption of the universe.[124] It is, on the other hand, Madhva's contention that Śiva, like Brahmā and the other gods, is penetrated with Viṣṇu's essence and therefore is worthy of adoration, provided that the worshipper is conscious of this fact and does not identify Śiva or other gods with Viṣṇu or consider them as equals, because those who nurse these erroneous ideas work their own destruction.[125] That is why the Mādhvas accord also worship to Śiva and visit his sanctuaries. According to the biography of their founder the god obviously reciprocated this homage, because Madhva was, on his initiative, splendidly entertained on the occasion of a visit to the sacred place Hṛṣīkeśa.[126] Accordingly, the famous Śaiva monastery at Śṛṅgiri in Mysore, which was founded by Śaṅkara, and the Mādhva temple of Udipi maintained friendly relations.[127]

These facts could not however prevent Śaiva leaders from engaging in polemics. This may have been their reaction to a piece of active intolerance on Madhva's side. This Viṣṇuite teacher, while promoting the institution of debates between the representatives of different creeds, advised the Vaiṣṇavas present to prevent a dissentient speaker from scoring a triumph; besides, the king was expected to punish an unsuccessful and non-conforming opponent, who of course never was a Vaiṣṇava.[128] In an interesting section of the Śivaite Saura-Purāṇa[129] we are told that the realm of the 'orthodox' king Pratardana was so completely free from all unsocial and anti-traditional people that Yama and other gods felt annoyed, because there were no longer evildoers to be punished. Reluctantly, it is true, they ordered a *kiṃnara*,[130] disguised as a Viṣṇuite, to exterminate the cult of Śiva.[131] Nobody in the kingdom discovered the imposture and many influential people joined the movement started by the *kiṃnara* who preached Śiva's subordination to Viṣṇu and refused to pay homage to those brahmans who wear the distinctive marks of Śivaite communities: Viṣṇu is the only God proclaimed by the Veda, Śiva is a cruel and barbarous deity, the ashen garment and the rosary of his adherents are worthless. The *kiṃnara*'s scornful description of Śiva as a frequenter of places where corpses wait for cremation, as a nudist adorned with ropes of snakes[132] elicits the king's reply that the god has many forms unknown to men. Yet the ruler thinks him a blockhead rather than a deceiver. Meanwhile, as a result of the neglect of Śiva's cult, the hells are filled again and the world is on the point of perishing. Viṣṇu wakes up and is requested by Lakṣmī to stop the general ruin. He however answers that Śiva is his lord and that there are many beings of his own rank. The only unforgivable sin is contempt for Śiva. Then the divine couple goes to Mount Kailāsa to praise Śiva, to whom the gods apologize for their fraudulence, and the *kiṃnara* is decapitated. The rest of the story is narrated in the form of a prophecy. In the Kali period the illegitimate son of a brahman called Madhu, a notorious hater of Śiva, will introduce a heresy. Now, illegitimacy, being practically identical with excommunication, played an important part in these polemics; the South, being for the greater part unaryan and incompletely brahmanized, was an in many respects ritually impure region and Madhva's name was, probably on purpose, mutilated. The followers of this teacher have only the outward appearance of human beings, in reality they are on the way to hell. Surrendering themselves to detestable vices and more depraved than Buddhists or Jainas, they defile everybody who comes into contact with them. Studying the scriptures only with a view to detect errors they believe in a system without a sound foundation, viz. the doctrine that there is nothing else but *māyā*, and that the *saṃsāra* is real and essential. This objection and their stigmatization as disguised Cārvākas[133] were no doubt based on the author's interpretation of Madhva's standpoint that the phenomenal universe is a reality. Opposing these false doctrines with determination the compiler of the Saura-Purāṇa maintains that all great founders of schools and authoritative manuals of Hindu philosophy, Jaimini, Kapila, Patañjali, the purāṇas and itihāsas, despite some mutual contradictions in matters of secondary importance, assign to Śiva a rank higher than the highest.

Yet the Hindu is inclined to revere the divine whatever its manifestation and so Śivaites are nevertheless strongly dissuaded from vilifying Viṣṇu.[134] In practice this trait of character may lead to curious forms of compromise and to attempts to consider both deities as complementary powers, whose co-operation is needed for the progress and prosperity of world and mankind. An almost endless collection of rites and customs could be brought together in which both gods—whether with or without the third member of the Trimūrti, Brahmā[135]—figure conjointly and indiscriminately. A man who is ill to death must, according to some authorities,[136] remember or hear the sacred names of both. In an enumeration of a number of *tīrthas* belonging to all parts of India the author of the Viṣṇusmṛti (ch. 85) inserted also some which are sacred to Śiva. Places are not rare in which the worship of both gods is recommended.[137] The partly Viṣṇuite, partly Śivaite Agni-Purāṇa combines in one chapter[138] the ordinary form of worship of both deities. It is, however, often difficult to decide whether we are in these cases concerned with neutrality or indifference or with a tendency to compromise or inclusion. Moreover, texts may have been rewritten, compiled or amplified in another milieu.[139] But there can be no doubt that these phenomena must be viewed in the light of the syncretistic tendencies which are in the last millennium increasingly forging ahead in Hinduism.

First, an instance of compromise. In Benares, where Śiva is the presiding deity and all the principal temples are dedicated to him,[140] his supremacy is also acknowledged by those Hindus for whom he is not the Highest Being, but no more than Viṣṇu's servant. This anomaly is accounted for by the belief that Viṣṇu-Rāma, gratified by Śiva's religious behaviour—for thousands of aeons the god used to mutter Rāma's mantra—had granted him the privilege to effect the final emancipation of everybody who dies in his sacred district at Benares.[141] Such a story helps us in understanding how both religions could for long periods co-exist in the same sacred place, for instance at Kāñcī (Conjeeveram) in the South and how, for instance, Viṣṇu so often figures in Śivaite legends.[142]

There is, further, indeed a curious trend to represent the two great divine powers as complementary.[143] A random example of a prescription which was to influence the social life of the faithful: Viṣṇu is said to be the tutelary deity of all articles which are given as a present enumerated in a special list, but any articles not mentioned in that list should be regarded as sacred to Śiva, and so the formula used in making a donation is: 'I make this gift composed of such and such articles, respectively sacred to Śiva or Viṣṇu. . . .'[144] Many traces of these complementary and co-operative functions of both gods survive in popular tales and beliefs. Śiva reciting a hymn in praise of the Ganges states that sinners dying, through the grace of God and as a result of their karma, in the waters of that river are relieved from all sins and become his attendants, dwelling by his side, but also that if a dead body of a person falls into these waters, that person will abide with Viṣṇu for many years.[145] Śrī-Kṛṣṇa is much pleased with his adorers' observance of the fast of the Śivarātrī[146] on the fourteenth day of the dark half of the month Phālguna. According to popular tradition his cult is not efficacious without this observance.[147]

Sometimes a mythological achievement or undertaking of great importance requires the co-operation of both divinities. When the army of the gods was defeated by the asuras, the devas, making Brahmā-Prajāpati their leader, approached Śiva and Viṣṇu for help with the result that the goddess Devī, Caṇḍikā, the Great Goddess was created from the tejas of the bodies of the gods.[148] Mythologizing popular tales even speak of ties of affinity, Viṣṇu having given his sister Devī in marriage to the other great god together with wedding presents.[149] Sometimes also both gods are, in more or less popular stories, even said to co-operate for the good of men who are on the wrong track. Thus once Viṣṇu, disguised as a woman,[150] accompanied Śiva who intentionally behaved as a Don Juan in a forest inhabited by ascetics who without knowing Śiva's true nature worshipped him.[151] A more philosophical account of this co-operation on a cosmic level is furnished in those purāṇic passages[152] which regard Viṣṇu as an integral part (*aṃśa*) of Śiva, as his *śakti* not different from himself; the whole universe consists of the essence of these two highest gods, Śiva being the *puruṣa* and Viṣṇu the *prakṛti* of Sāṃkhya philosophy.

Many purāṇic legends indeed give evidence of the conviction that the great divine powers complement each other and that they are to co-operate for the well-being of world and mankind. This is for instance apparent from part of those numberless popular legends and local traditions which, accounting for the name, origin or holiness of some temple, river or place of pilgrimage, assign a prominent part to one of the chief gods or to both of them. Thus the Kāśī-khaṇḍa of the Skanda-Purāṇa, the legendary history of Benares, narrating the origin of the famous Maṇikarṇikā well, says that Viṣṇu dug that well with his discus, and filled it with the perspiration from his own body. When the work was finished he began to practise austerities, no doubt to supply the energy spent in performing the arduous task. Meanwhile Śiva-Mahādeva came and looked into the well. Seeing in it the radiance of a hundred million suns, he was so enchanted that he began praising Viṣṇu loudly, and declared that he would give him anything he might ask. Viṣṇu, much gratified, replied that he only desired that Mahādeva should always live there with him. Mahādeva was so pleased with this compliment that his whole body shook with delight, and an ornament called Maṇikarṇikā fell from his ear into the well. He then declared that the well should henceforth be known by that name, and that it should be the most efficacious of all the places of pilgrimage.[153]—When the *asura* Gaya, who was a devout Vaiṣṇava, endowed with great strength and vigour practised rigorous austerities for many thousands of years, the gods, oppressed and alarmed, repaired to Brahmā for aid and protection. Brahmā, as usually, took no action himself, but remitted the case for intervention to Śiva. This god however referred the devas to Viṣṇu who, being equal to the occasion, proceeded to intervene and found also solutions in the ensuing succession of predicaments.[154] In another story Viṣṇu acts as Śiva's teacher: he enters the latter's heart and gives him insight into the intricacies of creation, preservation and absorption.[155] A last example: when Śiva, bewildered after Satī's death, went with her body on his shoulders to the eastern provinces, Brahmā, Viṣṇu and other gods, in order to relieve him of the corpse, cut it into pieces and made these fall at certain places on earth which henceforth were considered sacred.[156]

In particular cases however the historical development of a theme reveals that the motif of co-operation or more or less forced or inclusive co-existence has at a given moment been introduced, and replaced an antagonistic attitude, no doubt as a result of the increasing influence of one of these religions which wanted its god to be concerned in an important mythical event.[157]

There is an interesting purāṇic story about the Mātṛkās 'Divine Mothers' created by Śiva to help him in destroying the formidable demon Andhaka.[158] When these deities, though sucking the blood of the demon to the point of satiety, did not succeed in acquitting themselves of their task, Śiva had to resort to Viṣṇu for help. Viṣṇu then created a female being Śuṣka-Revatī, who in a moment killed all the demons. The troupe of Śiva's Mātṛkās however was not satisfied and wished to devour demons, gods and men all and sundry. In order to prevent these beings from being killed Śiva propitiated Viṣṇu-Narasiṃha who created another group of Mātṛkās from his own limbs. These mothers were capable of creation as well as destruction, and when they overpowered Śiva's Mātṛkās the latter applied to Narasiṃha who pointed out to them that their duty was to protect the world. Thus their malevolent nature was changed, their task henceforth being to worship Śiva, not to afflict his devotees, to protect those who remember Viṣṇu-Narasiṃha, to fulfill all the desires of those who offer oblations, and to maintain order. This narrative suggests not only the co-operation of both great gods but also Viṣṇu's superiority, and especially his benevolent nature, noble spirit and peaceable disposition.

A very instructive example of gradual recast and transformation is furnished by the legend of the son of the *daitya* Hiraṇyakaśipu, Prahlāda, who, while yet a boy, became an ardent devotee of Viṣṇu. This so enraged mighty Hiraṇyakaśipu, that he ordered the youth to be killed,[159] with no success, because his devout love to Kṛṣṇa and fervent religiosity made him invulnerable. This story of unswerving loyalty against brute hostility and self-exaltation, pathetically narrated in black and white, was a great favourite of many apologists. In the course of time Prahlāda—who had already in the Bhagavadgītā[160] been mentioned as a *vibhūti* or manifestation of Kṛṣṇa's power and majesty—even became the principal character of the myth of Viṣṇu's Man-lion *avatāra*, to which he originally did not belong. Originally the Man-lion had made his appearance to punish the king of the daityas for his arrogance and the dethronement of the gods. Later on it was to avenge Prahlāda,[161] as well as to vindicate his own insulted majesty that Viṣṇu became incarnate as Narasiṃha and slew Hiraṇyakaśipu.[162] The presentation of this legend reached its poetical and theological culminating point in the Viṣṇu- and Bhāgavata-Purāṇas of about the IVth and IXth centuries A.D. In later versions it was on the one hand abridged and revised and, on the other, amalgamated with other material according as the particular theological standpoints of the compilers might require. All these later adaptations have in common a reduction of the philosophical content of the legend to the simple form of a popular devotional narrative. Among the authors there were not only Viṣṇuites, but, interestingly enough, also Śivaites. As the narratives we owe to them throw much light on the mutual relations between both religions it may be permitted very briefly to summarize here part of the results ensuing from the investigations of Professor Hacker of Münster, who wrote an interesting book on the Prahlāda legend.

Whereas up to a definite stage of development[163] of the story Śiva does not play any part in it, this god appears, in the Viṣṇuite Narasiṃha-Purāṇa (ch. 40 ff.), on the scene as the leader of the gods who, being alarmed by Hiraṇyakaśipu's tyranny, proceed on the advice of Bṛhaspati,[164] to praise Viṣṇu. It is Śiva who after adoring Viṣṇu with a hymn, consisting of names and epithets—among which are also his own names Śaṅkara and Maheśvara!—without any formulation of a request for help, induces Viṣṇu to appear and to promise Hiraṇyakaśipu's ruin in case he should lay violent hands on his son. Quite another role is destined for Śiva by the compiler of the sixth book of the Padma-Purāṇa.[165] Although he is introduced here as the narrator of the story, the legend is reduced to a specimen of anti-Śivaite propagandism. In one of the many narratives with which the god instructs and entertains his wife Umā he relates that it was due to a boon granted by himself—and not, as in the older versions, by Brahmā[166]—that his fervent adorer Hiraṇyakaśipu had, after millions of years spent in rigorous ascetic discipline, obtained the government of the universe. This role of Śiva, whose worshipper is in the course of the story represented as being much impressed by Viṣṇu's omnipotence, is no doubt due to the author's wish to proclaim the inferiority of heretical[167] Śivaism, which is inculcated here, with the highest authority of Śiva himself.[168] Another no less tendentious trait of this version is the alternative with which

Prahlāda is presented by his father: he should either revere Hiraṇyakaśipu as the lord of the three worlds, or worship, after the Pāśupata tradition, Śiva, the guru of the universe, the lord of the gods, who is the god of the demons and from whom all dominion derives. The priests of the king add that Rudra is the highest god, through whose favour Hiraṇyakaśipu has risen to his royal position.[169] Here again it is not the philosophical or theological system of the rival religion which is combated and refuted but its socio-ritual practices which provoke the author's deep-rooted aversion.

Turning now to some Śivaite adaptations we first confine our attention to a version contained in the Śiva-Purāṇa,[170] which, though dependent on the Bhāgavata, quite intelligibly lacks those features which the successive generations of Vaiṣṇava devotees had added to the story in order to make its hero a champion of their own faith and, on the other hand, does not fail to intimate that Narasiṃha is not quite too powerful, because he needs four milliards of years to conquer the demon. Another version preserved in the same purāṇa[171] gives us a different picture. In reading the story proper one has the impression that it is Viṣṇuite, but just before the end Śivaization forges ahead. In deviation from other versions the blaze of Narasiṃha's fury cannot be quenched before Śiva, praised and implored by the gods, transforms himself into a *śarabha*, a terrible monstrous animal with eight legs which was believed to kill lions.[172] As soon as the Man-lion catches sight of this opponent he bids him welcome with respectful benedictions and disappears. In the two Śivaite adaptations with which I must bring the survey to an end, Prahlāda is no longer the central figure of the story, because the Śaivas, once they had introduced the śarabha, made it an *avatāra* of their god which soon became the hero of a new mythical tale, various versions of which occur in Śivaite literature. Thus this tale developed into an element of the theological polemics into which Śaivas and Vaiṣṇavas found themselves engaged. In a third passage of the Śiva-Purāṇa, rightly called 'The story of the *śarabha*',[173] the traditional Prahlāda legend has now been converted to the simple introduction to an account of Śiva's intervention. In order to help the gods he sends his own frightful manifestation (*bhairavaṃ rūpam*), called Vīrabhadra[174] and his *śārabhaṃ rūpam*, which he normally assumes on the occasion of the reabsorption of the universe. After an unsuccessful attempt at conciliating Narasiṃha by means of friendly words—which are only to intensify the lion's fury and to make him boast of his omnipotence—Vīrabhadra reveals his identity and explodes with a torrent of abuse, saying that the Man-lion sinks into complete insignificance beside Śiva, finally to drag him along towards heaven. Now, in the power of his antagonist, Narasiṃha resolves to praise and implore him:[175] 'Whenever I think, my mind defiled by arrogance, "These are my commands" I pray Thee, O Lord, to take this inclination away from me.' Finally the monster incorporates Narasiṃha in the literal sense of the term: he makes him part of his body, declaring that now Viṣṇu is completely included in Śiva, like water poured into water.[176] Vīrabhadra tears off the lion's skin, which is henceforth worn by Śiva.[177]

A comparison between this Śivaite version and the anti-Śivaite form of the story presented by the Padma-Purāṇa is very instructive. The Śaiva author takes the intervention of the Man-lion as arrogance which results in nothing but Śiva's revenge. Whereas the Vaiṣṇava text condemns the cult of the rival religion without engaging in a discussion of its mythological presuppositions, the Śaiva makes the mythological imagery of both parties[178]—which actually is a symbolization of functional aspects of the characters of the two gods—a weapon to combat his rivals without caring for their cult. The last point is worth noticing, because Hinduism in general is inclined to attach, in these questions, more value to the socio-ritual side of a doctrine or religion than to its theoretical foundation. As long as we have no exact information on the author's times and milieu we cannot feel sure that it was his inability to suppress the cult of the rival religion—Professor Hacker's supposition[179]—which made him take this stand.[180] Whereas, finally, the Vaiṣṇava author does not wish to interfere with Śiva's position of authority provided that he is Viṣṇu's inferior,[181] the Śaiva is willing to permit the worship of Viṣṇu-Narasiṃha, but only on the understanding that actually Viṣṇu is completely identical with Śiva.[182] Śivaism indeed, though often decidedly inclined to adoptive inclusivism,[183] actually contented itself in many particular cases with the recognition of the equality of both gods;[184] with the pronouncement that by worshipping Viṣṇu, who is ever victorious by the grace of Śiva, one delights and satisfies the latter;[185] or with the simple statement that as compared with Śiva, Viṣṇu is, in point of fact, no more than a mirage.[186]

Doctrinal tolerance is, finally, one of the most remarkable aspects of Hinduism. Yet, here also, a distinction should be made.[187] The systematic philosophical treatises expounding or defending the tenets of a definite school of thought are of course bent on establishing the views of their community, and consequently much inclined to reject dissentient views. For those authors who believe in a personal God and in a well-considered doctrine about His nature, attributes and omnipotence it is no matter of indifference whether God is Śiva or Viṣṇu. Poets, mystics and other exponents of more emotional forms of religion are, on the other hand, inclined to neglect, notwithstanding their allegiance to either god, doctrinal distinctions and ritual differences and to emphasize the attainment of the ultimate Oneness into which not only all human, but also all divine persons may ultimately merge.[188]

A few instances of comprehensive broad-mindedness may be recalled here. The exploits of the family of Raghu, in which those of Rāma, who is Viṣṇu, are the most important, open in Kālidāsa's famous poem with an invocation of Parameśvara (Śiva) and Pārvatī, while his other epic, the Kūmarasambhava, which is a story of Śiva, contains a long and elaborated prayer to Brahmā (2, 4 ff.). On the whole this poet, despite many sympathetic references to Śiva, praises the two other members of the triad so devotedly that he cannot have been a narrow-minded partisan of one of them.[189] In later times also Tulsīdās begins his poem of the deeds of Viṣṇu in his incarnation as Rāma, the Rāmacaritamānasa, with a prayer addressed to the other great god of Hinduism. That in spite of metaphyical differences the two religions were in definite times and regions drawing nearer together is also apparent from inscriptional evidence. Temple inscriptions dating from the XIIth century[190] open with the invocation of one sacred name and close with the other and pious kings openly profess themselves worshippers of both gods. A donation to the Lord Śiva may begin with an invocation of Vāsudeva.[191] A complete collection of all relative legends, literary texts and other documents would no doubt be a welcome addition to our knowledge of interconfessional relations in Hinduism.

The two deities—'the two highest who are one'[192]—may even be invoked under the joint title Pradyumna-Īśvara,[193] that is Hari-Hara, a figure which—whatever inspiration sculptors might derive from it to express the coincidence of opposites mutually supporting each other[194]—never rose to real importance in religious praxis.[195] Both gods are sometimes praised as being, each of them, one half of the highest God, or the original form of God is said to be composed of two 'halves' known individually as Śiva and Viṣṇu.[196] In illustration of the difference in attitude between a mystic and a philosopher belonging to the same Viṣṇuite tradition I may recall[197] that, whereas the saint and poet Nammālvār saw no difference in a so-called sectarian mark on the forehead made with sacred dust and one made, in the Śivaite way, with ashes, the philosopher Vedāntadeśika preferred to interpret in the poet's work the word for 'ashes' to mean the dust under Viṣṇu's feet in order to avoid any thought of ashes.

Teachers and preachers, enraptured with their visions of the truth, did not hesitate to identify the Highest Being of every denomination with the Highest Principle of Vedantic monism. The plurality of doctrines and of divine names does not last when the higher insight has dawned or the experience of the Oneness has been realized. 'May Hari, the ruler of the threefold universe, worshipped by the Śivaites as Śiva, by the Vedāntins as Brahman, by the Buddhists as Buddha . . . by the Jainas as the liberated . . . grant our prayers.'[198] Then it is explicitly taught that the doctrine one adopts and the philosophy one professes are matters of indifference. Avoiding all polemics the author of the Yogavāsiṣṭha-Rāmāyaṇa[199] makes an attempt to recognize the truth of all Hindu traditions, to adopt them and to weld them into something higher. 'Many names have been given to the Supreme Spirit by the learned for practical purposes such as Order (*ṛtam*), Self (*ātmā*), the High Brahmā, Truth; it is called . . . Brahman by the Vedāntins, . . ., the Void (*śūnya*) by those who proclaim the doctrine of the Void[200] . . ., Śiva by the worshippers of the god whose ornament is the digit of the moon'.[201] Similarly, authorities on Kṛṣṇaite *bhakti* express the opinion that in praising God's glory and majesty one should not consider him, Kṛṣṇa, different from Śiva.[202] 'Just as one substance with many qualities (becomes manifold) through (the apprehension of) the senses working in different ways, even so the Holy One (*bhagavān*) is conceived of in different ways through the (diversity of the) scriptural traditions.'

VI

Śiva and Viṣṇu in Folklore, Myth and Literature

IT NEED HARDLY BE SAID that after a survey of some main doctrines and of the institutionalized rites of both religions it will not be improper now to cast a glance at the customs, convictions, folklore, mythological and literary traditions related to the cult of the two great gods. As however it would lead us too far to review Indian religious folklore as far as it is concerned with Viṣṇu and Śiva, I shall limit myself to a few remarks on traditional popular belief, abandon any attempt at examining sources written in languages other than Sanskrit and mainly focus attention on these gods as they appear in the post-epic classical literature, covering the period in which the Hinduism of literate Indians may be said to have consisted mainly of these two religions, Śaiva-Śākta and the variants of Viṣṇuism.

A phenomenon which has, for many centuries, been of special importance in religious practice and which must have played a role in the interrelations of both religions concerns an obvious parallelism in cults and customs, beliefs and ceremonies. Evil is, in India also, averted by the utterance of certain names. When an Indian hears a lizard chirp he may repeat four or five times the name of Kṛṣṇa, but if his house be pestered with snakes he writes one of Śiva's names on the walls.[1] Mention has already been made[2] of Śiva's drum and of Viṣṇu's conch,[3] and Kṛṣṇa's flute is only too well known: it may be added that the Vaiṣṇavas have a predilection for the flute and the cither, leaving the cymbals, drums and bells mostly to the Śaivas and Tantrists.[4] Since the harp is the preference of Buddhist gods, it is clear that with regard to musical instruments the Indian religions tended to evince a certain partiality. These observations have a wider application. The main annual Viṣṇuite festivals and ceremonies and those in honour of Śiva *cum suis*, which are determined by the lunar calendar,[5] alternate, so as to constitute some striking cases of correspondence. The great Śivarātrī is for instance held on the fourteenth day of the dark fortnight of Phālguna (February-March) and Kṛṣṇa's and Rādhā's Dolayātrā (Holi) on the full moon day of the same month.

Rather than repeat some well-known relations of the great gods with definite animals I would insert here a short account of their associations with the vegetable kingdom. Whereas of course many plants play no role in this connection and other plants and trees seem to waver in their sympathy,[6] a number of them are widely sacred to one of these gods or to their wives—that is, they are regarded as representatives or manifestations of the power complexes for which these divine names stand—and are as a rule worshipped accordingly. Thus the *tulasī*[7] (basil or *ocimum sanctum*) is all over India an object of veneration for Viṣṇuites, who, for instance, make necklaces of bits of its stem. This most sacred and respected plant which is believed to destroy mosquitoes, diseases and demons, is a great purifier of the atmosphere;[8] many Indians are convinced that evil spirits never dare come to a place where a *tulasī* is planted. Being 'dear to Hari' and found before every temple of the god it is married to him on the eleventh day of the bright half of the month of Kārtika, when his image is worshipped with its leaves. Interestingly enough this plant is believed to be the meeting point of heaven and earth; Brahmā and other gods and goddesses reside on its leaves. It grants children to the childless, wealth to the needy and opens the gate of heaven to the devout worshipper. A Viṣṇuite tradition relates that when the chastity of Vṛndāvatī—who is sometimes identified with Rādhā—sustained the life and power of her husband, the demon Jalandhara, Kṛṣṇa however, by deceiving Vṛndāvatī in the guise of that demon, succeeded in killing him. When Vṛndāvatī came to know of this fact she declared that she would be reborn as the *tulasī* and cursed Viṣṇu: he would have to bear her leaves on his head for the wrong he had done her. The god, full of remorse, accepted her in the form of that plant to be his permanent companion.

According to the Agni-Purāṇa (202, 3 ff.) the *mālatī* (*jasminum grandiflorum*) heads the list of flowers given in propitiation of the god, while an act of worship made with *tamāla* flowers grants enjoyment and salvation to the votary himself. A *pūjā* performed with the jasmine called *mallikā* absolves the worshipper of all sins, etc.[9] The tree sacred to Kṛṣṇa is the *kadamba*, under which he dances with the *gopīs*.

As Kṛṣṇa-Viṣṇu is fond of the leaves of the *tulasī*, so Śiva is said to appreciate those of the *bilva* (*bael*, *bel*, wood-apple tree or *aegle marmelos*),[10] which is mainly associated with Śaiva and Śākta cults. Its wood is not burned as fuel for fear of rousing the indignation of the god of destruction.[11] Its trifoliate leaf 'symbolizes' the three functions—creation, preservation and destruction—of the Lord as well as his three eyes. According to the Śivaite mythical tradition of its origin[12] Lakṣmī used to worship Śiva every day with a thousand lotus flowers. Accidentally, one day two flowers were missing and, pondering over an alternative, she remembered that her husband had casually remarked that her breasts were as beautiful as blooming lotus flowers. Then she decided to offer these parts of her body. When she was cutting them off with a sharp weapon the god appeared, declaring himself satisfied and restraining her from completing what she had begun. One breast however was already cut off; it was, the god said, to be planted and would become one of the most sacred fruits in the world. Among the plants prescribed in the worship of Śiva are also the *dhustara* (thorn-apple) and the 'magical' and calamitous *arka*,[13] which elsewhere is said to cause the displeasure of the gods in general.

Rice is sacred to Lakṣmī, the goddess of fortune and prosperity, who already at an early date was closely connected with the yellow ripe corn and who up to the present day is, at her festival, represented by a corn-basket filled with unhusked rice. She is sometimes even believed to exist or to manifest herself in the shape of seedlings grown in the winnowing-basket.[14] Durgā, the goddess of uncultured tribes, is associated with plants of another type. Among the food offered to her is the aphrodisiac pulse which is also given to the spirits of the deceased.[15] Manifesting her nature in several aspects this goddess is also represented by different sacred trees. One of these—usually nine[16]—plants is the *kadalī* (the plantain tree or *musa sapientum*) which, representing vegetative power, is the centre of a ritual performed by women in order to have children.[17] In the Devī-Māhātmya the goddess is made to say: 'When rain and water shall fail for a hundred years, I shall, propitiated by the munis, be born on the earth but not from a womb, support the whole world with the life-sustaining vegetables which will grow out of my own body until the rains set in again.'[18] We are strongly reminded of widespread beliefs and well-known customs related to the Corn-mother.[19]

Generally speaking and barring geographical differences the main fig trees are assigned[20] to different gods. The big *pipal*, *aśvattha* or *ficus religiosa*, is, for instance in Gujerat, often seen near a shrine of Śiva and believed to be the abode of snakes, the god's pets. Elsewhere however the *aśvattha*—sacrosanct and the most prominent of all trees[21] —is sacred to Viṣṇu whose embodiment it is:[22] among all trees I am', Kṛṣṇa said (*BhG.* 10, 26), 'the *aśvattha*'. This tree, which is supposed to represent fertility, to give children, and to avert disasters, plays an important part in the ancient cosmological speculations of the Indians.[23] I only recall AV. 5, 4, 3 where it figures as the celestial seat of the gods who there gained the sight of 'immortality' (*amṛtam*) and *ChU.* 8, 5, 3 mentioning a 'soma-yielding' (*somasavana*) fig-tree in the Brahmaloka.[24] Although the great epic (*Mbh.* 13, 135, 101) calls Viṣṇu, that is identifies him with, three species of the ficus, this god was according to a purāṇical legend cursed to become an *aśvattha*, and Śiva to become the banyan or Indian fig tree (*nyagrodha*),[25] which, like the god himself, has phallic associations.[26] Not rarely the banyan is indeed said to be a form of Śiva, the *aśvattha* a form of Viṣṇu, and the *palāśa*—i.e. the butea frondosa—a form of Brahmā,[27] another instance of a threefold assignment[28] or distribution in relation with the three members of the Indian trinity.[29]

In studying these relations of the great divine figures one should not forget that there are, in India, very clear examples of plant theophanies attesting to the people's consciousness of the divinity and the highly important function of the vegetable kingdom. Says Durgā: 'Then, O Gods, I shall support (nourish) the whole universe with these life-sustaining vegetables which grow from my own body until the rains set in again. I shall then become glorious upon the earth as the 'Bearer of vegetables' (Śākambharī) and then I shall destroy the great *asura* Durgama (i.e. the personification of drought).'[30] Lakṣmī is adored in, and in the form of, a basket filled with unhusked rice[31] or represented by a corn-measure filled with grain and adorned with flowers.[32] The belief moreover obtained that worship of the genii of trees and plants—and among these is Śiva[33]—may lead to the position of such a deity in one's next existence.[34]

Similar instances of what may be called a complementary tendency[35] in rites and practices might be collected from other provinces or nature. The Viṣṇuites for instance believe that their god is present in every *śālagrāma*—a black fossil found in the Gandak river—, while the adorers of Śiva are convinced that this deity resides in every round white pebble found in the Narmadā.[36] The Śivaite Liṅgāyats never part with a small *liṅga* assumed to be the representative of their God, the Viṣṇuite followers of Kabir wear a pearl of *tulasī* wood or a *tulasī* collar.

These great gods maintain, for instance, relations with those mountains which occupy a prominent place in Indian cosmology and mythology, but their preference lies in different directions. Thus Kālidāsa often alludes to the Kailāsa, a mountain formed of crystals, as an abode of Śiva and Pārvatī[37] and the poet's liking for this mountain may probably be closely bound up with this fact.[38] His 'affection for the Himālaya'[39] is too well known to be recalled here.[40] Viṣṇu is on the other hand said to be worshipped on Mount Mandara,[41] the mountain which, already in the Great epos, was made the churning staff when the ocean had to yield the *amṛta*.[42]

It would be an endless task to collect all legends connected with sacred mountains, rivers and other places in which Viṣṇu or Śiva play a more or less prominent part,[43] or current in regions or localities which are considered to have been the scene of their earthly activities. Let it suffice to observe that in these traditions also both gods remain true to their character. Viṣṇu-Madhusūdana is said to stay on Mount Mandara in Bhāgalpur, keeping his foot placed on it, because this is the mythical mountain of the same name which the god had thrown upon the trunk of the dangerous demon Madhukaiṭabha[44] in order to prevent his bones being a cause of damage.

The general public does not hesitate to ascribe to the objects of their veneration thoroughly human qualities and imperfections. Thus the dissatisfaction expressed by Garuḍa,[45] his *vāhana*, at Viṣṇu's indifference to the suffering of the plover whose eggs had been stolen (washed away) by the sea and his refusal to convey his master to Amarāvatī in order to promote the interests of the gods brought the Exalted One to see his error[46] and to order the sea to give back the eggs. When on the other hand king Parāntaka of Uraiyūr in the region of Trichinopoly had omitted to punish a gardener who had appropriated some flowers which were set apart to be offered to Śiva, the god became so angry that he destroyed, by means of a dust-cloud, town and royal house with the exception of the queen, for she would give birth to a son who, by Śiva's grace, was to be king in after years.[47] It would not be difficult to collect a considerable number of interesting stories of this type, especially from narrative literature and popular traditions. Kṛṣṇa is known as a trickster[48] but his colleague is, if the occasion presents itself, no more averse from pranks and deceit. An interesting story is told by Somadeva[49] in which Śiva himself, almost bound to grant a boon whatever it might be, finds himself compelled to become a party to the trick played upon the innocent Kaliṅgasenā[50] by allowing a strange man to substitute himself surreptitiously for her husband. When a playwright[51] could put an accusation of theft into the *vidūṣaka's* mouth against the same god one might feel reminded of those poets who call their god a thief of men's hearts or say that Kṛṣṇa has stolen the hearts of the *gopīs*. Elsewhere[52] Śiva-Parameśvara is reviled because he had joined an ill-matched pair in marriage.

The gods' main activities gave, quite intelligibly, rise to an endless number of legends and popular tales. Thus a king of South-Indian Madura who took great pains to learn to dance, was very distressed, because Śiva at Chidambaram proved to be able to dance without interruption and always on the same foot. As the god did not notice his urgent demands to take a rest or to change, at least, his foot, the king committed suicide; it was only then that Śiva condescended to dance on his other foot.[53]

Needless to say that in these tales the exalted superhuman God of philosophers and theologians often hides himself behind His aspect of a mighty and reliable helper of his devotees and punisher of their adversaries, who however in this function is not rarely bound by, and subject to, general norms of *dharma* or moral or to other limitations which may impress the reader as imperfections or infringements of His omnipotence. Śiva is not able to get rid of the blue colour which he contracted in drinking the poison: there are things which cannot be helped.[54] As a good colleague Viṣṇu declares, in a Śivaite context, it is true, that he is unable to remove the calamity which Śiva had caused, although Brahmā had pronounced another opinion.[55] This tendency may result in the idea that even these great gods must atone for transgression of the *dharma*. Thus Viṣṇu had according to a purāṇic story[56] to incarnate himself—as a result of a curse—seven times on earth for having beheaded a woman, viz. the mother of Bhṛgu, with whom the *asuras* had taken refuge.

Nor is there much need to cite many examples of the popular belief in more or less direct intervention of the great gods in mundane events and especially in the vicissitudes of individuals. They may for instance appear in bodily form[57] or in dreams and give helpful advice.[58] In these tales myth is no less mixed up with legend than in the many compilations and more or less original compositions written in praise of their god by Śaiva and Vaiṣṇava devotees who in the course of time developed a very extensive hagiography.[59]

I make, in passing, mention of the abundant literary and inscriptional[60] evidence of worship,[61] of the great gods being invoked by men in distress and agony,[62] by those who observe a vow or entertain a hope or desire, in normal and exceptional circumstances. We hear of King Puṣpabhūti, who did not even in dreams take food without worshipping the god whose emblem is a bull, the Lord of beings, the unborn and ageless guru of the immortals, the upholder of the universe, the creator and annihilator of all existence; who was honoured by his vassals and subjects with presents customary in Śiva's worship, and gratified by white bulls, and conceived for a great Śaiva saint Bhairavācārya a deep affection as towards a second Śiva who initiated him in the god's ritual.[63] Definite aspects of cult, piety and adoration come to the fore as circumstances may require. For propitiating Śiva with *tapas* in order to be united with one's beloved one may go to a temple of Gaurī and recall the god's union with her, his eternal consort.[64] Hearing the holy story of the Rāmāyaṇa, which relates the heroic deeds of Viṣṇu who had descended to the earth in order to save mankind, was for many centuries to come a dependable way to long life, moral purity and good fortune.[65]

It is generally speaking not by mere chance that an invocation of a god's protection is not infrequently accompanied by a reference to one of his important aspects or great exploits.[66] Śiva, who laughs at the memory of his violent but effortless proceedings against Dakṣa, and Kṛṣṇa-Viṣṇu, who made the gods happy by slaying Kaṃsa, will no doubt prove competent and reliable helpers.[67] God's victory indeed brings the victory of His worshippers in its wake,[68] and the poets do not omit emphasizing this continued efficacy of the divine activity in the reality of the *hic et nunc* by resorting to a parallelism in sentence structure: 'It is Viṣṇu-Keśava who is victorious after having killed Keśin . . ., it is (our king) Chandragupta who is victorious . . .'[69]

However, references to the cult and adoration of the great gods may in many literary works be frequent, it does not follow that they often supply us with a wealth of information about little known particulars. Many topics and descriptions are traditional,[70] and not rarely an author confines himself to a bare mention of a name or ceremony which then may serve to insert a simile or to embroider a descriptive passage.[71] Yet one of the sources of interest in definite poems or prose works lies in their contribution to our knowledge of popular belief and worship and of the position, character and significance of the gods in the estimation of their adherents. For even the boundless phantasy of the story-tellers can hardly have come into flagrant collision with fixed public opinions about the character and behaviour of these great figures. We may for instance learn from classical Sanskrit works that Śiva was, at least in the eyes of some authors,[72] much more interested in the weal and woe of his worshippers than Westerners are often prepared to assume.[73] We hear, in Bāṇa's Kādambarī which yields pre-eminence to this god, not only of oblations offered to him at cross-roads,[74] of a devotee marked with the dust of his feet clasped in her devotion and even bearing on her head these feet marked with the god's name and fastened with a band of hair;[75] of adoration of pictures of the same god which were believed to have been carved on a rock by Pārvatī,[76] but also of a shrine dedicated to the service of Durgā[77] and of the oblations offered to this goddess. In the Kathāsaritsāgara Śiva, whether he is propitiated[78] or not, often intervenes in the course of events,[79] bestowing favours and advantages upon his devotees,[80] lending them a helping hand,[81] and, very often, granting them the birth of a son,[82] giving orders[83] which appear to be their salvation. He is pleased by their austerities,[84] appealed to for advice[85] and believed to be (as Bhairava) invisibly present in cemeteries,[86] to appear in dreams so as to come into personal contact with his worshippers[87] and to secure the abodes of his followers against evil powers[88] and misfortune.[89]

The pity and love of God for all creatures is especially illustrated by innumerable stories about the great power and wonderful results of *bhakti*. It is not only the belief of a devotee that his *bhakti* will result in divine intercession with regard to the consequences of his actions, the performance of a vow with faith and devotion will also lead to the attainment of every power and pleasure, to freedom from pain and disease, and to all other divine graces.[90] And, what is more, God's heart may feel pity even for those whom he is, by the force of circumstances, to punish or to destroy. Did not Śiva, after shooting the fatal arrow at Tripura repent his deed, and lament the death and destruction which he had brought about?[91] Human sentiments, moral considerations and sympathy with the misfortune of those who have to pass through the successive states of worldly existence are indeed by no means foreign to the great gods. On hearing the stunning news of Kāma being destroyed by the fire which emanated from Śiva's third eye, Pārvatī, disconcerted, complains of her unfortunate beauty to her father:

'It is true that every aim can be attained by asceticism, but the world is vain and plunged into misfortunte. It is better to die than to lead a miserable existence.'[92]

After the comprehensive characterization of the Indian stotras given by the Indian scholar S.K. De[93] it would be needless to expatiate on the general features of this type of devotional literature. Only seldom reaching the standard of great religious poetry and therefore almost ignored by many Sanskrit scholars, this very productive genre which in the epics, purāṇas, tantras and even in *kāvya* works occurs as mere insertions, developed, by the VIIth century A.D., into a distinct form of literature to enter upon its flowering-time together with the medieval cults and denominations. As is only natural, these poems are devotional rather than doctrinal. They are mostly expressions of popular religion and may be appreciated as sources of knowledge of the mentality, the creed and credulity of their authors and those who were edified by them. Although not rarely traditional many effusions, prayers and lamentations are more or less poetic recasts of religious truths. If one dies at Benares Śiva gives the knowledge of the highest truth.[94] 'When shall I be a dweller in Kāśī? When look back on sorrow from those groves of gladness? With Ganges water and with leaves of *bel* (*bilva*) I will worship Śiva, my lord. Whether on water or on land it matters not, only let me die away there at Benares and salvation will be mine. She who feeds the world (i.e. Annapūrṇā, a manifestation of Durgā[95]) is there as queen, that golden one in whom I will take refuge. There will I dance. . . .'[96] However, Śiva's character remains ambiguous, and this fact finds expression in prayers quoted as models of 'love to a deity': 'When shall I pass my days as a moment, dwelling in Vārāṇasī here on the bank of the divine river (Gaṅgā), wearing (only) a small waist-cloth, holding my hands joined on my head, and crying out: "O Lord of Gaurī, Destroyer of Tripura, three-eyed Śambhu, be propitious"':[97] the god, though benevolent, remains always capable of mischief on an inconceivable scale.

Generally speaking the more popular and edifying literature which is mostly written in the language of the masses, enables us to form a very good idea of the religious experience and the practical piety and devotion of the faithful.[98] The authors and singers are in touch with the fundamental tenets of their denominations but do not preach these. Expressing the religious truths and values in the language of their hearts they remain true to the image of their gods as depicted by their more 'theoretical' co-religionists, who, on their part, tried to formulate what was living religion.

Devout Viṣṇuites are inclined to emphasize God's omnipotence and the far-reaching effects of His grace. 'The hot-rayed (sun) turns to coolness, the ocean, difficult to pass over, to a small river, the day-labourer to a kinsman (of the rich), Indra's thunderbolt to a flower, the hungry pauper to a man of substance, the highest position (*paramapadam*) of (Viṣṇu,) the discus-bearer, to an (open) door (to all devotees), even *saṃsāra* becomes (that highest) position when the Lord, the husband of Lakṣmī, is pleased.'[99] But those who do not prove themselves worthy of His grace, fall victims to Yama.[100] However, Yama himself owes his dominion in the world of the Fathers likewise to divine grace: it is Śiva who granted him this favour.[101]

It would be interesting to institute a comparative study of the places dealing with God's grace. From these it would appear that it does not only enable man to acquire final emancipation; it is also fruitful in many other ways. There are purāṇic stories of men who secured health, wealth and happiness, or a residence in the celestial regions, through the Lord's grace and one Brahmadatta could through Viṣṇu understand the language of the creatures. It is on the other hand believed that the grace of Śiva enables even the perpetrators of diabolical deeds to obtain the highest attainments.[102]

Although I cannot of course pretend to adding anything essential to the images of the central gods of Hinduism as they are present to the mind of every student of Indian history, it may be worth while to institute a brief comparison between those main features of each divine personality which are over and over again made theme and motif, or condensed into epithets or mere references, in the works of the classical authors. We have every reason to draw the so-called polite letters also into this comparative survey, because, according to the Indians, poetry and literary composition in general may help a man to attain religious merit. They make his mind receptive to higher ideas and are an important means of self-realization and of unification with the divine essence, 'for instance through the praise of the lotus-feet of the divine Viṣṇu-Nārāyaṇa',[103] and through the re-activation of the power inherent in the divine histories and the myths and legends of the gods and their manifestations.[104] The epic poets also told their stories about worldly struggle and worldly pleasure mainly to lead the mind eventually to the Lord.[105] It will however appear that it is not always easy to characterize the literary portraits of these two great figures, because the poets, like their adherents in general, will quite naturally emphasize those traits of character which should, on a particular occasion, come to the fore and the same occasions will present themselves to Śaivas and Vaiṣṇavas alike, both praying in the same distress for the same divine assistance and both being inclined to attribute to their God the same indescribable qualities.[106]

It would to begin with be interesting to contrast the characterizations which the followers of either god give of themselves. A single instance may show that there indeed is a tendency to emphasize different qualities and activities. In the Kriyāyogasāra which was, probably at a later date, attached to the Padma-Purāṇa, Viṣṇu himself is (a. 2) said to have enumerated the characteristics of the Vaiṣṇava: he has to look upon Brahmā, Viṣṇu and Rudra as equal, to wear garlands made of *tulasī* wood and *dhātrī* fruits, to mark his limbs with the figures of conch, discus, club and lotus, to bathe regularly in the waters of the Ganges, to study the Bhāgavata, to construct new Viṣṇu temples or to repair old ones, to serve cows and superiors, to have no regard for heretics, to be devoted to Śiva and to worship Viṣṇu.[107] According to another authority,[108] the best of the Bhāgavatas include those devoutly worshipping Śiva. The faithful servant of God is himself like God,[109] and his feet hallow the ground on which he treads. The Śivaite on the other hand should first and foremost worship his spiritual preceptor like Śiva himself, follow the path of his God, always meditate on Him, considering Him to be present in himself, and dissociate himself from all opinions which are incompatible with the Śivaite creed.[110]

Homage to Śiva[111] is not rarely paid in secluded or uninhabited places,[112] for instance on the bank of a mountain stream,[113] on the fourteenth day of the month.[114] This devotion, which may be attended with meat offerings,[115] very often consists in the observation of austerities (*tapas*).[116] One of the characters of the Kathāsaritsāgara is said to have, at Benares, remained with his body steeped in the water of the Ganges, worshipping Śiva three times a day, performing *tapas*, like a hermit, by living on roots and fruits, his wife sharing all his devotions and privations.[117] The performance of *tapas* in places sacred to the god[118] may of course bring him to special concessions. Śiva is moreover believed to appear in his terrible form, as Bhairava, with drawn sword and lolling tongue, making an appalling roar, to punish breakers of the divine commandments,[119] but he may also, pleased and adorable, grant a benevolent vision of himself.[120] Viṣṇu is on the other hand, as Rāma's, i.e. Lakṣmī's, husband, worshipped with flowers by people who, wishing to purge away the results of their evil deeds, live on fruits and bathe in tanks.[121] But it is also Viṣṇu who is credited with the willingness to grant his devotees a boon by which they may, for dishonourable purposes, change their sex at will,[122] for Kṛṣṇa-Viṣṇu, who loves his worshippers more than Brahmā, Śiva or Śrī,[123] is not able to resist the call of those who invoke him.[124]

Śiva is characterized by several attitudes assumed for the expression of important aspects of his being, that is for the due performance of his functions and duties. It is these poses, which attracted the special attention of the poets who over and over again glorify the great god's power; he embodies service to the world and mankind; in these he is the prototype of all ascetics,[125] the human ascetic boasting of a joy which, like his god and prototype, 'he has found in being alone in the heart of the infinite'.[126] Śiva is also the originator of the eternal rhythm of the universe, the destroyer[127] and the author of life and regeneration. In his headdress is the crescent moon[128] which drips the nectar of everlasting life[129] and hence is often invoked for protection:[130] as is well known, the waxing moon, giving a bath to the fresh shoots of trees and creepers, brings about growth and fruitfulness,[131] and so its excellent virtues made it worthy of its high position on Śiva's head.[132] The poetess Phalguhastinī describes the rise of the crescent, which is just a spot of whiteness in the midst of surrounding darkness as a nail-mark on the hip of Lady Eve, as the smile on the face of Night, as the bow of Kāma and as a flower on the dark matted locks of Śiva.[133] Through the god's locks flows the heavenly Ganges, Umā's sister,[134] the sacred and pre-eminently purifying river which as a destroyer of sin and source of prosperity and redemption[135] streams in heaven, earth and nether world[136] and which the god consented to bear[137] lest the earth should be crushed when Gaṅgā was willing to supply her badly needed waters to its inhabitants.[138] It is he, the arch-ascetic, seated in splendid isolation on a solitary summit of the Himālayas, who relents at the evil plight of the superhuman saints who by their *tapas* have succeeded in putting an end to the terrible drought. To him mankind is indebted for the possibility of coming into contact with this goddesss, who may transform a devotee's personality so as to enter Viṣṇu's abode or to become immortal as Śiva's attendant.[139] Directing their attention readily to the god's head and headdress[140] the poets are inclined to combine in their prayers and eulogies moon and river with his matted hair—which characterizes him as the great ascetic[141]—, his necklace of skulls[142]—the symbols of death and transitoriness—and his frightful serpent garlands.[143]

One could easily start a large collection of descriptions of, and statements about, these central gods from which to deduce, not so much a systematic parallelism of qualities as varied oppositions in regard to traits of character, outward appearance etc.[144] Viṣṇu's Man-lion aspect[145]—the main exception to the general preponderance of kindly, human traits in this god—corresponds to Śiva's shape of terror;[146] the whiteness of the latter's teeth[147] to that of the garland which Lakṣmī gave to her bridegroom;[148] the third eye in the former's forehead to the double pair of arms of the other god;[149] the crescent of the former to the *kaustubha* jewel suspended on the breast of the latter.[150] Viṣṇu is described as appearing together with the goddesses of Fortune, Glory, Victory (Lakṣmī, Kīrti and Jayā) and other female deities, whereas Śiva is, in the same context, said to be accompanied by Pārvatī, the Gaṇas, demons and Mother-goddesses (the energies of the principal deities represented as divine persons).[151] Both gods are able to issue other beings from their own body, but whereas Śiva's Vīrabhadra had to stop Dakṣa's sacrifice and to assist the lord of the demons,[152] the Māyāmaha, turning out to be the Buddha, who emanated from Viṣṇu, made the demons apostatize from the Veda so that they, losing their power, could be overcome by the gods.[153]

Descriptions of Śiva's, Kṛṣṇa's, Viṣṇu's physical appearances and references to their special attributes occupy an important place in the devotional literature of the Indians, without however being absent in other literary genres. Viṣṇu's sleep[154] and waking up on the serpent;[155] his body producing, at the beginning of an aeon, the animate world;[156] his powerful arms[157] and other limbs;[158] his dark form and beautiful body;[159] his relations with the lotus;[160] his ornaments such as the *kaustubha* gem;[161] the many heroic feats performed in his *avatāras*,[162] when he has come to the rescue of man and world,[163] are no less celebrated than Śiva's third eye[164] manifesting his superior power, by which he had burnt Kāma,[165] his dark neck,[166] his bull,[167] his elephant-hide,[168] his drum[169] and the skulls in his hand,[170] his heavy step,[171] his wild laugh,[172] his wrath,[173] his drinking the poison Kālakūṭa,[174] his *gaṇas* or host,[175] his asceticism.[176] In reading these references to the gods' nature and appearance, one should take them, with the Indians, as indications of their aspects, functions and faculties. Śiva's black neck reminds them of the god's willingness to help and rescue men and world: he indeed had swallowed the poison *lokarakṣārtham*,[177] that the world might be safe.

Many works of literary art are replete with mythological allusions, the divine figures and histories being a source of inspiration which never dries up.[178] The evening is dark like Śiva's neck,[179] to which may also be compared the azure throat of a peacock.[180] The star-swarms fill the sky with their clusters like *kuṭaja* buds in the forest of his hair when it tosses in his dance,[181] and the splendour of the eyes of the god who is white from the sacred ashes smeared on his body is seen in an autumnal cloud with flashing lightnings.[182] A country is graced with ponds like Viṣṇu's navel,[183] in which fine birds (*dvijottama*, which also refers to Brahmā) are seated upon lotus-stalks.[184] A line of kings issues from an ancestor as the lotus from this god,[185] who is also the source of all variations of existence.[186] Holy grass is said to have been formed from Viṣṇu's hair.[187] The goddess of autumn may on account of her (its) whiteness be compared with Śiva's body which is smeared with ashes.[188] A queen who is the centre of all creatures' love, confidence and felicity is compared to Lakṣmī,[189] the much beloved lotus goddess,[190] who has arisen from the ocean.[191] A tall man, his chest broad like a rock of the Himālayas, his shoulder rising over it like the hump of Śiva's bull, may be described as white like mount Kailāsa.[192] Rāma uplifting his weapons in battle is said to be like Nārāyaṇa.[193] Śiva's city[194] is as famous as for instance Viṣṇu's sword.[195]

From these stray remarks it is clear that a comparative examination of the more or less detailed descriptions of the gods' persons and outward appearances[196]—as these are sometimes given in purāṇas and works of literary art—would be worth instituting. In order to avoid repetition I confine myself to the observation that the strikingly stereotyped features of these portraits, which are in essential harmony with the ritual and the iconographical handbooks,[197] may not be regarded as evidence of poverty of ideas on the part of the authors, but rather as a token that they understood very well what, from the religious point of view, was essential and that they attached much value to the commemoration and confirmation of the divine qualities and power through the medium of literature.[198] 'Concentration on the glorious beauty of God's form',[199] on his outward appearance, emblems and attributes is an essential element in yoga; any commemoration of the divine person may be a little help to attain final emancipation.

Śiva's complicated character[200] and his widely divergent interests may occasion conflicting situations. 'Although his beloved takes up half his body, he is an ascetic, free from phenomenal qualities.'[201] It is not surprising that poets could not resist the temptation to weld seemingly conflicting sides of his character into a harmonious whole: 'Śiva, though free from the hue of passion (*rāga*), abounds in colours (*rāga*), the skilful painter who is ever producing new and wonderful creations.'[202] What strikes us is that a poet of Kālidāsa's standing, in describing for instance the interruption of his ascetic practice by the appearance of Umā and the ensuing wedding, conceived a very dignified and truly exalted idea of the god's character and behaviour. As contrasted with the epic and purāṇic ascetics who lost their self-control and gave up their ascetic ideals under the influence of physiological processes or as victims of tricks and seduction,[203] Śiva remains, even at this juncture, the highest expression of the poet's conception of divinity, whose *yoga* obviously was the necessary preparation for his marriage and fatherhood[204] and, when Umā approached him, he discontinued this *yoga* of his own free will, to restrain his emotions after a short time.[205] The same god is in virtue of his descent and the openness of many of his adherents to Tantrist and Śāktist currents of thought not rarely invoked for aid in magical rites.[206]

Viṣṇu on the other hand does not, if I am right, give us the impression of one who is likely to get into a conflict situation. His adaptability and versatility seem to be accepted as natural and self-evident. The story of his appearance as Mohinī, the fascinating young woman who tricked the *asuras* out of the possession of the newly produced *amṛta*, must, for instance, have enjoyed considerable popularity. The older sources confine themselves to a short statement:[207] that, disguised as an anonymous woman, Viṣṇu-Nārāyaṇa recovered the *amṛta*. Or that a beautiful maiden who declares herself to be Viṣṇu's *mohinī māyā* 'deluding creative power' appears as a result of Brahmā's intervention by means of *mantras* in Viṣṇu's conflict with Madhu and Kaiṭabha.[208] According to a later version Viṣṇu-Mohinī distributed the *amṛta* among the gods, cheating the demons out of their share.[209] Śiva did not like this and refused to accept his share until a second distribution was made to all those who had taken part in the churning of the ocean. A second churning takes place but now only poison is produced and when this is about to consume the universe, Śiva drinks it, on the advice of Hanumat, to save the universe.[210] The Dutch clergyman Baldaeus who, in 1672, published an interesting book on what he called the 'Idolatry of the East-Indian heathens',[211] relates a long and complicated story[212] in which Viṣṇu tries to get his compeer Śiva out of the difficulties arisen from the amorousness of the wives of the *munis*: he assumes the form of an attractive girl and reduces their husbands to the same state of infatuation. According to another version[213] Śiva himself became enamoured of Mohinī and went to Viṣṇu's heaven to ask his colleague to assume that shape again. After Viṣṇu had complied with this desire Śiva tried to do her violence, but then Viṣṇu assumed his male form and Śiva embraced him and became one with him. In another form of this version[214] Śiva ran, on this occasion, after the female Viṣṇu, establishing out of his semen, which dropped in several places, beautiful shrines of images.

Some years ago it was observed[215] that the favourite myth of the Indian poets describing Śiva's feats of arms is the destruction of Tripura, the Triple City of the *asuras*. It was suggested that the popularity of that tale[216] was perhaps due to the fact that the demons had themselves chosen their destruction. They had indeed sought and obtained the boon that they might rule the three worlds for a thousand years and that after that period a god would destroy their stronghold.[217] It is difficult to judge whether this sentimental motive was so decisive. I would rather suppose that it is the antiquity and signficance of the theme and its inherent possibilities of reinterpretation and of application in religious practice which made it so attractive. It may be recalled that in the brāhmaṇas a 'threefold stronghold' is an absolutely secure protection and that the *asuras*, terrified, are said to run away from it.[218] Or the gods made three ritual citadels[219] and instituted a tripartite sacrificial rite[220] called 'victories' of the nature of an arrow to overpower the asuras who had made earth, atmosphere and heaven three fortresses.[221] Agni, Viṣṇu and Soma were the component parts of that arrow. According to another form of the mythical tale the asuras made three citadels in the three parts of the universe obviously to hold them against the gods,[222] but here also the gods succeeded in chasing their enemies away from these places by ritual means. By repeating *hic et nunc* this divine deed by ritual techniques one will chase away one's rivals and enemies.[223] In another version[224] of the same myth the gods did not however succeed in conquering their antagonists and after making a special arrow they invited Rudra, the fierce one, to shoot it. Proceeding to do so this god cleft the strongholds and drove the asuras away from these worlds. As a reward he became the overlord of the animals. The tenor of this myth is evident: by resorting to a ritual technique originating in the divine reality before the beginning of phenomenal time, the man who knows is able, when imitating Rudra's achievement, that is the destruction of the world-dominion of the demoniac powers, to stimulate the power of the three great gods Agni, Viṣṇu and Soma, into a display of superiority to the wicked designs and malign influences of all inimical beings.[225]

In the Mahābhārata version,[226] reference to which I have already made, the same three gods were transformed into an arrow, but Brahmā —who acts as a charioteer—and other important beings and entities co-operated also.[227] Shooting his weapon Śiva consumed the Triple City together with all its inhabitants. Other sources give different details,[228] speaking for instance of subtle assistance lent by Viṣṇu.

Two interesting details strike us here: first, before Śiva's success Indra had failed; and in the second place, the demons knew that they would be defeated after having seized the reins of world government for a thousand years. Moreover, the Vedic rite could in later times be replaced by worship of the god who occupies a central position in the mythical event. 'I pray these flames, born of the arrow of the Triple City's seizer, may burn away your ills.'[229]

Now, with what thoughts did the myth inspire the great post-epic poets? Kālidāsa mentions it as an important feat commemorated by celestial singers.[230] A reference to the god's victory may however also serve to celebrate, confirm and consolidate his omnipotence and absolute superiority: 'What was the purpose of drum-beating when you wanted to burn up the Three Cities, which were no more than grass to you?'[231] However, the repetition *hic et nunc* of God's mythical exploit does not fail deeply to affect our own lives. God will continue to destroy all our sins and distress as his arrow burnt away Tripura: 'Praise to the victor of the Triple City, to the slayer of the sins of man'.[232] The practical effect is that the story of destruction becomes not only praise and fortification of the god who destroys our sins and evil, but also a promise of his help in the future: 'May the dance of the conqueror of Tripura protect you.'[233] The terrible god, who appears as Kāla, the Time of Death,[234] may on the other hand show also softer sides of his character and therefore be expected to have mercy on the innocent: he indeed let fall the bow from his hand at the pitiable sight of the demon women who were on the verge of death by fire.[235]

However, the scene of these events is not on our earth,[236] it is cosmic and those involved in them are superhuman.[237] This contrasts strikingly with the terrestrial scene of Viṣṇu's great deeds when he descended in the form of an animal or a man in order to help and save mankind. In the stories of the Man-Lion the Dwarf, both Rāmas and Kṛṣṇa the scene is mostly laid in our world, even in India, in regions and places well-known and mentioned by name. They may be full of the wonderful and marvellous and embellished by phantasy, the central figures, for all their extremities of vice and virtue, make the impression of human characters; their actions and reactions are within the limits of our understanding; the conflict between the brahmans and the arrogant *kṣatriyas*, or that between Rāma and the demon Rāvaṇa, however heroic and extravagant, remain within earthly proportions. Their immediate causes are very human, struggle for political supremacy and for the possession of a woman. Although Śiva is, in his hymnology, not rarely represented as a vital and colourful divine personality, Viṣṇu's character, as for instance manifested in the hymns of the Ālvārs, is more absorbing and more varied, often appearing as the intimate companion of his adherents and the hero of many stories which are likely to touch upon a tender chord or to exhibit a view of humanity.[238]

A side of no mean interest in the images of these gods is their relation to their female partners. Just as the character of an individual man cannot be understood without a thorough knowledge of his social and erotic connections with his natural complement; as an evaluation of a human culture is impossible without an insight into the position of the female half of creation, the being and essence of gods hide from a correct appreciation, when their sexual relations and married life are left out of consideration.

Viṣṇu, it is emphasized, is in all his incarnations united with Śrī-Lakṣmī who, like her husband, is eternal and omnipresent.[239] Already at an early moment the texts attempt to make clear all theological and philosophical implications of this important union which makes God 'Lord or husband of Śrī': he is the creator, she creation, she is the earth, he the support of it, he is one with all male, she with all female beings, etc.[240] And the poets never tire of recalling that Viṣṇu's feet are graced by the attentions of his spouse Śrī-Lakṣmī.[241] If however we peruse the stories of the god's married life more closely Laksmī, notwithstanding her—according to some authorities[242] reciprocated—love at first sight and spontaneous embrace as soon as she came forth from the ocean,[243] does not appear to be free from fits of a very feminine love of teasing and jealousy,[244] for which, it is true, her husband with his 'thousand other loves' gives just cause. Passing over in silence other alliances his second consort, Bhūdevī, the Earth,[245] a well-known figure in art and eulogies,[246] stamps him as a bigamist. As to his relations with the different incarnations of his eternal spouse they often are such as to appeal to his devotees for the elements of youthful passion and reckless adventure by which they are characterized, and by the possibilities they offer of viewing human—not rarely but too human—emotions, not only as natural to exalted superhuman beings, but often also as truly divine and hence as eternal and universal, as sanctioned and hallowed.

He ravished Rukmiṇī, although she has been intended for Śiśupāla,[247] whom he beheads with his discus, and in the ensuing slaughter he only spares her brother Rukmin because she intercedes for him. He married her, the Viṣṇu-Purāṇa observes, in due form, after however first having made her his own in the *rākṣasa* way, that is, by violence. Already in the Harivaṃśa—in which the episode has swelled to an uncommon size[248]—Rukmiṇī is said to be an incarnation of Śrī, destined to marry, as Bhīṣmaka's daughter, the hero Kṛṣṇa, whom she loves, and in the course of time she is explicitly represented as being his accomplice: she sends to invite Kṛṣṇa to carry her off and instructs him how to proceed, because she wants to marry him against her brother's will.[249] I need not repeat here the story of Viṣṇu's *avatāra* as Rāma or expatiate upon the significance of this incarnation as another repetition of the myth of the champion of the cosmos against the demoniac powers,[250] nor recall the qualities of character which made Rāma—deified by the later poets—the exemplary king and blameless husband—in the orthodox Indian sense of the expression—and Sītā the type of a faithful and affectionate wife.[251]

And Rādhā, Kṛṣṇa's chief mistress when he was a youth among the cowherds,[252] described as a typically Indian beauty with solid breasts, a narrow waist and great buttocks[253] and the partner in his eternal love-affair, displays all reactions and sentiments to which a human soul may be subject when it has conceived an ardent passion for an equally human beloved, or a fervent devotion for God, feelings inextricably blended in the eyes of Indian exegetes. Does not, in the many poems on

Kṛṣṇa's and Rādhā's love-adventures, the hero, at the time he first met the maiden, watch her when she was bathing; is not she timid and bashful; are not her pangs of love, her hopes and anger, her anguish and languor, misgivings, sulkiness and other reactions to her lover's behaviour eminently human? Does not the endlessly repeated story represent the ideal type of all phases of earthly love, advances, disappointment, jealousy, reconciliation, and union which Rādhā whispers to be beyond words: is it dream or truth?[254] Nay, does not in popular tales and dramas originated under the influence of the Bhāgavata cult Lord Kṛṣṇa, now entirely divested of his heroic character, appear as a common husband, pleasing his wife or as a young cowherdsman playing pranks among the maidens?[255] At the same time however, the romance of this perpetual love-affair is a symbol and interpretable as mystic-and-erotic relations between the devout human soul and God. Rādhā is the soul which, yearning for God, has found the way to Him and is worthy of His love; Kṛṣṇa's overtures are God's willingness to extend his kindness and grace; the *gopīs*, the less advanced souls which earn their beatitude by witnessing, as sympathizing spectators, the divine love-affair; Vṛndāvana and Gokula, the scene of the romance, the human heart and the paradise in which God and soul find each other in supreme love and devotion. In short, the mystery of the union of soul and God is, in this pre-eminently Viṣṇuite cycle, consistently conceived in terms of human love. Hence the poets' endeavour faithfully to express the transfigured personalities in their art, and strictly to follow the sequence of the story.[256] The constant celebration of God's love for Rādhā, that is, for the prototype of the human soul, wrought by the post-Caitanya poets into a model of perfection, came to be, beside bhakti and the chanting of songs recounting God's deeds, a means of attaining to salvation.[257] Hearing the sacred history is indeed the best means of attaining God himself in his paradise Vaikuṇṭha.[258] God's romance, moreover, presented the poets and thinkers with the opportunity for various interpretations. The Bhāgavata-Purāṇa prefers to view this biography as a manifestation of divine love and favour, the Brahma-Purāṇa makes an attempt to explain it in the light of Vedānta philosophy, the Brahmavaivarta-Purāṇa considers it a cosmic love-play of God and his eternal 'partner', the soul, their grief and joy, separation and union being the great drama of the universe.

Turning now to Śiva's wedlock with Pārvatī I cannot but subscribe to Keith's appreciation of the presentation of this mythical event by Kālidāsa:[259] this alliance is not an adventure, no mere sport, no episode of light love. 'Their nuptials and their love serve as the prototype for human marriage[260] and human love, and sanctify with divine precedent the forces which make the home and carry on the race of men.' The principal figures—the parents of creation[261]—and the scene of the events are truly superhuman. Umā[262] is no ordinary girl, not even a princess, she is of divine descent and no other than the Great Mother herself,[263] the exact female likeness of her consort, whose nature and character is reflected in hers. She is the daughter of the greatest, wildest and most unconquered scenery of the world, the Himālayas, and as such the female representative of nature itself. The day of her birth was a blessing for the universe,[264] she herself, as a maiden, the quintessence of all virtue, beauty[265] and loveliness, destined to marry Śiva and to become the other half of his body.[266] On him she waits and him she worships, in compliance with her father's request, with flowers and with water and holy grass for his service.[267] The god accepts her homage, although this is incompatible with the severe asceticism to which he devotes himself in his abode, the classical region for austerity, thc very Himālaya. No explanation is, in the Kumārasambhava, given of the motive and purpose of the asceticism. It is part of God's essence. But we have to recollect that he had in a preceding period been insane with grief because of the goddess's sudden death when she had become his bride as Satī, daughter of Dakṣa.[268] And now as Umā-Pārvatī she devotes herself, to summon her husband again to demanding austerities, proving herself to be worthy of him.[269] Their union—considered a model of conjugal love after a previous period of amorousness[270]—is a necessity for the maintenance of the universe, for they are to procreate the power destined to slay the unconquerable demon Tāraka, who menaces the world with destruction. When Kāma approaches the ascetic god new life and love awakes everywhere: the well-known sympathy of nature[271] with the weal and woe of one of its fellow-members.[272] But despite Śiva's willingness to receive Umā's homage and to bless her with the prospect of a husband who will never have another wife, despite Kāma's bowshot,[273] Umā's victory cannot be consummated into a union without her ascetic preparation and the test of her steadfastness and without the sanction of the Prājāpatya marriage, in which her father is to give her away to her bridegroom. No love, in this exemplary myth, without a valid wedding and this explains also why Kāma should be reduced to ashes,[274] from which he is to arise when Śiva will have taken Umā to spouse.[275] The proposal and wedding ceremonies, described with abundance of detail, take place in complete accordance with the traditional rules.[276] The poet does not omit mentioning that after the regular proposal the god is very eager for his marriage and that in view of his feelings it is no great surprise that human beings under the circumstances feel strong emotion (*Kum.* 6, 95).

We now understand why the frank description of the joys of the newly married pair, so abhorrent to a former generation of Western readers,[277] was a necessity. Twenty-five years were like one night, but the god's thirst for the pleasures of love was not satisfied.[278] Kālidāsa's description of this union is modest and moderate as compared with the aeon-long periods of love joy which the Indian power of imagination already before his times[279] allotted to these ideals of sexual potency.[280] This model of conjugal inseparability,[281] this most important Indian representation of the idea of the androgynous primeval being[282] Ardhanārīśvara, 'the Lord who is half female (and half man)', presiding over procreation, which is a development of the upaniṣadic myth of the Ātman 'who was as large as a man and a woman closely embraced,'[283] has given rise to many mythological tales,[284] part of which show its cosmological relevance.[285] It brings about, not only the periodic revival of the moon,[286] and the birth of Skanda, the champion of the gods against the asuras but, according to some authorities even that of Viṣṇu and other gods.[287] Representing the intrinsically dual nature of the universe and its living inhabitants, Śiva and his spouse 'are reborn on earth in every man and every woman'.[288] And so it is Pārvatī—who is never removed from her husband when he shows the friendly sides of his nature—who prevails upon her husband to show his kindly aspects, reducing him so to say to more human dimensions[289] and making him an indulgent father. Hence the consequence most consistently realized by the Śāktists: 'Whoever is blissfully embraced by a beloved woman who is Pārvātī's counterpart assumes Śiva's wonderful figure and will, liberated, continue the joys of amorous sport.'[290] Up to the present day Indians like to regard the married life of this divine couple as an ideal for mankind, their devotion and asceticism, their constancy and sublime activities being focused on the good of the world and society.[291] And yet it is Viṣṇu-Kṛṣṇa, not Śiva who is worshipped as a youth and a lover.

Śiva is the king or patron of dancers, actors and musicians and as such he is still today worshipped in different parts of India.[292] Dancing the life-process of the universe and its creatures the god is also their prime and eternal mover. Whatever the origin of his various dances, they are an extremely clear image of his being and function.[293] In the beginning of time he once stood on a demon which he held in one of his hands, sounding the world's first rhythm. The 'monstrous serpent Vāsuki undulates,' to quote Subandhu, 'beneath the bond of the mass of the god's tangled locks',[294] among which the divine river Ganges is commonly represented by the sculptors incidentally to pour to the earth in a powerful cascade.[295] According to the tradition handed down in Bharata's Nāṭyaśāstra[296] Lord Śiva had, before the dawn of history, on seeing, in heaven, one of the newly invented dramatic productions, suggested that dances should be included in stage-plays. The first drama which was performed in the presence of this god was the Amṛtamanthana ('the Churning (of the ocean) for the amṛta'), the second the Tripuradāha ('the Burning of Tripura')[297] in which Śiva himself executed the destructive Tāṇḍava dance which he is, as Bhairava, believed to repeat in crematoria.[298] That is to say, when the story of the god's feat had been recited, he danced and rendered it through this mimetic dance, performed in a very vigorous tempo, stamping his feet and causing the earth to quake.[299]

Nevertheless his wild dance is so graceful that a famous beauty can be said to possess, as it were, 'his sportful dancing with his quivering serpent'.[300] The dance is, quite intelligibly, part of the god's cult,[301] which is to fortify him in the fulfilment of his functions.[302] So it is not surprising to read that king Trivikramasena, the hero of the Vetāla tales, after completing his task spent a day in worshipping Śiva, in dancing, music and similar enjoyments,[303] or that a South-Indian poetess appreciated the dance of the god surrounded by demons so passionately that she identified herself with these uncanny spectators[304] and hence was reputed to have changed herself into a demon.[305] We also hear of people who, having fled to Śiva for protection, danced in front of him,[306] not to mention the well-known dancing girls attached to the god's temples.[307]

However, there is also a tale about a princess who, having attained supreme skill in music, was always singing to the lyre the hymn of Viṣṇu which this god himself had bestowed on her,[308] and the nymph Rambhā is in the same collection of stories[309] said to have danced a new piece before that same god.[310] Dancing is also in Viṣṇuism a form of cult. 'Vain is the tongue which does not sing the praise of him, Nārāyaṇa, the shelter of mankind. May the god we honour through his love-dance here show mercy on us now, for fear has spread upon our heads.'[311] And nothing could of course prevent a playwright from invoking Nārāyaṇa as the stage-manager of the main plot, prologue and epilogue of the triple world.[312]

It is largely due to the emphasis laid by Śivaism on cosmic structure and processes and on its god's greatness as natural force and his being the embodiment of the power of asceticism that it has been less productive of myths and mythical narratives than Viṣṇuism which was always inclined to give special prominence to God's interest in humanity, in human events and the bodily and spiritual needs of mankind and which worships its God especially in his incarnations part of which did not fail to make a powerful appeal to the emotions and imagination of poets and devotees. Yet it is worth while to examine here also some Śaiva 'legends' or mythical tales more closely.

An important event in the life of the *prajāpati* Dakṣa—to which I have already referred[313]—was his sacrifice. A no doubt comparatively original version of this narrative may be regarded as reflecting Rudra-Śiva's admission to the regular sacrifices of the brahmans. According to this short epic episode[314] Dakṣa[315] was engaged in sacrificing when Rudra-Śiva, furious and shouting loudly, suddenly and ruthlessly, pierced the sacrifice with an arrow, so that the gods present were alarmed, the sacrifice (in its embodied form) fled away and the whole universe became confounded. No mention is made of his motives. The *ṛṣis* made an attempt to appease the angry god, but in vain. He knocked out the teeth of Pūṣan who was eating an oblation. Finally the gods succeeded in conciliating him: they bowed humbly and 'apportioned to him a distinguished share in the sacrifice, and through fear resorted to him as their refuge'. Viṣṇu does not enter on the scene here. When, according to another version contained in the Northern recension of the Mahābhārata,[316] which clearly reflects an existing antagonism between both religions, Dakṣa, in the days of yore, made arrangements to perform a sacrificial rite on a top of the Himālayas—to attend which all gods with their wives had approached—the *ṛṣi* Dadhīci warned him, saying that the rite was not valid, because Rudra-Śiva—whom he by the power of his yoga beheld seated with Umā and Nārada—was not invited and adored. Dakṣa replied that he, it was true, knew the eleven Rudras, but did not know who was this Maheśvara: an unmistakable model of a man who wishes to keep aloof from ascendant Śivaism. In reply to Dadhīci's assurance that as there is no higher deity than Śiva, Dakṣa's sacrifice would be a failure, the latter even added that it was his intention to offer the whole oblation, duly consecrated by formulas, on a golden vessel, to Viṣṇu, the omnipresent lord.[317] As Umā was very much upset and not content with her husband's statement that his priests worship him in the sacrifice of true meditative wisdom, where no officiating brahmans are needed, Śiva created a terrible being, Vīrabhadra, a sort of double of his own nature and the living embodiment of his rage, which together with Umā, who assumed her terrible form of Mahākālī, and with a number of spirits created from the pores of Rudra's body, proceeded to destroy the sacrifice and to set fire to everything. Dakṣa, humiliated, took refuge with the mighty god, whose anger is better than the blessings of other deities and was restored to his favour.

The variants of the story told in Śivaite purāṇas tend to insert references to Śiva's power and superiority. The version preserved in the Vāyu-Purāṇa mentions, for instance, that the gods, desirous of assisting at Dakṣa's rite, respectfully intimated their purpose to Śiva-Mahādeva who gave them permission to go. In the Liṅga-Purāṇa (100, 32) Viṣṇu, who joins battle with Śiva, is beheaded and his head is blown, by the wind, into the fire. The moderate-minded compiler of the Kūrma-Purāṇa (15, 68), though a Śaiva, makes Brahmā interpose between both gods who had joined hostilities in which both occasionally prevailed. Viṣṇuite purāṇas are on the other hand inclined to ascribe Dakṣa's neglect of Śiva to his filthy practices, his going naked, smearing himself with ashes, carrying a skull and behaving as if he were drunk or crazy—allusions of course to the manner of life of Śaiva mendicants.[318] According to another variant tradition Rudra-Śiva was present at a former assembly and was there even censured before the other guests by his father-in-law so that he departed in a rage; the company is cursed and it is predicted that all worshippers of Śiva will be heretics of impure and detestable habits. In the Harivaṃśa[319] Viṣṇu compels his rival to capitulate after taking him by the throat and nearly strangling him.

These observations bring me to broach the subject of another tendency which makes its appearance in the literature of Hinduism, to wit what might be called Viṣṇuization or Śivaization of traditional themes. I shall not dwell on those cases in which an ancient theme was remodelled under the influence of the rise of both religions and their mutual antagonism: whereas for instance the story of Dakṣa's sacrifice illustrated, in its older versions, Rudra's isolated position among the gods, the purāṇas emphasize the antagonism between Śiva and Viṣṇu. The ancient love-story of mortal Purūravas and the apsaras Urvaśī, which for many centuries had nothing to do with Viṣṇu,[320] may rather be quoted as an example. According to the Mahābhārata[321] Purūravas' mother, Ilā, was also his father. In later times, in the Viṣṇu-Purāṇa, her sex was changed through the favour of Mitra and Varuṇa whom she had worshipped, but under a malediction of Śiva she, that is the male Sudyumna, was again transformed into a woman. After she had given birth to Purūravas, she again became Sudyumna, but now through the favour of the mighty Viṣṇu.[322] According to the Matsya-Purāṇa Purūravas was a devout worshipper of Viṣṇu-Janārdana, whom he propitiated on a top of the Himālayas and to whom he owed his dignity of universal sovereignty. In another chapter the same purāṇa[323] informs us that Purūravas, after seeing the erotic sports of the nymphs, worshipped the god of gods Janārdana and had a dream that his desire would be fulfilled. The same god had created out of his thigh the ravishingly beautiful Urvaśī in order to enchant Indra, who had attempted, likewise by sending nymphs, to disturb the former's serenity of mind when he practised austerities. This part of the story is in harmony with Kālidāsa's version:[324] all the nymphs who were seducing the sage Nārāyaṇa felt ashamed at the sight of this lady who was then produced from his thigh, but in the famous play of the great poet it is Indra who reunited the couple. In his Kathāsaritsāgara Somadeva (XIth century) introduces Purūravas in the very beginning of the narrative (17, 4 ff.) as an earnest worshipper of Viṣṇu who, being worried by the sufferings of his devotees, orders Nārada to make Indra give Urvaśī to the king, who at the end of the story recovers her, after the painful separation, through Viṣṇu's help, which the god, propitiated by Purūravas' *tapas*, willingly renders to him.

It would be most interesting to possess a large collection of instances of this Viṣṇuization or Śivaization which, in Indian religious literature, is a frequent occurrence.[325] It would not only show that not rarely one of the new great gods ousted Indra and others from a central place in a legend or narrative but also deepen our insight into the mutual relations between Śiva and Viṣṇu themselves.[326] I need not recall the well-known fact that already at an early date Viṣṇu was credited with part of Indra's achievements:[327] in one of the plays attributed to Bhāsa[328] Upendra's, i.e. Viṣṇu's foot, 'which is a great treat to all the worlds and which with its slender dark-red nails sent Namuci whirling through the sky', is invoked to protect the audience: in older texts this deed is Indra's. Is it however not interesting that Viṣṇu is also in two Śivaite purāṇas said to have combated Prahlāda and the demons Namuci and Śambara, whereas the older version of this story ascribed the latter feat also to Indra?[329]

Attention may for a moment be drawn to similar instances of Śivaization.[330] Thus the story of the Tāraka battle seems to have shifted, in the course of time, from the Indra mythology to Śiva's sphere. In the Great Epic Indra is credited with the demon's destruction,[331] but once (7, 148, 56) it reads: '... as Indra together with Skanda formerly killed Tāraka'. Later on the deed is Skanda's, and Indra's share is reduced to that of a mediator who, for instance, seeks the aid of Kāma to win Śiva's heart for Umā.[332]

The development of this modification of ancient mythological themes and figures cannot however be reduced to a question of mere chronology. It depends to a considerable extent on the divergent aims of the authors and compilers and on the different characters of their works. The tendency to replace Indra by Viṣṇu and to ascribe to the latter feats which in older texts were performed by the former, is for instance much more pronounced in the Viṣṇu-Purāṇa—which may have been composed between the IIIrd and Vth centuries A.D.—than in the Mārkaṇḍeya which, dating back to about the IIIrd century A.D., is not onesidedly Viṣṇuite or Śivaite.[333] Not rarely, moreover, Śivaism proceeded, in this matter, more superficially. Thus the Viṣṇuization of the traditional purāṇic accounts of the creation of the universe is in the Viṣṇu and Padma Purāṇas carried through more thoroughly than the Śivaization in Liṅga, Vāyu and Brahmāṇḍa.[334]

This tendency affects also narratives which, being foreign to the pre-epic literature, originally did not relate with special religious convictions or with the cult of a particular god. A remarkable instance, though chosen at random, is Śrīharṣa's (XIIth century) Naiṣadhacarita. Although this author does not seem to have been a staunch devotee of any deity,[335] both great gods are, in contradistinction to the famous epic episode of Nala and Damayantī, more than once mentioned in his work. It is not surprising that in the XIIth century Nala should be represented as offering prayers to the Sun, Śiva and Viṣṇu and using many imageries from older texts,[336] that reference is made to Kṛṣṇa's sport with the milkmaids as well as Śiva's amorous dalliance in the Devadāru grove;[337] to prayers to different incarnations of Lord Viṣṇu;[338] to a *liṅga* of Śiva Yāgeśvara[339] and to the god's evening-dance;[340] to a wreath of the fabulous *cintāmaṇi*-gems—which are supposed to yield its possessor all desires—offered as a dowry to Nala by his father-in-law who had received it from Śiva;[341] to a rosary of *rudrākṣa*[342] berries and one of lotus-seed beads used while repeating mantras for Śiva and the Viṣṇu-sūkta ṚV. 1, 154 respectively;[343] to Lakṣmī, reposing on the bosom of a great king, and thus forsaking her own home, the bosom of Viṣṇu, so that his *kaustubha* gem looks, on account of the open void, like no more than a cobweb made by spiders settling there;[344] to the threefold universe being contained in the cavity of Viṣṇu's abdomen,[345] and so on, and so on.[346]

The concentration of the hearer's attention upon one definite deity may be furthered by a combination of themes. In the Great Epic there is a story about the erratic Durvāsas, a reputed incarnation of a portion of Śiva,[347] who, while given the cold shoulder by everybody else, was invited by the hero Kṛṣṇa to dwell in his house but made himself guilty of terrible bad conduct finally to bless his host and his wife Rukmiṇī because they had always subdued their anger: 'As long as gods and men will like food, so long will everybody cherish the same liking for thee' (13, 144, 35). However, this *ṛṣi* has nothing to do with the churning of the ocean, told in 1, a. 15, 11 ff., which was undertaken, on the advice of Nārāyaṇa, by the gods and the *asuras* in order to obtain the *amṛta*. In the Viṣṇu-Purāṇa (1, 9) another story of the same eccentric is, by way of introduction, told to explain why it was necessary to acquire that draught. Durvāsas wandering and possessed by religious frenzy offered to Indra a garland of celestial flowers which had been presented to him by a nymph. As the god treated the gift disrespectfully, the *ṛṣi* laid a curse upon him: his dominion over the universe should be whelmed in ruin; to Indra's excuses and entreaties he remained adamant. From that time Indra himself and the threefold universe lost their vigour, all plants withered and died, and the Daityas and Dānavas, agitated by ambition, overcame the gods in battle. On Brahmā's advice, they repaired, for aid, to Viṣṇu, 'the god of high and low, the tamer of demons, the unconquerable remover of grief', who at the end of their long reverential address deigned to show himself and enjoined them, in alliance with the demons, to churn the ocean. The gods and *asuras*, the narrator proceeds, were assigned their stations by Kṛṣṇa (I, 9, 84), while Hari himself, in the form of a tortoise, served as a pivot for the mountain which was taken for the churning-stick (st. 87). The holder of mace and discus was in other forms present among both parties, assisting to drag the serpent Vāsuki (the rope), and in another body he sat, as Keśava, upon the summit of the mountain. Invisible, he, Hari, sustained with part of his *tejas* the serpent, with another part he supported the gods (st. 90).[348] It may be remembered that in the Mahābhārata it was Brahmā, who, when the gods were tired, prevailed upon Nārāyaṇa to infuse new strength into them (I, 16, 30). There is another interesting point of difference. Whereas in the Mahābhārata (I, 18, 34) Śrī is one of the beings and objects which came forth from the ocean and her appearance is described in no more than one line,[349] the Viṣṇu-Purāṇa (st. 99 ff.) dwells at great length on her, adding a long passage to give a vivid account of the praise and worship offered to the goddess by the sages and by Indra himself, who seated on his throne eulogized her, the mother of all beings, who abides on the breast of the god of gods, in a long address in which she is identified with the highest ideas and principles. Being gratified by his praise the goddess fulfils Indra's wishes. The first of these is that the threefold universe may never again be deprived of Śrī's presence, the second, that she will never forsake the man who worships her by repeating the hymn of praise, pronounced by the god. The narrative ends with a list of Śrī-Lakṣmī's incarnations: when Viṣṇu was Kṛṣṇa, she was Rukmiṇī, etc.

The story was also modified in Śivaite milieus. Durvāsas, incensed, because the garland he had presented to Indra fell from the neck of the god's elephant, uttered the curse that Indra and Kamalā (Lakṣmī) would henceforth be separated. Lakṣmī found, together with the rice, moon, *amṛta* and other precious things at her command, shelter in the ocean, which now was churned by Indra and his colleagues who were much annoyed by her absence. Thus the valuable objects were one by one recovered. When Viṣṇu in the guise of a beautiful woman distributed the *amṛta* among the gods, Śiva took offence at the demons being cheated out of their share. He suggested a second churning, but this produced only poison which threatened to consume the universe. Everybody left the place, except Śiva, his bull and Hanumat, who had pulled Vāsuki's (the rope's) tail, and who now advised the god to drink the poison in order to save the universe. He did so and fell senseless on the ground and was thought to be dead, but then cured by his daughter Manasā.[350]

A good example of a theme which obviously is revised more than once and therefore shows Viṣṇuite as well as Śivaite features is furnished by the well-known story of the descent of the Ganges. According to the Mahābhārata[351] Gaṅgā promised to Bhagīratha to descend in order to purify the ashes of the sixty thousand sons of his ancestor, king Sagara, who had been consumed by the wrath of the sage Kapila. Bhagīratha however gratified Śiva, who received the weight of the river when she fell from the sky on his forehead. Greater stress on this point—only Śiva could in this way prevent the mass of water from crushing and shattering the surface of the earth—as well as on the miraculous power of the ascetic saint is laid in the Rāmāyaṇa version.[352] In a different version preserved in the Vāyu-Purāṇa Gaṅgā is detained amidst the god's tresses[353] because of her arrogance. Or her purificatory power is explicitly ascribed to her intimate contact with the mighty god.[354] The Viṣṇu-Purāṇa[355] however makes, in this connection, no mention of Śiva, but does not forget to emphasize that the river issues from the nail of the great toe of Viṣṇu's feet or even from Viṣṇu's 'highest abode' (*viṣṇoḥ paramaṃ padam*).

The recast of a theme or narrative and the desire to make it subservient to the glorification of either god or the propagation of their religions sometimes entails curious insertions[356] and transformations. For instance, Bhavabhūti departs from his sources in making Rāvaṇa offer his heads to Śiva instead of Brahmā.[357] The Prahlāda story as told in the Śiva-Purāṇa[358] begins with Lakṣmī's wish to witness a fight. Complying with her request Viṣṇu takes the opportunity to intervene when Jaya and Vijaya, the celestial door-keepers, are cursed by the Kumāras, beings belonging to the Śivaite sphere. The god takes part in the ensuing dissensions, those concerned in the conflict descend from heaven, becoming *avatāras*—a probably Śivaite extension of the *avatāra* idea[359]—Viṣṇu becoming the Man-Lion, Jaya and Vijaya Hiraṇyākṣa and Hiraṇyakaśipu, one of the Kumāras Prahlāda, and so Lakṣmī has her fight.

I can only touch on those numerous narratives which in post-epic times propagate the superiority of one of the great Hindu gods over the older more or less parochial deities. According to a figurative purāṇic description[360] Indra, after slaying Vṛtra, had his residence rebuilt—notice the post-Vedic idea of periodicity!—by Viśvakarman. As his demands became ever more exacting the divine craftsman turned to Brahmā—himself but an agent of Viṣṇu—for help, with the result that this god, in the guise of a boy, informed Indra of the serious limitations of his power and duration of life and of his being but one in an endless series of Indras.

It would not however be out of place in this connection to recall once again the numerous compositions which followed the model of the highly successful and favourite Viṣṇuite Bhagavadgītā,[361] imitations likewise in the form of dialogues not only written in Sanskrit but also in modern Indian languages.[362] These *gītās*, regarded as compendia of religious doctrine and precepts, recited in a sing-song manner, and often even intended to be memorized, profess to have been revealed by a definite deity and preach the worship of that god or goddess. The authors saw it as their main task to prove and to proclaim that the Supreme Brahman is identical with the deity of their choice. Some of these works are even aggressively sectarian. The Devī-Gītā,[363] for instance, contends that Brahmā, Viṣṇu, Rudra, Īśvara and Sadāśiva lie at the feet of the Great Goddess; that means, of course, that the other gods are unworthy of a special independent worship, and that any other cult is only preparatory to the path of salvation through the help of Devī. Another feature of these works which were presumably intended for the general public is the readiness of their gods to perform miracles and so to demonstrate their omnipotence. Some of them imitate, for similar reasons, the famous theophany of the Bhagavadgītā. The imitation is obvious and beyond doubt in cases such as the Śiva-Gītā,[364] which—being in fact a compendium of Śaiva theology—does not omit to enumerate Śiva's *vibhūtis* (ch. 6) and has chapters corresponding to and bearing the same names as the chapters X and XI of the Bhagavadgītā.[365] This is not the only point in which that ancient work was in structure and composition taken as an example. Like their great predecessor these authors attempted to synthetize conflicting views and thus to place their own teachings on a firmer basis in the hope that they might be a foundation of a universal cult, and first of all to show what is, in their eyes, the best way to salvation. Thus the Śivaite Devīgītā speaks, like the Bhagavadgītā, of the three paths of *jñāna*, *karman* and *bhakti*.[366] This does not however alter the fact that these purāṇic *gītās*, the Śiva, the Devī, etc., appear, on closer examination, to prefer the *jñāna* to the *bhakti*. None of these works seems to have escaped the influence of the upaniṣads, and so Śiva is, in a Śivaite context, said to be, not only the Brahman of those texts but also that which the Vedas establish, the ultimate reality.[367] The same work[368] quotes a well-known upaniṣadic story about Brahman's appearing before the gods without being recognized by them. When all the gods were completely at a loss, a celestial form appeared and declared the greatness of Brahman, which now is known and worshipped by the gods. That this *gītā* uses this story in order to show the superiority of Śiva who is Brahman[369] is not surprising.[370]

It would take too long to discuss here also the frequent instances of minor reminiscences, when a Tamil poet calls Śiva the One Who condescends to appear in the heart of His devotee in whatever form the latter might choose to contemplate Him[371] or when, in another part of India, a eulogy upon the same god[372] teaches that the fruit of every work should be (renounced and) laid down on him.[373]

It may be true that each religion, to a certain extent, impresses us to have been to its own adherents sufficient in itself, yet I am not the first to draw attention to the catholicity and comparative impartiality of many Indian authors in matters of religion. To Kālidāsa God takes specially the form of Śiva,[374] the Great Lord (Maheśvara),[375] by whose glory and greatness he is much impressed, but Viṣṇu, the Puruṣottama,[376] also receives his meed of devotion. In the tenth canto of the Raghuvaṃśa he is extolled in a long devotional outpouring: though unborn, he creates himself for the protection of the pious; though free from action he slays enemies; though immersed in yogic sleep, he is watchful and vigilant in the preservation of his creation; unconquered, he is always victorious, and now he promises to incarnate himself as Rāma in order to kill Rāvaṇa.[377] However much the poet emphasizes, in the Raghuvaṃśa, the yogic aspects of religion and philosophy, the sons of Daśaratha, who are reflexes of Viṣṇu himself, embody the four aims of existence, viz. duty, the pursuit of possessions and enjoyment and, as the fourth, release from earthly existence.[378] Similar observations might be made in connection with other authors. Judging by several passages in his dramas, Bhavabhūti (VIIIth century) had at least strong Śivaite tendencies. Nevertheless he salutes also the Sun, Brahmā and invokes Viṣṇu as Varāha.[379] That Buddhist authors might evince the same impartiality appears for instance from Vidyākara's anthology. After devoting three chapters to his own religion this monk and scholar—who probably lived about 1100 A.D. at the Jagaddala monastery in Bengal—inserted four other chapters on Śiva, Viṣṇu and Sūrya, further on to quote from the poetry of Hinduism.[380]

This tendency to inclusive 'tolerance' and what Europeans might name liberality accounts also for the considerable number of places in which both gods are described as associating with one another or as co-operating for the same purpose. Thus the waves of the Ganges are not only present at the feet of Viṣṇu who abides in them, but also on the head of Śiva who lives at their tips.[381] We are even informed that intentional amalgamations of mythological traditions, for instance combining of the story of Kālī with that of Hari (Viṣṇu) was believed to give strength and merit.[382]

In connection with Satī's marriage with Śiva there exists the tradition[383] that once Brahmā, in deep meditation, praised the Mother of the World, 'whose quintessential being is both life-redeeming world-transcending enlightenment, and the world-beguiling life-tormenting ignorance of every creature, the Queen who wants no rest yet remains unmoved for all eternity, the Lady whose body is both the tangibility of the world and the supersensuously subtle material of heavens and hells'. When the goddess at last appeared to him he asked her to beguile Śiva, who remains a solitary, because no other woman is capable of ravishing his poised mind. 'Should he take no wife, how is the creation of the world to continue in its course?' She consents to marry the god. It is however Viṣṇu who advises Śiva to constitute such a couple with the goddess as he himself forms with Lakṣmī and as his colleague, filled with emotions by Kāma, readily agrees, dissuades him from killing Brahmā who, on seeing Satī's beauty, falls in love with her: 'We are three, but in substance one; and this is why you are not to murder Brahmā.'[384]

So, notwithstanding the endless diversity of Indian religious life, notwithstanding the co-existence of a few great religious currents and many sects and denominations, the conception of the fundamental unity of all aspects and manifestations of the divine is not lost and the quest for that unity has, also in the classical period, left an impress upon many passages in Indian literature.

NOTES

CHAPTER I

1. The reader desirous of more detailed information may be referred to my books *Die Religionen Indiens*, I, Stuttgart, 1960; II, 1963; French translations: *Les religions de l'Inde*, I, Paris, 1962; II, 1965; or to Ch. Eliot, *Hinduism and Buddhism*, 3 vols., [2]London, 1954; R. C. Zaehner, *Hinduism*, London, 1962, etc. For more recent literature see also the bibliographical notes added to my article on the Indian religions in *Storia delle religioni, fondata del P. Tacchi Venturi*, Utet, Torino (Turin, Italy), 1970.

2. For details see my book *Aspects of early Viṣṇuism*, Utrecht, 1954; [2]Delhi, 1969.

3. I refer to E. Arbman, *Rudra*, Uppsala, 1922.

4. For details see also A. Bergaigne, *La religion védique*, 3 vols., Paris, 1878–1883, [2]1963; A. A. Macdonell, *Vedic Mythology*, Strassburg, 1897; K. F. Geldner and J. Nobel, *Der Rig-Veda*, IV, Cambridge, Mass., 1957; A. B. Keith, *Religion and philosophy of the Veda and Upanishads*, Cambridge, Mass., 1925. Traits applicable to any god are left out of consideration here.

5. Macdonell, op. cit., p. 37.

6. ṚV. 6, 49, 13; 69, 5; 6.

7. For particulars see Arbman, op. cit., pp. 24 ff.

8. *VS.* 3, 61; 16, 51.

9. *Aspects of early Viṣṇuism*, pp. 73 ff.; cf. e.g., ṚV. 1, 155, 1; 8, 31, 10.

10. Macdonell, op. cit., p. 76.

11. ṚV. 3, 55, 10; 7, 100, 6.

12. ṚV. 2, 1, 6; cf. *ŚB.* 6, 1, 3, 10.

13. A. Hillebrandt, *Vedische Mythologie*, II, Breslau 1899, p. 199 (cf. also Arbman, op. cit., p. 26) was among those who consider only factors of chronological order, disregarding differences in emphasis, choice, presentation, etc. dependent on differences in the social and cultural milieu of the authors, the ends they had in view in expressing their thoughts, etc. ('Vor allem widerspricht der ausschliesslichen und ursprünglichen Beziehung Rudras auf Gebirge und auch auf Wälder die Auffassung unseres ältesten Textes, des ṚV., von Rudra als einem Himmelsgott', Hillebrandt).

14. *Aspects of early Viṣṇuism*, p. 172.

15. See also *Die Religionen Indiens*, I, p. 236 and cf. e.g. *Mbh.* 5, 10, 293, vulg. 'This entire universe is pervaded by Thee'.

16. F. B. J. Kuiper, 'The three strides of Viṣṇu', in *Indological studies in honor of W. Norman Brown*, New Haven, Conn., 1962, pp. 137 ff.

17. See my book *The Savayajñas*, Amsterdam Academy, 1965, pp. 131; 230. Cf. e.g. *TS.* 5, 5, 10, 2; 4; *AiB.* 8, 14, 3.

18. As Varuṇa's opponent (I refer to *Die Religionen Indiens*, I, p. 81) one might rather expect Indra to be the regent of the East (see e.g. W. Kirfel, *Die Kosmographie der Inder*, Bonn, 1920, p. 34*). Those comparatively few texts which address Viṣṇu and Varuṇa conjointly (A. Hillebrandt, *Vedische Mythologie*, II[2], Breslau, 1929, pp. 69; 325; Kuiper, op. cit., p. 144) do not in my opinion prove that Viṣṇu belonged also to the other (Varuṇa's) moiety (for AV. 7, 25 cf. *Aspects of early Viṣṇuism*, p. 110 and W. B. Bollée, *Ṣaḍviṃśa Brāhmaṇa*, Thesis, Utrecht, 1956, p. 38); nor do they inform us of a special position of Varuṇa in the cosmic classification. Both gods are, moreover, invoked together with many other deities, a fact which does not add to the demonstrative force of the joint occurrences of Viṣṇu and Varuṇa.

19. It may be asked whether this association of these gods with the quarters of space goes back to an early, prehistoric, period or is the result of later speculation or interpretation.

20. Also on the strength of the term *dhruva* which interestingly enough denotes also the non-manifested part of a whole, the manifested parts of which are transitory or of a

temporary nature or the idea of a whole or total including and encompassing the constituent parts (see my remarks in *Change and continuity in Indian religion*, The Hague, 1965, p. 122 f.).

21. I refer to my observations in *Loka, world and heaven in the Veda*, Amsterdam Academy, 1966, p. 43 f. (with bibliographical notes).

22. *Aspects of early Viṣṇuism*, pp. 81 ff.; see especially M. Eliade, *The sacred and the profane*, New York, (1959) 1961, pp. 36 ff.

23. See e.g. Eliade, op. cit., pp. 34 ff.; ṚV. 10, 89, 4; AV. 10, 7.

24. *Die Religionen Indiens*, 1, p. 160; e.g. *ŚB.* 5, 2, 1, 10 ff.

25. *Aspects of early Viṣṇuism*, pp. 81 ff.

26. This relation with the 'mountain(s)' does not in my opinion exclude other associations with them.

27. Eliade, op. cit., pp. 37 ff.

28. See also M. Eliade, *Patterns in comparative religion*, London and New York, 1958, p. 99 f.

29. Kuiper, op. cit., p. 144. I ask myself whether an argument can be derived from *Mbh.* 6, 21, 12 cr. ed. *yataḥ Kṛṣṇaṣ tato jayaḥ* (quoted by Kuiper, op. cit., p. 150), because not all epic statements with regard to Kṛṣṇa may be taken to apply without comment to the early Viṣṇu.

30. I fail to see how AV. 11, 6, 2 imploring Varuṇa, Mitra, Viṣṇu, Bhaga, Aṃśa and Vivasvant to free those speaking from *aṃhas* ('closeness, oppression, distress': see *Indo-Ir. Journal*, 1 (1957), pp. 33 ff.) may substantiate this contention. In supplications or deprecations of this type each parochial god was obviously supposed to grant the speaker's request in his own way and as far as he is concerned or is considered able to lend assistance.

31. Macdonell, op. cit., p. 161. See also *AiB.* 6, 15, 11.

32. *Die Religionen Indiens*, 1, p. 57 f.

33. Hence his being 'a victor' (ṚV. 6, 69, 8), a trait explicable without the assumption of a 'two-sidedness of his nature'.

34. Kuiper, op. cit., pp. 145; 151.

35. *Aspects of early Viṣṇuism*, pp. 77 ff.; 85 f.; *Die Religionen Indiens*, 1, p. 90. Cf. e.g. ṚV. 1, 164, 35; 2, 3, 7.

36. ṚV. 1, 154, 5; 3, 55, 10; 1, 22, 20 f., etc. See my remarks in *The meaning of the Sanskrit term dhāman*, Amsterdam Academy, 1967, p. 42 f.

37. As a representative of any part of the *axis mundi* he may indeed be said to fulfil the function of a connecting link; hence identifications such as *ŚB.* 3, 4, 4, 14 f.; *KS.* 25, 1: 102, 13 ff., discussed by Kuiper, op. cit., p. 115 (cf. *Aspects of early Viṣṇuism*, p. 35).

38. *Aspects of early Viṣṇuism*, p. 115 f.; *Die Religionen Indiens*, 1, pp. 84; 90; Kuiper, op. cit., p. 146.

39. As is well known Viṣṇu is, in 'the prayer for a child' ṚV. 10, 184, 1 (a text believed to be promotive of successful conception: *Aspects of early Viṣṇuism*, p. 18) besought 'to prepare the womb'; this function of the god in ritual may be a *hic et nunc* reiteration of his mythical concern with Aditi's womb.

40. ṚV. 6, 69, 5; 7, 99, 1 f.; 100, 4; AV. 7, 25, 1.

41. Kuiper, op. cit., pp. 149; 150.

42. *sakhe* (ṚV. 4, 18, 11; 8, 100, 12); *úpa mitrásya dhármabhiḥ* (ṚV. 8, 52, 3). Compare also ṚV. 8, 31, 10 *śárma . . . víṣṇoḥ sacābhúvaḥ* 'the protection of Viṣṇu, the companion'. The term 'associate' should not be taken to express subordination or lack of full status. See also *Aspects of early Viṣṇuism*, pp. 32 ff.

43. ṚV. 4, 18, 11; 8, 12, 27; 52, 3; 100, 12.

44. It may be recalled that Viṣṇu also pressed soma for Indra (ṚV. 2, 22, 1; 10, 113, 2; cf. 6, 17, 11; 8, 3, 8; 8, 12, 16) by which the latter was fortified.

45. One should say that Viṣṇu complied with Indra's request because he represented—before 'creation', it is true, in a latent form—the cosmic pillar rather than that 'he rose up . . . so he is connected with the pillar'.

46. Cf. also ṚV. 10, 1, 3. ṚV. 8, 15, 9 is not completely clear, 8, 29, 7 is ambiguous; in 8, 69, 7 Viṣṇu seems to be the speaker, saying that he goes, with Indra, upwards, but he also goes home.

47. ṚV. 1, 154, 1 *yáḥ pā́rthivāni vimamé rájāṃsi*; ibid. 3; 6, 49, 13; the verb *mā-* does not

exactly mean 'to measure' (nor *vi-mā-* 'durchmessen', Geldner), but rather 'to convert (that which has been mentally conceived) into dimensional actuality' (see *Four studies in the language of the Veda*, The Hague, 1959, p. 168). See also ṚV. 1, 155, 4; 7, 100, 3 f.

48. Cf. also ṚV. 1, 22, 17c; whatever the exact meaning of *áto dhármāṇi dhāráyan* in 1, 22, 18 it refers to a world-wide and inaugurative achievement.—For another view: G. Ch. Tripathi, *Der Ursprung und die Entwicklung der Vāmana-Legende in der indischen Literatur*, Wiesbaden, 1968, pp. 7 ff.

49. As is Kuiper's view, op. cit., p. 147. Nor does ṚV. 1, 154, 4 *yá u tridhā́tu pṛthivī́m utá dyā́m éko dādhā́ra bhúvanāni víśvā*, which indeed may mean 'who alone supports in a threefold manner heaven and earth, all places containing living creatures', suggests any ascension on Viṣṇu's part.

50. Sāyaṇa; 'der irdische Raum und der sichtbare Himmel' (K. F. Geldner, *Der Rig-Veda übersetzt*, II, Cambridge, Mass., 1951, p. 269). The text runs as follows: *ubhé te vidma rájasī pṛthivyā́ víṣṇo deva tvam paramásya vitse.*

51. Thus Kuiper, op. cit., p. 149.

52. Although in principle inaccessible (to ordinary men: ṚV. 1, 155, 5).

53. I refer to my observations in *Adyar Library Bulletin*, XXIX (1965), p. 29.

54. Notwithstanding ṚV. 1, 156, 5 (see above).

55. Kuiper, op. cit., p. 148. Does ṚV. 1, 154, 4 exclude the conception of a tripartite universe?; *bhúvanāni víśvā* may imply what is between heaven and earth. *ŚB.* 3, 3, 2, 2 cannot, as far as I am able to see, be adduced in favour of an original cosmic dichotomy, because it deals with the qualities of *satya* and *anṛta*, gods and men. Notwithstanding the frequent occurrence of a dual distinction with regard to the main constituents of the universe (*dyā́vapṛthivī́, ródasī*), the tripartite division—which plays an important part in the ritual—was well known already to the poets of the Ṛgveda (1, 52, 13; 1, 73, 8; 1, 115, 1; 2, 12, 2 f.; 10, 59, 7; 10, 88, 3; 10, 139, 2; 10, 149, 1, etc.) and is, though obviously not always relevant, so to say implied in the dichotomy (1, 160, 1; 7, 104, 23; 10, 89, 4). See also H. Lüders, *Varuṇa*, Göttingen, 1951–1959, p. 57. According to Kuiper, op. cit., p. 148 the dual division, Indra's creation, is likely to be older than the tripartite one, 'and the ritualistic interpretation of the Yajurveda (e.g. *VS.* 2, 25 *diví víṣṇur vyakramiṣṭa . . . antárikṣe . . .pṛthivyā́m*) may not reflect the mythical meaning'. The creation or stabilization of the atmosphere—the area of the divine activity: e.g. 3, 22, 2; 10, 65, 2; 10, 88, 3—is however more than once mentioned as an essential element in Indra's organizing endeavour (ṚV. 2, 15, 2; 3, 30, 9; 3, 34, 10; 6, 69, 5; 10, 153, 3).

56. It would appear to me that there is much truth in Heiler's (F. Heiler, *Erscheinungsformen und Wesen der Religion*, Stuttgart, 1961, p. 7) verdict: despite the important contributions made by ethnological and sociological research to the history of religions, these studies have not always avoided the risk of reducing religion to views of life and world or to the structure of society. I for one could not follow those who ultimately basing themselves on E. Durkheim's 'dualistic' sociological explanation of religion and without being able to put the existence of a Durkheimian dual society in pre- and proto-historic India beyond question, are inclined to consider in the highly complicated Vedic religion any duality as original. (For duality in the Veda see S. Kramrisch, 'Two', in *Festschrift Norman Brown*, pp. 109 ff.) Is it at all possible to find and reconstruct, in ancient India, a phase of *weltanschauliches* thought and religious belief characterized by undiluted homogeneity?

57. Cf. Heiler, op. cit., p. 471.

58. See especially W. Norman Brown, 'The creation myth of the Rig Veda', *JAOS*, LXII (1942), pp. 85 ff. and the same, ibid, LXI (1941), pp. 76 ff., and compare Lüders' chapter 'Der Vṛtrakampf als vedischer Weltschöpfungsmythus', in *Varuṇa*, pp. 183 ff., which must have been written or drafted before World War II.

59. I refer to G. van der Leeuw, *Religion in essence and manifestation*, London, 1938, p. 698, o.v. celebration.

60. The Indra-Vṛtra combat and the ensuing establishment of our world is, as a real myth, eternally present and is reiterated in history. Indra's hand could be seen and felt in any positive suprahuman display of power for the benefit of world and mankind.

61. ṚV. 1, 155, 4; 6, 49, 13; 6, 69, 5; cf. also AV. 6, 4, 3.

62. Cf. *ŚB.* 1, 9, 3, 9 f.; *Aspects of early Viṣṇuism*, p. 63.

63. Cf. e.g. ṚV. 1, 1, 4; 1, 177, 4; 4, 58, 10; 10, 80, 4; 10, 188, 3. I may also refer to a paper on *adhvará* and *adhvaryú*, published in *Vishv. Indol. Journ.* III (1965), Hoshiarpur), pp. 165 ff. One is reminded of Viṣṇu's relations with Pūṣan (*Aspects of early Viṣṇuism*, p. 110 f.), the knower of the paths.

64. ṚV. 6, 69, 1; 8, 25, 12; cf. also *ŚB.* 1, 1, 2, 13.

65. Cf. e.g. also ṚV. 6, 48, 14.

66. Like Viṣṇu Soma is in the navel of the earth (ṚV. 9, 72, 7), and the pillar of Heaven (9, 86, 46 *skambhó diváḥ*; cf. 9, 2, 5; 9, 74, 2, etc.); he was also concerned in the separation of heaven and earth (9, 70, 2); he is the king of the universe (9, 66, 2). It is quite intelligible that Viṣṇu—to whom the soma belongs according to *ŚB.* 13, 4, 3, 8; cf. ṚV. 6, 69, 6) —should press the divine beverage for Indra (see above).

67. The stanza recurs, with some variants, *VS.* 5, 19; *TS.* 1, 2, 13, 2; *MS.* 1, 2, 9, etc.; cf. also *ŚB.* 3, 5, 3, 22.

68. Cf. the well-known story *AiB.* 6, 15, 11; *KS.* 19, 11.

69. *JB.* 2, 68 (cf. AV. 17, 1, 6) *unnetar un mā naye 'ty āha, viṣṇur vā unnetā, yajño vai viṣṇuḥ, yajña evainaṃ tat sarvasmāt pāpmano vimucyonnayati.* The formula 'Viṣṇu must lead you up' is interestingly enough prescribed (*MGS.* 1, 11, 18) to accompany, in the wedding ceremonies, the seven steps to be taken by bride and bridegroom. For other ritual application: *ĀpŚS.* 13, 21, 3.

70. *ŚB.* 1, 1, 2, 13; 1, 9, 3, 9 f.; 3, 6, 3, 3. For particulars see *Aspects of early Viṣṇuism*, pp. 63 f.; 80, etc. Cf., e.g., *ŚB.* 1, 9, 3, 8 ff.

71. *TS.* 1, 7, 5, 4; *ŚB.* 3, 2, 1, 17.

72. Cf. e.g. *ŚB.* 1, 9, 3, 10. For the idea *svargaloka* see *Loka*, p. 167 s.v. It may be of interest to observe that the sacrificer, in making the strides, 'may begin either with the stride on earth or with that in the sky' (*KātŚS.* 3, 8, 11, 12; cf. *ŚB.* 1, 9, 3, 11 f.). This fact is not in favour of the supposition that Viṣṇu moves, in principle, only upwards. Cf. also *TS.* 1, 7, 6, 2.

73. It is in my opinion very difficult to say whether definite speculations on Viṣṇu and the number three (e.g. *VS.* 9, 31 f.; *TS.* 1, 7, 11, 1 associating him with three syllables; Kuiper, op. cit., p. 150, n. 86) are due to later reinterpretation of one single original significance of the number. Being characterized by the number three which expresses totality and hence also completion Viṣṇu's role is on the other hand intelligible in cases such as *JB.* 1, 180; 181; 2, 243 (quoted by Kuiper, pp. 145 f.; 149 f.) also when one is disinclined to accept Kuiper's starting-points. The co-ordination of Bṛhaspati with the devas and the upper world (see e.g. *ŚB.* 5, 1, 1, 4; 5, 3, 1, 2; 5, 5, 1, 12) does not by itself prove Viṣṇu's nature as a representative of the totality. Some importance may however be attached to the repeated statement that the whole of existence (*bhuvana*: the world and the living beings contained in it) is in the cosmic pillar (AV. 10, 7, 35; 10, 8, 2). Compare also my remarks in *J.A.O.S.* LXXXVII, p. 425. The number three may also be described as the higher synthesizing unity of which the other two are individual aspects.

74. Cf. ṚV. 1, 153, 3 with Geldner's note and Lüders, op. cit., pp. 66 ff.

75. Cf. also ṚV. 1, 154, 6. AV. 17, 1, 6 f. Viṣṇu and the sun are invoked conjointly, the former to arise with splendour, the latter to lead those praying to the highest expanse of heavens.

76. However, part of the ritualists (Taittirīyas, Kaṭhas) wanted to extend the number of the strides to four (the last one to be made without moving!), the last stride being intended 'to step across the quarters of space', which means to master the whole of the universe (cf. J. C. Heesterman, *The ancient Indian royal consecration*, Thesis, Utrecht, 1957, p. 104 f.); see e.g. *TS.* 1, 6, 5 (and the note by A. B. Keith, *The Veda of the Black Yajus School*, Cambridge, Mass., 1914, p. 88); 1, 7, 5, 4; *ĀpŚS.* 4, 14, 6 ff. (and see especially the note by W. Caland, *Das Śrautasūtras des Āpastamba*, 1, Göttingen and Leipzig, 1921, p. 125); 13, 18, 9; 16, 10, 12; but 18, 12, 10 three strides are to be taken; *ŚŚS.* 4, 12, 1 ff.; compare also *VS.* 2, 25 and 12, 5. In both cases the successful performer of the rite is convinced to have gone to 'heaven' (*ŚB.* 1, 9, 3, 14; *ŚŚS.* 4, 12, 7). The theoretical basis of the fourfold ceremony is no doubt the assumption of a tripartite universe consisting of equivalent parts.

77. *Aspects of early Viṣṇuism*, pp. 11 ff.

78. Cf. e.g. also *ŚB.* 4, 3, 4, 24 ff. (*TĀ.* 3, 10, 2). His name occurs quite naturally among a large number of divine powers to which oblations are due if untoward events were to

prevent an intended soma sacrifice (*ŚB.* 12, 6, 1, 29). Cf. also *ŚB.* 3, 2, 4, 20; 3, 3, 1, 2; 13, 3, 4, 3 ff.

79. See Macdonell, op. cit., p. 76.

80. *ŚŚS.* 3, 4, 1 ff.; cf. 3, 5, 6.

81. *ŚB.* 9, 1, 1, 15; 18; 25.

82. Aitareya, Kauṣītaki, Śatapatha. See also A. B. Keith, *Rigveda Brāhmaṇas*, Cambridge, Mass., 1920, p. 25 f.

83. Here Īśāna is neither identical with Rudra, nor the Supreme God.

84. Cf. also *TB.* 3, 11, 4, 2 (Maruts, Rudra, Indra, Bṛhaspati); 1, 7, 4, 1; *TĀ.* 3, 2, 1 (Earth, Heaven, Rudra, Bṛhaspati); *JUB.* 1, 8, 7.

85. Thus Bh. K. Goswami, *The bhakti cult in ancient India*, Benares, 1965, p. 89 f. is of the opinion that 'as the original sacred fire was for the uninterrupted good and safety of humanity, Rudra gradually came to be regarded as peaceful Śiva. When the upanishads later on taught the doctrine of a peaceful soul in its purity they unhesitatingly identified it with this Śiva'. I am afraid this view cannot be substantiated by textual evidence.

86. Cf. e.g. *JB.* 3, 26, 2; *ŚB.* 1, 7, 3, 8; 5, 2, 4, 13; 5, 3, 1, 10; 6, 1, 3, 13; 9, 1, 1, 1; 9, 2, 3, 32; see also *Mbh.* 3, 220, 9 'Agni is called Rudra by (the) brahmans'; *AgniP.* 1, 13, etc. For the relations between Agni and Śiva now see also W. D. O'Flaherty, in *History of Religions*, IX (1969), p. 4 ff.

87. *Aspects of early Viṣṇuism*, especially p. 166 f.

88. For *prāṇāḥ* see e.g. E. Abegg, *Indische Psychologie*, Zürich, 1945, *passim*; E. Frauwallner, *Geschichte der indischen Philosophie*, I, Salzburg, 1953, pp. 80 ff.

89. I cannot, for want of space, repeat here what I have written in *Aspects of early Viṣṇuism*. pp. 78 ff., etc.

90. See e.g. J. N. Farquhar, *An outline of the religious literature of India*, Oxford, 1920, p. 92 and for the uncertainty of any attempt at dating L. Renou, in L. Renou and J. Filliozat, *L'Inde classique*, I, Paris, 1947, p. 298 f. The Maitrāyaṇīya Upaniṣad must in any case have gone through a long process of extension, refashioning and rearrangement (J. A. B. van Buitenen, *The Maitrāyaṇiya-Upaniṣad*, The Hague, 1962).

91. *MaiU.* 5, 2; 6, 16; 6, 38 (cf. 7, 3; 7, 7); 6, 23.

92. *MaiU.* 6, 35; *BĀU.* 5, 15, 1 (=*ĪśaU.* 15).

93. Pūṣan, who maintains relations with the sun, is the god who knows the paths. Translations such as 'for one whose law is the Real to see' (Hume, cf. Senart), 'so that I who love the truth may see' (Radhakrishnan), disregard the value of the construction with the double dative. Cf. ṚV. 1, 12, 7; 5, 63, 1; 10, 34, 8, etc.; *Mbh.* 13, 135, 69.

94. Cf. F. Edgerton, *The Bhagavad Gītā translated and interpreted*, II, Cambridge, Mass., 1944, p. 32. However, this scholar, while nursing ideas with regard to the character of the Vedic Viṣṇu which now must be regarded as antiquated, underrated the significance of the figure in Vedic thought. See my résumé in *Die Religionen Indiens*, I, p. 236.

95. See also E. W. Hopkins, *Epic mythology*, Strassburg, 1915, pp. 202 ff.; 219 ff.

96. See e.g. *Mbh.* 7, 173, 10; 13, 14, 86 (a younger passage: *sarvagata*); 7, 102, 1 ff.; 173, 9.

97. *Mbh.* 1, 59, 16; cf. 5, 95, 3; Hopkins, op. cit., pp. 34; 81 f.

98. See e.g. *ĀśvGS.* 2, 2, 2.

99. As to Viṣṇu, cf. *Mbh.* 5, 10, 6: 'In former times Thou pervadest the three worlds in three strides . . . the entire universe is pervaded by Thee.'

100. *Mbh.* 12, after 274 (App. I, 28, 168).

101. Cf. also 7, 145, 59; 12, 65, 32. Indra and Viṣṇu are identified in 1, 21, 12.

102. *Mbh.* 1, a. 17. See also *Mbh.* 3, 102, 18 ff.; 194, 8 ff.

103. Cf. e.g. *Mbh.* 3, 102, 19 ff. and a younger passage after 3, 256, 28.

104. See the detailed descriptions of this god in *Mbh.* 7, a. 173; 12, after 274 (App. I, 28, 160 ff.); 13, a. 14–18 (an interpolated passage).

105. See e.g. *Mbh.* 12, after 274 (App. I, 28, 201).

106. Which he violently interrupted because he was not invited. The germ of the story is found in *TS.* 2, 6, 8, 3, where it is related that when the other gods had excluded him from a sacrifice he pierced it with an arrow. See *Mbh.* 7, 173, 42; 12, 274, 18 ff. (adding that on this occasion fever originated from a drop of sweat from Śiva's brow to spread among men and animals). The purāṇas reproduce the episode with many embellishments. We shall have to revert to it (ch. VI). For epic variants: Hopkins, op. cit., p. 223.

107. This point is often brought to the fore: see e.g., 1, 157, 11; 3, 41, 25; 104, 13; 5; 5, 189, 8; 12, app. 28, 399, etc. Cf. ṚV. 1, 114, 3, etc.

108. T. A. G. Rao, *Elements of Hindu iconography*, Madras, 1916, II, p. 65; A. K. Coomaraswamy, *Geschichte der indischen und indonesischen Kunst*, Leipzig, 1927, pp. 35; 42.

109. *Mbh.* 12, 160, 46; 13, 17, 74.

110. Cf. e.g. *Mbh.* 7, 173, 91 *yac ca viśvaṃ mahat pāti madādevas tataḥ smṛtaḥ.*

111. *Mbh.* 12, 64, 7 ff.

112. *Mbh.* 12, 337, 62 (*jñānaṃ pāśupatam*; cf. 13, 76, 29); 12, 59, 86 ff.

113. *Mbh.* 1, 16, 274* (in some mss.); 12, 330, 47.

114. Cf. however *ŚvU.* 3, 9: 'He stands like a tree established in heaven, the One' and the interesting place VāP. 10, 59 *ūrdhvaretāḥ sthitaḥ sthāṇur yāvad ābhūtasaṃplavaṃ / yasmāc coktaṃ sthito 'smīti tataḥ sthāṇur iti smṛtaḥ*: he is called Sthāṇu because he remains, in chastity, standing like a trunk or post (*sthāṇu*) until the dissolution of the universe.

115. *Mbh.* 7, 173, 92; 13, 146, 10 (because he is *sthitaliṅga*).

116. *Mbh.* 7, 173, 89. Other interpretations are 'with three mothers', and 'with three eyes'; for Vedic occurrences see Macdonell, *Vedic Mythology*, p. 74.

117. See *Die Religionen Indiens*, I, p. 245 f.

118. I refer to my relative article in *A.B.O.R.I.*, XLVIII–XLIX (1968), pp. 83 ff.

119. *Aspects of early Viṣṇuism*, p. 107.

120. *Die Religionen Indiens*, I, pp. 45 f.; 85.

121. At least according to the Indian interpretation.

122. See Bipinchandra Pal, *Bengal Vaiṣṇavism*, Calcutta, 1962, p. 4.

123. An inserted passage: 3, 256, after 28 (App. I, 27, 28 ff.).

124. See my relative paper which is to appear elsewhere.

125. See e.g. *PadmaP.* 6, 265, 50.

126. *TS.* 4, 5; *VS.* 16, a litany accompanying 425 oblations and addressed to the hundred forms and powers of Rudra (see e.g. A. B. Keith, *The Veda of the Black Yajus School*, p. 353).

127. Cf. e.g. *Mbh.* 12, a younger passage after a. 274 which is in substantial agreement with *Vāyu-Purāṇa* 1, 30, 79 ff. and *Brahma-Purāṇa* a. 38–40; 13, 17, 30 ff., which occurs in about the same form in *Liṅga-Purāṇa*, a. 65 (Śiva); 13, 135 (Viṣṇu). Texts such as the later additions to the Ṛgveda khilas (J. Scheftelowitz, *Die Apokryphen des Ṛgveda*, Breslau, 1906, p. 169 f.) represent an intermediate form. The Viṣṇusahasranāma in *Mbh.* 13 was translated by V. Raghavan, *The Indian heritage*, Bangalore, ^{2}1958, pp. 421 ff.; see also K. E. Parthasarathy, *Śrī-Viṣṇu Sahasranāmam*, Madras, 1966.

128. It is worth mentioning that the Viṣṇusahasranāmastotra (see also *Nārada-Pāñcarātra* (4, 3; 8), *Garuḍa-Purāṇa* 15) has remained practically unaltered since the days of Śaṅkara. See S. N. Tadapatrikar, in *A.B.O.R.I.*, x, p. 330. Compare also *Viṣṇu-Smṛti*, ch. 98.

129. Even robbers, while unwittingly pronouncing Śiva's name Hara (which also means 'take away'), acquire, according to popular tales, much merit.

130. The number 1000 (which in fact is not exact) means 'the All, totality' (*sarvam*: e.g. *ŚB.* 4, 6, 1, 15) and indicates divinity, celestial life, etc. (*Loka*, p. 88, n. 70). Incidentally there is an attempt to bring the sum total to 1008 which, like 108 (a multiple of 18), is a favourite and auspicious number (*aṣṭau* 'eight' being 'etymologically' connected with *aś-* 'to obtain').

131. Not including about twenty names occurring in two variants, one being given to Śiva, the other to Viṣṇu (e.g. Hutāśana, Hutabhuj). In his commentary on *Mbh.* 13, 17, 30 Nīlakaṇṭha draws attention to the fact that the inclusion of lexicographical synonyms does not entail tautology, because for instance, the merit of pronouncing the words Sarvātman and Viśvātman is not the same.

132. The reader may be referred to my relative study in *Four studies in the language of the Veda*, the Hague, 1959, ch. III.

133. He is also Bhayāpaha, Bhayanāśana ('a remover or destroyer of fear'), Chinnasaṃśaya ('the one whose, or by whom, doubt is dispelled, who inspires confidence'), Śarman ('the shelter or refuge'), Śatānanda ('of hundredfold bliss'), Mahābhāga ('the highly distinguished one'), Mahāmāya ('of great incomprehensible creative power'), Ojas ('inaugurative or creative power'), Prāṇada ('the one who gives or saves life'), Sahiṣṇu ('the forbearing one'), Siddhida ('the one who confers success or beatitude'), etc., etc.

134. *Mbh.* 10, a. 7; cf. e.g. also 3, a. 40, 57 ff. There are stories in the sacred books of

Hinduism which give the name a power even greater than that of its possessor. See e.g. J. Abbott, *The keys of power*, London, 1932, p. 40 f.

135. *Mbh.* 12, a. 43.

136. See e.g. Bh. S. Upadhyaya, *India in Kālidāsa*, Allahabad, 1947, pp. 305 ff.; D. H. H. Ingalls, *An anthology of Sanskrit court poetry*, Cambridge, Mass., 1965, pp. 68 ff.; 93.

CHAPTER II

1. Many scholars have advanced other views on this point. See e.g. R. E. Hume, *The thirteen principal upanishads*, Oxford, 1934, p. 8; S. Radhakrishnan, *Indian philosophy*, I, London (1927) 1948, p. 513; M. Falk, *Il mito psicologico nell'India antica*, Rome Acad., 1939, p. 434 (146); A. Silburn, *Śvetāśvatara upaniṣad*, Paris, 1948, p. 20. For a detailed exposition of my opinions see *Tijdschrift voor Philosophie* (Louvain), XIV, p. 19 f.

2. See Silburn, op. cit., p. 53 (or 'Le brahman, comment est-il cause?'). The text admits of the readings *kiṃkāraṇaṃ brahma* and *kiṃ kāraṇaṃ brahma*. Other translations proposed are 'What is the cause? (Is it) brahman?' (S. Radhakrishnan, *The principal upaniṣads*, London, 1953, p. 709); 'Woher stammt das Brahman?' (R. Hauschild, *Die Śvetāśvatara-Upaniṣad*, Leipzig, 1927, p. 3).

3. See my paper 'Pratiṣṭhā', in *Studia indologica internationalia* (Poona and Paris), I (1954).

4. Cf. *ŚvU.* 2, 16: *VS.* 32, 4; *ŚvU.* 3, 3: ṚV. 10, 81, 3, etc.; *ŚvU.* 3, 4 f.: *TS.* 4, 5, 1 cd; *VS.* 16, 2 f.; *ŚvU.* 3, 8: *VS.* 31, 18; *ŚvU.* 3, 14: ṚV. 10, 90, 1; *VS.* 31, 1; *ŚvU.* 3, 15: ṚV. 10, 90, 2; *ŚvU.* 4, 2: *VS.* 32, 1; *ŚvU.* 4, 3: AV. 10, 8, 27; *ŚvU.* 4, 6: ṚV. 1, 164, 20, etc. (see also the notes added to Hauschild's edition of the text). Such quotations do not occur in the Bhagavadgītā although there are reminiscences (3, 13: ṚV. 10, 117, 6; 11, 10: ṚV. 10, 90, 1).

5. I refer to Silburn, op. cit., p. 17. Compare e.g. also *ŚB.* 1, 7, 3, 8 and Eggeling's note (S.B.E., XII, p. 201).

6. Cf. *ŚvU.* 2, 1 ff.: *TS.* 4, 1, 1a–e; *VS.* 11, 1–5.

7. The stanza ṚV. 10, 81, 3, describing Viśvakarman's creative activity as that of a blacksmith, is *ŚvU.* 3, 3 quoted after a stanza in which Rudra is glorified as the sole ruler and creator.

8. *ŚvU.* 3, 4 '... the ruler of everything who of old created Hiraṇyagarbha'; 4, 12.

9. See also Silburn, op. cit., p. 15, who (p. 14 f.) over-estimates the solar contribution to the conception of a Supreme Lord.

10. *ŚvU.* 3, 3: ṚV. 10, 81, 3.

11. Cf. ṚV. 10, 129, 1 and 2, and *BhG.* 9, 19. For *sat* and *asat* see W. Norman Brown, in *J.A.O.S.*, LXI (1941), pp. 76 ff.; LXII (1942), pp. 85 ff.

12. P. M. Modi, *Akṣara*, Baroda, 1932; J. A. B. van Buitenen, in *J.A.O.S.*, LXIX, p. 176.

13. *tad akṣaram, tat savitur vareṇyam*: *ŚvU.* 4, 18.

14. Commentators refer to *KaṭhaU.* 6, 1.

15. Cf. *KaṭhaU.* 4, 13 and the term *nirvāṇa*.

16. For the religious significance of the bridge see C. J. Bleeker, *The sacred bridge*, Leiden, 1963, pp. 180 ff.

17. ṚV. 10, 90, 2, quoted *ŚvU.* 3, 15; cf. *ŚvU.* 3, 16.

18. In older texts this term is of considerable frequency: see *Change and continuity*, pp. 131 ff. Cf. *ŚvU.* 3, 7; 12 (*Change*, p. 145); 3, 20; 4, 7; 10 f.; 5, 3, and see also 3, 1 (*Change*, p. 155), 6, 16. The Bhagavadgītā has likewise adopted *īśa*, *īśvara*, etc.: 4, 6; 11, 44; 13, 28, etc.

19. Cf. *TĀ.* 10, 31, 1 *tvaṃ rudraḥ tvaṃ brahmā tvaṃ prajāpatiḥ*.

20. Cf. e.g. *ŚvU.* 3, 13 on the *puruṣa* 'of the measure of a thumb'.

21. See also L. Renou, *Religions of ancient India*, Jordan lectures 1951, London, 1953, p. 68.

22. See *ŚvU.* 1, 10; 3, 2; 4; 11; 4, 12; 14; 18; 21.

23. Cf. *ŚvU.* 3, 7.

24. Cf. *ŚvU.* 3, 6 'O dweller among the mountains, the arrow which thou holdest in thy hand ...'; 4, 22.

25. *ŚvU.* 4, 22: ṚV. 1, 114, 8; *TS.* 3, 4, 11, 2; *VS.* 16, 16. See also Silburn, op. cit.,

p. 39. I would not, with Silburn, op. cit., p. 38, contend that this upaniṣad incorporates popular elements connected with an ancient Śiva cult in order to raise this deva to a higher rank.

26. I cannot enter here into a discussion of those terms, images, etc., which both works have in common and which need not integrally be regarded as due to borrowing on the part of the Gītā (Silburn, op. cit., p. 24, n. 4). Mention may however be made of a term of great future: *prapad-* *ŚvU.* 6, 18; *BhG.* 4, 11, and of *māyā*: *ŚvU.* 4, 9 f; *BhG.* 7, 25.

27. According to *ŚvU.* 6, 18 God has created Brahmā and delivered to him the Vedas; according to *BhG.* 15, 15 the Veda is known by Kṛṣṇa and effective for knowledge of him; to 6, 44; 8, 28 the ascetic transcends the Vedic ritual and its merits.

28. Some terms used by Śvetāśvatara are of considerable frequency in the Gītā, e.g. *avyaya* 'imperishable'; *kṣetrajña* 'knower of the field', *puruṣa* (see further on); others (e.g. *sahasrākṣa*) are wanting.

29. Cf. also *ŚvU.* 3, 21; 4, 11; 15 f.; 5, 13 f.; 6, 12; 20.

30. Cf. also *BhG.* 7, 29; 8, 24; 13, 12; 17; 4, 39; 5, 29, etc. Cf. also *BhG.* 10, 3 'who knows God as birthless, etc. is released from every sin'.

31. *ŚvU.* 3, 19; *BhG.* 7, 3; 26.

32. But compare *BhG.* 13, 12.

33. *ŚvU.* 3, 20: *TĀ.* 10, 10, 1 and, with slight variation, *KaṭhaU.* 2, 20. It may be remembered that the reputed author ascribes the proclamation of his doctrine to the power of his asceticism and the grace of the god (*deva*): *ŚvU.* 6, 21.

34. *BhG.* 18, 62, cf. also st. 56; 58, etc. For another occasion for God's grace see 11, 25; 44.

35. *deve parā bhaktiḥ.*

36. I may refer to my relative article in *Tijdschrifj voor Philosophie* (Louvain), x, pp. 607 ff.

37. But compare Pāṇini, 4, 3, 98 (see V. S. Agrawala, *India as known to Pāṇini*, Lucknow, 1953, p. 430 f.).

38. Compare e.g. A. Barth, *Oeuvres*, IV, Paris, 1914, p. 396; L. de la Vallée Poussin, *Indo-européens et Indo-iraniens. L'Inde jusque vers 300 av. J.-C.*, Paris, 1936, p. 317; J. Przyluski, in *Archiv Orientální*, 4 (1932), pp. 261 ff.

39. The term might be taken here in an elementary and general sense.

40. I refer to my remarks in *Orientalia neerlandica*, Leiden, 1948, pp. 312 ff.

41. With Mrinal Das Gupta, 'Craddhā and bhakti in Vedic literature', *The Indian Hist. Quarterly*, VI (1930), (Calcutta), pp. 315; 487; see especially p. 493, whom I cannot however follow in every respect.

42. *BhG.* 11, 54; cf. 18, 55.

43. *BhG.* 9, 13; 15, 19.

44. Compare *BhG.* 4, 36 f. and 9, 30.

45. Compare *BhG.* 5, 29 (see also 6, 15) and 9, 31. It is probably not right to contend that the author makes a badly concealed attempt at harmonizing a *jñāna* and a *bhakti* way to salvation. One should rather say that the *jñāna-* and the *bhakti-mārgas* are considered parallel methods of attaining the highest goal (cf. 7, 17), the latter being subject to greater emphasis as soon as the personal aspect of the Highest comes to the fore.

46. For the Kṛṣṇaite parallel see *BhG.* 15, 15; 18.

47. *BhG.* 2, 46; 52; 6, 44; 8, 28; 11, 48; 53. The Gītā does not on the other hand omit suggesting that it is expounding the truths already expounded in the Vedas, Upaniṣads, etc.: 13, 4 and cf. 15, 15.

48. *BhG.* 7, 7 ff.; 10, 14 ff.

49. *BhG.* 10, 12; cf. 9, 4 ff. and also 12, 3; 13, 12; 18, 50. This identity remains, for obvious reasons, in the background. For particulars see *Die Religionen Indiens*, I, p. 268.

50. *BhG.* 4, 11; 7, 21 f.; 9, 32.

51. Cf. e.g. *BhG.* 13, 24 f.

52. Cf. *BhG.* 2, 47; 3, 3 ff.; 21 ff.; 4, 12; 5, 2 f.; 6, 1 f.; 18, 1 ff. and see *Die Religionen Indiens*, I, p. 269 f.

53. This stanza (11, 55) is traditionally and rightly considered the substance of the whole teaching of the Gītā. See also *BhG.* 3, 9; 30 ff.; 4, 23 f.; 39; 9, 27; 34; 12, 2; 7; 20.

54. *BhG.* 7, 23; 8, 5; 9, 34; 10, 10; cf. 18, 65; 66 and 6, 31.

55. *BhG.* 2, 12; 4, 6; 10, 2; 3; 12; 11, 18.
56. *BhG.* 7, 7; 24; 11, 37 f., etc.; 6, 30 f.; 9, 4; 10, 12; 16; 11, 20; 40; 13, 13, etc.
57. *BhG.* 7, 6; 9, 5; 7 ff.; 10, 6; 8, etc.; 7, 5, 7; 9, 5; 18; 10, 39, etc.; 7, 6; 9, 7; 18; 10, 32. I need not point here the author's substantial agreement with the Śvetāśvatara-Upaniṣad.
58. *BhG.* 8, 14; 11, 31; 35 ff.; 9, 29; 7, 22.
59. Cf. e.g. also 9, 26; 11, 44.
60. The use of the term *māyā* in the Śvetāśvatara-Upaniṣad (4, 9 'nature is *māyā*, the great Lord the one who possesses and wields the *māyā*'; cf. *BhG.* 7, 25; 18, 61) is not essentially different from that found in older texts. Cf. *Change and continuity*, pp. 170 ff.
61. *BhG.* 4, 7 f.
62. *Die Religionen Indiens*, I, p. 249.
63. It may be recalled that according to the Bhagavadgītā only the deluded attribute acts—which really are done by our material nature—to the soul which is an inherent and integral fragment of God (15, 7): 3, 27 and see also 5, 13 (cf. *Śv.* 3, 18).
64. *BhG.* 5, 18; 6, 9; 6, 32; 9, 29; 10, 61; 13, 28; 14, 24 f.
65. *BhG.* 12, 2; 13 f.; cf. 6, 10; 32; 46, etc.
66. Ch. 2; cf. also Silburn, op. cit., pp. 18 ff.
67. Cf. especially *BhG.* 3, 40; 6, 10 ff.; 7, 1; 8, 14; 12, 14.
68. *BhG.* 2, 31; 48; 50; 53; 4, 42; 5, 7; 11; 6, 1; 8; 20; 23, etc.
69. *BhG.* 4, 9; 7, 19; 23; 9, 25; 28; 34; 10, 10; 18, 65.
70. Even those who like Edgerton, *The Bhagavadgītā*, p. 31 are firmly convinced of Kṛṣṇa's being, in the Gītā, an avatāra or manifestation of Viṣṇu will have to admit that the text itself does not offer strong proofs. *BhG.* 10, 21 'of the Ādityas I am Viṣṇu, of the celestial luminaries the sun, etc.' only shows that in the ages of the author Viṣṇu occupied a prominent place among those gods who are known as Ādityas. The vocative *viṣṇo* put into Arjuna's mouth (10, 24; 30) seems to express the latter's conviction that the divine manifestation of which he is a witness cannot be but the highest god known to him; in his eyes the epiphany cannot be simply Kṛṣṇa's but must be that of a more exalted being. So he suggests Kṛṣṇa's being a manifestation of Viṣṇu. Kṛṣṇa himself is, however, silent on this point.
71. I refer to *Die Religionen Indiens*, I, pp. 236 ff.
72. S. C. Mukherji, *A study of Vaiṣṇavism in ancient and medieval Bengal*, Calcutta, 1966, p. 3.
73. See e.g. W. Norman Brown, 'The sources and nature of *puruṣa* in the Puruṣasūkta', *J.A.O.S.*, II, pp. 108 ff. According to this scholar the hymn (p. 108) 'contains a number of lexical and mythological integers drawn from the sphere of the related deities Agni, Sūrya and Viṣṇu', so that 'it seems probable that Puruṣa has his chief importance as a blend of these derivate elements, which are treated with a rudimentary personification, perhaps faintly re-echoing an old folk notion (cf. P. Mus, in *Hommage—L. Febvre*, II, Paris, 1953, pp. 11 ff.), and for the nonce posited as the substance offered at the primal cosmological sacrifice' (p. 113 f.); 'Puruṣa seems, then, to be a blend of characteristics of (1) Agni, as the typical male, as the essence of plants, ... as the lord of immortality, as the lord of the sacrifice and the sacrifice itself; (2) Sūrya, as rising above the worlds to the place of immortality; (3) Viṣṇu, as the encompasser of earth, air and sky ...'. As the author has been the first to notice that the evidence is not in all respects conclusive and as part of the terminology applied to Puruṣa and these three gods occurs—in a minority of cases, it is true—also in connection with other deities—whatever, moreover, the advantages of an interpretation based exclusively on Ṛgvedic parallels, it involves the risk of relying on *argumenta e silentio*—it would be more cautious to say that the poet of this *sūkta* has largely drawn on the vocabulary known to other Ṛgvedic poets and adapted ideas occurring in other hymns with a remarkable predilection for some ideas and expressions which are comparatively speaking frequently found in connection with Agni, Sūrya, and Viṣṇu. I would therefore hesitate unreservedly to subscribe to the author's conclusion (p. 114): '(Puruṣa) is a combination of characteristics derived from them, fused in a rather shadowy way in a new unity, with special reference to the sun', but there seems to be much truth in his observation 'The emphasis in the hymn is not on the man-like nature of Puruṣa, but on his qualities of universality and his functioning as the sacrifice, which last is of

predominant importance'. Other more recent literature on this subject is: P. Mus, 'Du nouveau sur Ṛgveda 10, 90?' in *Indol. Studies in honor of W. Norman Brown*, New Haven, Conn., 1962, pp. 165 ff. (whose interesting, though partly speculative argument need not detain us here); L. Renou, *Hymnes spéculatifs du Véda*, Paris, 1956, pp. 97; 247 f.; the same, *Études védiques et pāṇinéennes*, XVI, Paris, 1967, pp. 148 ff.

74. This idea also was adopted by later thinkers: *ChU*. 3, 12, 6; cf. *MaitrU*. 6, 4 and see S. Dasgupta, *A history of Indian philosophy*, II, Cambridge, 1932, p. 523 f.

75. *Aspects of early Viṣṇuism*, p. 67 f.; T. M. P. Mahadevan, *The philosophy of Advaita*, London, 1938, p. 193, and see my remarks in *Indo-Ir. J.*, VIII, p. 23. For the idea of children begetting their parents and the bisexual character of primeval cosmogonic beings see Norman Brown, in *J.A.O.S.*, LI, p. 116 and my remarks in *The Savayajñas*, p. 344 f.

76. We are quite significantly not told to whom the oblation was made and what deities were engaged in the rite.

77. For particulars see *Die Religionen Indiens*, I, p. 173 (with a bibliography); W. Kirfel, 'Der Aśvamedha und der Puruṣamedha', in *Festschrift—W. Schubring*, Hamburg, 1951, pp. 39 ff. For the Puruṣa idea now see also P. Mus, in *Mélanges d'Indianisme—L. Renou*, Paris, 1968, pp. 539 ff. Compare also N. J. Shende, *The Puruṣa-sūkta in the Vedic literature*, Publ. Centre Adv. Studies in Sanskrit, Poona, A4, Poona, 1965.

78. I need not go into particulars; see J. Eggeling, *The Śatapatha-Brāhmaṇa*, v, Oxford, 1900, pp. XXXIII ff.

79. Anukramaṇī.

80. I refer to my article 'The Mudgalopaniṣad', in *Festschrift—E. Frauwallner, W.Z.K.S.O.* XII–XIII (1968–69), p. 101 ff.

81. *ĀpŚS*. 20, 20, 2 and compare W. Caland, *Das Śrautasūtra des Āpastamba*, III, Amsterdam Academy, 1928, p. 253. For a one-sided characterization of this rite see also M. Eliade, *Patterns in comparative religion*, London and New York, 1958, p. 97.

82. *Die Religionen Indiens*, I, p. 173; J. Eggeling, *The Śatapatha-Brāhmaṇa translated*, v (S.B.E., XLIV), Oxford, 1900, p. XXXIII.

83. For details see Heesterman, *The ancient Indian royal consecration*, pp. 66 ff.; 219.

84. Gold means immortality.

85. For particulars see *Change and continuity*, ch. IV.

86. The Puruṣasūkta: *VājS*. 31, 1–16; the Uttaranārāyaṇa litany: 31, 17–22.

87. For particulars see M. Eliade, *Myth and reality*, London, 1964, pp. 21 ff.

88. *Ṛgvidhāna* 3, 26, 1 ff.; cf. Eliade, op. cit., p. 30 f.

89. *ViDhŚ*. 64, 23. See S. Kramrisch, *The Indian temple*, Calcutta, 1946, pp. 357 ff.

90. The origin and background of which may here be left out of consideration. For the *śrāddha* see P. V. Kane, *History of Dharmaśāstra*, IV, Poona, 1953, pp. 265 f.; 439; 444; 449; 488; 507; for sins ibid., pp. 45; 48; 304; 320; for bathing ibid., II, Poona, 1941, p. 661 f. and cf. *Atri-Saṃhitā* 27, 28.

91. The prescription of this hymn in an expiation for a definite mortal sin (*Manu* 11, 252) may be due to the fact that the recitation of a cosmogony is enough to cure imperfections. Cf. also *Atri-Saṃhitā* 31, 18.

92. For details see e.g. S. Lévi, *La doctrine du sacrifice*, Paris, 1898; L. Silburn, *Instant et cause*, Paris, 1955, ch. II.

93. Renou, *Hymnes spéculatifs*, p. 12.

94. *Śaun*.; the hymn (except *Śaun*. 7 and 8) occurs also in *AVPaipp*. 9, 5. For details: W. D. Whitney and Ch. R. Lanman, *Atharvaveda Saṃhitā*, Cambridge, Mass., 1905, p. 902 f.

95. Both texts are quoted in *VaitS*. 37, 19 as accompanying, in the Puruṣamedha, the release of the human victims. See also the introductory remark in the commentary ascribed to Sāyaṇa.

96. *asmin sūkte puruṣasya arthād manuṣasya māhātmyaṃ varṇyate* (comm.).

97. *AVŚ*. 10, 7, 32; 33; 34; 36, 8, 1.

98. Cf. e.g also *AVŚ*. 10, 7, 40 and probably 41.

99. Cf. texts such as AV. 10, 10, 30 and especially AV. 10, 7, 17 which may be said to be in a way the résumé of the author's expositions: 'Whoever know the Bráhman in the Puruṣa know the most exalted one (*parameṣṭhin*); whoever knows the most exalted one, and whoever knows Prajāpati, whoever know the chief *bráhman* power (see *The Savayajñas*,

pp. 153; 433), they know also the *chambha*.' One may read Deussen's introduction to these hymns (P. Deussen, *Allgemeine Geschichte der Philosophie*, I, I, [4]Leipzig, 1920), pp. 310 ff., to which I cannot however subscribe in every respect.

100. *ŚB*. 6, 7, 2, 12 ff.; 6, 7, 4, 7 f.

101. *ŚB*. 6, 1, 1, 5. Formulations such as 'in the brāhmaṇas Prajāpati takes the place of Puruṣa' may lead to misunderstanding. For Prajāpati see *Die Religionen Indiens*, I, pp. 185 ff.

102. *ŚB*. 13, 6, 1, 1; also 12, 3, 4, 1.

103. Cf. e.g. *BĀU*. 1, 4, 1 ff.; 2, 5, 1 ff.; *ChU*. 3, 2, 1 ff. Places such as *KaṭhaU*. 6, 8; *MuU*. 1, 2, 11 must be left out of consideration.

104. Which is repeatedly said to be the source of creatures, to be everything, including Brahman, being beyond death (*MuU*. 2, 1, 5; 10). Cf. also *PrU*. 6, 5; *MaiU*. 2, 5. It cannot be my task here to picture the development of the Puruṣa idea in general, for instance its relation to the *ātman* concept, its being the immortal substratum of the human soul, its use in Sāṃkhya theories, etc.

105. The Puruṣa is primal, cosmic, one with Brahman, ātman, and the All; he is immanent in every individual being, the cosmic and the individual *puruṣa* being one (*BĀU*. 1, 4, 1; 2, 5, 1 ff.; 5, 15; *MuU*. 2, 1, 2; 4, 10, etc.).

106. See above, p. 20.

107. Cf. also S.Ch. Chakravarti, *The philosophy of the Upaniṣads*, Calcutta, 1935, p. 151 f.

108. See e.g. *Mbh*. 7, 173, 22; 13, 15, 42; 44, etc. (also in some younger and inserted passages).

109. Edition, translation and notes by J. Varenne, *La Mahā Nārāyaṇa Upaniṣad*, 2 vols., Paris, 1960.

110. According to Varenne, op. cit., II, pp. 5 ff. at the latest in the IVth century B.C. In any case it impresses us as belonging to the middle group of predominantly metrical upaniṣads.

111. See e.g. R. G. Bhandarkar, *Vaiṣṇavism, Śaivism and minor religious systems*, Strassburg, 1913, pp. 5 ff., etc.; J. E. Carpenter, *Theism in medieval India*, London, 1921, pp. 265 ff.; N. Chaudhuri, in *I.H.Q.* XX, pp. 275 ff.; *Die Religionen Indiens*, I, p. 246 f.

112. *Mbh*. 3, 145, 37 ff.

113. *Mbh*. 5, a. 48. When in the days of yore several gods went to Brahmā, two ancient deities (*pūrvadevau*, st. 5), viz. the ṛṣis Nara and Nārāyaṇa, who so to say draw into themselves the minds and energies of the gods present, left the place without worshipping him. Brahmā explained that they, endued with ascetic merit and illuminating heaven and earth. had come from one *loka* to the other (i.e. from the 'world' of men to the 'world' of brahman, Nīlakaṇṭha). Having become mighty through their own asceticism, and being of great strength of character and heroic energy they permanently (*dhruvau*) contribute to the happiness of the world; worshipped by the gods and the gandharvas they exist only for the destruction of the asuras. As at that time the gods had been much alarmed because of a war with the asuras, Indra, after having gone to the spot where Nara and Nārāyaṇa were practising austerities, asked and obtained the boon that they would assist him in the battle. Thereupon he succeeded in vanquishing, with their aid, the anti-gods. The text continues by stating that Nara (st. 14), i.e. Arjuna (st. 15), slew in battle many enemies of Indra, among whom was the asura Jambha, to state further on (st. 17) that Nārāyaṇa also has, in this world, destroyed numberless other anti-gods.

114. which is also handed down as the 10th book of the Taittirīya-Āraṇyaka.

115. Cf. *MNU*. 14; 25; 71 ff.; 226; 238; 263; 284; 289 f.; 536, etc.; see Varenne, op. cit., I, p. 144 f.; II, p. 37.

116. Varenne translates this term by 'Être'; however, his expositions on this point (II. p. 31) do not always tally with the facts.

117. *MNU*. 15 f.; 19 ff.

118. *MNU*. 226; cf. Varenne, op. cit., I, p. 152.

119. *MNU*. 444 ff. The epithets are *harita*, *piṅgala*, *lohitākṣa*, and (71) *sahasrākṣa*.

120. *MNU*. 22; 25 f.; cf. 269.

121. For the expression *brahmaṇaḥ sāyujyaṃ salokatām āpnoti* cf. *ŚB*. 2, 6, 4, 8 and my remarks in *Loka*, Amsterdam Academy, 1966, pp. 114; 157. Cf. also Varenne, op. cit., II, p. 50.

122. *MNU*. 176 f.; cf. *KaṭhaU*. 3, 6, 9; ṚV. 1, 22, 20.

123. See Varenne, op. cit., p. 49.
124. *MNU.* 2; 8.
125. *MNU.* 12; 25.
126. *MNU.* 38; 53; 55; 59, where the text has the words *dhāmāni veda bhuvanāni viśvā* which literally means: 'he knows all residences-and-manifestations of divine power (for *dhāman* see my publication *The meaning of the Sanskrit term dhāman*, Amsterdam Academy, 1967 and see e.g. Nīlakaṇṭha on *Mbh.* 12, 342, 69 *vulg.*: *dhāmaśabdo lokasāravācī ṛtam abādhitaṃ dhāma sattāsphūrtirūpam*) and the worlds and their inhabitants (see *Vishveshv. Indol. Journ.* (Hoshiarpur), v (1967), pp. 42 ff.). For the content of these ideas see R. Pettazzoni, *The All-knowing god*, London, 1956 (cf. p. 122).
127. *BhG.* 11, 39; cf. also 10, 23; 15, 14.
128. Other references to various aspects of the god's nature are: he is able to give inspiration or mental illumination (67 ff.; 384), an old Vedic function; he helps, saves, and protects men, destroys enemies and makes his worshippers surmount difficulties (164 ff.; 305 ff.).
129. Varenne, op. cit., pp. 147; 153.
130. See above.
131. *ŚvU.* 4, 2 (the third god is Āditya; for this triad see further on, p. 97); *PrU.* 2, 5; *MaiU.* 5, 1.
132. Hopkins, *Epic mythology*, pp. 180; 196; 207; 222; 227. Cf. e.g. also *TĀ.* 1, 12, 1.
133. The relation is more complicated than can be suggested in a few lines.
134. Cf. e.g. *ŚB.* 6, 1, 1, 5; 10, 4, 1, 12; *Die Religionen Indiens*, I, pp. 191 ff.
135. See especially the Nārāyaṇīya section *Mbh.* 12, a. 321–339 and compare Carpenter, *Theism in medieval India*, pp. 264 ff.
136. *Mbh.* 12, 326, 20; 41; 122, etc.; cf. 12, 351, 3, etc.
137. Cf. e.g. also *Mbh.* 12, 51, 2 *namas te bhagavan viṣṇo lokānāṃ nidhanodbhava . . . // viśvakarman namas te 'stu viśvātman viśvasaṃbhava / apavargo 'si bhūtānāṃ pañcānāṃ parataḥ sthitaḥ // namas te triṣu lokeṣu namas te paratas triṣu . . . tvaṃ hi sarvaparāyaṇam . . .*
138. The reader may be referred to W. D. P. Hill, *The Bhagavadgītā*, Oxford and London, 1928, pp. 18 f.; 28 f.
139. *BhG.* 10, 12; 11, 18; cf. 10, 15; 11, 3; 15, 18 and also 7, 30 and 8, 4. This repetition is not meaningless.
140. *BhG.* 8, 8; 10; 22; 11, 38; 15, 4; 17.
141. *BhG.* 10, 12 f.; 11, 38. Places such as 13, 22 are not discussed here.
142. *BhG.* 15, 4; 6; the expression *dhāma paramam* (cf. ṚV. 1, 43, 9) is later explained as *vaiṣṇavaṃ padam*); see also *Dhāman*, p. 81 f.
143. *Mbh.* 3, 13, 49; 186, 13; 7, 124, 16; 12, 43, 4; 8 etc.
144. *Mbh.* 7, 124, 16; 165, after 39. It has already been observed that the epic Śiva also claimed this title, which is also given to Sūrya (3, 3, 23).
145. *Mbh.* 1, 1, 22 *ādyaṃ puruṣam īśānam . . . brahma . . . sanātanam // asac ca sac caiva yad viśvaṃ sadasataḥ param / . . . viṣṇum*; 13, 135, 4 ff.; cf. also 12, 323, 29.
146. *Mbh.* 3, 187, 45; 12, 203, 9 *vāsudevaḥ sarvam idam . . . // puruṣaṃ sanātanaṃ viṣṇum yat tad vedavido viduḥ.*
147. *Mbh.* (Beng. and Dev. versions) 3, App. I, 27, 85.
148. *Mbh.* 3, 19, 27. Cf. *Aspects of early Viṣṇuism*, pp. 96 ff.
149. Renou, in *J.A.*, CCXXXVII (1949), pp. 7 ff.; Gonda, *Notes on brahman*, Utrecht, 1950, pp. 57 ff.
150. *VS.* 23, 49; 51; *ŚB.* 13, 5, 2, 14 f.; *ŚŚS.* 16, 6, 1; 3.
151. I cannot enter here into a discussion of the *puruṣayajñavidyā* explained *ChU.* 3, 16 f. to Kṛṣṇa (see e.g. H. Raychaudhuri, *The early history of the Vaishnava sect*, Calcutta, 1936, p. 78 f.).
152. *Hariv.* 1, 1, 51; *BrP.* 1, 53 f.; *ŚivaP.* Dh. 51, 26 f., the earliest purāṇic treatise on creation (W. Kirfel, *Das Purāṇa pañcalakṣaṇa*, Bonn, 1927, p. 5).
153. The intimate relation of this Ṛgvedic *sūkta* with Viṣṇu appears for instance from the *Mānavaśrautasūtra* which (11, 4, 5) among various prescriptions for a definite ceremony states also that Savitar is to be addressed with a Savitar formula, Soma with a Soma mantra, etc., but Viṣṇu with the Puruṣasūkta. In the *Taittirīya-Āraṇyaka* (10, 11, 1) the first word of the sūkta, viz. 'thousand-headed', is made to begin a characterization of Nārāyaṇa

as the highest god. In a long and interesting—though no doubt later—passage (3, 26, 1 ff.) the *Ṛgvidhāna* explains how to pay, with this *sūkta*, homage to Viṣṇu with a view to reach absorption in brahman as well as the practical rules relating to a *nyāsa* rite of tantric character—*in casu* fixation of the meaning of the stanzas in the limbs and part of one's body—to be performed with this text and to *pūjā*, i.e. worship of Viṣṇu with the stanzas of the sūkta, etc. The author advises the adept also to mutter the *sūkta* for the sake of reintegration: the man who does so while dwelling in the wilderness and who loves the god Nārāyaṇa, the eternal creator, truly, will see Him.

154. Cf. e.g. *Hariv.* 1, 1, 1 ff. *ādyaṃ puruṣam īśānaṃ puruhūtaṃ puruṣṭutam / ṛtam ekākṣaraṃ brahma vyaktāvyaktaṃ sanātanam // asac ca sad asac caiva yad viśvam sadasatparam / parāvarāṇāṃ sraṣṭāraṃ purāṇaṃ param avyayam // maṅgalyaṃ maṅgalaṃ viṣṇuṃ vareṇyam anaghaṃ śucim / namaskṛtya hṛṣīkeśaṃ carācaraguruṃ harim* . . . The process of identification does not draw to a close here. Among the epic names of Viṣṇu-Kṛṣṇa is also that of the Vedic Viśvakarman, who, being all-seeing, and having a face, eyes, arms, and feet on every side, produced heaven and earth (ṚV. 10, 81, 3) and who in the brāhmaṇas was expressly identified with Prajāpati (*ŚB.* 8, 2, 1, 10, etc.; see also Norman Brown, *Man in the universe*, Calcutta, 1966, p. 25 f., whose remarks on Brahmaṇaspati should not be regarded as final). Surviving on the other hand as an individual deity, the artificer of the gods, he could also fuse with the Puruṣa when viewed as the great architect of the universe (*Mānasāra*, 2, 2 ff.). For Kṛṣṇa see also S. N. Tadapatrikar, 'The Kṛṣṇa problem', *Ann. Bhand. Or. Res. Inst.* (Poona), x (1930), pp. 269 ff.

155. See E. W. Hopkins, *Epic mythology*, Strassburg, 1915, pp. 206; 208; 215 etc.; A. Guruge, *The society of the Rāmāyaṇa*, Maharagama (Ceylon), 1960, pp. 161 f.; 222 ff.; 248 ff. etc.

156. *Rām.* 2, 4, 33 crit. ed.

157. Cf. e.g. Dasgupta, *History of Indian philosophy*, III, Cambridge, 1940, p. 105. Compare also places such as *AgniP.* 58, 27 'hymns should be sung to Hari as laid down in the Vedic Puruṣasūkta'.

158. See e.g. *SauraP.* 19, 27; 42, 36.

159. Which could easily be multiplied. The Mandasor stone inscription of 404 A.D. for instance begins with an invocation of the 'thousand-headed Puruṣa who is one with Viṣṇu-Nārāyaṇa. Cf. H. P. Shastri, in *Epigr. Ind.*, XII, pp. 320 ff.

160. V. Rangacharya, 'Historical evolution of Śrī-Vaiṣṇavism in South India', in H. Bhattacharyya, *The cultural heritage of India*, IV, Calcutta, 1956, p. 174; cf. Dasgupta, op. cit., III, p. 155.

161. Cf. e.g. Rāmānuja, *Vedārthasaṃgraha* 127; 131 (translated by J. A. B. van Buitenen, Poona, 1956, pp. 283; 287).

162. *Vaikhānasa-Smārtasūtra* 10, 7. I cannot discuss here the use made of this text in other communities. Cf. e.g. *AgniP.* 59, 47; 60, 24; 63, 15.

163. In later handbooks of the same community, which maintain the identity of Viṣṇu, Brahman, and Puruṣa, the popularity and great importance attached to this ancient text are much in evidence. On various occasions, for instance the construction of the god's image (I refer to the *Kāśyapa-Saṃhitā*, translated by T. Goudriaan, Thesis, Utrecht, 1965; see esp. ch. 43 (transl. p. 135); 46 (p. 140); 48 (p. 143); 49 (p. 145))—which we know to be an object of worship as well as a means of attaining by way of meditative concentration communion with God—it is recited together with the Viṣṇusūkta and other typically Viṣṇuite texts; it is of course to accompany the oblations to be offered to God's manifestation as Puruṣa, but it also accompanies ritual acts which are to accentuate, and hence to promote, the realization of the identity of the individual and the Universal 'Self' (*Kāśyapa Saṃhitā*, ch. 78 (p. 237); ch. 57 (p. 166); compare also ch. 60 (p. 175); ch. 67 (p. 195); ch. 73 (p. 215), etc.). Similar prescripts obtaining with regard to the recitation of this ancient text in worship whilst installing a new image, etc., occur in the handbooks of other communities (see e.g. *MatsyaP.* 265, 26; *BhāgP.* 10, 1, 20).

CHAPTER III

1. Cf. *Mbh.* 1, 1, 20 ff. *ādyaṃ puruṣam īśānaṃ puruhūtaṃ puruṣṭutam / ṛtam ekākṣaraṃ brahma vyaktāvyaktaṃ sanātanam / . . . viṣṇum . . .*; 1, 57, 83 f. the *avyaktam akṣaram brahma* is Kṛṣṇa; 10, 7, 257 Brahman is identified with Śiva, etc.

2. For a systematic account I refer to *Die Religionen Indiens*, II, pp. 194 ff. V. S. Agrawala, *Śiva Mahādeva*, Varanasi, 1966, is a subjective attempt at explaining, from a non-historical point of view, Śivaite symbolism, special emphasis being laid upon macro-microcosmic correspondence.

3. Cf. also ṚV. 1, 84, 7, etc.

4. I refer to *Change and continuity*, The Hague, 1965, pp. 140 ff.

5. Ibid., pp. 142 ff.

6. Ibid., p. 144. See *BĀU.* 4, 4, 13 ff. and 1, 4, 11.

7. *Dīgha Nikāya*, 13 (Tevijja Sutta), 25, p. 244.

8. ?, Mahinda ?, cf. *GGS.* 4, 7, 37 ff. where Mahendra occurs beside Indra.

9. See also Bh. Kumarappan, *The Hindu conception of the deity*, London, 1934, pp. 13 n.; 46. For *KB.* 6, 8 see further on.

10. See e.g. *Mbh.* 1, 1, 20; 12, 326, 37 (Viṣṇu = Aniruddha); 3, 31, 21; cf. also *ViP.* 5, 2, 20.

11. It is interesting to notice that Śiva's rise as a god is reflected in Buddhist sources. By the time of Buddhaghoṣa he is no longer next to Varuṇa the fourth in an enumeration but given a seat near Sakka (Indra): for references see G. P. Malalasekera, *Dictionary of Pāli proper names*, I, London, 1937, p. 329. According to the Jainas Śakra and Īśāna are the two Indras of the lowermost celestial sphere (W. Kirfel, *Die Kosmographie der Inder*, Bonn and Leipzig, 1920, pp. 16*; 233).

12. *ŚvU.* 3, 11, etc.; R. G. Bhandarkar, *Vaiṣṇavism, Śaivism*, Strassburg, 1913, p. 108 f.; S. Chattopadhyaya. *The evolution of theistic sects in ancient India*, Calcutta, 1962, p. 18.

13. See e.g. also M. Singer, *Krishna*, Honolulu, 1966, pp. 151 ff. According to the Śivaite *Atharvaśiras-Upaniṣad*, 57 f., the Lord is called Īśāna because He is the One who rules all the worlds with His ruling powers, with His generative powers and His highest energies (cf. *ŚvU.* 3, 1) and because He rules the movable and immovable (ṚV. 7, 32, 22); He is called Bhagavān Maheśvara because he causes the devout worshippers to participate in higher knowledge and favours them with it, because He gathers and releases (utters) the Word (of the Veda), because giving up all conditions (states) He is exalted by His knowledge of the Ātman and the lordly power of His yoga. There is also a variant version of the latter paragraph; see *The Śaiva Upaniṣads*, edited by Pt. A. Mahadeva Sastri, Adyar, 1950, p. 31. Another definition of *bhagavān* is: 'He who knows the origin and dissolution (of the world), the coming and going of the beings and knowledge and ignorance' (Śaṅkara, on *ChU.* 7, 26, 2).

14. *ĀpGS.* 7, 20; the other deities are Mīḍhuṣī and Jayanta (for the latter see also J. N. Banerjea, *The development of Hindu iconography*, Calcutta, 1956, p. 86). According to the commentator Haradatta these three deities are represented by their images. For these rites see A. B. Keith, *The religion and philosophy of the Veda and Upanishads*, Cambridge, Mass., 1925, p. 364 f. Mīḍhuṣī and Jayanta play a part in the śūlagava rite (also called Īśānabali: see further on; for the rite see A. Hillebrandt, *Ritual-literatur*, Strassburg, 1897, p. 83 f.) which is to propitiate Śiva and to avert plague in cattle.

15. See e.g. G. Jouveau-Dubreuil, *Archéologie du Sud de l'Inde*, Paris, 1914, II, fig. 33. For a popular tradition explaining his accession to the position of *dikpāla* see R. Dessigane, P. Z. Pattabiramin, J. Filliozat, *Les légendes çivaïtes de Kāñcipuram*, Pondichéry, 1964, p. 69.

16. *GGS.* 4, 7, 37 ff.; similarly, but with Prajāpati in the centre *SāmavB.* 3, 3, 3; cf. Hillebrandt, *Ritualliteratur*, p. 81 f.

17. In connection with the king who is said to have been created from particles of these eight gods; for this passage see my treatise *Ancient Indian kingship from the religious point of view*, Leiden, 1966, pp. 10; 25 ff.; 30 (= *Numen*, III (1956), pp. 45; 60 ff.; 65), and my paper 'The sacred character of ancient Indian kingship', *Atti dell'VIII Congresso Intern. di Storia delle Religioni* 1955, p. 173 f.

18. Cf. also *Manu*, 7, 2 ff.

19. For some particulars see also Banerjea, *The development of Hindu iconography*, pp.

519 ff.; H. H. Wilson and F. Hall, *The Viṣṇu Purāṇa*, London, 1864, I, pp. 153 ff.; II, p. 86; E. W. Hopkins, *Epic mythology*, Strassburg, 1915, pp. 149 ff.; A. Guruge, *The society of the Rāmāyaṇa*, Maharagama, 1960, p. 257.

20. See Kirfel, op. cit., p. 95.

21. Cf. e.g. *LiP.* 1, 104, 26: *yamāgnivāyurudrāmbusomaśakraniśācaraiḥ / diṅmukhe diṅmukhe nityaṃ sagaṇaiḥ pūjitāya te.* The Liṅga Purāṇa seems to be a manual of Śivaites who extolled the worship of the *liṅga* over the image of Śiva himself, inculcating also the adoration of the *pañcavaktra* (see further on).

22. See e.g. also *ViP.* 3, 14, 30; Varāhamihira, *BS.* 43, 57; 46, 10; 48, 26.

23. For particulars see e.g. P. V. Kane, *History of Dharmaśāstra*, II, Poona, 1941, pp. 871; 899; S. Stevenson, *The rites of the twice-born*, Oxford, 1920, pp. 87; 359; H. Meinhard, *Beiträge zur Kenntnis des Śivaismus nach den Purāṇas*, Thesis, Bonn, 1928, pp. 23 ff.; Somadeva, Kathāsaritsāgara, 116, 88 Indra himself is said to dismiss the *lokapālas* to their several stations after honouring them.

24. Banerjea, op. cit., p. 485; *AgniP.* 51, 15; 56, 28 f.; 96, 32.

25. The trident is his emblem as the *vajra* is Indra's, etc.: *LiP.* 1, 84, 60 ff. (*taṅka* 'hatchet'); 2, 28, 50 ff., etc.

26. Banerjea, op. cit., p. 529.

27. *ViDhP.* 3, a. 55–58, and compare especially M. Th. de Mallmann, *Les enseignements iconographiques de l'Agni-Purāṇa*, Paris, 1963, p. 136 f.; B. Bhattacharyya, *The Indian Buddhist iconography*, Calcutta, 1958, p. 361: among the Hindu gods adopted by the Vajrayāna are the eight *dikpālas*, Īśāna being represented as white in colour, holding trident and skull-cap, wearing the crescent on his matted hair, etc.

28. Meinhard, op. cit., pp. 25; 27; cf. *LiP.* 2, 28, 52 and especially 54; see also *ViDhP.* 3, a. 55.

29. *ŚivaP.* 6, 29, 22; *LiP.* 1, 104, 26, etc.

30. It occurs *TĀ.* 10, 1, 5 ff. together with some variations addressed to other deities.

31. See e.g. *LiP.* 2, 48, 18 ff. and especially 25. Compare also Meinhard, op. cit., p. 25 f. It is worth observing that according to *AgniP.* 56, 28 the mantra ṚV. 7, 32, 22cd (originally addressed to Indra) is used in invoking Īśāna: *íśānam asyá jágataḥ svadṛ́śam íśānam indra tasthúṣaḥ* 'ruler of the movable and immovable'.

32. For these variations see my article on the Indian mantra, *Oriens*, XVI (1963), pp. 244 ff., esp. pp. 292 ff.

33. *LiP.* 1, 82, 40 f.; 102, 17 ff., etc. Cf. also Hopkins, op. cit., p. 149; Meinhard, op. cit., p. 26.

34. For Īśānapuruṣa see *MatsyaP.* 266, 26.

35. For particulars see Meinhard, op. cit., p. 27. These texts adduced by Meinhard occur in the Liṅga-Purāṇa; the versions of these myths found in the Mahābhārata, Vāyu-, Kūrma-, and Śiva-Purāṇas make no mention of Īśāna.

36. As is contended by Meinhard, op. cit., p. 26.

37. Cf. e.g. *LiP.* 1, 72, 60; 1, 102, 19; Wilson and Hall, op. cit., I, p. 131 f., etc.

38. *LiP.* 2, 27, 245 ff.

39. AV. 15, 5, 1 ff.; cf. M. Bloomfield, *The Atharva-Veda and the Gopatha-Brāhmaṇa*, Strassburg, 1899, pp. 52; 82; E. Arbman, *Rudra*, Uppsala, 1922, p. 29 f.

40. *Die Religionen Indiens*, I, p. 85.

41. Up to the present day Śiva is often called 'the Lord'; see e.g. also W. Koppers, *Die Bhil in Zentralindien*, Horn and Wien, 1948, p. 171 f.; G. W. Briggs, *The Ḍoms*, Mysore, 1953, p. 73.

42. *Die Religionen Indiens*, I, p. 45 f.

43. See e.g. *The Savayajñas*, pp. 128; 389.

44. W. D. Whitney and Ch. R. Lanman, *Atharva-veda Saṃhitā*, Cambridge, Mass., 1905, p. 779 translate 'the formidable god'.

45. See Lecture I, p. 6.

46. Although the division of this text made by the manuscripts and the *anukramaṇī* is opposed to its sense, sixteen subdivisions may be made by reckoning the last words of all stanzas only to stanzas 1 and 7; see Whitney and Lanman, op. cit., p. 778. For the number sixteen see *Change and continuity*, ch. IV.

47. For a different group of 'guardians' of the regions see *ŚB.* 13, 4, 2, 16.

48. See e.g. AV. 1, 31 and *Kauś.* 38, 11; *The Savayajñas*, p. 421 f. For an enumeration of relevant facts see e.g. also Sacred Books of the East, XXVI, pp. 467 and XLIV, p. 563 s.v.

49. See e.g. *The Savayajñas*, pp. 120; 138; 259 and see, for instance, AV. 12, 3, 24; *Kauś.* 61, 32 (*The Savayajñas*, p. 162 f.). Compare also the *digbandhana* rite to be mentioned in Lecture IV, p. 70, l. 13 ff.

50. See e.g. ṚV. 10, 51, 9; 10, 128, 1; AV. 5, 3, 1; 9, 2, 11; compare *The Savayajñas*, p. 389.

51. *The Savayajñas*, pp. 128; 240; 254; 259 f. and see e.g. AV. 4, 14, 9.

52. See also *MGS.* 2, 5, 3 and the note by M. J. Dresden, *Mānavagṛhyasūtra*, Thesis, Utrecht, 1941, p. 127.

53. W. Kirfel, 'Ist die Fünfzahl der symbolische Ausdruck einer bestimmten Kultur?', *Geistige Arbeit*, Berlin, VI. 4 (1939), pp. 3 ff., quoting, among others, G. Haloun, 'Die Rekonstruktion der chinesischen Urgeschichte durch die Chinesen,' *Japanisch-Deutsche Zs. f. Wissenschaft und Technik* (Kobe),' 1925, p. 248 ff. (the five Chinese 'god-emperors' are 'ausgesprochene Repräsentanten der Farbensymbolik, mithin die Beherrscher der Weltgegenden') and expressing the opinion that this 'Farbensymbolik' is the most important of all groups of five, because there are Buddhist and Hinduist parallels. The importance of the quarters of the universe in rites is for instance apparent from ṚV. 10, 131, 1 requesting Indra to drive away the enemies who are in the East, in the West, in the North and in the South; the stanza is also used in the ritual (e.g. *ŚŚS.* 12, 3, 5; 12, 13, 1; *ŚGS.* 6, 5, 6 one performs while looking to the four cardinal points; *TB.* 2, 4, 1, 2; *ĀśvŚS.* 7, 4, 7; 8, 3, 2, and compare *AiB.* 6, 22, 1; 8, 10, 8: 'from all sides freedom from foes and danger becomes his, prosperity ever increasing he attains . . .'); from AV. 12, 3, 7, etc. (*Kauś.* 61 1 ff.; compare *The Savayajñas*, pp. 79; 128). See also further on p. 42. I cannot, moreover, unreservedly subscribe to Kirfel's attempt (see also his book *Die dreiköpfige Gottheit*, Bonn 1948, pp. 14; 41 ff.) to assign the origin of the (pentadic) correlative system under consideration to 'a lunar culture dominating in the North and the West'. For the importance of the number five as the symbol of the middle, which is under the immovable highest point (zenith), in China see H. Köster, *Symbolik des chinesischen Universismus*, Stuttgart, 1958, pp. 50 ff.

54. *oṣadhayo vanaspatayaḥ* 'the herbs and the trees'.

55. *sa eṣo 'ṣṭanāmāṣṭadhāvihito mahān devaḥ.*

56. For the date of this brāhmaṇa see A. B. Keith, *Rigveda Brahmanas*, Cambridge, Mass., 1920, pp. 42 ff.

57. *ŚB.* 6, 1, 3, 7 ff.; cf. further on *PGS.* 3, 8, 6.

58. *ŚB.* 6, 1, 3, 18 significantly adds Kumāra as the ninth form of Agni.

59. That is to say, he again occupies the place which in a ritual *pradakṣiṇa* enumeration corresponds to the North-East.

60. Rudra = Agni; Śarva = the waters; Paśupati = the plants; Ugra = Vāyu (the wind or air); Aśani = lightning; Bhava = Parjanya; Mahān devaḥ = the moon = Prajāpati; Īśāna = the sun.

61. For which see e.g. also J. M. Nallasvami Pillai, *Studies in Śaiva-Siddhānta*, Madras, 1911, pp. 229 ff.

62. *HirGS.* 2, 8, 6. The same names occur, in a somewhat different order, Īśāna being the third, in *BhārGS.* 2, 8 and *BaudhGS.* 2, 7, 18. Compare also A. B. Keith, in *J.A.O.S.* (1907), p. 933 f.

63. *ĀśvGS.* 4, 8, 19 ff.

64. *KGS.* 52, 6.

65. *PGS.* 3, 8, 6.

66. See Lecture I, p. 11.

67. Aśanin is *Mbh.* 13, 17, 42 one of Śiva's names.

68. and in omitting Kumāra at the end.

69. I cannot go into the formulas of the Śatarudrīya litany, for which see *TS.* 4, 5 and Keith's note, *The Veda of the Black Yajus School*, Cambridge, Mass., 1914, p. 353.

70. *ĀpGS.* 19, 13 ff.

71. *ĀpGS.* 20, 5; 12 f.; 16.

72. For its popularity in later times and circles see also A. Getty, *Gaṇeśa*, Oxford, 1936 p. 76 f.

73. Cf. Haradatta on *ĀpGS.* 19, 13 *atha īśānabalir nāma pākayajño vakṣyate, śūlagava iti*; compare also Arbman, op. cit., p. 105 f., n. 5.

74. For particulars see Arbman, op. cit., pp. 104 ff.

75. I refer to Arbman, pp. 106 ff.

76. *ŚŚS.* 4, 17. See also W. Caland's note (*Śāṅkhāyana-Śrautasūtra*, Nagpur, 1954, p. 99) in explanation of this, at first sight, curious fact.

77. See above, p. 38 f.

78. With Caland, loc. cit.

79. *Mbh.* 13, 16, 23 *bhūr vāyur jyotir āpaś ca* are followed by *vāg buddhis tvaṃ* (v.e. *khaṃ*) *matir manaḥ / karma satyānṛte cobhe tvam evāsti ca nāsti ca.* Cf. also Hopkins, *Epic mythology*, p. 223.

80. For more details see Meinhard, op. cit., pp. 9 ff. and compare *Die Religionen Indiens*, II, p. 204 f.

81. See *LiP.* 2, 12, 3 ff.; 1, 41, 36; 86, 131; 103, 42, etc.; *LiP.* 2, 28, 3 enumerates *bhūr āpo 'gnir marud vyoma bhāskaro dīkṣitaḥ śaśī* (differences in order are often due to the exigences of versification). Compare also Kālidāsa, *Śak.* 1, 1. It seems worth noticing that the sacrificer is (after the sacrifice, it is true) part of a correlative system consisting also of the earth, the air, the sky, heaven, and immortality in *ŚB.* 8, 7, 4, 12 ff.

82. We also find: fire=Paśupati, air=Īśāna, sun=Rudra, sacrifice=Ugra (*LiP.* 1, 41, 29 ff.; 2, 13, 3 ff.).

83. Kirfel, *Kosmographie*, pp. 4* f.; 55. The shell of the mundane egg is enveloped by seven sheaths.

84. Cf. *LiP.* 1, 70, 51 f. ... *anyonyasya samāśrayāt // puruṣādhiṣṭitatvāc ca avyaktānugraheṇa ca / mahādayo viśeṣāntā hy aṇḍam utpādayanti te.*

85. *LiP* 1, 70, 52 ff. The eight coverings are st. 59 called the eight prakṛtis: cf. *Mbh.* 13, 16, 54 *aṣṭam prakṛtayaś caiva prakṛtibhyaś ca yaḥ paraḥ* (sc. *śivaḥ*) and Nīlakaṇṭha's note: *aṣṭau bhūmir apo 'nalo vāyuḥ khaṃ mano buddhir ahaṃkāraś ca paraḥ māyāvī.*

86. *LiP.* 2, a. 12; cf. 1, 28, 15 ff. *devadevasya mūrtyaṣṭakaṃ idaṃ jagat*; 1, 103, 42 *asya devasya rudrasya mūrtibhir vihitaṃ jagat.*

87. Compare also R. Garbe, *Die Sāṃkhya-Philosophie*, Leipzig, 1917, pp. 305 ff.

88. The doctrine of the *aṣṭamūrter ananyatvam*: *LiP.* 1, 86, 131 ff.; 2, 13, 19 ff.

89. Cf. ṚV. 10, 90, 13 and remember *KB.* 6, 1 ff.

90. *LiP.* 1, 28, 16.

91. *LiP.* 2, 12, 5 f. (comm.) *tena* (*ātmanā*) *śivasyāṣṭamūrtitvena agnihotre sūryātmani sūryarūpe mahātmani paramātmani arpite sati tathā vṛkṣaśākhopaśākhāsadṛśās tadvibhūtīs tadaṃśāḥ sarvadā tṛpyanti.*

92. See *ViṣṇuP.* 1, 8, 2 ff.; *MārkP.* 49, 2 ff.; *VāP.* 1, 27, 1 ff.; *BmḍP.* 1, 10, 1 ff. (Vā. Bmḍ. represent an elaborate version); *KūrmaP.* 1, 10, 18 ff.; *SauraP.* 23, 1 ff., etc.

93. As in the *ŚB.*, not in the *KB.* version.

94. *sthānāni ViṣṇuP.* 1, 8, 5; *PadmaP.* 1, 3, 201; *MārkP.* 49, 69, etc.

95. For these names—with regard to which the purāṇic tradition is not homogeneous—see Meinhard, op. cit., p. 11 f.

96. For some exceptions see Meinhard, op. cit., pp. 12 ff.

97. Described by Hemādri, *Caturv.* I, 798, 13 ff.

98. See above, p. 39, n. 62.

99. *LiP.* 2, 45, 30 ff.

100. The Vedic *svāhā* is replaced by *namaḥ*; the Vedic triad *bhūr bhuvaḥ svaḥ* extended by *mahar janaḥ*, etc., the names of the higher celestial worlds.

101. Śivaites also claim that the 'Lord of eight-fold worth' is a reference to Śiva (see e.g. H. A. Popley, *The sacred Kural*, Calcutta, 1958, p. 90), the eight qualities being self-existence, pure essence, intuitive pure knowledge, omniscience, freedom from evil, graciousness, omnipotence, infinite bliss.

102. We also find *śivasya svarūpāṇi* (*LiP.* 2, 14, 2), or *mūrtayaḥ pañca* (ibid. 5) 'the five embodiments'. The term 'face' may be considered in the light of expressions such as *viśvatomukha*, which in the Ṛgveda (1, 97, 6) characterizes Agni and AV. 10, 8, 27 the One reality underlying the All as 'facing all sides' (the latter stanza is *ŚvU.* 4, 3 quoted to apply to Rudra-Śiva, the Īśvara), *caturmukha*, Brahmā's well-known epithet (which was also given to Śiva; cf. Meinhard, op. cit., p. 15, n. 3), etc. Compare R. Pettazzoni, *The*

All-knowing God, London, 1956, p. 125. For the 'face' as a mode of revelation of God's nature see also H. Ringgren, *Israelitische Religion*, Stuttgart, 1963, p. 79. Has *vaktra*—which in the famous epiphany *BhG.* 11, 23, 27 ff. is used in connection with Kṛṣṇa's divine outward appearance—been preferred to distinguish the term from the above *bahuvrīhi* compounds, or to mark it as Śivaite?

103. *TĀ.* 10, 43–47; *MNU.* 277–290.

104. See Lecture II.

105. In the *Mahābhārata*, Suvaktra is one of Śiva's thousand names: 13, 17, 43; 14, 8, 16.

106. Cf. also J. Varenne, *La Mahā Nārāyaṇa Upaniṣad*, Paris, 1960, I, p. 153; II, p. 38.

107. Cf. *TĀ.* 3, 14, 1.

108. *sadyojātaṃ prapadyāmi . . . bhavodbhavāya namaḥ.*

109. The expression *sadyo jātaḥ* occurs *PB.* 18, 1, 24 'In him who knows thus there is not even so much guilt as in a new-born child' (*kumāre sadyo jāte*).

110. With some variants.

111. The name is also found in a long enumeration of divine names *BaudhDhS.* 2, 5, 5 between the *nakṣatras* and the Bhūḥpuruṣa; Bhava, Śarva, etc. follow further on. Cf. also AV. 10, 8, 27?

112. Wilson and Hall, op. cit., I, p. 79.

113. He is here identified with Sanatkumāra, at the end of a chapter containing the instruction of Nārada by that 'Eternal Boy'. (For some particulars see S. Radhakrishnan, *The principal upaniṣads*, London, 1953, p. 468.)

114. 'Of the other seers, to whom the various books of the Ṛgveda are assigned . . . Vāmadeva, etc., there is still less reason to disbelieve the historic existence' (A. B. Keith, *The religion and philosophy of the Veda and the Upaniṣads*, p. 227).

115. *KB.* 28, 2; 29, 3; 30, 1; cf. also *AiB.* 3, 46.

116. See e.g. *AiB.* 6, 18, 2; *GB.* 2, 6, 1; *PB.* 13, 9, 27, and compare, in general, A. A. Macdonell and A. B. Keith, *Vedic Index*, II, [2]Benares, 1958, p. 286 f.

117. *AiB.* 4, 30, 2.

118. *AiĀ.* 2, 5, 1=*AiU.* 2, 1, 5 (=4, 5); cf. the note by R. E. Hume, *The thirteen principal Upanishads*, Oxford, 1934, p. 299 f.

119. ṚV. 4, 27, 1.

120. Cf. *BĀU.* 1, 4, 10.

121. ṚV. 4, 26, 2. According to the Anukramaṇī either the *ṛṣi* Vāmadeva praising himself as Indra or Indra is represented as engaged in self-praise. Compare also Sāyaṇa's note: . . . *garbhe vasan vāmadevaḥ utpannatattvajñānaḥ san sārvātmyaṃ svānubhavaṃ manvādirūpeṇa pradarśayann āha: ahaṃ vāmadeva indro vā manur abhavaṃ sarvasya mantā prajāpatir asmi; aham eva sūryaś ca sarvasya prerakaḥ savitā cāsmi.* From the Ṛgvedic point of view only Indra can be the person speaking.

122. *GB.* 2, 3, 23: 210, 4: *te 'bruvan vāmadevaṃ tvaṃ na imaṃ yajñaṃ dakṣiṇato gopaya, madhyato vasiṣṭham*, etc.

123. *AiĀ.* 2, 2, 1; in this connection the name Vāmadeva is explained: 'he who is dear to all of us' (the gods are speaking); cf. *ŚāĀ.* 2, 16.

124. *ŚāĀ.* 1, 2 'This is the *praüga śastra* of Vāmadeva . . . containing the word Ka (=Prajāpati). Vāmadeva indeed is Prajāpati; in Prajāpati so do they obtain all desires.'

125. *Mbh.* 3, a. 192; 2, 7, 15.

126. *Rāmāyaṇa*, 1, 7, 3, etc. For other information about persons called Vāmadeva see also V. R. Ramachandra Dikshitar, *The Purāṇa Index*, III, Madras, 1955, p. 190 f.

127. *MatsyaP.* 4, 27 f. *vāmadevas tu bhagavān asṛjan mukhato dvijān / rājanyān asṛjad bāhvor viṭchūdrān ūrupādayoḥ.*

128. See e.g. 23, 35 f. (=*PadmaP.* 1, 12, 30 f. and *Hariv.* 14842) and compare S. G. Kantawala, *Cultural history from the Matsyapurāṇa*, Baroda, 1964, p. 178 f. See also *VāyuP.* 97, 190; *BhāgP.* 2, 6, 36.

129. Compare e. a. *SauraP.* 5, 11 (a *muni*); 69, 38 (with Aṅgiras, Bharadvāja and other worshippers of Śiva); 47, 71; 48, 22 (=Śiva). According to *BhāgP.* 3, 12, 12 Vāmadeva is one of the eleven Rudras; 2, 6, 36 he is identical with Śiva; *BrP.* 2, 32, 99 the name belongs to a descendant of Aṅgiras and composer of Vedic hymns, etc. Compare Dikshitar, *The Purāṇa index*, III, p. 190. Meinhard's contention (op. cit., p. 19) that Vāmadeva unlike Aghora appears only as a member of the *pañcavaktra* can create misunderstanding.

130. He is also said to be a form of Maheśvara (in the 32nd *kalpa*); then he is all black (*VāyuP.* 23, 29).

131. For particulars see Meinhard, op. cit., p. 19 f.

132. For the force of adjectives beginning with the privative *a-* in general see my *Four studies in the language of the Veda*, The Hague, 1959, pp. 95 ff. The above adjective is especially used in connection with the idea opposite to that of the evil eye (e.g. AV. 7, 60, 1; 14, 2, 12; cf. ṚV. 10, 85, 44), for which see *Eye and gaze in the Veda*, Amsterdam Academy, 1969. For the use of *aghora* compare also *ĀpŚS.* 9, 16, 11; 16, 16, 4; 16, 25, 2; *MGS.* 1, 12, 3 f., etc.

133. *VS.* 16, 2; *TS.* 4, 5, 1, 1; *MS.* 2, 9, 2: 120, 18; *KS.* 17, 11. Among Śiva's thousand names is Aghoraghorarūpa (*Mbh.* 12, 10375C.).

134. I refer to H. Oldenberg, *Vorwissenschaftliche Wissenschaft*, Göttingen, 1919, pp. 100 ff.

135. See e.g. AV. 11, 4, 9; 14, 2, 50; *KS.* 36, 13: 79, 12 f.; *ŚB.* 10, 1, 3, 2; 4, etc.; AV. 1, 33, 4; *TS.* 2, 2, 2, 3 ('Rudra is his dread form'); cf. also *ŚB.* 12, 8, 3, 11. The adjective *ghora* is equivalent to Ugra (e.g. Sāyaṇa on *TĀ.* 10, 45).

136. Cf. also *NīlarU.* 1, 8 and *ŚāṇḍU.* 3, 1 *athāsya devasyātmaśakter ātmakrīḍasya bhaktānukampino ... tanūr avāsā indīvaradalaprakhyā caturbāhur aghorāpāpakāśinī* (the last two words being borrowed from the above stanza).

137. *TĀ.* 10, 45 *aghorebhyo 'tha ghorebhyo aghoraghoratarebhyaḥ / sarvataḥ śarva sarvebhyo namas te rudra rūpebhyaḥ.* According to the commentary attributed to Sāyaṇa this *mantra* 'states' the Southern face.

138. See however *LāṭyŚS.* 10, 13, 4 *tatpuruṣasya nārāyaṇasyāyanam.*

139. *TĀ.* 10, 46; *MNU.* 284, cf. e.g. also *TPVNārU.* 7, 43.

140. For *tat* (*etat*, cf. *idam*) in this sense see *Rām.* 6, 117, 25 Bo. *naitad asti tvayā vinā.*

141. See *LiP.* 1, 17, 89 f.; 2, 25, 91 ff. (prescribing the *mantras īśānamūrtaye svāhā*, etc., which accompanying *nyāsa* practices enable the worshipper to introduce the Divine Person into his own body: *LiP.* 1, 26, 37 f.; cf. Lecture IV, p. 82).

142. It may be remembered that the elements, though widely accepted as five in number, do not always and everywhere comprise the same provinces of nature (see W. Kirfel, *Die fünf Elemente*, Walldorf, 1951, pp. 7 ff.).

143. The twenty-fifth 'spirit' is co-ordinated with *prakṛti*, *buddhi*, etc. and, interestingly enough, identified with Īśāna (*LiP.* 2, 14, 6). For the development of this doctrine compare also A. B. Keith, *The Sāṃkhya system*, 2Calcutta, 1949, pp. 35 ff.

144. *pañcaviṃśatitattvātmā pañcabrahmātmakaḥ śivaḥ* (*LiP.* 1, 14, 33).

145. *ŚB.* 10, 1, 3, 4; *AiB*, 5, 25, 21 *eṣa kṛtsnaḥ prajāpatiḥ.*

146. *pāṅkta*: *ŚB.* 10, 4, 2, 23.

147. *Die Religionen Indiens*, I, pp. 191 ff.

148. *ŚB.* 6, 1, 2, 17 ff.

149. i.e. the space between earth and air and that between air and heaven.

150. Cf. *ŚB.* 1, 5, 2, 16 dealing with the fire-offerings: 'There are five utterances (ritual formulas) ...; fivefold is the sacrifice, fivefold the animal victim, five are the seasons of the year: this is the one measure of the sacrificial rite, this its completion'.

151. Cf. *Change and continuity*, p. 122 f.

152. *AVŚ.* 1, 30, 4 *yeṣāṃ vaḥ pañca pradiśo vibhaktāḥ.*

153. Cf. also ṚV. 2, 13, 10; *JUB.* 1, 34, 6.

154. *AVŚ.* 3, 4, 2; 13, 3, 6; see e.g. *VS.* 10, 10 ff. *ŚB.* 5, 4, 1, 3 ff. and compare J. C. Heesterman, *The ancient Indian royal consecration*, Thesis, Utrecht 1957, pp. 103 ff.

155. ṚV. 9, 86, 29.

156. See e.g. ṚV. 1, 89, 10 (=*AVŚ.* 7, 6, 1); 3, 59, 8; 4, 38, 10; 5, 86, 2; 6, 61, 12; 7, 69, 2 etc.; *AVŚ.* 6, 75, 3; 12, 1, 15; 12, 1, 42, etc. The expression *pañca janāḥ* does not, in the brāhmaṇas, refer to a confederacy of five peoples (W. Rau, *Staat und Gesellschaft im alten Indien*, Wiesbaden, 1957, p. 19, n. 2; cf. also B. Schlerath, *Das Königtum im Rig- und Atharvaveda*, Wiesbaden, 1960, p. 51 f.). Compare L. Renou, *Études védiques et pāṇinéennes*, IX, Paris, 1961, p. 97.

157. Cf. also *AVŚ.* 11, 6, 22 'the five divine directions' (*yā devīḥ pañca pradiśaḥ*); 3, 20, 9 and especially 3, 24, 3 'these five directions which there are, the five races of men (*kṛṣṭayaḥ*)'.

158. See also *AVŚ*. 13, 1, 18.

159. *AiB*. 8, 28, 2 (lightning, rain, moon, sun, fire: *pañca devatāḥ*).

160. See also *ŚB*. 6, 1, 2, 32. For fivefold ritual acts etc. see *AVŚ*. 4, 14, 7; 9, 5, 8 and see also 8, 9, 4; 11, 3, 18. For five rice-dishes see *AVŚ*. 9, 5, 37. See also *AVŚ*. 8, 6, 22 (five-footed); ṚV. 1, 122, 13 (twice five foods).

161. *AiB*. 1, 19, 8 five stanzas; 2, 14, 3; *ŚB*. 1, 9, 1, 17 five prayers; 2, 2, 3, 14 five potsherds; see e.g. also 2, 1, 1, 12; 2, 4, 4, 25; 5, 1, 2, 4; 5, 4, 5, 13; 5, 5, 1, 1; 8, 2, 1, 13; *JB*. 1, 256; *PB*. 9, 5, 10; *MŚS*. 5, 2, 2, 4.

162. For the five sensory organs (*indriyāṇi*) 'with "mind" (*manas*) as the sixth' see *AVŚ*. 19, 9, 5.

163. See also *The Savayajñas*, p. 130 f. The question as to how far the five fingers (see e.g. ṚV. 4, 6, 8; 8, 72, 7; 9, 98, 6; *ŚB*. 1, 1, 2, 16) and customs adopted in counting exerted influence in creating this system cannot be discussed here. For the 'five kingdoms of plants' see *AVŚ*. 11, 6, 15; for five (classes of) creatures 11, 2, 9.

164. Other places of interest are ṚV. 10, 55, 3; 2, 34, 14 and 3, 7, 7 (five officiants).

165. Cf. AV. 8, 9, 15 returning *PGS*. 3, 3, 5 and elsewhere; 9, 5, 25 f.; *ŚB*. 1, 8, 1, 39; *PB*. 6, 7, 12.

166. See e.g. *ŚB*. 1, 7, 2, 8; 2, 1, 1, 12; 5, 2, 4, 8; 14, 1, 2, 14; *PB*. 9, 9, 15; *AiB*. 3, 23, 5; 5, 18, 20; *JUB*. 2, 3, 6; 2, 4, 5; *ŚŚS*. 14, 4, 3.

167. *ŚB*. 2, 4, 4, 24 'he thus (by a definite ritual act and the accompanying *mantras*) effects a union (*mithunīkaroti*) between the quarters and the seasons'. In this connection the five seasons come likewise very much into prominence.

168. *ŚB*. 6, 1, 2, 17; 19; 9, 5, 1, 39.

169. *ŚB*. 2, 4, 4, 25 'five (four officiants and the sacrificer) partake of that . . ., for the seasons are five and so that *rūpa* of the seasons is thereby obtained'.

170. Attention may also be drawn to groups of five consisting of four homogeneous elements and 'a fifth', e.g. *ŚB*. 8, 6, 1, 11 (cf. 14).

171. See e.g. *TS*. 1, 5, 1, 3; *ŚB*. 1, 5, 3, 1 'The fore-offerings are the seasons; hence there are five of them, for there are five seasons'; 2, 2, 3, 14; 3, 1, 4, 5 (five libations); 5, 1, 2, 9; 5, 4, 4, 6 (*diśah*: regions); 6, 1, 2, 18; 9, 4, 3, 10; 9, 5, 1, 39; *PB*. 12, 4, 8; 21, 15, 5 'this five-day rite is a complete *vrata*, for there are five seasons' (see also *AiB*. 1, 7, 15); *ĀpŚS*. 18, 9, 10 f. and compare Oldenberg, op. cit., p. 46; *Die Religionen Indiens*, 1, p. 177 f. It may be observed that the number five may also be obtained more or less artificially, for instance by adding heterogeneous entities: *ŚB*. 5, 2, 4, 9.

172. *ŚB*. 5, 4, 4, 9 ff.; *ŚŚS*. 16, 18, 3 ff.

173. *ŚB*. 8, 6, 1, 22.

174. *JUB*. 4, 7, 1; *ChU*. 3, 13.

175. *TU*. 1, 3, 1.

176. For other upaniṣadic pentads see *BĀU*. 4, 4, 17 'that (him) in which the five groups of five (explained as *gandharvas*, Fathers, gods, demons and *rākṣasas* or the five *varṇas*, including the outsiders, Śaṅkara) are established, that (him) alone I regard as the Self'; *PrU*. 3, 12 fivefold *vibhutvam* (faculty of powerful extension). In later upaniṣads, etc., there are more groups of five.

177. *MaiU*. 2, 6, 6, cf. 7 and 9; compare *PrU*. 2, 3.

178. See e.g. *MS*. 2, 8, 10 (cf. *MŚS*. 6, 2, 2, 5); *ĀpŚS*. 5, 18, 2 (cf. *TB*. 1, 1, 10, 1–3 and 6); 18, 9, 10 f.; 21, 21, 11; 14; *ŚB*. 11, 7, 4, 4; *MŚS*. 5, 2, 2, 4; 6, 2, 4, 17 (the mantras being: 'To him sitting in the trees; . . . in men; . . . in the water; . . . in the sacrificial grass; . . . in the wood, hail!'; *Kauś*. 57, 21.

179. *BĀU*. 1, 4, 17: 'Now his (man's) completeness (*kṛtsnatā*) is (as follows): mind . . ., etc., fivefold is this All . . .' (*pāṅktam idaṃ sarvaṃ yad idaṃ kiṃ ca*). Compare *The Savayajñas*, p. 241 f.

180. Cf. *MuU*. 3, 1, 9.

181. *TU*. 1, 7. Compare *ChU*. 2, 21, 3 and also *ŚB*. 10, 2, 6, 16 ff.

182. *ŚŚS*. 16, 24, 2.

183. *ChU*. 5, 10, 10.

184. It may also be remembered that the sacrifice is called *pañcayāman* (ṚV. 10, 52, 4; 10, 124, 1); that ṚV. 5, 42, 1 speaks of five sacrificial priests, 1, 164, 13 of a wheel with five spokes, etc.

185. It distinguishes (see e.g. *PadmaP.*, *Śivagītā*) five forms of final emancipation, viz. *sālokya* (being in the same 'world' with God, residence in the same 'heaven' with God), *sārūpya* (similarity of form), *sārṣṭya* (equality in rank, condition or power), *sāyujya* (intimate union or communion with God, absorption), *kaivalya* (isolation, 'being absolute'). Remember also the doctrine of the five *kañcukas* (*Die Religionen Indiens*, II, p. 204); the five purifications (of the body, the place, the utensils, the *mantra* and the *liṅga*), the formula *namaḥ śivāya*, (five syllables), etc.

186. Not to forget the *pañcāyatana-pūjā* (*Die Religionen Indiens*, I, p. 321 f.).

187. Hence his name Pañcamantratanu, compare *Sarvadarśanasaṃgraha*, 7, 59 f. For some details see Meinhard, op. cit., p. 17 f.

188. Compare also their use in the Sakalīkaraṇa ritual (see Lecture IV, p. 84 and see above, p. 42). See e.g. also *Somaśambhupaddhati*, I, 39.

189. H. Brunner-Lachaux, *Somaśambhupaddhati*, I, Pondichéry, 1963, p. XXXIII.

190. See e.g. Brunner-Lachaux, op. cit., pp. 32 (preparation of sacred ashes made of cow-dung); 40 (ritual bathing); 188 (a fourfold rite of invocation and installation, God being considered 'complete' with the fifth *mantra* addressed to Īśāna); compare *LiP.* 1, 27, 29 ff.; 2, 24, 23. For a last (and central) place of Īśāna—who is beyond the comprehension of even the yogins (Banerjea, op. cit., p. 460)—see also *LiP.* 1, 81, 14 ff. Mention is also made of a fivefold division of the sacrificial rites corresponding to the five mantras and 'faces' (ibid., p. 256); of a fivefold sequence of the acts pertaining to the *dīkṣā* (*LiP.* 2, 21, 32 ff.). See also Meinhard, op. cit., pp. 18 f.; R. G. Bhandarkar, *Vaiṣṇavism, Śaivism etc.*, Strassburg, 1913, p. 124, n. 1; R. V. Joshi, *Le rituel de la dévotion kṛṣṇaite*, Pondichéry, 1959, p. 31 f.

191. Brunner-Lachaux, op. cit., p. 180.

192. Brunner-Lachaux, op. cit., p. x. For Śiva's functions see *Die Religionen Indiens*, II, p. 198. One may also consult J. Ch. Chatterji, *Kashmir Shaivism*, Srinagar, 1914, pp. 41 ff.—The influence of this Śivaite doctrine can for instance also be seen in Indian music: the origin of the five jātis is traced to Śiva's five faces; as Naṭarāja 'Lord of dancers' he is supposed to have worked these out in his dance (H. A. Popley, *The music of India*, New Delhi, [3]1966, p. 75).

193. See also *Sarvadarśanasaṃgraha*, 7, 61 ff.

194. The fivefold distinction is so important that this Sadāśiva (cf. *Die Religionen Indiens*, II, p. 202) conception is also said to constitute a pentad, for which see Brunner-Lachaux, op. cit., p. XI.

195. The name is explained as 'the Eternal, ever-existent Śiva', cf. Nīlakaṇṭhadīkṣita, *Śivatattvarahasya* quoted by H. Mitra, op. cit., p. 231, n. 2: *sadā sarvakāleṣu vartamānaḥ śivaḥ sadāśivaḥ . . . tatra brahmāviṣṇurudramaheśvaramūrtīnām uttarottaracirakālavartitve 'pi sadāśivākhyapañcamamūrtyapekṣayā kadācitkīṃ rudramūrtiṃ vyāvartayituṃ sadeti viśeṣaṇopādānasaṃbhavāt . . . yad vā paramaśive vā kevalayaugiko 'yam draṣṭavyaḥ. tatra kālāvac chedarahite sadāpadasāmañjasyāt.*

196. I refer to Banerjea, op. cit., p. 573, who adds some iconographical details and their underlying 'symbolism'. Īśāna—who is invisible—is, according to Mandana, quoted by Banerjea (p. 574) to be placed on the top because he stands for the celestial vault or space (*vyoman* or *ākāśa*). For Sadāśiva see especially Haridas Mitra, 'Sadāśiva worship in early Bengal', *Journal and Proceedings Asiatic Soc. of Bengal*, XXIX (1933), pp. 171 ff.; M. Th. de Mallmann, *Les enseignements iconographiques de l'Agni-Purāṇa*, Paris, 1963, pp. 54 ff. and compare also Brunner-Lachaux, op. cit., p. 180. Unlike the Tantric texts the Purāṇas contain only a few references to Sadāśiva's 'outward appearance': cf. *ViDhP.* 3, 48, 6 ff. The descriptions are in agreement that he represents the *ākāśa tattva* and his five faces the five elements. These descriptions were studied by H. Mitra, op. cit., There are, however, some differences among the Śākta tantras, the Āgamas and the purāṇas regarding Sadāśiva's position, etc.; the tantras for instance consider him only a manifestation of the Supreme Being, the Āgamas identify him. They agree, however, in identifying him with Īśāna. It seems that the worship of this figure—that is this variety of the Śivaite cult—was coeval with the Śaivāgamas and the tantras. He occupies an important position in tantric cosmogony. Archaeological remains seem (as far as Bengal is concerned) to point to the existence of his worship in the VIIIth–XVth centuries. The conception was probably introduced from the South before or about the Pāla period.

197. Cf. e.g. *LiP.* 2, 14, 1 f. *pañca brahmāṇi*; 3 *pañcabrahmātmakaḥ śivaḥ*.

198. The state in which—in the course of the evolution of the universe—there is for the first time the experience which may be 'spoken of' (*ākhyā*) as 'being' (*sad*); see Abhinavagupta, *Pratyabhijña-Vimarṣiṇī*, 3, 1, 2. For the Sādākhya of Kashmir Śaivism see Chatterji op. cit., pp. 65 ff.

199. Cf. Banerjea, op. cit., p. 479, and especially H. W. Schomerus, *Der Çaiva-Siddhānta*, Leipzig, 1912, pp. 70; 75; 135 f., etc. An image of Sadāśiva should be of white colour and have five faces which primarily represent the aspects Sadyojāta, etc. which in their turn are associated with the five Sādākhyas: D. N. Shukla, *Vastu-Sastra*, II, Gorakhpur, 1958, p. 252 f. For Śiva's fivefold *śakti* (his immanent, creative aspect), viz. the power of self-revelation, the power of realizing absolute bliss and joy, the will-power, the power of knowledge and the power of assuming every form (i.e. of creating) see Chatterji, op. cit., pp. 43 ff.

200. For the *kañcukas* see *Die Religionen Indiens*, II, pp. 204, 226.

201. Cf. e.g. *LiP.* 2, 23, 7 ff.; *Die Religionen Indiens*, II, p. 205.

202. See *Pañcabrahmop.* 1.

203. He is the Great God (Mahādeva), the Great Lord (Maheśvara), the Highest Lord (Parameśvara), etc.

204. Compare the 'theopanistic' passage *BĀU.* 2, 1, 20.

205. Notwithstanding the fact that the Pāñcarātrins asserted the orthodoxy of their creed (cf. *Die Religionen Indiens*, II, p. 120).

206. *BhāgP.* 4, 24, 33 ff. . . . *sarvasmā ātmane namaḥ || namaḥ paṅkajanābhāya bhūtasūkṣmendriyātmane | vāsudevāya śāntāya kūṭasthāya svarociṣi | saṃkarṣaṇāya sūkṣmāya durantāyāntakāya ca || namo viśvaprabodhāya pradyumnāyāntarātmane || namo namo 'niruddhāya hṛṣīkeśendriyātmane namaḥ paramahaṃsāya pūrṇāya nibhṛtātmane* . . .

207. Cf. *BhG.* 1, 15. In ancient works this name is derived from *hṛṣīka-* and *īśa-* explaining it as 'Lord of the senses' (*Hariv.* 14950=*Bh.* 279, 46). Following them modern translators speak also of 'the mover of everyone's faculties' (P. C. Roy).

208. See e.g. J. N. Farquhar, *An outline of the religious literature of India*, Oxford, 1920, pp. 98; 182 ff., etc. Renou in L. Renou and J. Filliozat, *L'Inde classique*, I, Paris, 1947, p. 647; Bhandarkar, op. cit., pp. 38 ff.; J. E. Carpenter, *Theism in medieval India*, London, 1921, pp. 220 ff.

209. For the name now see also V. Raghavan, in *J.A.O.S.*, LXXV, pp. 83 ff.

210. In an interpolated stanza *Mbh.* 12, 211, 612* (after 11). For Pañcaśikha see especially E. W. Hopkins, *The Great Epic of India*, New York and London, 1902, pp. 142 ff.

211. *Mbh.* 12, a. 321 ff.

212. It is worth noticing that *Mbh.* 12, 337, 63 ff. Bhagavān Nārāyaṇa, the Supreme Soul pervading the entire universe, from whom all acts are said to spring and who may be seen in all religious systems, is considered the promulgator and preceptor of the Pāñcarātra system. He is the sole object of the exposition and the sole object of worship. Those conversant with this religion will enter Hari (=Nārāyaṇa). Other references to Nārāyaṇa and the Pāñcarātra: *Mbh.* 12, 322, 24; 326, 100.

213. *Die Religionen Indiens*, II, p. 120.

214. I must refrain from entering here into a detailed examination of the relations between Pāñcarātra and Sāṃkhya, which are e.g. apparent from identifications such as that of Vāsudeva with the Paramātman, Saṃkarṣaṇa with the jīva, Pradyumna with manas and Aniruddha with ahaṃkāra (*Mbh.* 12, 326, 35 ff.; 12, 327, 26; cf. e.g. V. M. Apte, in Majumdar and Pusalker, *History and culture*, II, p. 447 and my above remarks, p. 41; compare also Śaṅkara, *Vedāntasūtra*, 2, 2, 42). There are also other correlations, for instance between the *vyūhas* (and Nārāyaṇa) on the one hand and the 'elements'—for which see e.g. R. Guénon, *Études sur l'Hindouisme*, Paris, 1966, pp. 45 ff.—on the other: *TriśBU.* 141 ff.; between the *vyūhas* (Vāsudeva being mentioned at the beginning as well as the end) and the fingers: *ŚukarU.* 2, 5.

215. Cf. Kumarappa, *The Hindu conception of the deity*, p. 102. The theory implies that the individual in his embodied form is regarded as derivable from God only after a series of emanations.

216. The Highest Being, Vāsudeva, is on the one hand 'bearer of the four *vyūhas*' and itself 'without *vyūhas*' (*KūrmaP.* 22, 245) and on the other characterized as *caturvyūha* (see

also R. C. Hazra, *Studies in the Upapurāṇas*, I, Calcutta, 1958, p. 133). Cf. e.g. also *GopUTU.* 35 ... *pradyumno 'haṃ sanātanaḥ*. For other views see further on (p. 53).

217. It is of course also an example of the Hindu habit of identifying one divine being with others by regarding the latter as forms of the former.

218. Farquhar, op. cit., p. 98. Wilson and Hall, *Vishṇu Purāṇa*, v, p. 16: 'arrangements' or 'dispositions'.

219. Banerjea, *Development of Hindu iconography*, p. 386.

220. S. Radhakrishnan, *Indian philosophy*, I, London, [5]1948, p. 491 ('form, manifestation', M. Monier-Williams, *Sanskrit-English Dictionary*, s.v.).

221. S. Dasgupta, *A history of Indian philosophy*, III, Cambridge, 1940, p. 37.

222. Thus the verb is used in connection with the teeth which while being arranged separately constitute a whole: *PGS.* 2, 6, 17; *HGS.* 1, 10, 1, etc., *annādyāya vyūhadhvam*, etc. The teeth have to stand in this way also for the sake of a long life and of brahmanical holiness. Compare also the military use of the term *vyūha* ('battle-array'; see e.g. R. P. Kangle, *The Kauṭilīya Arthaśāstra*, III, Bombay, 1965, p. 259) and its grammatical sense ('separation of the phonetic elements of a word for purposes of recitation'). These uses make the meaning 'aggregate, whole, structure' understandable. For a Buddhist use of the term see L. Silburn, *Instant et cause*, Paris, 1955, p. 203.

223. Cf. e.g. *ŚB.* 4, 5, 9, 1 (*tad yatraitad dvādaśāhena vyūḍhachandā yajate. tad grahā vyūhati vyūhata udgātā ca hotā ca chandāṃsi* ...) and the note by J. Eggeling, *The Śatapatha-Brāhmaṇa translated*, II, p. 418. See also *ŚB.* 4, 5, 9, 2; 4; 6, etc. and compare *KB.* 22, 1–3; 7; 23, 1; 3; *PB.* 2, 8, 1; 2, 10, 1; *KKS.* 46, 5.

224. *AiB.* 4, 27, 3 *chandāṃsi vyūhaty ayātayāmatāyai*.

225. A good explanation is furnished by the commentary: *svasvasthānaviparītatvenoḍhāni sthānāntare prakṣiptāni chandāṃsi yasmin dvādaśāhe so 'yaṃ vyūḍhachandāḥ*.

226. *tac ca vyūhanam asāratvaprayuktakālasya parihārāya bhavati*. See e.g. *ŚB.* 1, 5, 3, 25; 3, 1, 3, 8; *KB.* 14, 3; 26, 15; *JB.* 3, 104; and especially *ṢB.* 3, 7 ff.; *JB.* 3, 7; *PB.* 10, 5, 13; *ŚŚS.* 10, 2, 2.

227. Cf. also *ŚB.* 12, 3, 3, 2 'by means of the unexhausted element of the sacrifice they obtained all success that there is in the Veda'; 12, 4, 2, 8; *PB.* 14, 5, 7; 14, 11, 5; 15, 5, 5. A sacrifice which is exhausted in strength, passes as it were away from the performer (*ŚB.* 4, 5, 1, 13; 16).

228. *JB.* 3, 108 *tena viṣvañcaṃ pāpmānaṃ vyauhata* (subj. Prajāpati). According to *KB.* 27, 7 (cf. 27, 4) the performance in its transposed form serves to obtain all the metres.

229. *PB.* 2, 4, 2, and see the commentary; 3, 1, 2.

230. *TS.* 2, 6, 1, 5, the verb used being *vyauhan*. Compare also *TS.* 1, 7, 4, 2; *BhŚS.* 3, 5, 7, etc.; *TS.* 5, 2, 6, 3 f. sand is to be pushed asunder; if this act takes place after piling gravel (which has arisen from the interior reeds of Indra's vajra which had become crushed) the officiant may make a man rich in cattle. Compare also *KKS.* 31, 6.

231. *JB.* 3, 297; *PB.* 15, 11, 9.

232. *BĀU.* 5, 15, 2; *ĪśaU.* 16.

233. *ĀpŚS.* 3, 1, 2.

234. *TS.* 2, 3, 13, 3.

235. *ĀpŚS.* 18, 9, 11 f. See Caland's note in *Das Śrautasūtra des Āpastamba*, III, Amsterdam Academy 1928, p. 128. For the *mantras* see *TS.* 1, 8, 7c and d. Cf. also *ŚB.* 5, 2, 4, 6.

236. *JB.* 1, 237.

237. I also refer to *ĀpŚS.* 3, 19, 7.

238. *JB.* 2, 370; the passage refers to the 'pushing away' (*apauhat, apoḍha*) of evil. For a division of a sacrificial cake into eight parts see *ĀpGS.* 8, 22, 2.

239. Eggeling, op. cit., IV, p. 351; *ŚB.* 10, 4, 2, 4 ff.

240. Cf. also *TB.* 3, 3, 9, 1.

241. Morā is a village near Mathurā. See J. N. Banerjea, *Paurāṇic and tāntric religion (early phase)*, Calcutta, 1966, pp. 29 ff.; 37; the same, 'The holy Pañcavīras of the Vṛṣṇis', in *J.I.S.O.A.*, x, pp. 65 ff. and the same, *The development of Hindu iconography*, p. 93 f. The inscription—'probably of a considerably earlier date than the Kushan period' (Banerjea, *Iconography*, p. 93)—records that 'in the time of Mahākṣatrapa Rājavula's son Svāmī were enshrined, in the stone temple, the images of the worshipful (*bhagavatām*) pañcavīras of the Vṛṣṇis ...' (H. Lüders, *Epigr. Ind.*, XXIV, pp. 194 ff.).

242. *BmdP.* 2, 72, 1 f.; *VāP.* 97, 1 f. *manuṣyaprakṛtīn devān* ('gods of human origin') *devān kīrtyamānān nibodhata / saṃkarṣaṇo vāsudevaḥ pradyumnaḥ sāmba eva ca / aniruddhaś ca pañcaite vaṃśavīrāḥ prakīrtitāḥ.* Compare D. R. Patil, *Cultural history from the Vāyu Purāṇa*, Poona, 1946, p. 66 and V. Raghavan, in *Purāṇa* (Benares), III (1961), with reference to *MatsyaP.* 47, 23 f.

243. For two '*viras*'—not *vyūhas*—mentioned in the Ghosundi inscription (IInd century B.C.) see Banerjea, *Paurāṇic and tāntric religion*, p. 41; Kumarappa, op. cit., p. 99.

244. Of three of them, Vāsudeva, Saṃkarṣaṇa and Pradyumna, *dhvajas* (votive columns, 'reminding us not only of the memorial columns, one of whose early prototypes was the wooden *sthūṇā* of the Vedic burial mounds, but also of the yūpastambhas which were erected by kings and noble men of yore in commemoration of their performance of Vedic sacrifices', Banerjea, *Iconography*, p. 103), dating back to the Ist or IInd century B.C. were in all probability found at Besnagar (ibid., pp. 103 f.; 388, n. 1). See e.g. also B. N. Puri, *India in the time of Patañjali*, Bombay, 1957, pp. 183 ff.

245. V. M. Apte, in Majumdar and Pusalker, *History and culture of the Indian people*, II, p. 448 adds in explanation: 'probably because he was represented as the champion of solar worship in India and was very often identified with the Sun-god Himself' (see *Die Religionen Indiens*, I, p. 231, and for Sāmba, or Śāmba, A. Teeuw, *Bhomakāwya*, Thesis, Utrecht, 1946, pp. 11 ff.). One may also observe that Sāmba was Kṛṣṇa's younger son born of the non-Aryan Jāmbavatī and that under the influence of the tendency to view the Highest Being as fourfold he was likely to be eliminated. However, Varāhamihira, *Bṛhatsaṃhitā*, 58, 40 whilst omitting Aniruddha, makes mention of Sāmba after Kṛṣṇa and Baladeva and before Pradyumna, but the Viṣṇu-Smṛti (in its present form probably IIIrd century A.D.) mentions the four 'classical' figures (67, 2).

246. See e.g. *AgniP.* a. 308, 10. In Jaina texts the five Vṛṣṇi heroes are collectively described as the *baladeva-pamokkhā paṃcha-mahāvīrāḥ* (Banerjea, *Paurāṇic and tāntric religion*, p. 30).

247. Born of his chief queen Rukmiṇī.

248. *ViP.* 5, 18, 58 *oṃ namo vāsudevāya namaḥ saṃkarṣaṇāya te / pradyumnāya namas tubhyam aniruddhāya te namaḥ.*

249. For Saṃkarṣaṇa, etc., see e.g. *ViP.* 4, a. 15; 5, a. 1, and Dikshitar, *Purāṇic index*, III, p. 502 f.; for Pradyumna, *ViP.* 5, a. 27, etc. and Dikshitar, op. cit., II, p. 416 f.

250. Compare also Dikshitar, op. cit., III, p. 502 f.

251. See Varāhamihira, *BS.* 58 (57), 36 and cf. Banerjea, *Development of Hindu iconography*, p. 306; Hopkins, *Epic mythology*, pp. 12; 206; 212.

252. He is also called Lāṅgaladhārin 'Ploughbearer', etc. For his relations with the nāga cult see J. Ph. Vogel, *Indian serpent-lore*, London, 1926, p. 89; Banerjea, *Iconography*, p. 103.

253. Bhandarkar, *Vaiṣṇavism, Śaivism*, p. 3; Banerjea, *Paurāṇic and tāntric religion*, p. 10 f.: *Mahāniddesa* 89; 92.

254. *Mbh.* 1, 61, 91. See also J. J. Meyer, *Trilogie altindischer Mächte und Feste der Vegetation*, Zürich, 1937, I, pp. 206 ff.

255. See above, p. 42 f. and cf. e.g. Hopkins, *Epic mythology*, p. 227.

256. *ViDhP.* 3, 52, 13; cf. Banerjea, op. cit., p. 526. According to purāṇic records this eldest son of Kṛṣṇa and Rukmiṇī was Kāma in a previous birth (see Dikshitar, op. cit., II, p. 416). Cf. also W. Ruben, *Krishna*, Istanbul, 1943, p. 159.

257. I refer to my paper 'Viṣṇu's name Aniruddha', in the *Journal of the Akhila Bhāratīya Saṃskṛta Pariṣad*, 1 (1969), pp. 63 ff. For his adventures in purāṇic mythology, part of which are not recorded in the Mahābhārata, see Dikshitar, I, p. 54 f.; Hopkins, *Epic mythology*, pp. 48; 214; Ruben, op. cit., pp. 179; 193; 199.

258. Thus the name is used in connection with Viṣṇu's omnipresent might (*vaibhavam*) in the explanation of ṚV. 10, 90 given by the Mudgala-Upaniṣad.

259. *LakṣmīT.* 4, 10.

260. *Mbh.* 3, 327, 82.

261. *Mbh.* 12, 326, 37.

262. *Mbh.* 6, 61, 66; 12, 326, 37; 69.

263. Explanations of these divine names are not wanting in our sources. Thus according to a purāṇic account (*MatsyaP.* 248, 46 ff.) God owes his name Vāsudeva to the fact that

Brahmā and the other beings reside in him at the end of a yuga or alternatively that he resides in all creatures. Saṃkarṣaṇa is so called because he drags and unites (*saṃkarṣayati*) repeatedly in every period of the world. (Another explanation is given *ViP.* 4, 15, 15: he was drawn out of his mother's womb and placed in Rohiṇī.) Pradyumna is so named, because it is on account of him that gods and demons stand in opposing battle-arrays or because he knows (*pravidyuḥ*) all dharmas. The name Aniruddha is finally explained as the one who has no obstructor (*niroddhā*), or as the one whom nothing could deter in descending for the betterment and redemption of humanity (K. E. Parthasarathy, *Śrī-Viṣṇu Sahasranāmam*, Madras, 1966, p. 122, cf. p. 256).

264. See also K. Rangachari, *The Śrī-Vaiṣṇava Brāhmaṇas*, Madras, 1931, p. 27, etc., and compare e.g. *LakṣmīT.* 4, 8 ff.

265. *AnirS.* 2, 1 *aniruddhapraśastena pañcarātreṇa.*

266. *ŚB.* 11, 5, 8, 1.

267. *ŚB.* 11, 5, 5, 3 ff.

268. *ŚB.* 12, 3, 4, 1 ff.

269. *ŚB.* 6, 3, 1, 16.

270. *ŚB.* 2, 4, 2, 1 ff.; 6, 3, 1, 16.

271. *ŚB.* 10, 4, 2, 22.

272. *BhG.* 7, 19; 5, 29, etc.

273. The remark was already made by O. Lacombe, *L'absolu selon le Védânta*, Paris, 1937, p. 25, n. 4; see also Bhandarkar, op. cit., p. 12.

274. Cf. above, p. 41.

275. *BhG.* 7, 4 f.

276. *BhG.* 4, 6 . . . *prakṛtiṃ svām adhiṣṭhāya saṃbhavāmy ātmamāyayā*; for this stanza see E. Lamotte, *Notes sur la Bhagavadgītā*, Paris, 1929, p. 56 f.

277. *BhG.* 9, 8.

278. The reader may also be referred to Chattopadhyaya, pp. 32; 89 f.; W. Eidlitz, *Kṛṣṇa-Caitanya*, Stockholm, 1968, *passim.*

279. The ideas enunciated in the relative Pāñcarātra texts (cf. e.g. *Mbh.* 13, 326, 67 ff.) are far from uniform and the texts themselves in most cases difficult to date (VIIth–Xth century ?; see also Renou, in op. cit., I, pp. 647 ff.). Compare e.g. also Bhandarkar, op. cit., p. 7 f.; Farquhar, op. cit., pp. 97 ff.; Carpenter, op. cit., p. 221; Banerjea, *Iconography*, p. 387 f.; Patel, op. cit., p. 188 f.

280. Compare S. Dasgupta, *A history of Indian philosophy*, II, p. 545 f.

281. *Mbh.* 12, 336, 53 = 348, 57 Bo. and compare Nīlakaṇṭha's commentary. Compare also Dasgupta, op. cit., IV, p. 413; R. C. Hazra, *Studies in the purāṇic records on Hindu rites and customs*, Dacca, 1940, pp. 85; 225.

282. *Mbh.* 12, 331, 4 ff.

283. See Nīlakaṇṭha on *Mbh.* 12, 336, 4 (*nūnam ekāntadharmo 'yaṃ śreṣṭho nārāyaṇapriyaḥ / agatvā gatayas tisro yad gacchanty avyayaṃ harim: gatayaḥ gatīḥ aniruddhādīṃs trīn anupāsyaiva vāsudevaṃ gacchaty arthaḥ*).

284. Now see also E. Krishnamacharya, *Jayākhyasaṃhitā*, Baroda, 1967, pp. 18 ff.

285. *MārkP.* 4, 36 ff.

286. For other modified forms of the Vyūha doctrine see D. C. Sircar, in Majumdar and Pusalker, *History and culture*, III, p. 418.

287. Schrader, op. cit., p. 42; Banerjea, *Iconography*, pp. 235 f.; 388 f.; Dasgupta, op. cit., III, pp. 39 ff.

288. Some Pāñcarātra authorities are, significantly enough, of the opinion that all incarnations spring from Aniruddha.

289. *AhirbS.* 5, 50 ff.; 56, 2 ff.

290. For an enumeration and some observations about the composition of the list see Schrader, op. cit., pp. 42 ff.

291. See also Hazra, *Studies in the Upapurāṇas*, I, p. 133. The complication of the system led also to the assumption of a Vibhava-Saṃkarṣaṇa beside the *vyūha* of the same name; their iconic representations are however different.

292. *LakṣmīT.* 11, 47 ff.

293. D. L. De, quoted by Renou (Renou and Filliozat), op. cit., I, p. 647; Sircar, in Majumdar and Pusalker, *History and culture*, III, p. 418.

294. A. Hohenberger, *Rāmānuja*, Bonn, 1960, p. 31 f.

295. Rāmānuja, *Śrī-Bhāṣya*, 2, 2, 41.

296. Rāmānuja makes no use of the *vyūhas* to explain the evolution of the universe.

297. Rāmānuja, loc. cit.: *vibhavārcanād vyūhaṃ prāpya vyūhārcanāt paraṃ brahma vāsudevākhyaṃ sūkṣmaṃ prāpyate.*

298. They have nothing to do with the three guṇas of the Sāṃkhya system.

299. *AhirbS.* 5, 29.

300. For *śakti* in the Ṛgveda see also L. Renou, *Études védiques et pāṇinéennes*, IV, p. 55; V, p. 18 (ṚV. 3, 57, 3; cf. 3, 31, 14 where Geldner's translation 'gute Dienste' is inadequate). Cf. e.g. also AV. 3, 13, 3.

301. ṚV. 10, 88, 10: the god is Agni and *śakti* is in the plural. Compare 10, 134, 6 (see 3); from places such as ṚV. 2, 39, 7 (where the Aśvins are said to unite their *śakti* 'for us') it appears that this power is useful for the world; similarly 7, 68, 8 (not 'Geschicklichkeit', Geldner), and see also 10, 25, 5; *AiB.* 1, 29, 13, quoting ṚV. 1, 83, 3; AV. 2, 27, 7 Indra is requested to bless those praying with his *śaktis*; *VS.* 11, 63.

302. In ṚV. 5, 31, 6 Indra displays his *śakti* by separating the two halves of the universe which is a creative and inaugurative deed par excellence. See also *KB.* 23, 2 (Indra's *śakti* to slay Vṛtra); *VS.* 11, 57.

303. For some particulars see Schrader, op. cit., pp. 31 ff. The Pāñcarātrins speak of a chain of emanations, Saṃkarṣaṇa emanating from Vāsudeva in whom all the six guṇas are manifest, Pradyumna having *aiśvarya* and *vīrya*, from Saṃkarṣaṇa and Aniruddha with *śakti* and *tejas*, from Pradyumna.

304. See *ŚB.* 1, 1, 1, 22 *dvandvaṃ vai vīryam* ... *dvandvaṃ vai mithunaṃ prajananam*; 1, 9, 2, 6; 2, 3, 1, 23; 3, 8, 4, 7; 3, 9, 3, 34; 10, 5, 2, 8; 14, 1, 3, 1; *TB.* 1, 1, 9, 2, etc.; 5, 3, 3, 14 'they are double-named, for a coupling means strength'. One might also consider passages such as *PB.* 24, 12, 4 '... the Ādityas prospered (*ārdhnuvan*) pairwise: Mitra and Varuṇa, Dhātar and Aryaman, Aṃśa and Bhaga, Indra and Vivasvat; *ŚB.* 8, 6, 1, 22; *ChU.* 7, 4, 2; 7, 7, 1; *KB*, 14, 5; there are six seasons which are united in pairs and called 'summer, the rains, and winter'. For the dual deities which are a peculiar feature of Vedic mythology see A. A. Macdonell, *Vedic mythology*, Strassburg, 1897, p. 126.

305. For *tejas* see e.g. *ŚB.* 1, 2, 1, 13; 1, 2, 4, 7 (Vāyu).

306. *ŚB.* 1, 3, 2, 14; cf. also ṚV. 1, 80, 8. It might be recalled that the poet of ṚV. 1, 154 describes Viṣṇu's *vīryāṇi* (for Indra's *vīryāṇi* see 1, 32); for the Aśvins 1, 117, 25.

307. *PB.* 10, 1, 6; cf. *JB.* 2, 217 and see ṚV. 2, 22, 3.

308. *VS.* 11, 82.

309. *ŚB.* 11, 4, 3, 3; cf. also 6 ff.; compare also 12, 7, 1, 1 ff. describing the decomposition of Indra: from every limb his *indriyaṃ vīryam* (vital and psychical faculties and power) flowed away, from his mouth his *bala*, etc., and passages such as ṚV. 2, 16, 2.

310. For other combinations see e.g. *ŚB.* 13, 2, 6, 3; 5 *tejas* and *indriyam*; 13, 2, 6, 9; *PB.* 4, 2, 5, etc., *tejas* and *brahmavarcasa*; *PB.* 14, 9, 34 *tejas* and *haras* (probably 'conquering power'; see also J. Manessy, *Les substantifs en -as- dans la Ṛk-Saṃhitā*, Dakar, 1961, p. 184 f.). Compare also *ŚB.* 2, 5, 4, 8 Agni is *tejas*, Indra *vīrya*, etc.; similarly, 3, 9, 1, 19.

311. *indriyaṃ vīryam*: *ŚB.* 5, 2, 3, 8; 5, 3, 5, 7.

312. ṚV. 2, 16, 2.

313. *ŚB.* 3, 9, 1, 19; cf. 7, 4, 1, 39; 41.

314. *ŚvU.* 6, 8. This translation (cf. e.g. Silburn, *Śvetāśvatara Upaniṣad*, Paris, 1948) is decidedly to be preferred to '... die ... Tätigkeit, die aus seines Wissens Kraft besteht' (R. Hauschild). Note the occurrence of the term *śakti* in the same stanza.—The combination *jñānabalaiśvaryaśaktitejaḥsvarūpaḥ* occurs *TripViU.* 2, 15.

315. Rāmānuja, *Gītābhāṣya* 11, 19.

316. Cf. Hazra, *Studies in the Upapurāṇas*, I, p. 216. This important compilation (VIIth–Xth cent.), while being free from tantric influence and attaching little importance to the cowherd Kṛṣṇa who is foreign to the Pāñcarātrins (cf. Bhandarkar, op. cit., p. 39), shows special affinity with the Pāñcarātra current of thought. Emphasizing 'monotheism' in the Pāñcarātric sense (*ekāntabhava*) it recommends image worship and the use of Vedic and Hinduist mantras and teaches that final emancipation may be reached by entering Vāsudeva, Aniruddha, Pradyumna and Saṃkarṣaṇa.

317. Schrader, op. cit., p. 144 f.

318. Some information may be found in G. P. Malalasekera, *Dictionary of Pali proper names*, London, 1937–8, I, p. 108 f.; II, pp. 270; 858 f.
319. Cf. e.g. Apte, in Majumdar and Pusalker, op. cit., II, p. 449.
320. See my relative paper in *Festschrift-E. Frauwallner*, Vienna, 1968. This small work, whilst identifying Viṣṇu with the Primeval Person, is in substantial agreement with the main tenets of epic and post-epic, especially Pāñcarātric, Viṣṇuism. It contains occasional references to the Vyūha theory (cf. especially 1, 4 'Hari is the One of four *vyūhas*').
321. It may be remembered that *Mbh.* 12, 271, 61 Kṛṣṇa is said to be one quarter of Viṣṇu.
322. *AhirbS.* 59, 2–39; see also Schrader, op. cit., p. 143 f.
323. *AhirbS.* 59, 14 ff.
324. *AhirbS.* 59, 21.
325. See also *ChU.* 3, 12, 6.
326. See e.g. *BĀU.* 3, 7, and compare *Die Religionen Indiens*, II, p. 136, etc.
327. *AhirbS.* 59, 33 f. *purā sīdati kāryāṇi kārayan prāṇino 'khilān // phalāni puruṣebhyaś ca sanoti kriyayārcitaḥ / tataḥ puruṣa ity evam aniruddho 'bhidhīyate.*
328. See above, n. 320.
329. Cf. e.g. *GopUTU.* 42 *brahma māyayā catuṣṭayam*; *VāyuP.* 1, 1, 42 *maheśvaraḥ paro 'vyaktaś caturbāhuś caturmukhaḥ*; *KūrmaP.* 12, 13 *caturṣv api vedeṣu caturmūrtir maheśvaraḥ.*
330. For a 'quadruple' (*catuṣpādam*) brahman 'shining' in the four places' or receptacles (*sthānāni*) of the Puruṣa, viz. navel, heart, neck and skull, see *BrahmaU.* 1 f.
331. *Mbh.* 12, 321, 8 f.
332. *Rām.* 1, 14, 18 *tasya . . . viṣṇo putratvam āgaccha kṛtvātmānaṃ caturvidham*; 1, 16, 1.
333. *Mbh.* 12, 135, 28; 95, incorrectly regarded as a 'military epithet' by E. W. Hopkins, *The religions of India*, Boston, 1895, p. 442.
334. *ViP.* 2, 2, 14 ff.
335. See e.g. *LakṣmīT.* 8, 22, and compare also 10, 18 ff.
336. I cannot trace here the history of the Vyūha doctrine as far as this is known to us. There are no Vyūha images before the Gupta period, but then and afterwards their worship continued (cf. e.g. Banerjea, *Iconography*, *passim*; *Paurāṇic and Tāntric religion*, p. 58 f.). For some particulars, the various applications of the term (sometimes including also the incarnations) or the changed views on, or functions of, these divine persons see e.g. Bhandarkar, op. cit., pp. 53; 64; 84; Dasgupta, op. cit., III, pp. 157 f.; 475; IV, p. 27; Lacombe, op. cit., p. 326; Carpenter, p. 220 f.; H. von Glasenapp, *Madhva's Philosophie des Vishnu-Glaubens*, Bonn and Leipzig, 1923, pp. *26; 34 ff. etc.; Joshi, *La rituel de la dévotion kṛṣṇaite*, p. 49; Rangachari, *The Śrī-Vaiṣṇava Brāhmaṇas*, pp. 27 f.; 47 f.; 100; Kumarappa, op. cit., pp. 215 f.; 311 f. For some interesting iconographical details see De Mallmann, *Enseignements iconographiques de l'Agni-Purāṇa*, pp. 19 ff. (*AgniP.* 42 describes a Viṣṇu Viśvarūpa who seems to be a syncretistic aspect of the four *vyūhas*).
337. Banerjea, *Iconography*, p. 408 f.
338. *ViDhP.* 3, 47, 8 f.; cf. Banerjea, op. cit., pp. 572 f. and 409; Ch. Eliot, *Hinduism and Buddhism*, II, London, (1921), 1957, p. 198 f. Mention may also be made of the epithets beginning with *catur*-'four', part of which occur already in the Mahābhārata.
339. 'The lion- and boar-faces are thus primarily associated with the Pāñcarātra *vyūhas* and not with the Nṛsiṃha and Varāha incarnations, though the latter have helped to some extent the formation of this concept' (Banerjea, op. cit., p. 409).
340. Or is he called 'fierce, cruel' simply because none is his obstructor ?, or because presiding over final emancipation he is able to withold it ?
341. For another explanation see Banerjea, op. cit., p. 409.
342. *LakṣmīT.* 4, 19; *ViṣvaksenaS.* 125 ff. T. For the contradictory statements of the cosmic activities of the *vyūhas* see also Schrader, op. cit., p. 38.
343. There seems to have existed in Pāñcarātric circles whose system comprises five principal subjects—ontology (cosmology), liberation, devotion, yoga, and the objects of sense—, and who have five daily observances, admit the validity of five sacraments, and the existence of five focuses of obscuration by which the soul is infatuated (*LakṣmīT.* 12, 20 ff.), etc., a tendency to distinguish a fivefold Brahman from the fourfold Highest Reality. For particulars see Schrader, op. cit., p. 24 and see pp. 119; 171. Not all groups of five enumerated here are exclusively Pāñcarātric or Viṣṇuite. For 'five' in connection with Pañcaśikha see Hopkins, *Great Epic*, p. 144; for the fivefold activity of the Supreme

Brahman: *Mbh.* 12, 335, 83. The one Vāsudeva-Viṣṇu-Nārāyaṇa can moreover be conceived in five aspects: Para ('The Highest'), Vyūha, Vibhava, Antaryāmin and Arcā (the consecrated images).

344. *AhirbS.* 6, 25; God is Śrīvāsa, i.e. 'Lakṣmī never leaves His bosom' (Sarthaparvathy, op. cit., p. 244). *LakṣmīT.* 2, 11; 2, 18; 2, 55; 9, 2; 9, 54 f., etc.

345. Cf. also *JayākhyaS.* 4, 2 f.; 4, 60 f.

346. Cf. e.g. *LakṣmīT.* 2, 16 *lakṣmīnārāyaṇākhyātam . . . brahma sanātanam.* Yet, even in *pralaya* they 'become only as it were a single principle' (*AhirbS.* 4, 78). An interesting explanation of the essential unity of God (Viṣṇu) and his Śakti (Śrī-Lakṣmī), notwithstanding their appearance as two persons at the same time, is given at *LakṣmīT.* 8, 49: when the goddess arose from the ocean, she was only visible to the demons, while the gods saw only the male form.

347. E.g. *LakṣmīT.* 2, 16.

348. Viṣṇu himself being the *causa efficiens.* This is one of the favourite themes of the Lakṣmītantra. For a succinct survey see also H. von Glasenapp, *Entwicklungsstufen des indischen Denkens*, Halle (S.), 1940, p. 160 f. Viṣṇu is Śrīgarbha, an explanation of which is 'the whole cosmos is inside him both before and after creation' (Parthasarathy, op. cit., p. 175).

349. Cf. e.g. also *JUB.* 2, 4, 7.

350. ṚV. 1, 161, 1 *drúṇa íd bhūtím ūdima* 'we have only spoken of the origin (mode of formation) of the wood (which is to be the material for a goblet)': in st. 9 the question is discussed as to whether water or heat has contributed most to the genesis of wood.

351. *ŚB.* 11, 1, 5, 7. See also 12, 7, 2, 2; *PB.* 12, 13, 30. The term is in various contexts also translatable by 'prosperity, well-being', e.g. *TB.* 2, 5, 6, 5; 3, 7, 1, 3; *TĀ* 5, 8, 6 but *JB.* 1, 248 the opposite significantly is 'ruin, destruction'.

352. which also combines with other decidedly 'positive' concepts, e.g. ṚV. 8, 59, 7 *prajām puṣṭím bhūtím asmā́su dhattam.*

353. AV. 12, 1, 63 *śriyā́ṃ mā dhehi bhū́tyām.* Notice also *AiB.* 1, 13, 11 where *bhū-* and a derivative of *śrī-* run parallel: *yo vai bhavati yaḥ śreṣṭhatām aśnute* (cf. *Aspects of early Viṣṇuism*, p. 193).

354. *BhG.* 18, 78.

355. *ŚB.* 7, 2, 1, 17 '. . . he separates himself from evil, from annihilation. With "homage to Bhūti who has done this" they rise . . .'. See e.g. also *Rām.* 3, 44, 16.

356. In the Sītāyajña: *PārGS.* 2, 17, 9 f.; cf. *Aspects of early Viṣṇuism*, pp. 219; 224. Sītā 'the Furrow' is here the wife of Indra, the killer of Vṛtra.

357. *Mbh.* 12, 218, 8.

358. *Mbh.* 13, 135, 80.

359. *JUB.* 1, 46, 1 ff. (*bhūmānaṃ gaccheyam*).

360. I prefer this translation of *so ṣoḍaśadhātmānaṃ vyakuruta* to 'he divided himself into sixteen parts' (H. Oertel, *JAOS.*, XVI, p. 123). Among these aspects are *ābhūta sambhūti* and *śrī.*

361. *VS.* 31, 22.

362. *ŚB.* 11, 4, 3, 1; cf. *Aspects of early Viṣṇuism*, p. 223.

363. See e.g. *ĀśvŚS.* 5, 13, 10 etc.; *KŚS.* 16, 4, 24; *VaikhGS.* 1, 16: 1; *BhG.* 11, 48.

364. See above, p. 55. For particulars see Schrader, op. cit., pp. 30 ff.; Dasgupta, *History of Indian philosophy*, III, pp. 34 ff., esp. p. 52 f.

365. Schrader, op. cit., pp. 60 ff.

366. Schrader, op. cit., pp. 53 ff.

367. See e.g. also *LakṣmīT.* 8, 13 ff.

368. *LakṣmīT.* 3, 33.

369. *LakṣmīT.* 4, 40. Because the universe is produced from her, she is also called Prakṛti (ibid. 4, 51), see also ibid. 4, 42 ff.

370. See e.g. *LakṣmīT.* 4, 48.

371. See e.g. *LakṣmīT.* 13, 5 ff.; 15.

372. See my publication *Dhāman*, Amsterdam Academy, 1967, p. 32 f.

373. *saṃkoca*: *LakṣmīT.* 6, 36.

374. ṚV. 4, 22, 8; (cf. 1, 31, 18; *VS.* 11, 2; 18, 15); 1, 83, 3; for Indra's *śakti* (5, 31, 6 he is *śaktīvat*) see also 3, 31, 14 (where Geldner's translation 'nach deinen guten Diensten'

is inadequate); 7, 20, 10; AV. 3, 13, 3; *TS.* 5, 6, 1, 3; for the Aśvins' ṚV. 2, 39, 7; 7, 68, 8; for Soma's 10, 25, 5 (not 'Mitwirkung', Geldner); for Savitar's *VS.* 11, 63; *TS.* 4, 1, 6, 3; *TĀ.* 4, 3, 2.

375. AV. 2, 27, 7; ṚV. 10, 88, 10. For a 'materialization' of *śakti KB.* 23, 2.

376. See e.g. ṚV. 1, 106, 6; 4, 30, 17; 8, 14, 2; 8, 15, 13; 8, 37, 1; 8, 61, 5; AV. 1, 12, 10.

377. 'For by *śakti* ('power, emergy', Eggeling) one goes to the world of heaven' (*ŚB.* 6, 3, 1, 14). Cf. also *TS.* 4, 1, 1, 1.

378. *LakṣmīT.* 20, 7; cf. 50, 182, etc.

CHAPTER IV

1. One might, speaking quite generally and avoiding generalization, say that there are three classes of superhuman beings which largely correspond to the groups of the mainly vegetarian upper classes, the middle classes (mainly *śūdras*) and the scheduled groups: beside the above gods, the meat-eating partly benevolent and partly malevolent deities, who are more concerned with man's daily events, and the lowest group of the spirits, who have no permanent residence and contact with whom should be avoided, because they cause evil and misfortune. E. W. Harper, 'A Hindu village pantheon', *Southwestern Journal of Anthropology* XV (1959), (*Albuquerque, N. Mex.*), pp. 227 ff., dealing with a region in the Western Ghats of Mysore, draws attention to a terminological distinction: the term *dēvaru* is applied to the unique High God as well as to the gods of the highest group, the terms *dēvate* and *devva* to the members of the two other groups. Of course 'informants frequently differ in their opinions as to what or who a particular supernatural is' (Harper, op. cit., p. 234). One should not underestimate the significance of the cults of, and religious practices connected with, the various classes of divine and 'demoniac' beings in traditional Hinduism. Even in modern times religious activities may, in a village of approximately 2000 people in the North, occur on over 300 days of the year, every adult person being drawn into some rites or ceremonies. (For particulars: M. E. Opler, 'The place of religion in a North Indian village', *Southw. Journal of Anthrop.*, XV (1959), pp. 219 ff.; A. R. Beals, *Gopalpur, a South Indian village*, New York, 1962, pp. 54 ff.; compare e.g. also A. Daniélou, *Le polythéisme hindou*, Paris 1960, pp. 547 ff.; E. W. Harper (ed.), *Religion in South Asia*, Seattle, 1964, *passim.*)

2. It must be borne in mind that the name Vaiṣṇavas often covers worshippers of the *avatāras* Rāma and Kṛṣṇa. European authors and British administrators were not rarely inclined to use that term quite broadly; cf. e.g. H. A. Rose, *A glossary of the tribes and castes of the Punjab and the NW. Frontier provinces*, Lahore, 1919, I, p. 366, who even goes so far as to apply the term to any 'orthodox' Hindu who does not eat flesh, onions, or garlics and does not drink spirits, with the result that 'the numbers returned at our census as Vaiṣṇavas exceed greatly the numbers returned under any other sect'. In Sindh and elsewhere the term *Vaishnav* means only a 'vegetarian' (U. T. Thakur, *Sindhi culture*, Bombay, 1959, p. 134).

3. It should be emphasized that a worshipper of Śiva—who is often known as Mahādeva—is in a similar way not always a member of a Śivaite 'order' or community, although the term is generally applied to those who are more or less exclusively devoted to his worship (see also Thakur, op. cit., pp. 108 ff.). Like Viṣṇu, Śiva is known by many other names. Thus the Anāvils of Surat are, at least in the rural areas, almost all followers of Śiva under his name Śaṅkara, but Īśvar, Rudra, Hara, Sadāśiva, Mahādeva are also current designations of the god whose principal attribute is, here also, the power of destruction (T. B. Naik, in M. Singer, *Traditional India*, Amer. Folklore Soc., 1959, pp. 183 ff. (=*Journal American Folklore*, LXXI (1958), pp. 389 ff.). There may, moreover, exist numerous Śivaite sanctuaries in a village, and the villagers may regard the god as their guardian deity, this does not necessarily mean that they constitute a Śivaite community (see e.g. also T. K. Basu, *The Bengal peasant from time to time*, Calcutta, 1962, ch. VIII).

4. However, the greatest gods and the stories of their epic exploits are not well known in all villages.—It may be recalled that until the thirties of this century there was among the Indian population always a considerable demand for brahmans who, having memorized

part of the Veda, bear and hand down the 'Sanskritic' Hindu tradition consisting of doctrines, ritual prescriptions, rules of conduct, symbolism, versified texts concerning the ultimate truths, the nature of reality, the afterlife, final emancipation, etc. This tradition is only in part Vedic in character, other components may be called śāstric (resting on the smṛti literature and related religions and scientific subject-matter), purāṇic and more or less esoteric. Elements of this tradition are known very widely, but as an organized, systematic whole it is passed down within special groups or 'orders' of ascetics, part of which are bound together by worship of a particular god.

5. See e.g. above, n. 1 and W. Crooke, *The popular religion and folklore of North India*, Westminster, 1896 (new edition by R. E. Enthoven, *Religion and folklore of North India*, Oxford, 1926); D. C. J. Ibbetson, *Report on the . . . settlement of the Panipat Tahsil . . .*, Allahabad, 1883, p. 142; H. Whitehead, *The village gods of India*, Oxford, 1921; L. Dumont, *Une sous-caste de l'Inde du Sud*, Paris and The Hague, 1957, pp. 410 ff.; O. Lewis, *Village life in Northern India*, Urbana, 1958, p. 235.

6. The *nakṣatras* are already in Vedic texts (*KS*. 39, 13 etc.) presided over by definite deities (Agni, Prajāpati, Maruts, Rudra, Aditi . . . Viṣṇu, etc., cf. W. Kirfel, *Die Kosmographie der Inder*, Bonn and Leipzig, 1920, p. 35); Rudra and Viṣṇu are among those gods who are supposed to reside on various mountains (ibid., p. 103), etc., although in other contexts the same gods are co-ordinated with only a few prominent deities (Indra, Bṛhaspati, p. 101), or Viṣṇu's *avatāras* are, in a similar way, distributed over parts of the world. Compare e.g. also the *graha-śānti* described in VaikhSmS. 7, 13.

7. Some remarks on Varāhamihira's († 587) *Bṛhatsaṃhitā* may be subjoined here in substantiation. Together with Bṛhaspati, Indra, Agni, and eight other gods Viṣṇu is a lord of a lustrum (8, 21; 23; 26); diamonds belong, according to shape and colour, to Yama, Viṣṇu, Varuṇa, etc. (80, 8); names are said to be equal to synonymous terms of Agni, Viṣṇu, Indra, etc. (96, 16); Viṣṇu and Rudra-Śiva are among the lords of the *nakṣatras* (98, 4 f.), and the rulers of the lunar days (99, 1); there is a comet and a halo of Rudra-Śiva (11, 32; 34, 2); this god is (4, 30) mentioned in connection with the ornament on his head; prayers are, in a ceremony, addressed to Śiva, Nārāyaṇa and three other gods (48, 77); but in a long and solemn prayer Brahmā, Viṣṇu and Śiva precede the names of many other gods and powers (48, 55), a lustration of horses, etc., is to be performed when lord Viṣṇu awakes from his cosmic sleep (44, 1), and the same figure is as God and lord of Śrī praised by all the deities in order to obtain a powerful ensign, viz. Indra's banner (43, 3 f., cf. 30). For the worship of Viṣṇu see also 105, 6; 8, a passage obviously presupposing Viṣṇuite allegiance on the part of the reader: one should on definite days, for personal benefit, worship Viṣṇu and an asterism. Places such as 87, 22 and 25 (a bird in the South-West, the region of destruction, indicates the approach of a Kāpālika, a bird in the North meeting a Vaiṣṇava) are in harmony with widespread opinions (see Lecture V, p. 93). Nevertheless, there is an interesting contrast between the evil consequences of a portent appearing at images or emblems of both gods: in the case of Śiva it tends to the destruction of land and ruler; in that of Viṣṇu, of the 'worlds' (*loka*, i.e. of all positions of safety, etc.: 46, 8 and 11).

8. It should however be noted that both Śiva and Viṣṇu, besides their high qualities and main functions, have many other tasks and duties often corresponding to sub-manifestations of their personalities. This character of the gods imposes curious situations in religious practice. For instance, as no brahman would accept anything in charity in the name of Śiva who is known to be also the terrific god of destruction, no Sindhi brahman is willing to act as a temple priest of this god (Thakur, op. cit., p. 109). The terrific and orgiastic character of his religion has on the other hand often been exaggerated and unduly generalized. 'La voie du rituel śaiva (the authoress means the so-called Śuddha-śaiva sanskritic tradition of the South) se présente au contraire comme une voie saine et équilibrée, où les facultés de l'être sont utilisées et dirigées, ses besoins fondamentaux satisfaits et peu à peu transformés' (H. Brunner-Lachaux, *Le rituel quotidien dans la tradition śivaïte de l'Inde du Sud selon Somaśambhu*: *Somaśambhupaddhati*, I, Pondicherry, 1963, p. XL).

9. There are interesting cases of introduction of, for instance, Viṣṇu in an originally non-Viṣṇuite context. Thus Jagaddeva, Svapnacintāmaṇi 1, 129 (J. von Negelein, *Der Traumschlüssel des Jagaddeva*, Giessen, 1912, p. 136) 'who, in a dream, performs an act of worship etc. in connection with an image of the All-knowing one (i.e. Śiva) will be for-

tunate in all respects' was in a Viṣṇuite tradition of the text changed into the metrically incorrect '... of Viṣṇu'. I refer to lecture VI.

10. For these terms see e.g. M. N. Srinivas, *Religion and society among the Coorgs of South India*, Oxford, 1952; V. Raghavan, 'Variety and integration in the pattern of Indian culture', *The Far East Quarterly*, XV, pp. 496 ff.; D. Ingalls, 'The Brahman tradition', in M. Singer, *Traditional India*, pp. 3 ff. (*Journal Amer. Folklore* LXXI, pp. 209 ff.); M. Singer, 'Text and context in the study of contemporary Hinduism', *The Adyar Library Bulletin* XXV (1961), pp. 285 ff.; E. B. Harper (ed.), *Religion in South Asia, passim;* and my *Religionen Indiens*, II, ch. I. The distinction between 'Sanskritic' and 'non-Sanskritic' tradition(s) prevailing in modern anthropologic literature is not satisfactory so far as it is used to define contemporary phenomena, which should be studied not only from the historical but also from the functional point of view. Compare also V. Raghavan, op. cit., pp. 497 ff.

11. Thus for instance marriage ceremonies combine ancient (Vedic) sacramental rites with popular and local features and even members of the higher classes may, also with respect to religion and philosophy, accept a range of belief from the 'lowest (worship of plants, village deities, goddesses presiding over dire maladies, etc.) to the 'highest' (Vedantic philosophy). 'The lesser and popular belief is neither discounted nor discarded; rather it is conserved, integrated, refined, and informed by higher philosophy' (Raghavan, op. cit., p. 502). For the adoption of deities see e.g. R. C. Hazra, *Studies in the Upapurāṇas*, II, Calcutta, 1963, pp. 25 ff.

12. See e.g. Whitehead, *The village gods of South India*; W. Th. Elmore, Dravidian gods in modern Hinduism, University studies Nebraska 15, Lincoln, 1915, I (Madras 1925); N. Macnicol, *The living religions of the Indian people*, London, 1934, esp. pp. 48 ff.

13. C. G. Diehl, *Church and shrine*, Uppsala, 1965, p. 23.

14. This seems to be Whitehead's (op. cit., pp. 132 ff.) assumption. In studying this problem we should not overlook those cases in which the same local deity is equated by part of the population with Śiva, by others with Viṣṇu (see e.g. G. D. Berreman, *Hindus of the Himalayas*, Los Angeles, 1963, pp. 100; 376; cf. 102; 385 f.).

15. For a definition see Bhaṭṭa-Nārāyaṇakaṇṭha on *Mṛgendrāgama*, K. 8, I (*karmavāsanākṣapaṇapūrvakaṃ jñānadānena bhuktimuktiphalasādhanī, aśuddhasya iṣṭasādhanī śuddiḥ*).

16. The Vedic ceremony in which a brahman 'teacher' receives a boy as a pupil to give him instruction and to initiate him into one of the three twice-born classes (*Die Religionen Indiens*, I, pp. 119; 124). The semantically dominant element may change, so that the term is applicable to a period of ascetic abstinence and austerity, for instance in case of death etc.; see e.g. E. K. Gough, in Singer, *Traditional India*, pp. 254 ff.

17. For an historical survey of this institution emphasizing the similarities between Vedic and post-Vedic consecratory and initiatory ceremonies see my book *Change and continuity*, The Hague, 1965, ch. X.

18. See *Change and continuity*, pp. 277; 422, and compare e.g. the description of the ideal teacher in *Ahirbudhnya-Saṃhitā*, ch. 20.

19. *Change and continuity*, pp. 409; 413; cf. e.g. *VarP.* 127, 9 ff.; *Haribhaktivilāsa*, 2, 127–155.

20. Cf. also T. M. P. Mahadevan, *Outlines of Hinduism*, Bombay, 1956, pp. 201 ff.

21. In many particulars there are, in this connection also, variations in the prescriptions given by the authorities even when they belong to the same school of religious belief. See e.g. *Change and continuity*, loc. cit., *passim*; R. V. Joshi, *Le rituel de la dévotion kṛṣṇaite*, Pondicherry, 1959, pp. 11 ff.

22. For the *guru* see *Change and continuity*, ch. VIII.

23. Ibid., pp. 231; 234.

24. Cf. e.g. *Varṇāśramacandrikā*, Dharmapuram, pp. 57; 59.

25. See also *Change and continuity*, p. 280 f.

26. When a soul has, in the course of transmigration, reached a considerable state of purity so as to strive after omniscience—which leads to emancipation—Śiva, extending his grace, instructs it, manifesting himself as a *guru* or as an internal light. See also *Change and continuity*, p. 429.

27. *Change and continuity*, p. 394. See e.g. also Dumont, *Une sous-caste de l'Inde du Sud*, p. 418.

28. Cf. *Die Religionen Indiens*, II, p. 235 f.

29. Cf. *Ahirbudhnya-Saṃhitā*, a. 20.

30. S. C. Nandimath, *A handbook of Vīraśaivism*, Dharwar, 1942, p. 67; Shree Kumaraswamiji in H. Bhattacharyya, *The cultural heritage of India*, IV, [2]Calcutta, 1956, pp. 100 ff.

31. The term *samaya* means 'a ceremonial custom or observance which may have the character of a covenant'. See e.g. A. Avalon, *Kulārṇava Tantra*, Madras, 1965, p. 104.

32. but not obliged.

33. There are two higher grades, viz. the special *dīkṣā* (*viśeṣadīkṣā*) by which one becomes qualified for the fire cult and the *nirvāṇadīkṣā* by which the *ātman* is freed from all fetters and fit to be united with Śiva (Southern Śivaism).

34. They have of course Śaiva symbols branded on their bodies.

35. The last element is nowadays a formality.

36. An etymologically untenable explication of the term may help us in understanding what a *mantra* meant to them: the first syllable expresses the idea of omniscience, the second that of final deliverance (cf. e.g. *Mṛgendrāgama*, K. 1 comm.).

37. The requisites to be procured by him—and which are partly known from the Vedic *upanayana* and partly typically Hindu—are in harmony with the candidate's social status, a brahman presenting a black antelope's skin, a kṣatriya the skin of a black he-goat, etc.; see *Change and continuity*, pp. 409 ff.

38. According to some authorities the caste of the aspirant and the extent to which his *mala* has ripened are important factors to be considered.

39. I cannot enter here into a discussion of Tantrist *dīkṣā*, on which I made a few observations in *Change and continuity*, pp. 435 ff.

40. Viz. the *kriyāvatī* 'which is in accordance with the rites': Joshi, op. cit., p. 12.

41. This procedure is called the *varṇamayī* ('that connected with letters, sounds, syllables').

42. Compare also *Change and continuity*, p. 443.

43. For Viṣṇu's emblems and attributes see *Aspects of early Viṣṇuism*, pp. 96 ff.; see also pp. 217; 94 f.; 153. For the cosmic significance of the conch—which is also one of the treasures of the universal sovereign or *cakravartin*—compare C. Marcel-Dubois, *Les instruments de musique de l'Inde ancienne*, Paris, 1941, p. 8 f.; M. Th. de Mallmann, *Les enseignements iconographiques de l'Agni-Purāṇa*, Paris, 1963, p. 257 f. and see *Dīgha Nik.* 23, 19. For the discus De Mallmann, op. cit., p. 252. The above formulation takes into account the probability of reinterpretation, or rather of the multivalent nature of these emblems.

44. For *śālagrāmas* connected with the Vaiṣṇava cult see J. N. Banerjea, *The development of Hindu iconography*, Calcutta, 1956, pp. 82 f.; 647, etc.; Joshi, op. cit., pp. 59 ff. (Kṛṣṇa is often worshipped in the form of a *śālagrāma*); Kane, op. cit., II, p. 715 f. According to a mythological tale Viṣṇu was cursed to become, in his next birth, a *śālagrāma* stone. Sometimes an image of Viṣṇu and a *śālagrāma* are in a procession carried together through the streets.

45. Ocimum sanctum, the holy basil, a shrubby species which is very often planted around Hindu temples; rosary beads are cut from its wood.

46. For weapons as sacred objects see the short paragraph in F. Heiler, *Erscheinungsformen und Wesen der Religion*, Stuttgart, 1961, p. 97 f. (with some references); for the trident ('c'est l'une des armes de main les plus caractéristiques de Śiva, Devī et leurs acolytes', De Mallmann, op. cit., p. 250) see also Banerjea, op. cit., pp. 301; 466 ff., etc.; T. A. Gopinatha Rao, *Elements of Hindu iconography*, II, 1, Madras, 1916, p. 200; V. R. R. Dikshitar, *War in ancient India*, Madras, 1944, p. 114; recalling the Buddhist *triratna* (G. Jouveau-Dubreuil, *Iconography of Southern India*, Paris, 1937, p. 21) it is thought to have the iconographic features of Śiva.

47. For the *liṅga* see the not too clear and critical article by Hariharānand Sarasvati, 'The inner significance of *liṅga*-worship', *J. Ind. Soc. of Or. Art*, IX, pp. 52 ff.; cf. p. 57 'the *liṅga* symbolizes the Supreme Man (*puruṣa*); the *yoni*, the *prakṛti*'.

48. W. Kirfel, *Symbolik des Hinduismus*, Stuttgart, 1959, p. 22 f. may to a certain extent be right in considering the skull to be an *indicium* of the god's provenance (or rather, of that of one of his components; cf. also H. Meinhard, *Beiträge zur Kenntnis des Śivaismus*, Thesis, Bonn, 1928, p. 7 f.).

49. For the cosmogonic character of this hour-glass-like musical instrument see Miss Marcel-Dubois, op. cit., p. 9, quoting the medieval Tamil poet of the *Uṇmāi Vilakkam*, 36 'creation has issued from the drum' and adding (p. 10) '... les tambours rituels sont identifiés explicitement avec la divinité et ... le rite permet d'agir sur elle par leur intermédiaire' (cf. *ŚB.* 5, 1, 5, 6; *TB.* 1, 3, 6, 2). For the outward form of the instrument see Marcel-Dubois, op. cit., 66 and 67; De Mallmann, op. cit., p. 256.

50. The significance attached to symbols and emblems may be illustrated by an epic passage (*Mbh.* 13, 14, 102) where all men are held to be Śiva's creatures because they are distinguished by genitals and not by disks, lotus flowers or *vajras* which would stamp them as belonging to Viṣṇu, Brahmā or Indra. The Śaṅkaravijaya mentions six communities of Śivaites, recognizable by different symbols: the Raudras, for instance, had the trident branded on the forehead, the Ugras the *ḍamaru* branded on the two arms, etc. Some general remarks on emblems and symbols may be found in A. K. Coomaraswamy, *Geschichte der indischen und indonesischen Kunst*, Leipzig, 1927, pp. 48 ff. (Engl. edition, 1927; New York, 1965, pp. 43 ff.); Zimmer, *Myths and symbols*; Kirfel, *Symbolik*; K. Fischer, *Schöpfungen indischer Kunst*, Cologne, [2]1961, p. 45; J. N. Banerjea, *The development of Hindu iconography*.

51. I may refer to my paper (in Dutch) 'Het begrip *dharma* in het Indische denken', in *Tijdschrift voor Philosophie* (Louvain) XX, 1958, pp. 213 ff.; *Die Religionen Indiens*, I, pp. 288 ff.; R. C. Zaehner, *Hinduism*, London, 1962, pp. 134 ff.; W. Norman Brown, *Man in the universe*, Calcutta, 1966, pp. 10 ff. A paraphrasis such as 'the divinely ordained norm of good conduct, varying according to class and caste' (A. L. Basham, *The wonder that was India*, London, 1954, p. 113) is not incorrect but incomplete.

52. The willingness to tolerate another's opinion on intellectual issues is, in European eyes, often amazing but becomes understandable if we realize that the Indians are deeply convinced that on the intellectual plane no one of us knows the ultimate truth.

53. Hence, no doubt, the term *dharma* which belongs to the root *dhṛ-* meaning 'to hold, maintain, preserve'. I would not subscribe to Zaehner's definition (op. cit., p. 3) '*Dharma* is ... the "form" of things as they are and the power that keeps them as they are and not otherwise', suggested by the untenable etymology of Latin *forma*, which whatever its origin, can hardly have anything to do with the Sanskrit *dhṛ-*.

54. J. N. Farquhar, *The crown of Hinduism*, Oxford, 1913, p. 449. For *mantras* in general see my relative paper in *Oriens* XVI, pp. 244 ff., esp. pp. 276 ff. and compare e.g. F. E. Keay, *Kabir and his followers*, Oxford, 1936, p. 153; G. Tucci, *The theory and practice of the maṇḍala*, London, 1961, *passim*.

55. There are of course exceptions which are worth studying. When for instance Śiva's image is washed on the day of the great Śivarātrī-festival worshippers of Śrī-Kṛṣṇa take part in the ceremony which requires the utterance of the mantra *śivāya namaḥ* (R. V. Joshi, *Le rituel de la dévotion kṛṣṇaite*, Pondicherry, 1959, p. 7).

56. For particulars L. Renou and J. Filliozat, *L'Inde classique*, I, Paris 1947, p. 566.

57. 'Ceremonies express harmony among villages, harmony among relatives, harmony among friends and neighbours, and harmony within the family. Without such harmony, there can be no ceremony.' (Beals, op. cit., p. 54.)

58. For some particulars see *Die Religionen Indiens*, I, pp. 339 ff. (with a bibliography); S. Stevenson, *The rites of the twice-born*, Oxford, 1920, pp. 263 ff.; O. Lewis, *Village life in Northern India*, Urbana, 1958, pp. 197 ff.; R. Ch. Hazra, *Studies in the upapurāṇas*, Calcutta, 1958–1963, *passim*.

59. As on every other point of Hinduism the local differences are very great.

60. Cf. also Renou and Filliozat, op. cit., I, p. 586.

61. On the occasion of New Year's day Viṣṇu receives, in Kāṭhiāwār and elsewhere, the first fruits, 'because he is the protector of the universe and Indra, the god of the crops, obeys him.'

62. For instance, the Nṛsiṃhacaturdaśī is the anniversary of his appearance as the Man-lion.

63. I refer to *Die Religionen Indiens*, I, pp. 115 ff.; A. Hillebrandt, *Ritualliteratur*, Strassburg, 1897, pp. 41 ff.; A. B. Keith, *The religion and philosophy of the Veda and Upanishads*, Cambridge, Mass., 1925, pp. 358 ff.; V. M. Apte, *Social and religious life in the Gṛhyasūtras*, Bombay (1939) [2]1954, ch. XVIII; Ram Gopal, *India of Vedic kalpasūtras*,

Delhi, 1959, esp. ch. II; III; XVII; L. Renou and J. Filliozat, op. cit., pp. 564 ff.; 581 ff.; The Vaiṣṇava *Bṛhannāradīya-Purāṇa*, extolling *smṛti* which records *dharma* rooted in the Veda, urges people to follow their own gṛhyasūtras (22, 10; 23, 9; 26, 50 ff.).

64. The descriptions and prescriptions of the (Hindu) *smṛti* texts are on the whole in harmony with those of the (Vedic) gṛhyasūtras. In this India has been highly conservative. See e.g. J. Jolly, *Recht und Sitte (einschliesslich der einheimischen Literatur)*, Strassburg, 1896, and especially P. V. Kane, *History of Dharmaśāstra*, II, Poona, 1941, ch. XVII and XVIII; Stevenson, *The rites of the twice-born* (mainly based on data collected in Kāthiāwār), ch. X; one might consult also J. Auboyer, *La vie quotidienne dans l'Inde ancienne*, Paris, 1961, pp. 209 ff. (Engl. edition *Daily life in ancient India*, London, 1965).

65. A survey of the Śaiva and Vaiṣṇava ritual as performed nowadays in the South has been given by C. G. Diehl, *Instrument and purpose*, Lund, 1956, pp. 66 ff.; for Śaiva ritual in the South see Brunner-Lachaux, op. cit., (n. 8.), esp. pp. 1 ff. Some other important ritual texts have been edited by N. R. Bhatt and published by the French Indological Institute at Pondicherry: *Rauravāgama*, 1961; *Mṛgendrāgama*, 1962; *Ajitāgama*, 1964. For the ritual significance of the married head of the family who is the support of all other stages in the life of the twice-born see e.g. *Manu* 3, 77 f.; *GautDhŚ*.3, 3.

66. The manuals (see e.g. *Ajitāgama*, 19, 22 ff.) expatiate upon the bits of wood to be used or avoided, their length (if it has the breadth of eight fingers it may contribute to final liberation) and other qualities.

67. Among these gods are Brahmā, Viṣṇu, Rudra, Īśvara, Sadāśiva, Sarasvatī, Lakṣmī, etc.; see e.g. *Ajitāgama*, 19, 59 ff.

68. The reader may be referred to Kane, op. cit., II, pp. 696 ff.

69. A discussion of these topics in the relative handbooks (for which see also Diehl, op. cit., pp. 42 ff.; Kane, loc. cit.) may be preceded by remarks on the qualities required of the performer of the ritual: he must know the scriptures, the acts of worship, be of good character and conduct, bodily be of perfect shape, be married, and in circles of Saiva brahmans, have descended from the gotras of the five *ṛṣis* (Kauśika, Kāśyapa, Bhāradvāja, Gautama, and Agastya), supposedly born from the five faces of Śiva.

70. For a description of the ritual of (southern) Vaiṣṇavas see: K. Rangachari, 'The Sri Vaishnava brahmans', *Bulletin of the Madras Government Museum* (Madras) NS. II, 2, (1931).

71. 'But the *saṃkalpa* (which for practical purposes may be translated by 'intention') is still there and preserves to the *karma* (ritual act) a character of efficient instrument (the formulation of the 'intention' comprises also the result the worshipper has in mind), even if surrendered to the will and pleasure of Viṣṇu' (Diehl, op. cit., p. 85). See also Stevenson, op. cit., p. 219.

72. The day of the 'orthodox' (i.e. 'traditional') Śrī-Vaiṣṇava brahman is usually devoted to the following five pursuits: the rites for purifying one's own person (*abhigamana*); collecting the requisites for worship (*upādāna*); worship (*ijyā*); study and contemplating the meaning of the sacred books (*svādhyāya*); and meditative concentration on the Lord's image (*yoga*). So important are especially the morning and evening devotions to a brahman, that one who wilfully neglects them for three days is liable to slip back to the state of a *śūdra*. It may however be noted that the exact order of the ritual acts may vary very much, and that the acts themselves may also considerably be shortened for want of time.

73. 'He appears, for instance, as Nara-Nārāyaṇa at Badrināth, as Kṛṣṇa at Mathurā, Vṛndāvana, Gokula, and Dvārakā, as Jagannātha at Purī, as Viṭhoba at Paṇdharpūr, as Śrīnivāsa at Tirupati, as Varadarājā at Kāñcī, and as Raṅganātha at Śrīraṅgam' (Mahadevan, *Outlines of Hinduism*, p. 191).

74. It may be observed that the meticulous efforts to purify oneself from every kind of 'sin' or evil may involve also the observation of a variety of customs etc. with regard to the avoidance of inauspicious occurrences, etc.; see e.g. Stevenson, op. cit., pp. 210 ff. Ritual purity is 'the first path to *dharma*, the resting-place of the Veda, the abode of prosperity (*śrī*), the favourite of the gods, etc.', Hārīta, quoted by Kane, op. cit., II, p. 651.

75. See the possibly Bengal treatise by Trimalla, which has been edited and translated into German by Miss F. Nowotny, *I.I.J.*, 1 (1957). The gods mentioned here are Gaṇeśa, Brahmā, Viṣṇu, Rudra, Jīvātman, Paramātman and the illustrious guru. For the cakras in general compare e.g. A. Avalon, *The serpent power*, Madras, 1950, pp. 103 ff.

76. This rite (cf. e.g. Stevenson, op. cit., pp. 286; 409 f.; 413; Farquhar, *The crown of Hinduism*, pp. 322 f.; G. Tucci, *Tibetan painted scrolls*, Rome, 1949, pp. 308 ff.) is also performed in installing and consecrating an image of a god. Although it is often said that by going through the process the nature of the image changes because it becomes a container of supranormal power ('an image is a storehouse of concentrated energy', M. Ramakrishna Kavi, Preface to *Atri-Saṃhitā*, Tirupati, 1943, p. VIII), many Indians, especially among the theists, are convinced that the ceremony essentially serves to ennoble the worshipper, to realize God's presence in the image so that it becomes an effectual means of contact between God and himself. (For *pratiṣṭhā* see my relative paper in *Studia Indologica Internationalia* (Poona and Paris), I (1954), pp. 1 ff.)

77. For particulars see e.g. Rangachari, op. cit., p. 53; Brunner-Lachaux, op. cit., pp. 8 ff.

78. Selecting a place ('where God is usually brought or where Bhāgavatas bathe', Rangachari, op. cit., p. 53), smearing one's body with consecrated mud or earth in order to remove the dirt, sipping water (*ācamana*), sprinkling water over oneself.

79. The Northern school of this religion omits the (Vedic) syllable *Oṃ* when the mantra is taught to non-brahmans.

80. 'God with all His attendants ... begins to make Himself pleased with the most auspicious materials which are His own and some of which are intended for doing honour, some for creating pleasure by touch and some for eating, supplied by me who is His servant through my body, senses and mind all of which are given by Him' (Rangachari, op. cit., p. 54).

81. A very frequent formula, also occurring in variations (see M. Bloomfield, *A Vedic concordance*, Cambridge, Mass., 1906, p. 493 f.), used in taking a sacrificial implement (*VS.* 1, 24; 5, 22; 26; *ŚB.* 1, 2, 4, 4; *ĀpŚS.* 1, 3, 2, etc., etc.).

82. For the interpretation of this stanza see K. F. Geldner, *Der Rigveda in Auswahl*, II, Stuttgart, 1909, p. 9; the same, *Der Rigveda übersetzt*, Cambridge, Mass., 1951, I, p. 60, and L. Renou, *Études védiques et pāṇinéennes*, XV, Paris, 1966, p. 1 f.; for Jātavedas also J. Gonda, *Epithets in the Ṛgveda*, The Hague, 1959, pp. 85 ff.; 'to see the sun' of course means 'live'. This stanza is, in Vedic ritual, used to accompany an offering to the Sun etc. (cf. e.g. *ŚB.* 4, 3, 4, 8 f. 'He offers with two stanzas to the Sun ..., for ... dispelling the darkness by that light he reaches heaven'; otherwise *TS.* 1, 2, 8, 2), but in the domestic rites also for other purposes, e.g. *HGS.* 1, 9. 9 in performing the ritual acts connected with the bath at the end of studentship; *MGS.* 1, 2, 4 during the daily twilight devotion. For the numerous Vedic mantras accompanying the bath of a Vaikhānasa Viṣṇuite see *VaikhGS.* 1, 3.

83. The formula *avadhūtaṃ rakṣo avadhutā arātayaḥ* is, in Vedic ritual, used when the officiant shakes the black antelope skin which is thought to bestow bliss (*VS.* 1, 14; 19; *TB.* 3, 2, 5, 5; *ŚB.* 1, 1, 4, 4; *ĀpŚS.* 1, 19, 3; *MŚS.* 1, 2, 2, 6 etc.).

84. = *TU.* 1, 4, 2. It forms part of a teacher's prayer.

85. After having sprinkled water over his legs and head with the mantra ṚV. 10, 9, 1–3; *TS.* 4, 1, 5, 1, etc. (which like the preceding quotations are mis-spelled in Rangachari's survey, op. cit., p. 55), that is the beginning of the so-called *āpohiṣṭhīyaṃ sūktam* (the initial words are *āpo hi ṣṭhā mayobhuvaḥ*). In the domestic ritual the first stanza is prescribed when the teacher or spiritual guide makes his pupil at the end of his studentship wash himself (*HGS.* 1, 10, 2; *MGS.* 1, 2, 11) and when they take a bath at the end of the annual course of study (*HGS.* 2, 18, 9). Cf. also *MGS.* 1, 1, 24, etc.

86. Cf. e.g. *SomaśP.* 1, 20; 21; 23; 24; 27; 28.

87. One should of course preferably utilize mud taken from a pure place (mountain, bank of a river, *tīrtha*, etc.).

88. These mantras run as follows: *Oṃ haṃ ātmatattvāya namaḥ; oṃ haṃ vidyāttvāya namaḥ; oṃ haṃ śivatattatvāya namaḥ*. For the *tattvas* see e.g. H. W. Schomerus, *Der Śaiva-Siddhānta*, Leipzig, 1912, p. 134. The Tantrist Hindu *mantras* may begin with the Vedic *Oṃ* and consist, further, of the *bīja*, i.e. a syllable bearing, in a condensed form, the energy of the *mantra*, the significance of which is explained and handed down in esoteric oral instruction (the initial *h* 'symbolizes' Śiva), the name in the dative and one of the seven closing terms which were also, though differently, used in Vedic formulas (*namaḥ, svadhā, svāhā, huṃ, phaṭ, vaṣaṭ, vauṣaṭ*).

89. A *mudrā* expresses an idea and 'symbolizes' the transformation effected by the mantra. For some particulars see S. Srikantha Sastri, 'Śri Vidyārṇava Tantra' in the *Quart. Journ. of the Mythic. Soc., Bangalore*, xxxv, p. 12; Diehl, op. cit., p. 69; Brunner-Lachaux, op. cit., pp. 373 ff.

90. For *śānti* see D. J. Hoens, *Śānti*, Thesis, Utrecht, 1951.

91. The deified weapon of a deity plays a part in the daily ritual as well as in ceremonies for protection; it is also taken round the streets a short time before the deity inhabiting a temple goes out in procession.

92. See Diehl, op. cit., p. 71.

93. One should draw a quadrangular figure as it were right in the water and in the middle of that figure the Māyābīja and the Varuṇabīja, two monosyllables containing the essence of a *mantra*. See *Die Religionen Indiens*, II, pp. 33 f.; 47. For *prāṇāyāma* see ibid. I, p. 311; S. Lindquist, *Die Methoden des yoga*, Lund, 1932, p. 39 f., etc.; M. Eliade, *Le yoga*, Paris, 1954, pp. 67 ff.; 235 and Bhoja, on Patañjali, *YS*. I, 34: Since all other functions of the organs (of the human body) are preceded by respiration—there always exists a bond between respiration and concentration—the realization of concentration upon one single object ultimately rests on breathing discipline.

94. Cf. Patañjali, *YS*. I, 34 and Bhoja's commentary.

95. For the *aghamarṣaṇa* ceremony see also M. Monier-Williams, *Brahmanism and Hinduism*, London, 1891, p. 404 and Stevenson, op. cit., p. 220; Kane, *History of Dharmaśāstra*, IV, Poona, 1953, p. 45, etc.; the 'evil' consists for instance in the 'sins' of the previous night, from which one should be freed. The mantras used are ṚV. 10, 190, 1–3. For some additional acts see Brunner-Lachaux, op. cit., pp. 26 ff.

96. For details see *Rauravāg*. p. 32: one must first clean hands and feet, face the East, place the fingers in a particular position, etc.

97. Including unforeseen occurrences interfering with the worshipper's state of purity (sneezing, etc.).

98. For the often divergent technical details see Brunner-Lachaux, op. cit., pp. 30 ff.; *Rauravāg*. p. 34. The ashes of the cow-dung are to the accompaniment of the *hṛdmantra* gathered on lotus-leaves, small parts of it are dried in the sun, consecrated with mantras, brought into contact with the limbs of Śiva and placed on the worshipper's head, etc.

99. According to some authorities this rite ends up by applying the *tripuṇḍra* (see further on).

100. Stevenson, op. cit., pp. 214; 229 ff.; Kane, op. cit., II, pp. 668 ff.; 689 ff.

101. See above, p. 68 f.

102. It may be recalled that authorities sometimes distinguish between the purāṇic, smārta, āgamic and śrauta performance of a rite (Kane, op. cit., II, p. 653), the second being that which is laid down in smṛtis (*Manu*, etc.), the third that taught in the manuals of Śivaites and Viṣṇuites.

103. See also H. Oldenberg, *The grihya-sūtras translated*, I (S.B.E., XXIX), Oxford, 1886, (²Delhi, 1964), p. 120 f.

104. Cf. *ĀśvGS*. 3, 4, 1–5; *ŚGS*. 4, 9, 3; 10, 3 ff., etc.

105. See Kane, op. cit., II, p. 693. The formula of the Śrī-Vaiṣṇavas runs as follows: 'I satisfy all the gods from Brahmā downwards by (these) libations of water; I satisfy all the gods . . ., . . . all troops (*gaṇa*) of gods . . ., . . . all the wives of the gods . . ., . . . all the wives of the troops of gods . . .'; etc.

106. *VaikhSS*. I, 4. The gods of the *tarpaṇa* differ in each *sūtra*, the Vaikhānasas mentioning the deities of the quarters, the planets and some others.

107. Cf. *BDhŚ*. 2, 5, 9, 5 *Oṃ bhūr bhuvaḥ puruṣaṃ tarpayāmi*.

108. Diehl, op. cit., p. 73 mentions a *yakṣmatarpaṇa* with a mantra regretting the contamination of the water through dirt from the worshipper's body, Stevenson, op. cit., p. 231 an offering to the Sun coupled with a *tarpaṇa* of six gods (Brahmā, Viṣṇu, Rudra, Mitra, Sūrya, Varuṇa) who have been invited to take up their separate abodes in each of six corners of two interpenetrating triangles which have been traced in sandal-wood paste on a shallow copper dish.

109. Here also the descriptions are far from unanimous. Stevenson, op. cit., p. 216 f., for instance, says that the Śaiva worshipper, if he is at home, goes into the room set apart for worship, or, if he is on the river bank, to some lonely spot, and there opens the small

box, in which the ashes, which he has taken from some great sacrifice (see also Stevenson, op. cit., p. 348), are pressed together in the shape of a ball. Diehl, op. cit., p. 74 (see the interesting note 2) mentions inter alia the ritual act called, in Tamil, *tikkupantanam* (Skt. *dikṣu bandhanam* 'the binding or blocking in the directions', that is 'fortifying oneself on all sides by incantations invoking the protection of the tutelary deities of the eight quarters') which, being also known to the Vaiṣṇavas (Rangachari, op. cit., p. 56), plays a considerable part in the Śaiva ritual described by this author. It consists in throwing the *astra mantra* (*astrāya namaḥ* or *astrāya phaṭ* 'homage to the offensive weapon' which is a protection against evil powers)—which may be accompanied by flowers, clods of earth, etc.—towards all quarters of the universe.

110. For some details see e.g. *Ajitāgama*, p. 190: the length of the marks indicates the social class to which the Śaiva belongs, those of a brahman being longer than those of a kṣatriya, etc.

111. The left hand is not used in worshipping the gods. The marks are made with the right hand (thumb).

112. According to Śivaite authorities the three lines represent the gods of the Trinity (Brahmā, Viṣṇu, Rudra) as well as Śiva's trident. See also Brunner-Lachaux, op. cit., pp. 34; 36.

113. = *ṚVKh.* 2, 6, 9 (J. Scheftelowitz, *Die Apokryphen des Ṛgveda*, Breslay, 1906, p. 73). The stanza occurs also *TĀ.* 10, 1, 10; *MNU.* 110 f. in a series of formulas to be muttered during the ritual ablutions prescribed for a devotee who resigns all worldly affairs; *MGS.* 2, 13, 6 in the Ṣaṣṭhīkalpa (the rite to be performed on the sixth day of a lunar fortnight, the goddess of that day, Ṣaṣṭhī, being implored to grant the worshipper's wishes; *BDh.* 4, 5, 12, etc.).

114. I refer to *Aspects of early Viṣṇuism*, ch. III.

115. For the lustral function of, and beneficial power inherent in, clay, mud and moist earth in general see J. J. Meyer, *Trilogie altindischer Mächte und Feste der Vegetation*, Zürich and Leipzig, I, 1937, p. 125 f.; II, pp. 4; 23 f.; III, p. 229 f., etc.; A. Lonicer, *Kreuterbuch*, Frankfurt, a. M., 1564, p. 56; and also *Aspects of early Viṣṇuism*, p. 267. According to a passage of the *Skanda-Purāṇa*, quoted by Hemādri, *Caturvargac.* II, 2, p. 364 f., describing a Bhairava festival, 'the town is full of people, who are stiff because of the masses of clods of earth, ashes, faeces and urine smeared on their body'. See also Meyer, op. cit., I, p. 101.

116. Ashes are widely believed to avert evil and promote fertility, to purify and fortify those applying them to their body. 'Die Asche gilt . . . als mit besonders wirksamen, heilvollen Kräften ausgestattet, wohl deshalb, weil sie einerseits an die vernichtende Kraft des dämonenverscheuchenden Feuers erinnert, andererseits als Überrest des läuternden Feuers frei von dämonischem Stoff ist' (J. Scheftelowitz, in H. Bächtold-Stäubli, *Handwörterbuch des deutschen Aberglaubens*, I, Berlin and Leipzig, 1927, p. 611). See the many data collected by Meyer, op. cit., (Register, III, p. 288, esp. I, pp. 107 ff.); J. G. Frazer, *The Golden Bough* (abr. ed.), London, 1957, pp. 94 ff., etc.; C. H. Tawney and N. M. Penzer, *The Ocean of story*, X, London, 1928, p. 75; W. Crooke and R. E. Enthoven, *Religion and folklore of N. India*, Oxford, 1926, p. 442; W. Koppers, *Die Bhil in Zentralindien*, Horn and Vienna, 1948, p. 148 f. etc. 'Asche ist . . . voll starken Zaubers, wohl weil sie als Überrest, ja Essenz vom Holz, also vom Baum, und vom Feuer, die Gotteskraft beider in sich birgt und offenbar auch deshalb mächtig sein musz, weil sogar das Feuer sie nicht verzehrt' (Meyer, op. cit., I, p. 107). Hence also the belief that special ashes, for instance those remaining in the fireplace after a sacrifice, are extraordinarily powerful. Compare also *Suśruta Saṃhitā*, *KS.* 3, 13 ff., Engl. transl. by K. Kunja Lal Bhisagratna, Calcutta, 1911, II, pp. 696 ff. and *Devībhāgavata-Purāṇa*, 11, 14, 20 ff. where a bath in ashes is said to cure rheumatism, bile-complaints and various other diseases.

117. Rangachari, op. cit., p. 56 provides his readers with a paraphrastic translation based on tradition. This stanza is, also with the Vaikhānasas, very favourite and used to accompany and consecrate a large variety of ritual acts, for instance in worshipping Viṣṇu (*VaikhSS.* 3, 13; 4, 12, similarly, *ṚVidh.* 1, 25, 4).

118. The formula is *VS.* 5, 21 (not complete); *TS.* 1, 2, 13, 3, etc. 'Thou art the forehead of Viṣṇu; thou art the back of Viṣṇu; ye are the corners of Viṣṇu's mouth; thou art the thread (*syūḥ*, or needle, Mahīdhara on *VS.* 5, 21) of Viṣṇu; thou art the fixed point (firmly fastened knot) of Viṣṇu; thou belongest to Viṣṇu; thee to Viṣṇu' (the relative

section of the Vedic ritual deals with the construction of the shed for the sacrificial carts; a beam is addressed; 'ye' refers to the two ends of a garland of sacrificial grass resting on it; see W. Caland and V. Henry, *L'Agniṣṭoma*, Paris, 1906, p. 90 f. and Caland, on *ĀpŚS.* 11, 8, 1 (*Das Śrautasūtra des Āpastamba*, II, Amsterdam, 1924, pp. 209 ff.; Rangachari, op. cit., p. 56 explains *viṣṇoh syūr asi*: 'you are the one that connects us with Viṣṇu').

119. *TĀ.* 10, 1, 8; *MNU.* 91 ff. with some differences. Interestingly enough the words *MNU.* 94 *mṛttike brahmadattāsi kaśyapenābhimantritā* 'O lump of clay, thou has been given (to us) by brahman and Kaśyapa has consecrated thee' (*MNU.*) are omitted (see J. Varenne, *La Mahā Nārāyaṇa Upaniṣad*, Paris, 1960, I, p. 149). The stanzas run as follows: '(O clay,) thou hast been drawn up by the black boar (Viṣṇu-Varāha) with a thousand arms; (thou art) the earth, the milch-cow, the earth which bears the world of men; O clay, destroy my evil ('sin': *pāpam*), the evil actions (producing demerit) which I have done, freed from (that) evil (which has been destroyed) by Thee I live a thousand years; O clay, give me a well-nourished condition; on Thee every thing is established'. Similar passages occur in the *snānavidhi MtP.* 102, 10 ff. (translated by L. Renou, *Anthologie Sanskrite*, Paris, 1947, p. 155), with the addition *āruhya mama gātrāṇi sarvaṃ pāpaṃ pracodaya* and *Sauparṇa Purāṇa* 6, 12 ff., referring to the worshipper's new birth as a result of the application of the sacred clay.

120. *snānavidhimantrāḥ*; see e.g. *Manu* 6, 24, and compare Kane, op. cit., II, p. 664; Varenne, op. cit., I, pp. 35; 149; II, p. 35 f.

121. For another indication see above, p. 70, n. 95, à propos of the *aghamarṣaṇa-sūkta* (ṚV. 10, 190).

122. Which are called *nāmam* in the South.

123. A thirteenth addressed to Vāsudeva is added in Rangachari's description (op. cit., p. 57 f.).

124. Some of them may be translated here: '(1) I pay homage to Keśava who possesses four discs and is bright as gold. (3) I direct my thoughts towards Mādhava of the lustre of the cut surface of a gem and possessing four maces. (4) I take refuge with Govinda who(se face) is laughing like the moon's and who possesses four bows. (7) I meditate on Trivikrama of the colour of Agni (fire) who is in possession of four swords . . . .'

125. Keśava, Nārāyaṇa, Mādhava, Govinda, Viṣṇu, Madhusūdana, Trivikrama, Vāmana, Śridhara, Hṛṣīkeśa, Padmanātha, Dāmodara.

126. *BaudhDhŚ* 2, 5, 9, 10. Similarly, e.g. *Ṛgvidhāna*, 3, 27, 1 ff.

127. See also Kane, op. cit., II, pp. 653; 728.

128. In the South twelve Tamil stanzas praising each aspect of God are added to the above. After making the *puṇḍras* one should not—for obvious reasons—clean one's hands with water.

129. Two is the minimum, originally allowed to those who have no time or who are weak. For differences in the methods of painting the *ūrdhvapuṇḍra* in the case of Ekāntins or other Vaiṣṇavas see e.g. *Devībhāgavata-Purāṇa* 11, a. 12 ff.

130. Of non-Vedic origin. See also Stevenson, op. cit., p. 217. (For some remarks on Śivaite mantras see Brunner-Lachaux, op. cit., pp. IV ff.)

131. I refer to *Die Religionen Indiens*, I, p. 64, etc.; *Change and continuity*, pp. 38 ff.

132. See e.g. Diehl, op. cit., pp. 74; 77; 103; 105; 108; 122. The procedure is described as follows: 'From the spot between the eyebrows (*bindusthāna*, an element of the yogic-tantric conception of the body as a combination of organs and power centra, believed to be the seat of Śiva's highest aspect; see Lindquist, op. cit., p. 190; Nalini Kanta Brahma, *The philosophy of Hindu sādhana*, London, 1932, p. 295) one must draw the *amṛta* with the heart mantra (a very frequent mantra of the tantric type: *Oṃ aṃ hṛdayāya namaḥ*) having first shown the *aṅkuśa mudrā* (the *mudrā* of the elephant-driver's hook: a fist with the index-finger bent in the form of a hook) and then join it with the holy water of Śiva by means of the *dhenu-mudrā* ('entrelacer les doigts des mains, joindre l'auriculaire de chaque main à l'annulaire de l'autre, et le majeur à l'index' (Brunner-Lachaux, op. cit., p. 375 with a figure). Passing mention may be made here of some other Śaiva rites, considered by some authorities to be 'occasional' rather than obligatory (but see *SomaśP.* 1, 43 ff.), viz. the five 'baths' relating to Indra, Agni, heaven, Vāyu and mind, the first consisting in making seven strides towards the East when the sun shines through a rain-shower, the last in reciting the *mūlamantra* while holding one's breath.

133. In the isle of Bali the ritual preparation of *amṛta* by God, who directs the hand of the priest, being the second half of a complete ritual, was considered so important that the Balinese were in the habit of calling their religion *āgama tīrtha* (*tīrtha* = *amṛta*).

134. *Die Religionen Indiens*, pp. 36; 43; 233; N. K. Brahma, op. cit., p. 66; J. Woodroffe, *Introduction to Tantra Shastra*, Madras, 1952, p. 107; Eliade, *Le yoga*, p. 215 f. ('on "projette" les divinités en touchant divers points de son corps; on effectue, en d'autres termes, une homologation du corps avec le panthéon tantrique afin de "réveiller" les forces sacrées endormies dans la chair même'), See e.g. *Mahānirvāṇa-Tantra*, 3, 40 ff.; Kane, op. cit., II, p. 319.

135. For particulars see Diehl, op. cit., pp. 75 ff. The Śrī-Vaiṣṇavas have here again an interesting collection of mantras. Among these is a series of mantras each of which contains one or two words of the Sāvitrī or Gāyatrī stanza, ṚV. 3, 62, 10, amplified by other words; for instance while touching the heart one says *Oṃ tat savituḥ jñānāya hṛdayāya namaḥ*.

136. Compare *MNU*. 277 ff. *sadyojātaṃ prapadyāmi sadyojātāya vai namo namaḥ . . . vāmadevāya namo jyeṣṭhāya namaḥ . . . aghorebhyo 'tha ghorebhyo / aghoraghoratarebhyaḥ / sarvataḥ śarva sarvebhyo / namas te rudra rūpebhyaḥ / tatpuruṣāya vidmahe mahādevāya dhīmahi / tan no rudraḥ pracodayāt* (a later variant of ṚV 3, 62, 10; see my remarks in 'The Indian mantra', *Oriens*, XVI, p. 293 f.; another variant is the so-called *Śiva-gāyatrī*: *oṃ tan maheśāya vidmahe vāgviśuddhāya dhīmahi / tan naḥ śivaḥ pracodayāt* ('We make (let us make) the Great Lord the aim of our knowledge, let us contemplate him who is pure of speech. Śiva must stimulate us with regard to that') / *īśānaḥ sarvavidyānām īśvaraḥ sarvabhūtānām* . . . These *pañcasuvaktra* (*mantrāḥ*) '(formulas of) the five auspicious faces (of Śiva)' are muttered in order to promote meditation. The Tamilized formulas recorded by Diehl, op. cit., p. 76 are *Ōm hōm icānamūrtnē namaḥ. Ōm hem tatpuruṣavaktirāya namaḥ. Ōm hum akōrahrutayāya namaḥ. Ōm him vāmatēvakuhyāya namaḥ. Ōm ham satyōjātamūrttaye namaḥ*. For the *aghoramantra* see Meinhard, op. cit., p. 20.

137. Most people have no time for all three *sandhyā* performances, and limit themselves to the morning and evening rites. See also Kane, op. cit., II, p. 312 f.

138. For a brief description see Kane, op. cit., II, pp. 313 ff.; Renou and Filliozat, op. cit., I, p. 584 f.

139. 'It is not a very uncommon sight in . . . Bombay to see people like Waghris and Dheds (low castes) washing their faces at the municipal watertaps early in the morning and throwing a little water in the air . . . as for the Sun and going through the usual obeisance-gestures looking towards the East. And if the brahmin males offer 'mantric' prayers to the rising and the setting sun, women of brahmin and other high castes show their reverence to and their regard for the blessings of the Sun-god by going through more or less the same procedure as that mentioned above as being the practice of the Waghris. . . . But they do so only after their bath and preferably while offering worship to the basil plant' (G. S. Ghurye, *Gods and men*, Bombay, 1962, p. 8).

140. Homage paid to these goddesses adds to the success of one's (ritual) work done at twilight-time: *Ajitāgama* 19, 36. See also Stevenson, op. cit., p. 219 f. These adorations are also named Gāyatrī (the morning one), Sāvitrī (noon) and Sarasvatī (evening one). Tantrism personified them as Brāhmī (compare the comparatively ancient place *ViP*. 1, 5, 34, where Saṃdhyā is said to have arisen from a body abandoned by Brahmā; see also *BhāgP*. 3, 20, 28 ff.), Vaiṣṇavī and Raudrī, being manifestations of the Great Goddess as creating, conservating and reabsorbing. These three figures are also said to belong to the Seven Mothers (*brāhmī maheśvarī caiva kaumārī vaiṣṇavī tathā māhendrī caiva vārāhī cāmuṇḍā sapta mātaraḥ*), Brāhmī, Maheśvarī and Vaiṣṇavī being different aspects of the Gāyatrī (see e.g. S. Chattopadhyaya, *The evolution of theistic sects in ancient India*, Calcutta, 1962, p. 160 f.). The cult of these goddesses is described *AgniP*. a. 72; for the iconography see Mlle De Mallmann, op. cit., p. 167.

141. Monier-Williams, op. cit., p. 403.

142. Cf. e.g. *ĀśvGS*. 3, 7, 3 and 4; *MGS*. 1, 2; *KGS*. 1, 25; *VGS*. 5, 30 and also *BĀU*. 6, 3, 6. See also Hillebrandt, *Ritualliteratur*, pp. 55; 74.

143. Cf. e.g. *ĀpDhS*. 1, 11, 30, 8; *Manu* 2, 101; *Yajñ*. 1, 24 f.

144. *ĀpGS*. 3, 7, 21; *HGS*. 1, 23, 9; *PGS*. 1, 9, 3 f.; *ŚGS*. 1, 3, 14 f.; *Kauś*. 73, 2.

145. ṚV. 3, 62, 10 *tat savitur vareṇyam bhargo devasya dhīmahi / dhiyo yo naḥ pracodayāt*:

see J. Gonda, *The vision of the Vedic poets*, The Hague, 1963, pp. 98 f.; 291. The verb *dhīmahi* was in later times reinterpreted so as to express the idea of 'concentrating upon', no doubt under the influence of the high importance attached to *dhyāna* and the conviction that identification with the object of concentration resulted in 'obtaining' that object.

146. See also Kane, op. cit., II, p. 313.

147. Cf. *MGS.* 1, 2, 3b 'God Savitar approaches, possessing treasures . . . having in his hands many gifts for men . . .' (*MS.* 4, 14, 6). For 'confirmation' see G. van der Leeuw, *Religion in essence and manifestation*, London, 1938, pp. 430 ff.

148. According to *TĀ.* 2, 2 the evil spirits which fight the sun are 'appeased' (rendered harmless) by throwing up towards the East water consecrated by the Gāyatrī. The *Viṣṇu-Purāṇa* 2, 8, 45 ff. (see also H. H. Wilson and F. Hall, *The Viṣṇu-Purana*, II London, 1865, pp. 249 ff.) and the *Vāyu-Purāṇa* 50, 162 ff. record the belief that rākṣasas called Mandehas, desirous to devour the sun, assail it every day again; the gods and the brahmans however prevent them from succeeding by throwing at *saṃdhyā*-time the consecrated water which is of the nature of the *vajra* (Indra's weapon).

149. It is in view of the variants of the Gāyatrī or Sāvitrī-stanza interesting to notice that *MGS.* 1, 2, 3 makes mention of three different Sāvitrī-stanzas for the three twice-born classes of society.

150. See e.g. *ĀśvGS.* 3, 7, 3 ff. *yajñopavītī nityodakaḥ saṃdhyām upāsīta vāgyataḥ* 'Invested with the sacred cord, constantly fulfilling the prescribed duties regarding the use of water, he should perform the twilight devotion, observing silence'; Yājñ. 1, 22 f. *snānam abdaivatair mantrair mārjanaṃ prāṇasaṃyamaḥ / sūryasya cāpy upasthānaṃ gāyatryāḥ pratyaham japaḥ // gāyatrīṃ śirasā sārdhaṃ japed vyāhṛtipūrvikām / pratipraṇavasaṃyuktāṃ trir ayaṃ prāṇasaṃyamaḥ // prāṇān āyamya saṃprokṣya tṛcenābdaivatena tu / japann āsīta sāvitrīṃ pratyag ātārakodayāt // saṃdhyaṃ prāk prātar evaṃ hi tiṣṭhed āsūryadarśanāt.* From these stanzas it appears that the purification called *mārjana*, the worship of the sun, the Gāyatrī with the *vyāhṛtis* (*bhūr bhuvaḥ svaḥ*; cf. also *MGS.* 1, 2, 3a), 'breath-control' which are some of the principal constituents of more recent forms of the ceremony were then already (± 300 A.D.?) regarded as obligatory.

151. *ŚB.* 8, 5, 3, 7 '. . . the Gāyatrī is Brahman, and that Brahman is yonder burning disk'; *Maitr. U.* 6, 35.

152. Interestingly enough some later authors held a different opinion with regard to the relative significance of the elements of the rite. As to the character of the ceremony in its entirety Medhātithi (IXth century) on *Manu* 2, 101 observes that it essentially is a contemplation of the god called Āditya represented by the orb of the sun as well of the fact that the same 'intelligent being' dwells in one's own heart. We remember that the Śaiva and Vaiṣṇava worshippers have realized their identity with God before proceeding to perform this part of their daily rites. (The expression 'divine self-worship' used by Diehl, op. cit., p. 83 may create misunderstanding.)

153. Cf. *Change and continuity*, p. 364, etc.

154. Thus Śaiva authorities (e.g. *SomaśP.* 1, 51) expressly speak of Śaiva-saṃdhyā. The Nambūdiri brahmans of Kerala perform the saṃdhyā rites up to the present day in accordance with the Vedic prescriptions without the 'Hindu' elements added by other communities. For some information see K. Ramavarma Raja, 'The brahmins of Malabar', *J.R.A.S.* (1910), pp. 625 ff.

155. Kane, op. cit., II, p. 315 who is right in adding that this is hardly anywhere prescribed by any *smṛti* or commentator. These names of the 'standard twenty-four' forms of Viṣṇu are, each with the expression of obeisance, repeated at the beginning of every ceremony performed nowadays. The author of *ViP.* 2, 8, 51 on the other hand observes that the sun is supremely a portion of Viṣṇu, and its supreme stimulator is the syllable *Oṃ*, expressing (him), which (st. 50) is identical with Viṣṇu.

156. Mis-spelled by Diehl, op. cit., p. 87; see *TĀ.* 10, 32, 1; *MNU.* 479.

157. *MGS.* 1, 9, 15.

158. *ĀGS.* 1, 24, 13; *HGS.* 1, 13, 6; *KGS.* 24, 14, etc.

159. *GB.* 1, 1, 39. See M. Bloomfield, *The Atharva-Veda and the Gopatha-Brāhmaṇa*, Strassburg, 1899, p. 110 . . . *amṛtam asy amṛtopastaraṇam asy amṛtāya tvopastṛṇāmīti pāṇāv udakam ānīya . . .*

160. Diehl, op. cit., p. 246 f. It cannot be maintained (with Diehl, op. cit., p. 87, n. 4)

that the meaning of the mantra is in this connection of little significance. In *MNU.* 479 (referred to by Diehl, p. 87, n. 4) the *mantra* accompanies the rite of the agnihotra to the vital powers or the central life potencies (*prāṇas*) to be performed by the devotee who has renounced all earthly concerns at the beginning and the end of his meal. In *BDhŚ.* 2, 7, 12, 3 it accompanies the drinking of water in the *prāṇāhuti* (oblations to the *prāṇāḥ*) ceremony: *amṛta-* . . . *iti purastād āpas pītvā pañcānnena prāṇāhutīr juhoti.*

161. *Die Religionen Indiens*, 1, p. 141; P. E. Dumont, *L'Agnihotra*, Baltimore, 1939; Renou and Filliozat, op. cit., 1, p. 353.

162. Dumont, op. cit., p. 49 etc.; Kane, op. cit., II, p. 1001. Compare *ŚŚS.* 2, 6, 11; *ĀpŚS.* 6, 5, 4 and *TB.* 2, 1, 11, 1 'Order (*ṛta*) is fire (Agni), Truth (*satyam*) is the sun, . . . so he sprinkles, in the morning, the sun through fire', with the result, it is added, that the man who does so and knows the meaning of the rite will not fall into misfortune or 'come to an end'. In *MŚS.* 11, 9, 2, 4 the formula accompanies the sprinkling of food to be presented to brahmans, on the occasion of a *śrāddha.*

163. Among those mentioned by Rangachari, op. cit., pp. 64 ff. are the following. The sequence (*Oṃ*) *āpo jyotī raso 'mṛtaṃ brahma* pronounced by the worshipper while smearing the whole of his body occurs *TĀ.* 10, 15, 1; 28, 1 = *MNU.* 342; 472, likewise (and then already!) in the *saṃdhyā* ceremonies and as part of a series of mantras to be used in order to achieve internal purification; it is also found in dharma literature and in the *Prāṇāgnihotra-Upaniṣad*, 1 (cf. *AmṛtabU.* 10, etc.); it is the so-called *śiraḥ*, viz. of the Gāyatrī (which may precede) and is followed by the *vyāhṛtis* (*bhūr bhuvaḥ svaḥ*) and the *praṇava* (*Oṃ*); *MaitrU.* 6, 35 it occurs in a passage teaching that that which is in the middle of the sun is Brahman, the One. (For the relations between the *prāṇāgnihotra* and these mantras see also Varenne, *La Mahā Nārāyaṇa Upaniṣad*, 1, p. 154.) It is appositely followed by the words *arkamaṇḍalamadhyasthaṃ sūryakoṭisamaprabham / brahmādisevyapādābjaṃ naumi brahmaramāsakham* 'I praise the companion of Śrī who resides in the centre of the sun's orb, who is as brilliant as many millions of suns, whose lotus-feet are to be served (honoured) by brahmans and others.' The phraseology reminds us of that of definite later upaniṣads. The next stanza is *TĀ.* 10, 26, 1 = *MNU.* 329 f. (dealing with the *saṃdhyā* ceremonies '. . . des versets proprement upaniṣadiques s'insèrent entre certaines formules empruntées au rituel', Varenne, op. cit., 1, p. 79) *āyātu varadā devī akṣarabrahmasaṃmitam / gāyatrī chandasāṃ mātā idaṃ brahma juṣasva naḥ* (*me*) 'The goddess who fulfills requests must come! (The mantra) which is equal to the imperishable Brahman must come! The Gāyatrī, the mother of all metrical texts (must come)! Take delight (O, goddess) in this (manifestation of) Brahman of mine (which I dedicate to Thee)!' (Rangachari's transcription and translation are, here also, incorrect). These words are immediately followed by *TĀ.* 10, 26, 1 = *MNU.* 334 and the *āvāhana*, that is the invocation proper, the invitation addressed to God to be present: *ojo 'si saho 'si balam asi bhrājo 'si devānāṃ dhāma nāmāsi viśvam asi viśvāyuḥ sarvam asi sarvāyur abhibhūr Oṃ gāyatrīm āvahayāmi* 'Thou art energy, thou art overwhelming power, thou art (physical) power, thou art splendour, thou art the location and name of the divine being (see J. Gonda, *The meaning of the Sanskrit term dhāman*, Amsterdam Academy 1967, pp. 19 ff.); thou art all (things), the life(-time) of All, superior, Oṃ, I invite Gāyatrī (to be present).' Engaging in contemplation the worshipper then repeats the lines *prātar dhāyāmi gāyatrīm ravimaṇḍalamadhyagām / ṛgvedam uccārayantīm raktavarṇām kumārikām / akṣamālākarām brahmadaivatyāṃ haṃsavāhanām* 'At daybreak I meditate on Gāyatrī who resides in the middle of the sun's orb, who pronounces the Ṛgveda, is of red colour, a virgin, who has a rosary in her hand, whose god is Brahmā, whose mount is the goose.' (According to purāṇic conceptions she is a *śakti* and mind-born daughter of Brahmā and inseparable from him: cf. e.g. *MaP.* 3, 32; 4, 7; 9, 24; 171, 23.) This is the counterpart of the similar Śivaite stanza *Agni-Purāṇa* 72, 27.—Omitting the formulas which accompany the *nyāsa* and *digbandhana* (see p. 178 f., n. 109). I subjoin the stanzas to be pronounced in connection with the contemplation of Viṣṇu 'who is in the disk of the sun, the imperishable Highest ātman, with four arms (cf. also J. N. Banerjea, *The development of Hindu iconography*, pp. 76; 386 ff.; 428 f., etc.), etc.' (an enumeration is given of the god's ornaments and attributes, because the worshipper must mentally concentrate upon Viṣṇu in the form of a definite cult image of the god which, being in its turn made in accordance with traditional iconographic precepts, essentially is a means of promoting concentration and of realizing the worshipper's oneness with Him). The goddess

is invited to depart with the following mantra (*TĀ.* 10, 30, 1 = *MNU.* 343) which is pronounced with the hands in a praying position: *uttame śikhare devi* (*TĀ.*, *MNU. jāte*) *bhūmyāṃ parvatamūrdhani / brāhmaṇebhyo 'bhy anujñātā gaccha devi yathāsukham* 'O goddess, go with pleasure (home) to the highest peak on the earth on the top of the mountain, (where thou wast born, *MNU.*), allowed by the brahmans to depart!'

164. The sun is a remover of evil: *ŚB.* 13, 8, 1, 11.

165. This act may also be intended to send away the goddess of the Sandhyā (or, in general to bid farewell to any deity invoked to be present). See e.g. Krishnaswami Aiyar, *Popular Hinduism*, Madras, 1901, p. 95.

166. The first stanza is *TS.* 3, 4, 11, 5p (cf. also the almost identical *TĀ.* 4, 3, 2), etc. which is a variant of ṚV. 3, 59, 6 (see also A. B. Keith, *The Veda of the Black Yajus School*, Cambridge, Mass., 1914, p. 277, n. 2): 'The fame (ṚV. 'assistance') of Mitra, the supporter of men, of the god, which brings wealth (blessings, etc.), is true (fame), of most wonderful renown', belonging in *TS.*, etc., to the stanzas for the special sacrifices (*kāmyeṣṭis*), elsewhere however to those accompanying the attendance and worship of the sacrificial fires which follows the agnihotra (*VS.* 11, 62; *VS.* 6, 5, 4, 10; *ĀpŚS.* 6, 18, 1, etc.; *TĀ.* preparation of the Mahāvīra pot). Stanza 2 is *TS.* 3, 4, 11, 5q, which is a variant of 51, 1 of the Mitra hymn ṚV. 3, 59, 'Mitra stirs, with intelligence (discrimination), men (to activity); Mitra supports heaven and earth; Mitra regards the races of men with unwinking (eye); to the true one let us offer an oblation rich in ghee', *ĀpŚS.* 6, 27, 7 enjoins the man who has been on a journey to worship his fires with this stanza, whereas *MŚS.* 3, 2, 8 prescribes it in connection with the *agnihotra*; these are not the only Vedic uses. Compare also *BDhŚ.* 2, 4, 7, 11 *maitrībhyām ahar upatiṣṭhate mitrasya carṣaṇīdhṛtaḥ, mitro janān yātayatīti.* Stanza 3 is *TS.* 3, 4, 11, 5r = ṚV. 3, 59, 2 'Let that mortal, O Mitra, be distinguished as having benefits (satisfaction, refreshments, etc., see L. Renou, *Études sur le vocabulaire du Ṛgveda*, Pondicherry, 1958, p. 27 f.; P. Thieme, *Mitra and Aryaman*, New Haven, Conn., 1957, p. 44) who exerts himself for thee, O Āditya, by (keeping his) vow; being assisted by thee he is not slain, not oppressed; distress does not reach him neither from near, nor from afar'. It is used *ĀpŚS.* 6, 18, 1 (see above), etc. After these mantras the worshipper should pronounce a salutation: *sarvābhyo devatābhyo namo namaḥ* (cf. *s. d. svāhā HGS.* 1, 7, 18); and after pronouncing *kāmo 'kārṣīt* (*MNU.* 424) and *manyur akārṣīt* (*MNU.* 427) 'Desire had made (the mistake)' and 'zeal ...' (formulae of atonement, cf. *ĀpDhS.* 1, 9, 26, 13), salute the quarters of the universe, etc., finally to prostrate himself saying *Oṃ viṣṇave namaḥ*, for which compare *ŚGS.* 2, 14, 10; *ViS.* 67, 12, etc The long last formula to be recited is *dhyeyaḥ sadā savitṛmaṇḍalamadhyavartī nārāyaṇaḥ* ... which expresses the obligation or intention always to make God residing in the disk of the sun the object of one's contemplation, and after referring to His ornaments, etc., ends with homage to His manifestation as Kṛṣṇa Govinda who is the god of those who are devoted to the brahmans and their traditions, who is well-disposed to brahmans and cows and willing to extend his sympathy to the world and mankind.

167. For reasons of space I cannot discuss also other rites, for instance the so-called 'sacraments' (*saṃskāras*: Renou and Filliozat, *L'Inde classique*, I, p. 582) and the customary rites of various religious communities in case of death.

168. For a survey of the relevant facts in a comparatively early Hindu text (Kauṭilya's *Arthaśāstra*) see R. P. Kangle, *The Kauṭilya Arthaśāstra*, III, Bombay, 1965, pp. 156 ff.

169. For the Indian temple in general see S. Kramrisch, *The Hindu temple*, Calcutta, 1946; K. Fischer, *Schöpfungen indischer Kunst*, Cologne, 1959, pp. 51; 153 (with a bibliography), and my book *Die Religionen Indiens*, I, pp. 326 ff. I cannot enter here into a discussion of the regional differences in structure, of the attempts to draw a line between Aryan and Dravidian styles (cf. Elmore, *Dravidian gods in modern Hinduism*, pp. 3 ff.), of sociological distinctions (see Dumont, *Une sous-caste de l'Inde du Sud*, p. 319) and other problems (cf. also C. G. Diehl, *Church and shrine*, Uppsala, 1965, p. 23 f.). For regional differences see also H. von Glasenapp, *Heilige Stätten Indiens*, München, 1928, *passim.*

170. Nevertheless a definite shape of the temple originally implied a definite dedication which was also expressed by its name (see especially Kramrisch, op. cit., pp. 411 ff.). Thus specific shapes of the building were dedicated to specific groups, for instance the Śiva liṅga sanctuaries belong in the early 'medieval' period to another group of buildings than the Lakṣmī shrines.

171. For the emblems and attributes of the gods see also A. K. Coomaraswamy, *Geschichte der indischen und indonesischen Kunst*, Leipzig, 1927, pp. 48; 50 f.

172. For particulars see Kramrisch, op. cit., p. 275. As to the outside, a Viṣṇu temple may show some avatāras, the Śiva temple divinities most related to the god.

173. Von Glasenapp, *Heilige Stätten Indiens*, pp. 13; 23; 61 f. Cf. e.g. also *SauraP.* a. 67.

174. Von Glasenapp, op. cit., p. 14; S. Kramrisch, *The Hindu temple*, op. cit., p. 73.

175. Such as Mathurā, Dvārakā, Ayodhyā. See also P. V. Jagadisa Ayyar, *South Indian shrines*, Madras, 1920, p. 125 f.

176. Not rarely however two or more gods are supposed to have a predilection for the same resort. See e.g. Von Glasenapp, op. cit., *passim*; H. Zimmer, *The art of Indian Asia*, New York, 1955, I, p. 257 f.

177. Cf. e.g. Varāhamihira, *BS.* 54, 3; 86, 75; Kramrisch, op. cit., pp. 53; 233 ff.; H. Zimmer, *The art of Indian Asia*, New York, 1955, I, p. 323.

178. Kāśyapa, *Jñānakāṇḍa* 17, and others; cf. Goudriaan, *Kāśyapa's Book of Wisdom*, p. 67.

179. Kauṭilya, *AS.* 2, 4, 17; cf. R. P. Kangle, *The Kauṭilīya Arthaśāstra*, Bombay, II, 1963, p. 80; III, 1965, p. 156. Cf. also Renou and Filliozat, *L'Inde classique*, I, p. 577.

180. *Ajitāgama*, Kr. 6, 24 ff.

181. 'Die Götter sind auf diese Weise bis heute in einem Land angesiedelt, in dem der Mythus noch immer Wirklichkeit ist' (S. Kramrisch, *Grundzüge der indischen Kunst*, Hellerau, 1924, p. 31). Both animals could in the course of time be anthropomorphized.

182. *Change and continuity*, ch. III.

183. I refer to *Aspects of early Viṣṇuism*, pp. 101 ff., etc.

184. See also E. B. Havell, *The Ideals of Indian art*, London, 1920, p. 73; and my *Aspects of early Viṣṇuism*, p. 103.

185. One may, among other publications, consult Stevenson, op. cit., pp. 368 ff.; W. J. Wilkins, *Modern Hinduism*, London, 1887, pp. 209 ff.; Monier-Williams, *Brahmanism and Hinduism*, p. 144; J. N. Farquhar, *The crown of Hinduism*, Oxford, 1913, pp. 312 ff.; Ch. Eliot, *Hinduism and Buddhism*, II, London (1921), [3]1957, p. 174; Kane, op. cit., II, pp. 705 ff.; for some general remarks M. Weber, *The religion of India*, Glenco, Ill., 1958, pp. 21 ff.; L. S. S. O'Malley, *Popular Hinduism*, Cambridge, 1935, pp. 95 ff.; and, for more detailed information, Rangachari, *The Sri Vaishnava brahmans*; R. V. Joshi, *Le rituel de la dévotion kṛṣṇaite*, Pondicherry, 1959; T. Goudriaan, *Kāśyapa's Book of Wisdom* (Vaikhānasa Viṣṇuism, dealing inter alia with this subject) the same, 'Daily worship of the Vaikhānasas', to be published in *Indo-Iranian Journal*; Diehl, *Instrument and purpose*, pp. 95 ff. (Śivaite); F. Nowotny, 'Pūjāvidhinirūpaṇa des Trimalla', *Indo-Ir. J.*, I (1957), pp. 109 ff. (Śivaite); Brunner-Lachaux, *Somaśambhupaddhati*, esp. the Introduction and pp. 68 ff.

186. 'The great gods ... get their *nitya-sevā* (daily service) from their votaries of the upper castes. If the votary himself is a brahmin, it is well and good; otherwise he has to commission the services of a *pūjārī* brahmin, that is a professional brahmin priest' (Basu, op. cit., p. 145).

187. Thus in the great temple of Liṅgarāj at Bhubaneswar 'the god is represented by a natural block of stone' (O'Malley, op. cit., p. 96). See e.g. also Von Glasenapp, *Heilige Stätten*, p. 23; Zimmer, *Art of Indian Asia*, I, p. 280; Farquhar, *Crown of Hinduism*, p. 316 f. It may in this connection be observed that even the two great gods under discussion have not always a sanctuary in a definite region. See e.g. Thakur, *Sindhi culture*, p. 135.

188. This is the so-called *parārthapūjā*, lit. 'the worship (cult) for the sake of others' as distinguished from the *ātmārthapūjā*. Although there exist manuals for either variety many may serve both purposes. It seems worth recalling that in contradistinction to the Vedic rites these Hindu services may be held by any qualified member of the community. They are, moreover, obligatory.

189. Some particulars will be mentioned further on.

190. See W. Caland, *Vaikhānasasmārtasūtram*, Calcutta, 1929, p. xv f.

191. Yet the younger Vaikhānasa manuals did—probably under the influence of the Pāñcāratrins and the Śrī-Vaiṣṇavas—incorporate new elements which were fully developed in Śaiva and Śākta communities (see Goudriaan, *Daily worship*).

192. See e.g. Kane, op. cit., II, p. 739 f.

193. This point is, as far as the Vaikhānasas are concerned, recently elucidated by Goudriaan, *Daily worship*. Attention may be drawn also to some publications dealing with the

interesting modified survival of Śaiva ritual in the isle of Bali: C. Hooykaas, *Āgama tīrtha, five studies in Hindu-Balinese religion*, Amsterdam Academy, 1964; the same, *Surya-sewana, the way to God of a Balinese Śiva priest*, Amsterdam, Academy, 1966 (pp. 141 ff. a (tentative) comparison of Śaiva ritual in South India and Bali); Mrs. J. H. Hooykaas-van Leeuwen Boomkamp, *Ritual purification of a Balinese temple*, Amsterdam Academy, 1961.

194. I mean the so-called *prayogas* (manuals dealing with ritual practice or the application of rules) and *paddhatis* (guide-books for particular rites and ceremonies in which the course of the rites and the functions of the officiants are accurately described).

195. Cf. e.g. Hillebrandt, *Ritualliteratur*; Nowotny, op. cit., p. 120; Goudriaan, *Daily worship*; Renou, preface to Brunner-Lachaux, op. cit.

196. Cf. e.g. *Vis.* a. 65 (one of the earliest detailed descriptions of (Vāsudeva-)pūjā); *BaudhGPS.* 2, 14 (daily worship of Māhapuruṣa, i.e. Viṣṇu; a translation may be found in P. N. U. Harting, *Selections from the Baudhāyana-Gṛhyapariśiṣṭasūtra*, Thesis, Utrecht, 1922, p. 32 f.); for particulars see Kane, op. cit., II, pp. 729 ff.; V, pp. 34 ff.; Stevenson, op. cit., pp. 29; 233 ff., etc.; Brunner-Lachaux, op. cit., p. 339, mentioning (p. 332) varieties of Śaiva cult consisting of 12 and 24 *upacāras*. Minor variations in order and (of) terminology may be left unnoticed here. The sixteen *upacāras* are: invocation, offering of a seat, of water for washing the feet, of *arghya* water, of water for rinsing the mouth, of a bath, a garment, the sacred thread, perfumes, flowers, incense, a lamp, food, homage, a circumambulation and dismissal.

197. The historical development of the total complex of ritual acts known as *pūjā* may, in the main points, become clear by comparative study of the older handbooks and the younger manuals and commentaries which even in the Vaikhānasa community give a much greater place to practices of a Tantric character.

198. See also *Die Religionen Indiens*, II, p. 124 f.

199. See *Die Religionen Indiens*, II, pp. 131 ff.; Rangachari, op. cit., pp. 17 ff.

200. Until Rāmānuja's times there does not seem to have been much distinction between Smārta Hindus (*Die Religionen Indiens*, I, pp. 332 ff.; II, p. 93) and this school.

201. See *Die Religionen Indiens*, II, pp. 125 ff.; Rangachari, op. cit., pp. 7 ff.

202. Compare also Rangachari, op. cit., p. 40.

203. I cannot dwell here on the differences in importance attached, in later times, to the two schools of Śrī-Vaiṣṇava thought, the Tengalais who hold a one-sided *prapatti* view of life and emphasize the devotee's disposition and state of mind and the more conservative Vaḍagalais who are rather inclined to believe in the efficacy of rites, yoga, myths, etc. For these differences in general see A. Govindacharya, in *J.R.A.S.* (1910), p. 1103 f. Some ritual particulars are the following: during worship Sanskrit mantras predominate among the Vaḍagalais, Tamil among the Tengalais. On a *śrāddha* day the former offer food also to the *ācāryas* and brahmans representing the deceased ancestors, the Tengalais only to God. The Tengalais regard the hearing of a special mantra as equivalent to *prapatti*, the others reject this view. (See also Rangachari, op. cit., pp. 45 ff.).

204. See e.g. J. N. Farquhar, *An outline of the religious literature of India*, Oxford, 1920, p. 196 f.

205. Renou and Filliozat, *L'Inde classique*, I, p. 577 f.

206. The Vaikhānasas have not only preserved numerous Vedic mantras, mostly taken from the Ṛg- and Yajuḥ-Saṃhitās, but also possess a considerable number of Sanskrit formulas which are their own and not known from elsewhere. These mantras were collected and edited: Vaikhānasamantrapraśna, *Vaikhānasagranthamālā*, 7, Madras, 1920. (For the often incorrect Sanskrit of the Vaikhānasa texts see also W. Caland, *Over het Vaikhānasasūtra*, Amsterdam Academy, 1926, pp. 1 ff.) The Śrī-Vaiṣṇavas use both Sanskrit and Tamil (see the preceding note).

207. This has practically resulted in the development of an independent Tamil school of Śivaite thought and ritual based on Tamil works based on Sanskrit authorities, the oldest of which date back to the XIIth century.

208. The Indian name for such a community transmitting an established doctrine and traditional rites of their own is *saṃpradāya*.

209. Minor differences in execution should not detain us here.

210. For the very elaborate preparatory and other ritual acts of the Southern Śaiva community dealt with by Diehl, see op. cit., p. 100 f.; for the Vaikhānasas Goudriaan,

Daily worship, (see n. 185); cf. also Brunner-Lachaux, op. cit., pp. 90 ff.; Rangachari, op. cit., p. 134 f.

211. This act is accompanied by ṚV. 1, 22, 5 *hiraṇyapāṇim ūtaye savitāram upa hvaye / sa cettā devatā padam* 'I invoke Savitar, the golden-handed one, for help; among the gods he knows the track'. Cf. Kāśyapa, *Jñ.* a. 69; for another use made of the mantra: ibid., a. 85. This stanza belongs to the inviting and offering prayers accompanying oblations presented to Savitar, the first of the series being the Sāvitrī (ṚV. 3, 62, 10): see *VS*. 22, 10; *AiB*. 5, 19, 9; *ŚŚS*. 3, 13, 12, etc.

212. Here also the manuals are at variance with regard to particulars. For instance, *Ajitāgama*, Kr. 20, 33 ff. has the worshipper make a circumambulation (from left to right) of Śiva's sanctuary, enter it after having washed his feet, etc., and throw, while standing at the door, a flower on the ground for Brahmā; *Suprabhedāgama* 1, 8, 15 f. however prescribes a respectful libation of holy water to the Sun and entering the temple flower(s) in hand.

213. See also Kramrisch, op. cit., p. 314. For different doorkeepers see e.g. B. K. Barua *A cultural history of Assam*, I, Nowgong, 1951, p. 171 f. Lakṣmī, the goddess of fortune, though Viṣṇu's spouse, must however be visible also over Śiva's entrance: *AgniP*. 74, 2. For temple doors see J. C. Harle, *Temple gateways in South India*, Oxford 1963.

214. Authorities also agree in prescribing that he should place his right foot inside before the left without touching the threshold, lest he should disturb and offend the deities of that place (cf. Brunner-Lachaux, op. cit., p. 98, and in general Th. Zachariae, *Kleine Schriften*, Bonn and Leipzig, 1920, p. 400; H. Oldenberg, *Die Religion des Veda*, Stuttgart and Berlin, ⁴1923, p. 553, note). For the right and left side see e.g. J. Gonda, *The Savayajñas*, Amsterdam Academy, 1965, p. 215. The left hand is not used in worshipping the gods. For some information on a partly Vedic origin of respect paid to the deities of the door and the site of the building see Nowotny, op. cit., pp. 115 f.; 140.

215. According to some Vaikhānasa authorities the demons, men's jealous rivals, covet the merit of the ceremonies (Goudriaan, *Daily worship*).

216. Cf. also Stevenson, op. cit., p. 370.

217. See e.g. *SomaśP*. 3, 5.

218. *VaikhSmS*. 4, 10 ff.

219. The terms occur also in Pāñcarātra philosophy to characterize the two aspects of Viṣṇu's Śakti; see F. O. Schrader, *Introduction to the Pāñcarātra*, Adyar, Madras, 1916, p. 30.

220. *dhruvabera*.

221. *kautuka* (*bimba*).

222. For many details see Kāśyapa, *Jñānakāṇḍa*, a. 40 ff. (ed. Goudriaan, pp. 128 ff.).

223. Kāś. *Jñ.* a. 54. Other images are to be used for bathings and festivals. Worship cannot exist without *bhakti*, but may, by ascetics and hermits, be performed without the concrete support of an image.

224. This ritual method mainly consists in the assignment of Brahman to the worshipper's body by means of mental concentration, gestures and formulas, which, while apparently being proper to this community, are to bring about his identity with Brahman and Viṣṇu.

225. Viṣṇu, Puruṣa, Satya, Acyuta and Aniruddha. Cf. Kāś. *Jñ.* a. 77.

226. The mantra is ṚV. 1, 154, 2 (*TB*. 2, 4, 3, 4) *pra tad viṣṇu stavate vīryeṇa mṛgo na bhīmaḥ kucaro giriṣṭhāḥ / yasyoruṣu triṣu vikramaṇeṣu adhikṣiyanti bhuvanāni viśvā* 'Viṣṇu is thus praised for his heroism, like a dread beast that wanders at will, that haunts the mountains, (he) in whose three wide strides all beings dwell'. In Vedic ritual this stanza is *inter alia* prescribed to the sacrificer after touching the middle reed-mat of the cart-shed which is Viṣṇu (*ŚB*. 3, 5, 3, 23). *VaikhSmS*. 3, 13; 4, 12 has it pronounced to accompany, in worshipping this god, an oblation and the preparation of a seat of sacred grass.

227. The mantra (*VaikhMP*. 8, 20) is *bhūr asi bhūḥ pratiṣṭhityai, bhuvo 'si . . . / sānandaḥ sarveṣām antarātmā bhava, pūtaḥ pūtāntarātmā bhava . . . viṣṇum pratiṣṭhāpayāmi*. One of the elements of the complex of acts is Vedic. The arcaka fills the *praṇidhi* vessel (which, containing the lustral water, is elsewhere called *praṇītacamasa*; see Caland, *Vaikhānasasmārtasūtram translated*, p. 23) and uses it for sprinkling the site of the immovable image and for invoking Viṣṇu; in Vedic ritual it is especially used for supplying what is required for pressing the soma (cf. *KātyŚS*. 6, 7, 19 comm.).

228. Some particulars worth knowing about flowers may be found in Kane, op. cit., II, p. 732 f. and J. J. Meyer, *Sexual life in ancient India*, London, 1930, p. 266.

229. The invocation proper (*āvāhana*) takes place after the preparation of the requisites, among which the vessels (the *praṇidhi*, three for washing, sipping and bathing, and five for the arghya, the gifts offered to an honoured guest) are of special importance. Each of the utensils (flowers, perfumes, lamps, etc.) has its presiding deity, the grouping of whom throws light on the systematic structure of these rites and on the underlying theory.

230. *VaikhMP.* 5, 49; Kāśyapa's *Arcanakhaṇḍa* 3; see Goudriaan, *Kāśyapa's Book of wisdom*, p. 314.

231. Compare *VaikhSmS.* 4, 11 where Caland incorrectly translated *sakalam* by 'complete'.

232. See above, note 299. For the invocation of gods into this vessel see *VaikhSmS.* 1, 13; 3, 13.

233. In the case of an immovable image the invitation to come and the dismissal are omitted (*BaudhGPS.* 2, 14). The same rule obtains in places where a permanent *liṅga* has been installed (ibid. 2, 17).

234. It is emphasized that the formulas to be pronounced make God comply with the worshipper's request to enter the movable image. These mantras are the very frequently used stanza ṚV. 1, 22, 17 (*TS.* 1, 2, 13, 1, etc.) *idaṃ viṣṇur vi cakrame tredhā ni dadhe padam / samūḷham asya pāṃsure* 'Over this Viṣṇu strode; thrice did he set down his foot; (all) is gathered in its dust', which, expressing Viṣṇu's striding (*PB.* 20, 3, 2), is (*VS.* 5, 15; *AiB.* 1, 17, 7; *ŚB.* 3, 5, 3, 13, etc.) in Vedic ritual to accompany an offering made in the track on the right of the right soma cart, an expiatory ceremony in connection with the Agnihotra (*TB.* 2, 7, 14, 2; *ŚB.* 12, 4, 1, 4 f.), and other ritual acts (*ĀpŚS.* 2, 6, 1; 9, 1, 11; 9, 6, 11 etc., *ŚGS.* 5, 2, 6), and *VMP.* 8, 21 *āyātu bhagavān puruṣas sagaṇas sasainyas saśrīsahāyas saha devatābhir anumanyatām*, used Kāś. *Jñ.* 25 in inviting God's *śakti* to appear; 68 when the officiant causes water which is identical with God's power to flow on the head of the immovable image in order to consecrate it.

235. This part of the ritual which in an elementary form occurs already in the *sūtra* (4, 12) was in the course of time much enlarged; the number of the mantras accompanying each act, in the sūtra usually one, increased. For particulars see Goudriaan, *Daily worship*.

236. ṚV. 1, 154, 5; *TB.* 2, 4, 6, 2, which *AiB.* 1, 17, 7 occurs together with ṚV. 1, 22, 17 (see above).

237. Even in Tantric and Śāktist rites.

238. The relations between both types of ritual become clearer, on the one hand from some early descriptions in which the *pūjā* is included in a regular *homa* so as to effect a variety of a fire sacrifice (cf. *BaudhGPS.* 3, 7, cf. Harting, op. cit., p. XVIII), on the other hand from a survey of the complete ritual as performed in different communities. For the incorporation of the *bali* see Goudriaan, *Daily worship*.

239. According to Kāś. *Jñ.* 71 this oblation should have the shape of a lotus flower in which Viṣṇu is believed to be present; it is made the object of a meditation.

240. Compare W. Caland, *Een indogermaansch lustratiegebruik*, Amsterdam Academy, 1898.

241. For particulars see Kāś. *Jñ.* a. 73 (Goudriaan, *Kāśyapa's Book of wisdom*, p. 215).

242. With regard to the latter prescript (cf. also *ViDhŚ.* 65, 15; *VaikhSmS.* 4, 12) the Vaikhānasa authorities are unanimous, some of them adding other formulas.

243. This is already prescribed in the sūtra: *VaikhSmS.* 4, 12; see also *BaudhGPS.* 2, 14. The accompanying mantras are *Oṃ namo nārāyaṇāya* and *Oṃ namo bhagavate vāsudevāya*.

244. I refer to Rangachari, op. cit., pp. 135 ff.; V. N. Srinivasa Rao, Tirupati, Madras, 1949, pp. 1 ff.; Diehl, op. cit., pp. 152 ff. The *ṣaḍaṅganyāsa* to be observed by this community is only to a certain extent similar to the *brahmanyāsa* of the Vaikhānasas of which it is the counterpart. For the Śivaite counterpart see Nowotny, op. cit., pp. 115; 133.

245. See also Diehl, op. cit., p. 84 f.

246. At a certain moment God, who is always in the *arcaka*'s heart, is thought to come out through his right nostril. This is one of the views which these Viṣṇuites have in common with Śivaites (see p. 84 and compare e.g. also Nowotny, op. cit., p. 143).

247. Here also I present the relevant facts only in a very brief review.

248. Which again are largely of the type *Oṃ brūm trūm ādhāraśaktyai namaḥ*: *Oṃ*, the *bija(s)*, special power centre(s) of esoteric significance, the name in the dative, 'homage'.
249. The formula is *Oṃ namo nārāyaṇāya, āgaccha, āgaccha.*
250. This term for 'gratifying, propitiating' includes also ideas such as 'homage, adoration, worship' and is used also for 'service worship'. (See e.g. Diehl, op. cit., p. 284.)
251. It should be remembered that the rites observed in different temples are not uniform. Those performed in the Kālamēkaperumāl temple at Tirumocur (six miles east of Mathurai) for instance are, in details, more similar to the Śivaite service.
252. *Die Religionen Indiens*, II, pp. 177 ff.
253. For particulars see G. A. Deleury, *The cult of Viṭhobā*, Poona, 1960, pp. 65 ff.
254. I refer to H. von Glasenapp, *Madhva's Philosophie des Vishnu-Glaubens*, Bonn and Leipzig, 1923, pp. *18 and 84 f.
255. See Kane, op. cit., V, pp. 95 ff. and especially 113 ff.; Stevenson, op. cit., p. 260 f.; Joshi, op. cit., p. 106; B. A. Gupte, *Hindu holidays and ceremonials*, Calcutta and Simla, 1919, p. 47 f.
256. Cf. C. M. Padmanabha Char, *The life and teachings of Sri Madhvacharyar*, Coimbatore, 1909, p. 254.
257. Which largely prevails among the Vaiṣṇavas.
258. This term is not necessarily synonymous with 'comparatively late' or 'younger'. For tantric mantras see e.g. *Nārada-Pañcarātra* 5, 1.
259. For a general characterization see Joshi, op. cit., pp. 1 ff.
260. A distinction is made between images made by men and (the much less numerous) images which have appeared spontaneously.
261. See *PadmaP.* 6, 253, 11 ff. The body of the man who fails to apply them is even said to be similar to a burial place for corpses.
262. Alternatively earth taken from the roots of a *tulasī* may serve also.
263. Keśava (forehead), Nārāyaṇa, Mādhava, Govinda, Viṣṇu, Madhusūdana, Trivikrama, Vāmana, Śrīdhara, Hṛṣīkeśa, Padmanābha, Dāmodara.
264. *Haribhaktivilāsa*, 4, p. 176.
265. With some variation in the mantras. The worshipper must remain seated in the *padmāsana* posture (the cross-legged tailor-fashion) which is one of the favourite Indian attitudes for meditation.
266. For particulars see Joshi, op. cit., p. 89.
267. *Aspects of early Viṣṇuism*, p. 200 f., etc.; Stevenson, op. cit., pp. 161; 172, etc.; De Mallmann, op. cit., p. 257 f.
268. See Meyer, *Trilogie*, III, p. 319 f.
269. This gesture is one of the thirty-two enumerated by Mitramiśra, *Pūjaprakāśa* (XVIIth century), pp. 123 ff. For *mudrās* in general see H. Zimmer, *Kunstform und Yoga im indischen Kultbild*, Berlin, 1926, *passim*; A. K. Coomaraswamy and G. K. Duggirala *The mirror of gesture*, Cambridge, Mass., 1917; E. Dale Saunders, *Mudrā*, New York, 1960.
270. Neck, heart, navel, abdomen, anus and the place between the eyebrows. Compare *Mṛgendrāgama* K. 1, 2 *śakter nādo 'bhavad bindur akṣaraṃ mātṛkā tataḥ*, and the comm.: *bhagavataḥ saṃbandhinī nikhilavāṅmayajanītvān māteva mātṛkā*, and e.g. also Nārada-Pañcarātra, 3, 1, 22 ff.
271. The formulas are *aṃ keśavāya kīrtyai namaḥ*, etc., Kīrti being the *śakti* of Keśava.
272. *Haribhaktivilāsa* 5, 60 ff.
273. The first is *maṃ namaḥ parāya jīvātmane namaḥ*; the sound *ma* takes precedence, because it is a name of God (Brahman, Viṣṇu).
274. Cf. *Haribhaktivilāsa* 5, 141.
275. See above, and compare *Haribhaktivilāsa* 5, 28 ff.
276. In an interpolated passage of the *Mahābhārata* it is told that Yudhiṣṭhira being installed on the throne is consecrated by Kṛṣṇa himself who (after 12, 40, 15 cr. ed.) sprinkles him with water contained in his famous conch, the Pāñcajanya.
277. The texts descend to many details; see Joshi, op. cit., p. 93 f.
278. Not all *nīrājana* ceremonies are executed in the same way. Here lights are waved in front of God's image in order to ward off evil, elsewhere a solution of saffron or turmeric and lime serves this purpose.

279. For particulars see Diehl, op. cit., pp. 98 ff.; Brunner-Lachaux, op. cit. and other publications quoted in the preceding pages. I do not consider here the Pāśupata ritual, which is in many respects rather different; now see also J. N. Banerjea, *Paurāṇic and Tāntric religion*, Calcutta, 1966, pp. 92 ff.

280. There are other performers of rites, viz. the family priests and the *pūjārīs* who officiate at shrines which are neither Śivaite nor Viṣṇuite.

281. Among these is also a purification of the mantras: *SomaśP.* 3, 43.

282. *SomaśP.* 3, 16 ff.; Brunner-Lachaux, op. cit., pp. 102; 114 ff. Here also (Brunner-Lachaux, op. cit., p. 114; cf. Rangachari, op. cit., p. 138, etc.) the body is 'destroyed' after the *jīva* ('soul') has by means of a Tantric rite been temporarily 'put in safety' (*SomaśP.* 3, 11 ff.), 'car il est nécessaire que le jīva continue l'expérience de l'incarnation présente . . .; il sera temporairement uni à Śiva dans le séjour suprême, union symbolique où le jīva reste distinct' (Brunner-Lachaux, op. cit., p. 104, n. 1).

283. Cf. Brunner-Lachaux, op. cit., p. 130, n. 3; Nowotny, op. cit., p. 113.

284. Compare above, p. 80.

285. This fire as well as the recipient of the oblations is Śiva.

286. Cf. Brunner-Lachaux, op. cit., p. 138.

287. Cf. also *SomaśP.* 3, 33; the mantra *Oṃ hāṃ hauṃ śaktaye namaḥ* and the *dhenumudrā* effect the transformation. The main difference between Balinese and Indian Śiva worship lies in the officiant's activities after he has become the living abode of God. In Bali it is his task to make holy water, to cause God to descend into it and so sell it to the people; thus the preparation of the holy water has become the central act of the ceremonies.

288. The most excellent worship of this *mūlaliṅga* is the one which is just finished at sunrise.

289. Cf. e.g. *LiṅgaP.* 2, 19, 31 *smarāmi devaṃ ravimaṇḍalasthaṃ / sadāśivaṃ śaṅkaram ādidevaṃ*. As is well known, the supreme god of the Balinese is Śivāditya or Śivasūrya. Although Śiva is predominant both gods have been identified and are worshipped as a unity in duality. A pre-Hindu Balinese sun worship may have caused this greater emphasis on Śiva's solar aspect, but the name Śivāditya (and Śivāgni) occurs already at an earlier date, e.g. in the Old-Javanese Agastyaparwa (XIth century; see my relative note in *Agastyaparwa*, The Hague, 1936, p. 211). On Śiva and Āditya see e.g. also I. Scheftelowitz, *Acta Orientalia* (Leyden), XI, p. 314.

290. Cf. also *Mṛgendrāgama*, Kr. 2, 20 ff.: 'One should meditate on Sadāśiva who is in the disc of the sun and at the end of the mantra throw, from the hollowed palms, water, while calling him to mind, perform, after offering an *arghya*, a *pūjā* complete with incense, light, ointment, flowers, mutter the Śiva (*mūla*)*mantra* and the *aṅgamantras* (which invoke Sadāśiva's 'limbs' or 'powers') and finally take 'Agni's bath' (*āgneyasnāna*).' A more detailed description is provided in *SomaśP.* ch. 2. However, part of the Śaiva authorities do not mention the Sūryapūjā (see Bhatt, *Rauravāgama*, p. 195 f.) so that it does not seem to have been obligatory always and everywhere as it is nowadays. In any case two schools may among the ancient authorities be distinguished, one considering the Sūryapūjā an essential element of the daily worship, the other regarding it as optional.

291. Commentators quoted by Brunner-Lachaux, op. cit., p. 68.

292. In Diehl's account the order of the acts deviates from the text edited by Mme Brunner-Lachaux.

293. See Brunner-Lachaux, op. cit., p. 146.

294. Cf. *Mṛgendrāgama*, K. 3, 37; *SomaśP.* 3, 47.

295. *Die Religionen Indiens*, I, p. 250 f. It is believed to support the germ of the impure worlds (which is *māyā*) and the first cause or germ of the pure worlds and hence to support the whole phenomenal manifestation (Nirmalamaṇiguru on *Aghoraśivācārya-paddhati*, Chidambaram, 1927, p. 90 f.). The tortoise is believed to be Viṣṇu who represents the stability of the world (see also Kramrisch, *The Hindu temple*, p. 111).

296. . . . *mūrtiṃ tejorūpāṃ daṇḍākārām avibhaktāvayavāṃ śivatattvātmakaparabinduvyāptikām* . . . (*AghoraśP.* 95).

297. The lion-seat is associated with royal power; see J. Auboyer, *Le trône et son symbolisme dans l'Inde ancienne*, Paris, 1949, ch. III.

298. Kramrisch, loc. cit. One may compare the description of the Balinese *padmāsana*

or throne of God and the turtle bearing it provided by Hooykaas, *Āgama Tīrtha*, ch. III and esp. pp. 103 ff.

299. The so-called *yogāsana*, one of God's five seats which may be visualized by the *ācārya*, the complete throne being conceived as a fivefold whole, the parts of which are arranged in the form of a lotus. For particulars see *SomaśP*. 3, 47–56 and Brunner-Lachaux, op. cit., pp. 154 ff. ('L'essentiel semble être de comprendre que c'est le domaine entier de la manifestation, visible ou invisible, qui sert de trône à Śiva').

300. After the 'construction' of the throne a sequence of four ritual acts is obligatory: invocation (*āvāhana*, i.e. calling God near: *Mṛgendrāgama*, K. 3, 56), installation (*sthāpana*), presence (*saṃnidhāna*), and detention (*saṃnirodhana*). *SomaśP*. 3, 66 explains the term *āvāhana* as follows: '(succeeding in) making God attentively turn to oneself'.

301. See also *SomaśP*. 3, 68.

302. This phenomenon can be understood as subjective in nature, viz. as a modification of the worshipper's mind, as well as objective: as the mantra and Śiva are identical, the 'placing' of the former results in a special presence of the latter. The installation is (*SomaśP*. 3, 67) *bhaktyā sthāpanam* 'to make God take His place with love and attachment.'

303. The divine presence is again not inconsistent with God's omnipresence, and explained as a state of the worshipper's mind. 'Uninterrupted': this refers to the *saṃnirodhana* (see above, n. 300), which is stated to be the continuation of God's presence till the end of the ritual.

304. A special *mudrā* and *mantra* are to ensure God's invisibility to the undevout.

305. This term literally means: 'the making complete, putting in possession of all its component parts'. The explanation and translation given by Diehl, op. cit., p. 81, n. 3 are erroneous.

306. According to the *SomaśP*. 3, 61 ff. and the authorities quoted by Mme Brunner-Lachaux, op. cit., pp. 184 ff., the *mūlamantra* duly recited is brought to Śiva's abode; identical with Śiva it sparkles in the form of the *bindu* in the middle of the forehead, from there to appear through the right nostril (see n. 246).

307. Authorities are, here also, at variance with regard to particulars. The order of the elements of the formulas to be used depends on the worshipper's desires; if he wishes to realize worldly ambitions a definite order is prescribed; if he aspires to liberation, the reverse order.

308. For particulars see Brunner-Lachaux, op. cit., pp. 208 ff. See e.g. also *KālP*. a. 58 where Kālī's names are recited in a similar way.

309. One of the mantras recited on this occasion is the 'Annasūkta', a series of formulas beginning with *prāṇāya svāhā* 'Hail to out-breathing!' and in Vedic ritual used to accompany the presentation of oblations: *VS*. 22, 23 ff.; 23, 18; *ŚB*. 13, 2, 8, 2: by these mantras the vital airs are put into them so that they become truly living; cf. also *BĀU*. 6, 3, 2; *MNU*. 4, 73 ff., and especially *BaudhDŚ*. 2, 7, 12, 3 (see Varenne, op. cit., II, pp. 80 ff.). For particulars see also Stevenson, op. cit., p. 391. The *naivedyas* must not be eaten: *BṛhaddharmaP*. 2, 27; *Atri-Saṃhita*, 43, 109.

310. See *Die Religionen Indiens*, II, p. 207; 226; V. Paranjoti, *Śaiva Siddhānta*, London, ^{2}1954, p. 151.

311. *SomaśP*. 3, 102 f. adds the interesting remark that Śiva's cult may also take place in a state of profound concentration (*samādhi*), of physical asceticism or austerities (*tapas*), by means of a repeated recitation of mantras, on one's own body or on that of one's *guru* (that means: God may be invoked to 'enter' the latter's body); the worship may in a similar way be based on a sacred book, on the water contained in a vessel, on fire (as described in the following fire rite), on a painted image, etc. (these possibilities are not integrally and exclusively characteristic of this Śivaite tradition); however, the liṅga cult is by far the most excellent.

312. In describing this ritual also authorities disagree in particulars. See e.g. *Mṛgendrāgama*, K. 6; *Rauravāgama*, K. 15; *Ajitāgama*, K. 21 and the parallel texts, enumerated by Bhatt, *Ajitāgama*, p. 238.

313. The consecrated water which is respectfully offered to a guest and to divine beings.

314. On festive occasions in a special room of the temples, on other days in a permanent *kuṇḍa* (a round hole in the ground for receiving fire). For particulars see Diehl, op. cit., p. 124. For a Viṣṇuite parallel (*dīkṣā* ceremonies) Joshi, op. cit., p. 13 f.

315. They are represented by two substitutes (*kūrca*) made, in a particular way, of sacred grass. Vāgīśvarī is one of the names of Sarasvatī, the goddess of speech and learning. This would lead us to suppose that Vāgīśvara is Brahmā (thus Diehl, op. cit., p. 125), Sarasvatī's spouse, but he is always described as Śiva (cf. Brunner-Lachaux, op. cit., p. 237).

316. It can be taken from the sun through a kind of crystal called 'sunstone', by attrition through pieces of pipal wood, from the temple kitchen, from the house of the *ācārya* or of an initiated Śaiva brahman.

317. See e.g. *Die Religionen Indiens*, II, pp. 34; 38 f.; Lindquist, *Die Methoden des Yoga*, p. 190; M. Eliade, *Le yoga, immortalité et liberté*, Paris, 1954, pp. 237 ff.; A. Daniélou, *Yoga*, London, 1949, pp. 123 ff. The system of *cakras* is assumed on the ground of yogic experiences of a trans-physiological character. Mere austerity and psycho-physiological discipline cannot 'awaken' or 'penetrate' them. 'Les yogis . . . opéraient leurs expériences sur un "corps subtil", c'est-à-dire en utilisant des sensations, des tensions, des états transconscients inaccessibles aux profanes . . ., ils pénétraient dans les profondeurs de l'inconscient, et savaient "réveiller" les couches archaïques de la conscience primordiale' (Eliade, op. cit., p. 238). They were convinced to come, in this way, into contact with, or to merge their identity in, the eternal, divine One underlying all phenomenal existence.

318. The technique consists in inhaling (through the left nostril) and in exhaling (through the right nostril) the terrestrial fire, of course to the accompaniment of mantras.

319. The process is that of the *amṛtīkaraṇa* described p. 72, n. 132. Compare also Bhaṭṭa-Nārāyaṇakaṇṭha on *Mṛgendrāgama*, K. 6, 7 f.

320. See *Die Religionen Indiens*, I, p. 115 f.; Kane, op. cit., II, p. 188 f. The first *saṃskāra* is the *garbhādhāna* (conception), the second the *puṃsavana* (the ceremony to be performed in the 2nd or 3rd month of pregnancy to ensure the birth of a male child), next the *sīmantonnayana* (the parting of the hair of the prospective mother to be performed in the 6th month) which here is to make face and limbs of the embryo well-shaped.

321. Cf. Śabara on Jaimini, *PūrvamS.* 3, 1, 3 *saṃskāro nāma sa bhavati yasmiñ jāte padārtho bhavati yogyaḥ kasyacid arthasya.*

322. *SomaśP.* 4, 20 even prescribes a bath in order to destroy the impurities caught during its stay in the womb.

323. Some of these are to protect the baby-fire, others are to worship Brahmā, Viṣṇu, Rudra and Ananta (-Śiva), i.e. God and his manifestation as the Trinity, and the deities of the ten quarters.

324. I refer to Brunner-Lachaux, op. cit., p. 248.

325. See e.g. Eliade, op. cit., p. 240 f.

326. Together with the mantras and the deities who were concerned in the rite. See also Brunner-Lachaux, op. cit., p. 264.

327. *SomaśP.* 70 f. . . . *pūjāhomādikarma ca / gṛhāṇa bhagavan puṇyaphalam ity abhidhāya ca.*

328. They dwell, it is true, on the significance of particular acts, mantras and gestures, distinguishing between worldly fruits (*bhukti*) and transcendent merit (i.e. emancipation: *mukti*), the large majority of worshippers being, of course, desirous of the former.

329. It may therefore be said that the performer of these rites pursues the same object as the yogin.

330. The success of the rite depends on the perfection of his spiritual development. He must take part in it with his whole personality. From the above exposition it will be clear that the opinion which has long been current in the West, viz. that Śaiva rites are necessarily orgiastic, is untenable.

331. Cf. also *SomaśP.* 3, 95 . . . *tvaṃ gṛhāṇāsmatkṛtaṃ japam / siddhir bhavatu me yena tvatprasādāt tvayi sthite*, and H. P. Chatterji, *The Nārada Pancharātram*, Allahabad, 1921, p. 152. The same idea was very distinctly expressed in Vedic ritual, see *The Savayajñas*, pp. 186 ff.

332. The first-grade initiates obtain, by the ritual, access to Śiva, the higher-grade initiates may be said to remain, by it, in a 'state of holiness'.

333. The man who performs Kṛṣṇa's *pūjā* will be revered even by the gods (Nār. *Pañc.* 5, 4, 1).

CHAPTER V

1. I would avoid using the frequently adopted term 'sect' (which is e.g. preferred by S. Chattopadhyaya, *The evolution of theistic sects in Ancient India*, Calcutta, 1962, p. 46), because it cannot be said that Viṣṇuism and Śivaism were, and are, schismatic bodies of believers which had seceded from a more or less established church.

2. Now see also L. Renou, *Études védiques et pāṇinéennes*, xv, Paris, 1966, pp. 15 ff. and pp. 34 ff.

3. ṚV. 7, 40, 5. Translators disagree; even Renou's translation and note contradict each other (*E.V.P.*, iv, p. 103; v, p. 44); the adjective *mīḍhvas* may in any case apply to Rudra (cf. e.g. 1, 114, 3), and the particle *hi* must make sense.

4. Cf. 6, 49, 10 and 13; 7, 36, 5 and 9; cf. 5, 51, 9 and 13; 10, 66, 3 and 5; 92, 5 and 11; 8, 54, 3 and 4.

5. Cf. 5, 46, 2; 6, 50, 12; 10, 65, 1; 66, 4.

6. Some references to the *Rudrāḥ*, Rudra's sons (e.g. 8, 20, 17) can be left unmentioned here.

7. 'Il s'agit d'un poème mixte Viṣṇu-Marut's, ou plutôt, soit un poème aux Marut à l'imprégnation "viṣṇuite", soit un poème à Viṣṇu avec insistance sur l'alliance entre le dieu et les Marut' (Renou, *E.V.P.*, x, p. 96).

8. Cf. ṚV. 8, 94, 12. Viṣṇu is 1, 156, 4 said to be the ordainer associated with the Maruts; see also A. A. Macdonell, *Vedic mythology*, Strassburg, 1897, p. 40.

9. Cf. K. F. Geldner, *Der Rig-Veda*, Cambridge, Mass., 1951, I, p. 420; Renou, *E.V.P.*, xii, p. 114; xiii, p. 92. For Rudra = Agni see e.g. *TB*. 1, 4, 3, 6; 1, 6, 1, 2, and the references given above. For Viṣṇu and sexuality now see also I. Fišer, 'Indian erotics of the oldest period', *Acta Univ. Carolinae phil. mon.* xiv, Prague, 1966, p. 49.

10. Places such as *VS*. 21, 19 f.; 25, 3 and 5 are not relevant; nor are, in the brāhmaṇas, passages such as *TB*. 1, 4, 3, 6; *ŚB*. 5, 4, 2, 6 and 10.

11. See e.g. *AiB*. 6, 30 quoting ṚV. 6, 20, st. 2 of which refers to Viṣṇu and compare W. Caland and V. Henry, *L'Agniṣṭoma*, Paris, 1906, pp. 373 ff.

12. *MNU*. 71 ff.; cf. 277 ff. (and see J. Varenne's notes: *La Mahā Nārāyāṇa Upaniṣad*, 1, Paris, 1960, pp. 152; 153); in 401 ff. the poet tries to avert the god's anger.

13. See e.g. *Mbh*. 3, 187, 5 'I am Viṣṇu, I am Brahmā and I am Indra, the lord of the gods, I am king Vaiśrāvaṇa, Yama ...'. An author may indeed remain undecided whether or not he should consistently give the Highest Being the same name: cf. *MNU*. 260 'it is Brahmā, Śiva, Hari, Indra, the Imperishable One'; st. 223 it is Rudra who acts as the regent of the world. Elsewhere however Rudra and Viṣṇu are clearly distinguished.

14. For early evidence (± 100 B.C.): B. N. Puri, *India in the time of Patañjali*, Bombay, 1957, p. 188.

15. See *Die Religionen Indiens*, 1, pp. 241 ff.

16. One might for instance read the long invocation of deities and powers pronounced by Kausalyā in performing a farewell rite for Rāma: *Rām*. 2, 22, 2 ff. (See e.g. A. Guruge, *The society of the Rāmāyaṇa*, Maharagama (Ceylon), 1960, p. 256 f.) Compare also descriptions of rites, etc., such as *Manu* 3, 85 ff.

17. See *Die Religionen Indiens*, 1, pp. 332 ff., etc.

18. See e.g. *Manu* 12, 121.

19. See e.g. also H. D. Bhattacharyya, in R. C. Majumdar and A. D. Pusalker, *The history and culture of the Indian people*, ii, Bombay, 2 1953, pp. 462 ff.

20. I cannot enter here into a discussion of the interesting question as to how far in ancient times minor or local deities or rites became 'translated' into 'scriptural' types of gods or worship and conversely 'scriptural' gods or ceremonies, in casu Viṣṇu and Śiva, were transposed into a local setting. For lack of sufficient and reliable information on the religion of the lower classes many intricacies of these processes of 'universalization' and 'parochialization' regrettably elude our observation.

21. Or they are included in one recension of the text and omitted in another. For some particulars see Guruge, op. cit., p. 257.

22. With Guruge, op. cit., p. 257.

23. One should be sceptical about the demonstrative force of arguments derived from the infrequency of occurrences of the god's names in definite texts or from the

insignificance of the functions attributed to him. That Śiva is known to the author of the *Kauṭ. Arthaś.* (2, 29, 13) as the power of the thunderstorm which may destroy cattle or to the compiler of *ĀpGS.* (7, 19, 13 ff.) as the recipient of the Śūlagava or Īśānabali does not show that his position of unquestioned supremacy was not established at those periods (T. M. P. Mahadevan, in Majumdar and Pusalker, *The history and culture of the Indian people*, II, p. 453). These authors were interested only in one single aspect or function of the god.

24. E. W. Hopkins, *Epic mythology*, Strassburg, 1915, p. 231.

25. As such Viṣṇu combines with Fire and Sun to make the horrible form of Śiva (7, a. 173; 83, 117), although in passages where the latter is God he is said to have created Viṣṇu (13, 14, a younger passage after st. 1 in the N. rec.).

26. Cf. *Mbh.* 7, a. 57 f.; 12, 122, 36; 13, a. 14; a. 17; a. 145, etc.

27. *Mbh.* 7, 172, 51 ff. Afterwards Śiva grants boons to Vāsudeva-Nārāyaṇa (st. 73).

28. Cf. *Mbh.* 10, 7, 61; 7, 57, 63 ff. and several other places. There are several places in the Mahābhārata where Kṛṣṇa bows to, praises and adores Śiva or receives boons from this god and his consort Umā.

29. Cf. e.g. *Rām.* 6, 59, 128. Some particulars: A. P. Karmarkar, 'Religion and philosophy in the epics', in *The cultural heritage of India*, ed. by the Rāmakrishna Mission, II, Calcutta, [2]1962, p. 86.

30. Compare also *Mbh.* 2, a. 19; a. 38; a. 42; 3, 40, 2; 5, 22, 32; 5, a. 88.

31. I refer to Hopkins, op. cit., p. 213.

32. *ViP.* 4, 1, 8 ff. (*īśvarakopāt*; Wilson seems to have read *īśvaraśāpāt*).

33. *ViP.* 5, 23, 1 ff. See also *Hariv.* a. 110, 6164; a. 111, 6243 f.; a. 115, 6431; *BrP.* 14, 48 ff.; *PadmaP.* 6, 273, 2.

34. Compare also the Jarāsandha episode in *Mbh.* 2, a. 13 ff. (a summary may be found in S. Sørensen, *An index to the names in the Mahābhārata* (1904), [2]Delhi 1963, p. 354 f.), and see Hopkins, op. cit., pp. 213; 217.

35. J. N. Farquhar, *An outline of the religious literature of India*, Oxford, 1920, p. 47.

36. See also *Bhaṭṭikāvya*, 10, 7. For Śiva in the Rāmāyaṇa see also Hopkins, op. cit., p 219. This detail was also pointed out by the Dutch clergyman A. Rogerius who wrote a book on Indian religion etc.: *De open-deure tot het verborgen heydendom*, published Leiden, 1651; re-edited by W. Caland, The Hague, 1915; see p. 96. See also Ph. Baldaeus *Afgoderye der Oost-Indische heydenen* (a similar work by another Dutch clergyman), Amsterdam, 1672, re-edited by A. J. de Jong, The Hague, 1917, p. 82.

37. *Rām.* Bombay ed. 7, 31, 42 ff.

38. *Rām.* cr. ed. 2, 22, 18; B. ed. 7, 91, 7 (the commentator Rāma observes that this homage is paid for the sake of the undisturbed progress of the ceremony).

39. In a narrative belonging to the Rāma-Rāvaṇa cycle the latter abducted the goddess Umā who is rescued by Viṣṇu (P. Thomas, *Epics, myths and legends of India*, Bombay, 1961, p. 84).

40. Cf. e.g. *SauraP.* a. 34: Viṣṇu advises the gods to revere Śiva also, because the *asuras* are invincible as long as they worship that god.

41. *Mbh.* 1, 59, 20; 5, 61, 11; 5, 128, 47.

42. *ViP.* 5, ch. 32 f. An extract is found in *AgniP.* 12, 41 ff. Cf. also *BhāgP.* 10, 62, 2 ff.

43. In a Śivaite variant of the story (Maity, *Historical studies in the cult of the goddess Manasā*, p. 112 f.) Ūṣa wins the favour of Śiva himself by her extreme austerities; the god blesses her so that she becomes able to marry the youth who however later on irritated the god by his audacity: he was cursed and accordingly bitten by a snake.

44. H. H. Wilson and F. Hall, *The Vishṇu Purāṇa*, v, London, 1870, p. 120.

45. I refer to Wilson and Hall, loc. cit.

46. Another interesting episode is the story of Dadhīca in *LiṅgaP.* 1, 35 f.

47. The development of the relations between the two main currents of religious thought and belief as well as those between these and the other denominations cannot yet be described. The first prerequisite to any history of these events—without which no thorough understanding of Hinduism and a systematic, consecutive account of its history will be possible—is an analysis and text-critical examination of all written sources—first and foremost of the purāṇas and the enormous bodies of allied and subsequent literature—and an ascertainment of the relative, and, if possible, absolute, chronology of their

component parts. The foundations of this systematic research have been laid by W. Kirfel, in *Das Purāṇa pañcalakṣaṇa*, Bonn, 1927, and ensuing publications. An interesting collection of relative facts—which for reasons of space cannot be summarized here—may be found in H. Meinhard, *Beiträge zur Kenntnis des Śivaismus nach den Purāṇa's*, Thesis, Bonn, 1928, (Baessler-Archiv 12), pp. 34 ff. Books such as V. R. Ramachandra Dikshitar, *The Purāṇa Index*, 3 vols., Madras, 1951–1955, however useful and meritorious, can hardly contribute anything of value to these investigations, because they are planned as mere indexes of facts. R. C. Hazra's important compilations on the Upapurāṇas (*Studies in the Upapurāṇas*, Calcutta, 1958–1963, etc.) are likewise deficient in this respect. The opinion long ago expressed by G. Bühler (*The sacred laws of the Āryas*, I (S.B.E., II), [2]Oxford, 1896, p. XXX n.), which had the approval of H. Raychaudhuri (*Materials for the study of the early history of the Vaishnava sect*, Calcutta, 1936, p. 2): 'The early history of the purāṇas, which as yet is a mystery, will only be cleared up when a real history of the orthodox Hindu sects, especially of the Śivaites and Viṣṇuites, has been written' obviously expects too much from extra-literary sources. The contrary is nearer to the truth, although it must be conceded that once the chronological order of the texts has been established as firmly as will be possible and the history of the religious and philosophical ideas, etc. has been written, our insight into the structure and composition of the texts will also be considerably deepened. With regard to the purāṇas it may be said that, Brahmā being left out of consideration, it is Viṣṇu who as a rule occupies a position of pre-eminence in the earlier texts, whereas the later stratifications of purāṇic myths and legends not rarely testify to Śiva's coming to the fore, also to enact independently and alone the three great rôles of unfolding, preservation and reabsorption. The Śāka and Kushāṇa dynasties (Ist century B.C.–IIIrd century A.D.) were usually Śivaites or Buddhists. The popularity of Śivaism with foreign rulers continued. Several indigenous dynasties adhered to the same religion and numerous temples were, in the classical age and afterwards, erected in honour of its god. Before the end of the Vth century A.D. Śiva was worshipped in *liṅga* form even in inaccessible parts of Bengal. Although we know few precise details about the history of these religions before the end of the IXth century, Śivaism seems to have been dominant in many regions. In the times of Śaṅkara and the Bhāgavata-Purāṇa (VIIIth–IXth centuries) there does not seem to have been a universal strong antagonism. In all probability, Viṣṇuism gradually grew in popularity all over the Indian sub-continent from the middle or the end of the IVth century A.D., several royal personages assuming titles such as *parama-bhāgavata* or *parama-vaiṣṇava*. Viṣṇu also, represented by various divine figures, seems to have established his cult in Bengal by the Vth century A.D.; from the VIIIth century onwards its development is evidenced by many inscriptions. Yet it is only after about 1000 A.D. that this religion can be decidedly said to have come to the fore. Except in those regions which have remained loyal to certain forms of Śivaism and in Bengal where Śāktas have preserved a stronghold, Viṣṇuism may be held to have after that date enjoyed supremacy up to the present day. This development is reflected in the data concerning both religions in those oversea territories (Further India, Indonesia) which were drawn into the sphere of Indian influence (see e.g. G. Coedès, *Les peuples de la Péninsule indochinoise*, Paris, 1962, p. 209 and my article on 'The presence of Hinduism in Indonesia', *Vivekananda Comm. Vol.*, Delhi, probably 1970; cf. Majumdar in Majumdar and Pusalker, op. cit., III, p. 67). Although the family god of the early Cālukyas of Bādāmi (VIth century) was Viṣṇu they also worshipped Kārttikeya (who is associated with Śiva). An inscription found at Gangdhar and dated 423 A.D. records the erection of a temple full of the Ḍākinīs, i.e. a class of female imps, in honour of the Divine Mothers 'who utter loud and tremendous shouts of joy and stir up the oceans with the mighty wind rising from the 'magic' rites of their religion'. Nevertheless, the founder was a Vaiṣṇava and the conclusion that already in the Vth century a cult of Mother goddesses could influence Vaiṣṇava forms of worship, seems indeed warranted (cf. D. C. Sircar, 'Vaishṇavism', in Majumdar and Pusalker, op. cit., III, p. 421). A clear piece of evidence of such an early (Vth century) approach between Vaiṣṇava and Śaiva-Śākta worship is furnished by the Maukhari chief Anantavarman, who in one of the caves in the Nāgārjuni hill installed an image of Kṛṣṇa and also images of Bhūtapati and Devī, that is of Śiva and Durgā. The religious beliefs—or rather policy—of royal families, known to us from inscriptions, etc. cannot always be regarded as a fair index of the popularity of a definite denomination. So when Orissan kings of the XIth century profess, in their copper-plate grants, devotion to Viṣṇu 'without omitting to insert verses in praise of Śiva' (P. Mukherjee, *The history of medieval Vaishnavism in Orissa*, Calcutta, 1940, p. 13), this may only mean that the royal family while privately worshipping Viṣṇu respected the Śaiva sympathies or allegiance of part of their subjects. For Harṣa's reign (characterized by religious 'tolerance') see R. Mookerji, *Harsha*, Oxford, 1926, p. 160 f.; A. Scharpé, *Bāṇa's Kādambarī*, Thesis, Utrecht, 1937, pp. 88 ff. For historical data see e.g. also *Die Religionen Indiens*, II, pp. 115 ff.; 188 ff.; Majumdar and Pusalker, *The history and culture of the Indian people*, vol. II, etc., *passim*; K. A. Nilakanta Sastri (ed.), *A comprehensive history of India*, II, Calcutta, 1957, pp. 378 ff.; R. Dessigane, P. Z. Pattabiramin and J. Filliozat, *Les légendes çivaites de Kāñcipuram*, Pondicherry, 1964, p. III f. (the Pallava monuments of the VIIth and VIIIth centuries show that Viṣṇu Raṅganātha was associated with Śiva's cult; in Rāmānuja's times Śaiva teachers and pupils visited also Vaiṣṇava shrines, etc.); M. Singer and others, *Krishna*, Honolulu, 1966, p. 120; Chattopadhyaya, *The evolution of theistic sects in ancient India, passim*; Bh. Sh. Verma, *Socio-religious, economic and literary condition of Bihar*, Delhi, 1962, *passim*; R. C. Majumdar, *History of Bengal*, I, Dacca, ^{2}1963, p. 401 (although the Pālas and the early Senas were Buddhists and Śivaites respectively, they both also supported the Viṣṇuite cult which must have had many adherents). The Vijayanagara emperors and, also in later times, other rulers, though by personal religious persuasion Viṣṇuites, generally adopted religious policies which extended toleration and sometimes even temples and village grants to adherents of other religions.

48. I refer to G. Bühler, *The laws of Manu*, (S.B.E., XXV), Oxford, 1886, p. 595; R. P. Kangle, *The Kauṭilīya Arthaśāstra*, Bombay, 1965, p. 119; P. V. Kane, *History of Dharmaśāstra*, II, Poona, 1941, p. 1313 f.; Majumdar, in Majumdar and Pusalker, *The history and culture of the Indian people*, III, Bombay, 1954, p. 368.

49. However, stories of persecution are not wanting. The Rāmānujārya Divyasūricaritai makes, for instance, mention of a bigoted Śaiva Cola king who ordered the eyes of one of Rāmānuja's disciples to be put out. For a story of an impartial king see also B. Ziegenbalg, *Malabarisches Heidenthum*, edited by W. Caland, Amsterdam Academy, 1926, pp. 119 ff.

50. See P. Hacker, 'Religiöse Toleranz und Intoleranz im Hinduismus', *Saeculum* (Freiburg and München), VIII (1957), pp. 167 ff.

51. For references see Kane, op. cit., II, pp. 169; 665; 736; R. C. Hazra, *Studies in the purāṇic records on Hindu rites and customs*, Dacca, 1940, p. 201.

52. I refer to *Die Religionen Indiens*, I, p. 260; II, pp. 213 ff.

53. *Mbh.* 12, App. I, *n*° 28 (a. 285 *vulg.*), *passim.*

54. That is to say, Śiva is (185 ff.) said to be the lord of ghosts and spirits, to carry skulls, to be clad in leaves and rags, to laugh awfully, to be terrible to behold and to observe dreadful vows and practices, to be fond of cooked and uncooked meat, etc.

55. Two chapters in the *Varāha-Purāṇa* (70 f.) are directed against the Pāśupatas.

56. Kane, op. cit., II, p. 169 (Vṛddhaharīta, 9, 359; 363 f.).

57. See *Kūrma-Pur.*, I, a. 16, esp. 115 ff.; 2, 16, 15; 2, 21, 32.

58. 'In old days the sectarian bitterness between the followers of Śiva and Viṣṇu was so great that a 'good' Vaiṣṇava would not even use the common word 'to sew' (*siv*) because it resembled the name 'Śiva' (S. Stevenson, *The rites of the twice-born*, Oxford, 1920, p. 266). For Śivaites denouncing the Vedas and exciting anti-Viṣṇuite feelings see also Hazra, *Upapurāṇas*, II, p. 362 f. The *BrahmaP.* (56, 64 f.) expressly states that in the holy Puruṣottama ground a temple of Śiva was erected in order to repress the wranglings between both denominations (Śaivas and Bhāgavatas). Viṣṇu was sometimes regarded as a sorcerer (Meinhard, op. cit., p. 38). When in the temple at Cidambaram, which had long been a centre of Śivaite cult, Viṣṇuite symbols, etc. were introduced by new rulers who worshipped Viṣṇu-Viṭhobā, twenty priests are related to have committed, in protest, suicide, by throwing themselves down from the high towers (A. T. Embree and F. Wilhelm, *Indien*, Frankfurt M., 1967, p. 214). See also R. Otto, *Dīpikā-Nivāsa*, Tübingen, 1916, pp. V; XI; 55; 58; 75; A. Lehmann, *Die śivaitische Frömmigkeit der tamulischen Erbauungsliteratur*, Berlin, 1947, p. 49.

59. In a passage in the *Śaṅkaradigvijaya* (15, 1–28) Mādhava brings Śaṅkara into contact with the Kāpālikas. Their preceptor reproaches the philosopher for neglecting the rules of the Kāpālika worship of Bhairava (carrying a skull red with blood and wine, etc.).

There ensues a fight between king Sudhanvan, who accompanies Śaṅkara, and the Kāpālikas, who are killed in consequence of a curse pronounced on them by the philosopher. See also R. G. Bhandarkar, *Vaiṣṇavism, Śaivism and minor religious systems*, Strassburg, 1913, p. 127 f.

60. For some particulars see Hazra, op. cit., pp. 201; 234 f.

61. When Vedic sacrifices were abolished, the Veda was sold, etc.; here also heretics, Jainas and Kāpālikas are put on a par. Cf. also *VāP.* 58, 31 ff. According to *VāmanaP.* 12, 17 Śiva was not invited by Dakṣa because he had come to be known as Kapālin.

62. *MatsyaP.* 144, 40 f. *ūrdhavapuṇḍraṃ mṛdā śubhraṃ lalāṭe yasya dṛśyate / caṇḍālo 'pi hi śuddhātma viṣṇuloke mahīyate*; see also *VāP.* 58, 64 f.; *KūrmaP.* 1, 29, 14.

63. Bhandarkar, op. cit., p. 117. *ViṣṇuDhP.* 1, 74, 34; 2, 22, 133 f. mentions the scriptures of the Pāśupatas together with those of the Pāñcarātrins, the Vedas, purāṇas, dharmaśāstras, and 'Sāṃkhya-Yoga'.

64. See Hazra, op. cit., p. 225 f.; 233; see e.g. *KūrmaP.* 1, 12, 249 f.

65. *Vṛddha-Harīta-Smṛti* 2, 67; *BmḍP.* 2, 31, 65; *PadmaP.* 6, 252, 52 *vaiṣṇavo varṇabāhyo 'pi punāti bhuvanatrayam.*

66. See Hacker, op. cit., pp. 171 ff.

67. Hence *ekāntimārga* for 'monotheism'.

68. Cf. e.g. *VarP.* 70, 23 ff.: *yo viṣṇuḥ sa svayaṃ brahmā yo brahmāsau maheśvaraḥ*, and dissenters are wretches; *KūrmaP.* 1, 26, 89; 95; 1, 27, 10 ff.; *LiP.* 1, 19, 1–14; 1, 21, 14; 2, 4, 20 (*viṣṇubhaktasahasrebhyo rudrabhakto viśiṣyate*, etc.).

69. *Vṛddhahārīta-Smṛti* 2, esp. 42 ff.; 63 ff.; 4, 27 ff.; 4, 449 ff. Cf. e.g. 2, 44 where worship of Rudra and the Śivaite *tripuṇḍra* (the three horizontal lines on the forehead) are called *śūdra* manners (cf. 2, 47; 63). A Vaiṣṇava brahman should not even in an emergency apply ash to his body (2, 48). One should not even look at a human body which is without the distinctive marks of Viṣṇuism (*ūrdhvapuṇḍra*), for this is like a place for cremating corpses. This antipathy to the marks of the other community is often said to be mutual: 'Selon les vichnouistes, porter le *liṅgam* est le comble de l'abomination; selon leurs antagonistes, quiconque porte le *nahmam* (the Viṣṇuite perpendicular mark) sera tourmenté dans l'enfer . . .' (J. A. Dubois (1764–1848), *Moeurs, institutions et cérémonies des peuples de l'Inde*, ch. IX, new edition Pondicherry, 1921, p. 187. An English translation was published in London (1816)).

70. *GaruḍaP.* 1, a. 7 ff.

71. Hence also the statement, in a Vaiṣṇava context, that Viṣṇu is the Śiva proper (cf. e.f. *PadmaP.* 6, 265, 37). There are, of course, parallels in other religions. Many orthodox Dutch protestants still object to using the second member of the phrase Roman Catholic.

72. M. Weber, *The religion of India*, Glencoe, Ill. 1958, p. 21.

73. C. and H. Jesudasan, *A history of Tamil literature*, Calcutta, 1961, p. 246. For instances of poets who abandoned themselves to the use of a vocabulary of hatred, contempt and intolerance against non-Śaivas see ibid., p. 27 'Throw to the dogs the food of those who do not call upon Viṣṇu'; p. 132.

74. Dubois, loc. cit.

75. 'On voit ces fanatiques former quelquefois des attroupements pour soutenir de part et d'autre la préexcellence de leur culte, et là s'accabler des injures les plus atroces et les plus obscènes, vomir un torrent de blasphèmes et d'imprécations, ici contre Vichnou, là contre Siva . . .'.

76. Thus the poetess Cinnammā (who lived before the Xth century) prays, in a laborious stanza, Śiva 'to deliver us from the great delusion, Śiva who in his aggressive and overbearing Mahābhairava attitude conquered no less than five *avatāras* of his rival Viṣṇu: his stick is the huge skeleton of Trivikrama, i.e. the fifth *avatāra* slain by him at the time of the universal dissolution; he tied up Nṛsiṃha's hands with the serpent Śeṣa; he dug his nails into the flesh of the ancient boar and assuming the form of a fisherman overpowered both Fish and Tortoise when the universe was but a vast ocean' (see J. B. Chaudhuri and Roma Chaudhuri, *Sanskrit poetesses*, A, Calcutta, 1939, pp. VIII f.; 5 f.; 75).

77. See *Die Religionen Indiens*, II, pp. 125 ff.

78. Traditions of conversions must be left unmentioned here (see e.g. S. Krishnasvami Aiyangar, *Some contributions of South India to Indian culture*, Calcutta, 1942, p. 237 f.), and so must cases of religious revival viewed with dislike by the opposing party (cf. T. A.

Gopinatha Rao, *Sir Subrahmanya Ayyar lectures on the history of Śrī-Vaiṣṇavas* (1917), University of Madras, 1923, pp. 10; 27). Already at an early date the various religious communities borrowed their methods of proselytizing from each other as appears from the tradition that the Vaiṣṇavas of the South, on seeing the success achieved by Śaivism by the employment of the vernacular languages—which they had learned by watching Buddhist and Jaina preachers—proceeded in their turn to employ, with marked success, Tamil (Gopinatha Rao, op. cit., p. 13). There is no reason for doubt that competition and innocent animosity were often rife in the small village communities. Thus Rāmānuja had to settle a dispute about the identity of an idol in a temple which the Śaivas claimed as that of their deity Subrahmaṇya and the Vaiṣṇavas asserted to be Veṅkaṭeśa (Gopinatha Rao op. cit., p. 12. Cf. *Die Religionen Indiens*, II, p. 15).

79. He could not pull off the last little ring from one of that man's toes which obviously had been attached to it by virtue of that mantra which now on his request was communicated to him by his victim. Afterwards the same poet, in order to extend the famous Śrīraṅgam temple, plundered a Buddhist sanctuary.

80. Thereupon he was with all honours conducted through Jñānasaṃbandha's birthplace. See Gopinatha Rao, op. cit., p. 6.

81. See e.g. *SauraP.* 4, 21. The *Śiva-Gītā* (which forms part of the *PadmaP.*) 16, 6 warns against hating the other great god although Śaiva faith is the only true and perfect religion.

82. Hacker, op. cit., p. 177.

83. *AhirbudhnyaS.* a. 12, 51; 13, 16 ff. Cf. F. O. Schrader, *Introduction to the Pāñcarātra and the Ahirbudhnya Saṃhitā*, Adyar, 1916, pp. 109 ff.

84. *SauraP.* 31, 57 ff.

85. Cf. *Die Religionen Indiens*, I, pp. 344 ff.

86. Cf. e.g. *SauraP.* a. 11, dealing with the cult of Śiva, states at st. 8 *nirdambhaḥ satyasaṃkalpo bhaktaḥ syād uttamo mama / sūryavahīndubhaktānām uttamo vaiṣṇavaḥ paraḥ.*

87. Another attitude—much in evidence among Viṣṇuites—towards other cults and doctrines simply consists in ignoring them. This tendency may for instance have contributed to the at first sight curious fact that writings of one school of thought often do not give us much information about the tenets of their opponents or have a preference for anonymous polemics. For other teachers again it suffices to declare the god of the other religion, for instance, incompetent to help his adorers when they surrender themselves to sin and vice, e.g. by insulting one's own god (cf. e.g. *SauraP.* 4, 21).

88. Meinhard, op. cit., p. 34.

89. Cf. *LiP.* 2, 6, 85 f.; cf. also 1, 103, 17 ff.; 37 ff., etc.

90. Incidentally, the consorts of the members of the Trinity, Lakṣmī, Pārvatī and Sarasvatī, are said to co-operate for the benefit of men (e.g. *Gopālakelicandrikā* 4, ed. W. Caland, *Een onbekend Indisch toneelstuk*, Amsterdam Academy, 1917, pp. 131, 6 ff.).

91. See my paper 'The Hindu Trinity' in *Anthropos* LXIII (*Comm. Vol. Father W. Schmidt*), pp. 212 ff.

92. As far as we are able to see, with some exceptions (persecutions, etc.) on the whole in a peaceful way.

93. One may quote here Kālidāsa, *Kum.* 7, 44 where Brahmā's body is said to be threefold; all three component parts can, under the limiting conditions of phenomenal perception and thought, appear as the first or as the last and so Śiva may have precedence of Viṣṇu, and Viṣṇu of Śiva; Brahmā may be above or under the two other gods; Somadeva, *Kathāsaritsāgara*, 73, 170 'Until you perceive that Viṣṇu, Śiva and Brahmā are really one, you will always find the successes which are gained by worshipping them separately short-lived and uncertain'. The identity of Brahmā, Viṣṇu and Śiva is often taught, e.g. *KālikāP.* a. 11; *NāradaP.* (*BṛhannāradīyaP.*) 15, 74, praising Śiva worship, declares the unity of Śiva and Viṣṇu-Nārāyaṇa or Śiva's being a form of the latter (15, 74 cf. 3, 63); 6, 42 'Only the sinners merged in the ocean of nescience find distinction in the eternal gods designated as Hari and Śaṃkara'. In many particular cases a certain equality of both gods or their joint appearance in a rite or custom may rather be due to neutrality or indifference on the part of the worshippers. That for instance in worshipping Devī the three great gods are adored also is due to the well-known fact that they, together with Sūrya and Gaṇeśa, are the object of the *pañcāyatana-pūjā* (*Die Religionen Indiens*, II, p. 83).

94. Edited and translated by P. E. Dumont, *L'Īśvaragītā*, Baltimore and Paris, 1933.
95. For purāṇic *gītā* literature in general see Lecture VI.
96. Dumont, op. cit., p. 8.
97. This is the name of one of the sources of the Ganges and the neighbouring hermitage of Nara and Nārāyaṇa (*Hariv.* a. 284, 15079).
98. According to the author the Sāṃkhya school teaches the essence of Vedānta (2, 40).
99. Similarly at the end of his discourse before his departure (11, 119).
100. Cf. 1, 51; 5, 42; 46. Looking at another person, which is a form of coming into contact with him, may imply transference of power or blessing, bestowal of grace or favour, etc. For the Indian beliefs and customs connected with the human or divine look see my publication *Eye and gaze in the Veda*, Amsterdam Academy, 1969.
101. Some other places of interest may be quoted: 7, 4 'Among the Ādityas I am Viṣṇu' (*ādityānam ahaṃ viṣṇuḥ*: *BhG.* 10, 21); 7, 3 'Among those who wield the incomprehensible creative power I am Hari' (*māyāvinām ahaṃ devaḥ purāṇo harir avyayaḥ*); 7, 5 'Among the warriors I am Rāma'.
102. *ĪśvG.* 11, 108 *mayaitad bhāṣitaṃ jñānaṃ hitārthaṃ brahmavādinām / dātavyaṃ śāntacittebhyaḥ śiṣyebhyo bhavatā śivam.* Viṣṇu indeed teaches the doctrine to Arjuna (11, 131).
103. *ĪśvG.* 11, 111 *ayaṃ nārāyaṇo yo 'sāv īśvaro nātra saṃśayaḥ.*
104. Cf. e.g. *Mbh.* 3, 82, 16 'There, in the days of yore, Viṣṇu paid his adorations to Rudra for his grace, and obtained many boons difficult of acquisition even among the gods'.
105. See the *Mahimnastava*, an ode in praise of Śiva (ed. W. N. Brown, Poona, 1965), 19. This eye developed, to protect the universe, into Viṣṇu's famous discus.
106. *KūrmaP.* 1, a. 25.
107. *VarāhaP.* 73, 17.
108. See e.g. *Mbh.* 13, a. 17: Kṛṣṇa acknowledges Śiva as the creator and is described as hearing this god's thousand and eight names. Cf. also *SauraP.* 24, 27.
109. Cf. e.g. *SauraP.* 43, 12. Popular motifs (e.g. Viṣṇu as Śiva's wedding-guest (ibid. 57, 18)) are left unmentioned here.
110. Mere enumerations of names are, however, no reliable source of information, because the order may be traditional, due to the exigencies of the metre, etc. It is of course impossible to give here a survey of all variants of the theme exemplified by an episode of the Manasā cycle (P. K. Maity, *Historical studies in the cult of the goddess Manasā*, Calcutta, 1966, p. 120): the Creator, wishing to put the ability of Brahmā, Viṣṇu and Śiva to the test let his body, in the guise of a corpse, float on the current. Only the third, Śiva, recognized the body and tried to restore it to life.
111. The text continues: 'By making sixteen one attains all objects of enjoyment and emancipation'.
112. *SauraP.* 40, 4 ff.; cf. 38, 12 ff.
113. W. Jahn, *Das Saurapurāṇam*, Strassburg, 1908, p. XIII.
114. *SauraP.* 40, 6 *śrutismṛtipurāṇānāṃ siddhānto 'yaṃ yathārthataḥ.*
115. Cf. also ibid. 38, 5 Brahmā owes his function as the creator, Viṣṇu his being the object of meditation, and Indra his being Viṣṇu to Śiva.
116. *SauraP.* 38, 9 *tvattaḥ paraṃ prabhuṃ naiva prāyeṇa jñāsyati sphuṭam / viralāḥ kecid etad vai niṣṭhāṃ vetsyanti tattvataḥ* (Śiva is speaking).
117. Cf. e.g. *SauraP.* 49, 8.
118. I cannot discuss here the relations of both supreme gods to other gods, for instance Indra who is said to be unable to undo what is ordained or done by Viṣṇu and even seeks protection by entering the latter's body (*MatsyaP.* 274, 14; 47, 97 ff.).
119. *Mbh.* 5, a. 109, after 5 (452) *atra viṣṇuḥ sahasrākṣaḥ sahasracaraṇo 'ksayaḥ / sahasraśirasaḥ śrīmān ekaḥ paśyati māyayā.* Cf. also *Mbh.* 7, CXCIX (7, 172, 50 ff.): Nārāyaṇa has a visionary sight of Rudra.
120. Cf. e.g. *MatsyaP.* 47, 11 *so 'vatīrṇo mahīṃ devo praviṣṭo mānuṣīṃ tanum / mohayan sarvabhūtāni yogātmā yogamāyayā* (this work, partly non- (prae-) denominational, partly viṣṇuite and śivaite, may have assumed its present form approximately in the IVth century A.D.); see H. Zimmer, *Myths and symbols in Indian art and civilization*, Washington, 1946, pp. 28 ff.

121. Not infrequently inserted narratives and, especially, short passages or incidental remarks impress us as the result of a recast or secondary addition. Thus when Viṣṇu, in connection with a vrata implying his worship in his manifestation as the nakṣatra Puruṣa, is said to be 'but an incarnation of the divine essence of Śiva' (*AgniP.* 196, 8 *nakṣatrapuruṣo viṣṇuḥ pūjanīyaḥ śivātmakaḥ*).

122. *Die Religionen Indiens*, II, pp. 143 ff.; H. von Glasenapp, *Madhva's Philosophie des Vishnu-Glaubens*, Bonn and Leipzig, 1923.

123. Madhva, *Brahmasūtrabhāṣya*, 1, 1, 1; see also Von Glasenapp, op. cit., pp. 7; 29; 72. Deceit on a god's part with similar intention is a well-known motif.

124. According to Madhva this appears from texts such as ṚV. 7, 40, 5; 10, 125, 5. In the next period of the universe a last rebirth awaits Rudra and Umā, thereupon to come to Viṣṇu's presence.

125. Madhva, *BĀUBh.* 1, 5, p. 23a.

126. Von Glasenapp, op. cit., p. *6.

127. H. von Glasenapp, *Heilige Stätten Indiens*, München, 1928, pp. 70 ff.; 75.

128. See Von Glasenapp, *Madhva's Philosophie*, p. 13.

129. See A. Barth, 'Deux chapitres du Saurapurāṇa', in *Mélanges Ch. de Harlez*, Leyden, 1896, pp. 12 ff. and the additions and critical remarks by W. Jahn, *Das Saurapurāṇam*, Strassburg, 1908, pp. XIII ff.

130. A mythical being with a human figure and the head of a horse or with the body of a horse and the head of a man.

131. That the supremacy of either god can assume enormous proportions is in itself not surprising; the conclusion drawn from this that even social and religious unrest, rise of Śivaism and other cults, and apostasy from the Viṣṇuite religion, etc. take place on the initiative and authority of Viṣṇu through the agency of his servant and executor Śiva is however another indication of the extreme consistency with which Hinduism likes to follow up a definite line of thought. Some instances are (without references to the original texts!) given in W. Eidlitz, *Der Glauben und die heiligen Schriften der Inder*, Olten-Freiburg, i B., 1957, p. 77 f.).

132. See *Die Religionen Indiens*, I, p. 218.

133. Cf. *SauraP.* 39, 70; 73; 40, 52; 61. The main tenets of the 'materialists' called after their founder Cārvāka concern the exclusive reality of the phenomenal world, the sole authority of perceptual evidence and the denial of any statement or view with regard to the existence of a 'soul', survival after death, or the karmic effects of deeds. See e.g. S. Radhakrishnan, *Indian philosophy*, I, London, [5]1948, pp. 271 ff.; E. Frauwallner, *Geschichte der indischen Philosophie*, II, Salzburg, 1956, pp. 302 ff.

134. Cf. e.g. *SauraP.* 52, 58.

135. Other combinations—e.g. the Trimūrti with Indra or Sūrya; Prajāpati, Viṣṇu, Rudra (, Indra) etc. etc.—are likewise extremely frequent.

136. W. Caland, *Die altindischen Todten- und Bestattungsgebräuche*, Amsterdam Academy 1896, p. 9; E. Abegg, *Der Pretakalpa der Garuḍa-Purāṇa*, Berlin, [2]1956, p. 110.

137. Thus *MatsyaP.* 54, 4 Śiva is requested to tell the interrogator how the worshipper of himself and those who follow Viṣṇu can attain health, wealth, etc.

138. *Agni-Purāṇa*, ch. 21; this important work does not seem to have been compiled before the IXth century.

139. In some parts of the *Devī-Bhāgavata-Purāṇa* Viṣṇu is glorified as the highest deity (12, 8, 1), elsewhere Śiva (5, 1, 3; 20 f., etc.).

140. Besides, there are many shrines dedicated to some particular manifestation of the Supreme Īśvara.

141. *Rāmottaratāpanīya-Upaniṣad* 1; 4 (for a translation see P. Deussen, *Sechzig Upanishad's des Veda*, [4]Darmstadt, 1963, pp. 818 ff.); cf. Adhy. Rām. 6, 15, 62.

142. Origin legends and similar local traditions not rarely lift a tip of the veil hiding the history of the interrelations between both confessions in a definite region. According to a legend, handed down in purāṇas and the Kapila-Saṃhitā, there was, in the beginning, in Bhuvaneśvara (Orissa), only a single great mango forest. At a given moment Śiva decided to leave his residence in Benares because it had been spoiled for him by throngs of unbelievers, and to move on to that mango forest. However this site, known to only a few initiates, was already a dwelling place of Viṣṇu. This god, being honoured by his

colleague, gave him permission to settle in the neighbourhood on condition that he should never return to Benares. When Śiva explained that, and why, this was impossible, Viṣṇu declared that all the sanctuaries of Benares were also in the sacred mango forest at Bhuvaneśvara. Being contented Śiva moved in and settled down (see Von Glasenapp, *Heilige Stätten*, p. 94 f.). The legend clearly reflects the greater antiquity of Viṣṇuism in that place —it is perhaps warranted to hold (with H. Zimmer, *The art of Indian Asia*, New York, 1955, p. 272) that the Viṣṇu cult had taken possession of a pre-Aryan tree sanctuary—and of a harmonization of the rival cults emphasizing the importance of the new centre. See also Von Glasenapp, op. cit., p. 122 f. on the Viṣṇuite elements in Nepalese Śiva worship.

143. For the special development of this tendency in Indonesia (Bali!) which was doubtless furthered by indigenous views of the world now see P. Zoetmulder, in W. Stöhr and P. Zoetmulder, *Die Religionen Indonesiens*, Stuttgart, 1965, pp. 316; 322, etc.

144. *AgniP.* a. 209, 49; 60; 212, 15 f.

145. *BrahmavP.*, *KṛṣṇajanmaKh.* 34, 13 ff.

146. See e.g. B. A. Gupte, *Hindu holidays and ceremonials*, Calcutta, 1919, pp. 214 ff.

147. *Haribhaktivilāsa* 14, 63. The tendency to identify Śiva with Kṛṣṇa has no doubt contributed to this belief.

148. *Devimāhātmya* a. 2 (*MārkP.* a. 82). Compare also stories such as *Mbh.* 12, a. 160: Brahmā made a sword which Śiva, after slaying the dānavas, handed over to Viṣṇu.

149. *BmḍP.* 4, 15, 14 ff. I cannot pay attention here to places such as *MārkP.* 106, 65 '(the sun) who is praised by Viṣṇu on the lotus seat of Śiva'.

150. For Mohinī see Lecture VI.

151. The point of the story is not made explicit; it is probably to disapprove of the way of life of an onesidedly ascetic community of Śivaites.

152. Cf. e.g. *SauraP.* 24, 66 ff., adding also that Śiva is the sun, Viṣṇu the moon, Śiva the thinker, Viṣṇu thought, etc.

153. E. B. Havell, *Benares, the sacred city*, London, 1905, p. 137 f.

154. *VāyuP.* a. 105 f. = 44 f. For a translation see L. P. Vidyarthi, *The sacred complex in Hindu Gaya*, London, 1961, pp. 114 ff. The story recurs in the *Agni-Purāṇa*, 114, where no mention is made of Śiva. See also A. Rogerius, *De open-deure tot het verborgen Heydendom*, ed. W. Caland, The Hague, 1915, p. 163, and H. von Glasenapp, *Heilige Stätten Indiens*, p. 108 f. Compare e.g. also the story narrated SauraP. 41, referred to in Lecture V.

155. *KālikāP.* a. 24.

156. See e.g. *KālikāP.* a. 11; *BṛhaddharmaP.* 2, a. 10 (though glorifying Viṣṇu the latter work praises Caṇḍī or Devī and does not distinguish between Śāktas and Vaiṣṇavas).

157. Cf. also Von Glasenapp, *Heilige Stätten*, pp. 14; 29; 45.

158. See *MatsyaP.* 179, 9 ff. and for various narratives in connection with these deities T. A. Gopinatha Rao, *Elements of Hindu Iconography*, I. 2, Madras, 1914, pp. 379 ff.; S. G. Kantawala, *Cultural history from the Matsyapurāṇa*, Baroda, 1964, p. 194 f., and p. 158, and compare p. 169.

159. The motif of the father opposing his son's allegiance to one of the great gods recurs in a Śivaite setting in *MatsyaP.* a. 180, 5 ff.: Harikeśa, the son of the yakṣa Pūrṇabhadra, was so extremely devoted to Śiva that he meditated on him in whatever posture he should be in; his father, disagreeing with his behaviour, drove him away from home. The god however permitted him to settle in Benares.

160. *BhG.* 10, 30 *prahlādaś cāsmi daityānām.*

161. See *BhāgP.* 7, 4, 28.

162. For full particulars see the important publication by P. Hacker, *Prahlāda: Werden und Wandlungen einer Idealgestalt* (Akad. d. Wiss. u. Lit., Mainz, Abh. d. Geistes- u. Soz. Kl. 1959, 9 and 13), Wiesbaden, 1960.

163. More precisely in the versions contained in the *Mahābhārata*, *Brahma-Purāṇa*, *Harivaṃśa*, *Viṣṇudharmottara-Purāṇa* 1, 54; *Padma-Purāṇa* 5, 42; *Matsya-Purāṇa*, *Viṣṇu-Purāṇa* and *Bhāgavata-Purāṇa*, dealt with in volume I of Hacker's publication.

164. Usually the gods had recourse to Brahmā.

165. *PadmaP.* 6, 265, 1–156.

166. Cf. e.g. *ViP.* 1, 17, 2; *BhāgP.* 7, 4, 1 ff.

167. The term used, *pāṣaṇḍa*, denotes any person who, or doctrine which, is hypocritical, or heretical and falsely assumes the characteristics of 'orthodoxy'.

168. This seems also to be Hacker's opinion; cf. op. cit., p. 171: 'Dasz alles dies von Śiva selbst erzählt wird, erscheint uns als eine unbegreifliche Albernheit; der Verfasser wollte dadurch seine Lehren wirkungsvoller gestalten'.

169. *PadmaP.* 6, 265, 26 ff.

170. *ŚivaP. RudraS.* 5, 43. The Śiva-Purāṇa is in fact a conglomeration of *saṃhitās* ('collections').

171. *ŚivaP. JñānaS.* 59 ff. I cannot dwell here on some remarkable features of this version; see Hacker, op. cit., pp. 176 ff.

172. For particulars see e.g. Hopkins, *Epic mythology*, p. 18 f.; cf. e.g. Mbh. 3, 134, 14 *aṣṭapādaḥ śarabhaḥ siṃhaghātī.*

173. *ŚivaP. ŚatarudraS.* 10 ff.

174. Another Śivaite theme, also known from the episode of the destruction of Dakṣa's sacrifice (see e.g. the interpolated passage *Mbh.* 12, a. 285 *vulg.*; *VāmanaP.* a. 4 and 5).

175. The Liṅga-Purāṇa inserts a hymn of praise consisting of Śiva's names and pronounced by Narasiṃha (1, 96, 76 ff.). The same work maintains that the man who recites this episode is fortified in his struggle against Viṣṇu's *māyā*, which is the cause of continued mundane existence.

176. *ŚivaP. Ś.*, 12, 31.

177. For Vīrabhadra see also J. N. Banerjea, *The development of Hindu iconography*, Calcutta, 1956, p. 482 f.; W. Kirfel, *Symbolik des Hinduismus und des Jinismus*, Stuttgart, 1959, p. 29 f.; M. Th. de Mallmann, *Les enseignements iconographiques de l'Agni-Purāṇa*, Paris, 1963, pp. 62 ff.

178. One might compare W. Kirfel, *Symbolik des Hinduismus und des Jinismus*, Stuttgart, 1959, pp. 36; 38 f. and MatsyaP. 350, 7 ff. (translated by A. Hohenberger, *Die indische Flutsage und das Matsyapurāṇa*, Leipzig, 1930, p. 186).

179. Hacker, op. cit., p. 184.

180. We are indeed under the impression that religious quarrels on these points also could flame high.

181. Cf. also Rāmānuja, *Vedārthasaṃgraha* 112 'Does not the Viṣṇu-Purāṇa (1, 2, 66) tell us that the members of the Trimūrti are equal? No, it establishes the fact that the entire phenomenal world constituted by Brahmā, Viṣṇu, Śiva, etc. is ensouled by Viṣṇu-Janārdana alone'; Von Glasenapp, *Madhva's Philosophie*, p. 38. Many volumes were written for the purpose of proving Viṣṇu's (Kṛṣṇa's, Nārāyaṇa's) superiority.

182. For identification see also *Mbh.* 12, 330, 64.

183. Cf. e.g. *BrahmavP. KJKh.* 47, 50 ff. (see Zimmer, *Myths and symbols*, p. 9). This is of course not to say that there are no Viṣṇuite examples.

184. *AgniP.* 12, 51 f. it is Viṣṇu who assures Śiva of their equivalence and identity, adding that 'the man who sees difference goes to hell'. For the distinction between Śuddha-Śaivas who are exclusively worshippers of Śiva and Miśra-Śaivas who worship him along with other deities see S. K. Das, *Śakti or divine power*, Calcutta, 1934, p. 194. It is in this connection interesting to notice that ancient purāṇic traditions are in several cases more superficially śivaized than viṣṇuized.

185. See e.g. *SauraP.* 31, 59 ff.

186. *Śiva-Gītā* (*PadmaP.*) 2, 30 *taṃ tyaktvā tādṛśaṃ devaṃ yaḥ sevetānyadevatām / so hi bhāgīrathīṃ tyaktvā kāṅkṣate mṛgatṛṣṇikām.* Similar statements however occur also in Viṣṇuite works: *BhāgP.* 4, 7, 16 ff. Viṣṇu, being propitiated by Dakṣa after his reconciliation with Śiva, received offerings and was praised by all including Rudra, Brahmā, and Indra, after which he told Dakṣa that he was not different from Śiva and Brahmā. Those who are aware of this fact will find peace eternal. Cf. also 54 *trayāṇām ekabhāvānām yo na paśyati vai bhidām / sarvabhūtātmanāṃ brahman sa śāntim adhigacchati.* See also *Harivaṃśa*, 10660 f. *śivāya viṣṇurūpāya viṣṇave śivarūpiṇe / athāntaraṃ na paśyāmi tena te diśataḥ śivaṃ // anādimadhyanidhanam etad akṣaram avyayam / tad eva te pravakṣyāmi rūpaṃ hariharātmakam.* Cf. *MatsyaP.* 180, 2.

187. Hacker, in *Saeculum*, VIII, p. 175.

188. I cannot attach much value to such explanations of the alleged identity of both great gods as that proposed by Kantawala, op. cit., p. 186: 'Viṣṇu represents one of the solar aspects and Sūrya and Rudra are connected with each other', hence the oneness of Viṣṇu and Śiva.

189. See also Bh. S. Upadhyaya, *India in Kālidāsa*, Allahabad, 1947, p. 311.
190. I refer to J. E. Carpenter, *Theism in medieval India*, London, 1921, p. 382 f.
191. *Epigraphia Indica*, II, p. 354.
192. *Harivaṃśa*, 10660 f.
193. An inscription found at Deopara in Bengal (about 1100): *Epigr. Ind.*, I, p. 311.
194. H. Zimmer, *The art of Indian Asia*, New York, 1955, I, pp. 146 ff.; Banerjea, op. cit., p. 546 f.; S. Chattopadhyaya, *Theistic sects in ancient India*, Calcutta, 1962, p. 79. On Harihara and the association of gods in pairs in general: L. Renou, *Religions of ancient India*, London, 1953, p. 20 f.
195. The author of the *Relation des erreurs* (1644), edited by W. Caland, *Twee oude Fransche verhandelingen over het Hindoeïsme*, Amsterdam Academy, 1923, p. 25 mentions also Arigarputren, i.e. Hariharaputra, 'fils de Vichnou et de Rutren'; cf. also Baldaeus op. cit., p. 14; see *Die Religionen Indiens*, II, p. 14. Cf. also K. A. Nilakanta Sastri, *The development of religion in South India*, Bombay, 1963, p. 66.
196. Abhinanda, *Rāmacarita* (XIth century?), 9, 52; 24, 112 *ardhe puṃsaḥ purāṇasya devau hariharāv ubhau / ekaṃ tatra prapannasya pradveṣaḥ kas tavāpare*; Āryāvilāsa, *Saduktikarṇāmṛta*, I, p. 45.
197. Satyavrata Singh, *Vedāntadeśika*, Benares, 1958, p. 420 f.
198. S. Radhakrishnan, *The Hindu view of life*, London, 71948, p. 46 f.
199. H. von Glasenapp, *Zwei philosophische Rāmāyaṇas*, Mainz Academy, 1951, pp. 62 ff.
200. Śūnyavāda, the doctrine of the Buddhist philosopher Nāgārjuna and his school.
201. *Yogavās.* 3, 1, 12; cf. 3, 5, 6, 7; 5, 8, 19. See also S. Radhakrishnan, *Eastern religion and western thought*, Oxford-London, 21940, pp. 318 ff.
202. *Haribhaktivilāsa* 11, 283 ff. The Bhāgavata Vaiṣṇavas who produced the Bṛhannāradīya declare that the man who differentiates between Hari, Śaṅkara and Brahmā remains in hell as long as moon and stars exist (3, 45). Nowadays 'multisect *bhajana* (congregational devotional worship) may be seen as an . . . effort to unify Tamil and non-Tamil (groups), brahman and non-brahman, Śaivite, Vaiṣṇavite and all 'believers' in Hinduism' (M. Singer, *Krishna*, Honolulu, 1966, p. 123).

CHAPTER VI

1. J. Abbott, *The keys of power*, London, 1932, p. 43.
2. See above, 66.
3. The reading of a story about the worship of Viṣṇu is often punctuated by blasts from a conch shell.
4. C. Marcel-Dubois, *Les instruments de musique de l'Inde ancienne*, Paris, 1941, p. 109.
5. For a brief survey see K. W. Morgan, *Tle religion of the Hindus*, New York, 1953, p. 96 f.
6. There are—quite naturally—also geographical differences. Some useful data—though mixed with superfluous repetition—may be found in *Tree symbol worship in India, A new survey of a pattern of folk-religion*, edited by Sankar Sen Gupta, Calcutta, 1965.
7. Cf. also P. V. Kane, *History of Dharmaśāstra*, II, Poona, 1941, p. 731 f.; S. Stevenson, *Rites of the twice-born*, Oxford, 1920, p. 471.
8. Cf. e.g. *Tree symbol worship* (see above), pp. 12; 25 f.; 38; 54 f.; 87; 91; 129. According to P. Thankappan Nair, ibid., p. 93 the Nairs of Kerala consider this plant sacred to Śiva.
9. 'By offering a flower to a god the worshipper acquires a merit, a hundred times more than what he would have gained by offering gold' (202, 12).
10. See *Tree symbol worship*, pp. 28; 37 f.; 95; 130; 135.
11. In Kerala its fruits are not eaten, because they are thought to be Śiva's head (ibid., p. 95).
12. *Tree symbol worship*, p. 130.
13. Meyer, op. cit., I, pp. 69 ff. See *AgniP.* 202, 14; 248, 4.
14. Cf. e.g. *BhavP.* 28, 58, and see J. J. Meyer, *Trilogie altindischer Mächte und Feste der Vegetation*, Zürich and Leipzig, 1937, II, pp. 85 ff.; B. A. Gupte, 'Harvest festivals',

in *Indian Antiquary*, xxxv (1906), p. 61; J. Tod, *Annals and antiquities of Rajasthan*, Oxford, ²1920, pp. 665 f.; 695 f., and my *Aspects of early Viṣṇuism*, p. 218.

15. See e.g. *ViDhP.* II, 35, 10 f.; Meyer, op. cit., I, p. 121 f.; II, p. 42 f., etc.

16. For the number nine see *Aspects of early Viṣṇuism*, p. 94 f., etc.

17. For Durgā see *Tree symbol worship*, pp. 14; 49; 111; 113; 128; 134; 150; for the plantain tree also Meyer, op. cit., I, p. 104 f.; B. A. Gupte, *Hindu holidays and ceremonials*, Calcutta, 1919, p. 96.

18. 11, 43; 45, see V. S. Agrawala, *Devī-Māhātmyam, The Glorification of the great Goddess*, Benares, 1963, p. 141. In this function the goddess calls herself Śākambharī which is traditionally—and, if perhaps as a reinterpretation by way of popular etymology, probably correct—explained as 'bearer of vegetables' (see e.g. E. W. Hopkins, *Epic mythology*, Strassburg, 1915, p. 11 f.). I cannot follow Agrawala in his note, op. cit., pp. 218 f. ('supporter of the Śākas . . . the memory of whom was quite fresh').

19. See e.g. J. G. Frazer, *The Golden Bough*, abridged edition, London, 1957, pp. 542 ff.; M. Eliade, *Patterns in comparative religion*, London and New York, 1958, p. 261; 345 ff.

20. Not without exceptions, it is true; see *Tree symbol worship*, p. 98 f. etc.

21. Meyer, op. cit., II, p. 133.

22. e.g. *Mbh.* 13, 126, 5 B.

23. See Meyer, op. cit., *passim*; A. K. Coomaraswamy, *Yakṣas*, Washington, 1928–1931 (esp. II, 1, n. 63).

24. For other references see especially O. Viennot, *Le culte de l'arbre dans l'Inde ancienne*, Paris, 1954, pp. 26 ff.

25. See *Aspects of early Viṣṇuism*, p. 12; *Tree symbol worship*, p. 115.

26. Cf. Meyer, op. cit., III, p. 335.

27. *PadmaP.* 6, 117, 22 ff.; *SkandaP.* 3, 38, etc. The palāśa is in a similar way related to the brahmans and already in the Veda (e.g. *ŚB.* 12, 7, 2, 15) explicitly identified with brahman. See also J. N. Banerjea, *The development of Hindu iconography*, Calcutta, 1956, p. 341.

28. For a co-ordination with the three Aryan varṇas see Ilangō Adigal, *Shilappadikaram, translated by A. Daniélou*, New York, 1965, p. 134 f.: 'Having conquered the world the genius of the order of noblemen ruled it with justice, punished evil-doers and protected the world, like a new Viṣṇu'; the good genius of the *vaiśyas* resembles Śiva and that of the brahmans Brahmā.

29. I cannot continue this survey here and must also refrain from recalling, for instance, such well-known relations as that existing between Viṣṇu and his consort and the lotus (for which see *Aspects of early Viṣṇuism, passim*; H. Zimmer, *Myths and symbols in Indian art and civilization*, New York, 1947, p. 235. The Indian tendency to systematization led, for instance, also to a distribution of Viṣṇu's *avatāras* over different parts of the universe and the realms of devout rulers: as Hayagrīva he is worshipped by king Bhadraśravas in Bhadrāśravarṣa, etc. (*BhāgP.* 5, a. 18; cf. K. S. Ramaswami Sastri, *The supreme epic of devotion*, Tirupati, 1953, p. 48). See also R. C. Hazra, *Studies in the upapurāṇas*, I, Calcutta, 1958, p. 41. For the results of worshipping Viṣṇu with *tulasī* leaves in different months of the year see *BṛhaddharmaP.* 1, a. 8; for the benefits of worshipping Śiva with *bilva* leaves ibid. a. 11. Monday is the day for the worship of Śiva, Wednesday for Viṣṇu-Viṭhobā (Abbott, op. cit., p. 442). For different colours associated with both gods see A. Daniélou, *Le polythéisme hindou*, Paris, 1960, pp. 243; 330. For the power of colours see also Abbott, op. cit., ch. XII. Any cloth placed on an image of Viṣṇu must for instance be yellow. A correlation is for instance also assumed to exist between gods and the *rasas* in poetry, Rudra-Śiva being co-ordinated with fury, Yama with the pathetic, Indra with the heroic, Śiva-Mahākāla with the disgustful, Nārāyaṇa with the calm-and-peaceful (*Sāhityadarpaṇa*, 210 ff.). A Viṣṇuite passage in the *Ṛgvidhāna* (3, 27, 1 f.) prescribes the worship of Viṣṇu as Keśava in the month Mārgaśīrṣa, as Nārāyaṇa in the month Pauṣa, etc.

30. *Devīmāhātmya* 11, 45 f. (= *MārkP.* 91, 43 f.).

31. See also W. Crooke and R. E. Enthoven, *Religion and folklore of Northern India*, Oxford, 1926, p. 268; M. M. Underhill, *The Hindu religious year*, Calcutta, 1921, p. 107.

32. For more particulars see *Aspects of early Viṣṇuism*, pp. 212 ff.

33. I refer to Meyer, op. cit., II, p. 65 f.

34. Cf. e.g. *ViṣṇudhP.* 3, 221, 104.

35. See above, 103.

36. According to J. N. Farquhar, *The crown of Hinduism*, Oxford, 1913, p. 392, n. 3 Vaiṣṇavas may sip the water in which the fossil ammonite is washed to the chanting of the Puruṣasūkta for disinfecting their insides of 'the bacillus of sin'.

37. Kālidāsa, *Ragh.* 4, 80 (cf. 2, 35); *Kum.* 7, 30; 37; 8, 24; *Megh.* 58; 60; Bāṇa, *Kād.* 102; 113; 162; 224; 249; 253 ff.; 290; Subandhu, *Vās.* 31; Daṇḍin, *Dkc.* 1; Somadeva, *Kss.* 75, 59; 109, 61 ff.; *Sāhityadarpaṇa*, 257, comm. Compare also Sadhu Rama, *Essays in Sanskrit literature*, Delhi, 1965, p. 4 f.

38. See also S. C. De, *Kālidāsa and Vikramāditya*, Calcutta, 1928, p. 155, etc.

39. *Sāhityadarpaṇa*, 25 comm.

40. For the Gokarṇa, called Śivasthala, see e.g. *BṛhaddharmaP.* 1, a. 14.

41. See e.g. Kṛṣṇamiśra, *Prab.* 6, 9+; *MatsyaP.* 249, 16; 248.

42. However Śiva is sometimes also represented as residing on this mountain (S.G. Kantawala, *Cultural history from the Matsyapurāṇa*, Baroda, 1964, p. 178 f.).

43. The reader may for instance be referred to H. von Glasenapp, *Heilige Stätten Indiens*, München, 1928, *passim*; P. Thomas, *Hindu religion, customs and manners*, Bombay, n. d.; the same, *Epics, myths and legends of India*, Bombay, 1961.

44. In the epos Madhu and Kaiṭabha are two demons.

45. It is interesting to notice that the characters of the fable approach Viṣṇu through the intermediary of Garuḍa who acts as a minister.

46. *Pañcatantra*, 1, 15.

47. Von Glasenapp, *Heilige Stätten*, p. 81 f.

48. See e.g. Somadeva, *Kss.* 66, 50 *māyāṃ vaiṣṇavīm*; Kṣemendra, *Samayamātṛkā*, 4, 11. For the epic and post-epic Kṛṣṇa see W. Ruben, *Krishna*, Istanbul, 1943, p. 256 f.; M. Singer (ed.), *Krishna*, Honolulu, 1966.

49. Somadeva, *Kss.* ch. 33.

50. See also the note in C. H. Tawney and N. M. Penzer, *The ocean of story*, London, 1924 ff., III, p. 126.

51. Bhāsa, *Pratijñayaugandharāyaṇa*, 3, 0.

52. Budhasvāmin, *Bkśs.* 22, 147.

53. For other legends see e.g. E. Lamairesse, *Chants populaires du Sud de l'Inde*, Paris, 1868, pp. 84 ff.

54. *Hitopadeśa*, 3, 20.

55. Somadeva, *Kss.* 115, 99 ff.

56. *VāyuP.* 97 (=2, 35), 132 ff.; *MatsyaP.* 47, 92 ff., and compare D. R. Patil, *Cultural history from the Vāyu Purāṇa*, Poona, 1946, p. 41.

57. Somadeva, *Kss.* 36, 10 f. (Viṣṇu).

58. See e.g. *MatsyaP.* 21, 28 (Viṣṇu); Somadeva, *Kathāsaritsāgara* 22, 117 (Śiva); 38, 58 (Viṣṇu) and elsewhere.

59. Pious legends or fiction composed under the influence of popular belief may help us to deepen our insight into the character of these religions. Two worshippers of Śiva about to commit suicide adore the god embodied in the *liṅga* or perpetrate their deed before him (Somadeva, *Kss.* 119, 178 ff.). Once Śiva arose from a lake, in the form of a *liṅga*, composed of splendid jewels and approaching a woman who had bathed in that lake, gathered lotuses and meditated on him, was worshipped by her, and then she took her lyre and played upon it . . . (ibid., 120, 118 ff.). For stories about hidden or miraculous images or about their erection or disappearance (e.g. in connection with Viṣṇu's residence Jagannāth at Purī) see e.g. W. W. Hunter, *Orissa*, London, 1872, I, pp. 899 ff.; H. von Glasenapp, *Hinduismus*, München, 1922, p. 342; the same, *Heilige Stätten*, pp. 96 ff.

60. See e.g. D. C. Sircar and T. M. P. Mahadevan, in R. C. Majumdar and A. D. Pusalker, *The history and culture of the Indian people*, III, Bombay, 1954, pp. 414 ff.

61. For particular forms of worship see e.g. Kāl. *Megh.* 55 and Bāṇa, *Harṣac.* 4, p. 156 (Śiva's footprint; cf. 7, p. 246); 5, p. 171 (Śiva's temple resounding with the murmur of Rudra's *mantra*); *Kād.* 102; Kāl. *Megh.* 34 ff.; cf. also Budhasvāmin, *Bkśs.* 1, 1 ff.; 2, 67 f.; Bhavabhūti, *Māl.* 3, 0; 3, 15 +; Bhitari inscription of king Skandagupta (*C.I.I.* III, 52) who installed (an image of) Viṣṇu to increase the religious merit of his father.

62. Cf. e.g. Bāṇa, *Kād.* 335 (Bombay 1890) ('I sought the protection of Śiva, lord of

the three worlds, and helper of the helpless'); 639; Budhasvāmin, *Bkśs.* 4, 103 (Viṣṇu appearing in a dream); 4, 116; 4, 131; 18, 266 (Śiva and Pārvatī); 18, 463 (Śiva and Kṛṣṇa); 18, 504; 23, 30; 23, 66.

63. Bāṇa, *Harṣac.* 3, p. 110 ff.

64. Somadeva, *Kss.* 117, 97 f. Viṣṇu-Keśava, 'the sole refuge of all the weak whose minds are troubled by hardships (the Sanskrit text may also mean: of the fair ones troubled by him of the five arrows, i.e. Kāma), may be expected to help up the milk-maid who had fallen down because her sight was stolen by the dust raised by the cows (or: by her love for a cowherd)' (Viśvanātha, *Sāhityadarpaṇa*, 266).

65. *Rāmāyaṇa*, 7, s. 118; cf. e.g. also Bhavabhūti, *Uttar.* 7, 20.

66. In prayers man is often anxious to choose the most adequate name of his god (cf. F. Heiler, *Erscheinungsformen und Wesen der Religion*, Stuttgart, 1961, p. 276), who therefore may be addressed by several names at the same time. This well-known fact may have led the poet of the *Mṛcchakaṭika* to write stanza 1, 41: '. . . shout out, scream, cry loudly enough for Śambhu, Śiva, Śaṅkara, or Īśvara'.

67. Harṣa, *Ratn.* 1, 4; *Gopālakelicandrikā*, 1, 1 (p. 43). Some examples may suffice to show the importance of Viṣṇu's *avatāras* in popular belief (I refer to Abbott, op. cit., pp. 91; 149). At the ceremony of the sacred thread a Hindu boy is considered to have a special *śakti* so that the water in which his feet have been washed is a *tīrtha*, 'a place of pilgrimage', or a source of purity, because of his being like Viṣṇu in the Dwarf *avatāra*. Earthquakes are ascribed to Viṣṇu the Boar: sometimes the god has to change the earth which he holds up from one tusk to another. For the occurrence of the *avatāras* in dramas see e.g. Bhāsa, *Karṇabh.* 1, 1; *Avim.* 1, 1; *Bālac.* 1, 8. See e.g. also Somadeva, *Kss.* 57, 3, etc.

68. Cf. *Mṛcchakaṭika* 10, 46 'victorious is the destroyer of the sacrifice of Dakṣa, the god whose emblem is the bull, . . . and after him (king) Āryaka, who has killed his powerful enemy'.

69. Viśākhadatta, *Mudrār.* 6, 1 (see also 7, 19).

70. Cf. e.g. Bāṇa, *Kād.* 257.

71. Cf. e.g. Bāṇa, *Kād.* 7 f.; 64 f.; 75 ('he held a staff . . ., having on its top a leafy basket full of creeper-blossoms gathered for the worship of Śiva'); 91; 99; 116; 118; 162; 244; 247; 249; 259; 398, etc.

72. Compare also C. and H. Jesudasan, *A history of Tamil literature*, Calcutta, 1961, p. 211 (a story of Śiva carrying earth for the sake of a poor old woman).

73. This aspect is for instance not adequately stressed by H. von Glasenapp, *Die Religionen Indiens*, Stuttgart, 1943, p. 145 f.

74. Bāṇa, *Kād.* 135.

75. Ibid., 261.

76. Ibid., 278.

77. Ibid., 417 ff. Compare A. A. M. Scharpé, *Bāṇa's Kādambarī*, Thesis, Utrecht, 1937, p. 91.

78. Somadeva, *Kss.* 19, 4 ff.; 24, 16; 27, 142.

79. Ibid., 18, 337 ff.; 20, 175; 34, 226.

80. Ibid., 22, 167; 23, 11; 44, 11.

81. Ibid., 35, 19.

82. Ibid., 21, 142; 57, 55 etc.

83. Ibid., 45, 9; 43; 46, 33.

84. Ibid., 44 init.

85. Ibid., 29, 132 ff.

86. Ibid., 88, 45.

87. Ibid., 21, 143; 22, 116 ff.

88. Ibid., 102, 20.

89. Ibid., 105, 21; 32; 114, 120.

90. See e.g. *MatsyaP.* 55, 30 ff.; 60, 12; 72, 42 *rūpasaubhāgyasampannaḥ punarjanmani janmani / viṣṇau vātha śive bhaktaḥ saptadvipādhipo bhavet*. Compare also Kantawala, op. cit., p. 222.

91. See e.g. *MatsyaP.* 140, 47 ff.

92. *MatsyaP.* 154, 289 ff.

93. S. K. De, *Aspects of Sanskrit literature*, Calcutta, 1959, p. 110 f.

94. Householders and celibates residing in Śiva's city of Benares are by the grace of this god, to whom they are devoted, delivered (*MatsyaP.* 180, 70 f.).

95. *Die Religionen Indiens*, II, p. 210 f.

96. E. J. Thompson and A. M. Spencer, *Bengali religious lyrics*, London, 1923, p. 41 f.

97. *Sāhityadarpaṇa*, 240 comm.

98. For a characterization see A. Lehmann, *Die śivaitische Frömmigkeit der tamulischen Erbauungsliteratur*, Berlin, 1947, p. 28.

99. *Gopālakelicandrikā*, ed. W. Caland, Amsterdam Academy, 1917, p. 46.

100. R. D. Ranade, *Au-delà des marches*, traduits par M. Alpe-Roussel et A. S. Apté, Paris, n.d., pp. 71; 91.

101. *MatsyaP.* 11, 18 f.

102. *MatsyaP.* 20, 38; 184, 6 ff. and other places collected by Kantawala, *Cultural history from the Matsyapurāṇa*, p. 224.

103. Viśvanātha, *Sāhityadarpaṇa*, 2 comm. Some of the extremely numerous references to God's feet in prayers, devotional effusions, etc. are Kālidāsa, *Megh.* 9 (12); Bhāravi, *Kir.* 18, 48; Subandhu, *Vās.* 297; *BhāgP.* 4, 9, 8; Utpaladeva, *Śivastotrāvalī*, Benares, 1964, 9; 20 (*gāḍhagāḍhabhavadaṅghrisarojāliṅganavyasanatatparacetāḥ*). 'The world is blessed by the dust of the feet of Viṣṇu's servants' (Perumāl, *Tirumoli*, 4, 6); 'Where a Western mystic would have spoken of basking in the sunshine of God's love, a Tamil devotee would speak of reclining under the shadow of His feet' (X. S. Thani Nayagam, *Landscape and poetry. A study of nature in classical Tamil poetry*, London, 1966, p. 17). Hence statements about the print of Viṣṇu's feet being worn on his devotees' foreheads in sacred paste (Perumāl, op. cit., 5, *passim*); Sundaramūrti in F. Kingsbury and G. E. Phillips, *Hymns of the Tamil Śaivite Saints*, Calcutta, 1921, p. 78 'Linked to naught else in life, my mind thinks only of Thy holy feet'. Nārāyāṇa's foot is said to support the earth (*MārkP.* 56, 1). See e.g. also Bankey Behari, *Minstrels of God*, I, Bombay, 1956, p. 49. Worship of God's feet (for which see e.g. W. Kirfel, *Symbolik des Hinduismus und des Jinismus*, Stuttgart, 1959, p. 90) may lead to union with Him and therewith to enlightenment and salvation.

104. I cannot enter here into a systematic discussion of those works of literary art which deal with epic and other themes connected with the great gods, for instance Bhāravi's *Kirātārjunīya* describing how Arjuna, after practising asceticism, and being engaged in a conflict with Śiva, under the guise of a Kirāta, obtains the weapons which he desires from the god—the recurrence of the name of Lakṣmī in the concluding stanza of every canto is no doubt more than mere homage—; or Vāgīśvara's *Haravijaya* dealing with the slaying of Andhaka by Śiva (see e.g. A. B. Keith, *Classical Sanskrit literature*, London, 1927, p. 56 f.). In expanding traditional narratives are often enriched with episodes and digressions which tend to make the gods' images and the ideas associated with their characters increasingly varied and perfect. The story of the events preceding Skanda's birth—who after, in the *Mahābhārata* 1, 60, 20 f., having been Agni's son, is produced through this god's intermediary, from Śiva's seed—is made more attractive by the episode of Agni being sent in the guise of a parrot to Śiva and Pārvatī, by the description of the amorous sports and love-quarrels of that divine couple, and by references to Pārvatī's severe asceticism for the transformation of her dark complexion into a white one in order to please her husband (cf. *MatsyaP.* 158, 21 ff.).

105. Compare K. S. Ramaswami Sastri, *The supreme epic of devotion*, Tirupati, 1953, p. 20.

106. 'Somewhere in the ocean of Indian religious literature one may find each trait of the one god represented also in the other' (D. H. H. Ingalls, *An anthology of Sanskrit court poetry*, Cambridge, Mass., 1965, p. 93).

107. For a similar passage see Hazra, *Studies in the upapurāṇas*, I, p. 354.

108. *BṛhannāradīyaP.* 5.

109. Cf. e.g. Jesudasan, op. cit., p. 99.

110. *SāmbaP.* 69 ff.

111. As is well known some holy places bear names ending in *-īśvara* which are also given to the god himself, e.g. Siddhīśvara (Somadeva, *Kss.*, ch. 114 ff.).

112. Somadeva, *Kss.* 22, 109; 86, 132; 137; 103, 119; 108, 35; 111, 81 f.; for an empty sanctuary of Śiva see e.g. also 92, 26.

113. Bāṇa, *Kad.* 401; cf. 503.

114. Bāṇa, *Kad.* 290; Somadeva, *Kss.* 119, 85.
115. Somadeva, *Kss.* 93, 84.
116. Cf. e.g. *ibid.*, 110, 73; 114, 126.
117. Ibid., 103, 236 f.
118. Ibid., 107, 67; 122 ff.; 115, 93; Kailāsa; cf. 73.
119. Ibid., 106, 127.
120. Ibid., 107, 129.
121. Somadeva, *Kss.* 71, 200 f.
122. Somadeva, *Kss.* 89, 95.
123. *Gopālakelicandrikā*, p. 52.
124. Cf. *Gopālakelicandrikā*, p. 117 and Caland, *Een onbekend Indisch toneelstuk* (*Gopālakelicandrikā*), p. 32. See e.g. also Somadeva, *Kss.* ch. 73.
125. Ingalls, op. cit., 35; 81; and compare e.g. also Bhavabhūti, *Māl.* 5, 1 f.; Somadeva, *Kss.* 97, 23 ff.
126. B. Gargi, *Theatre in India*, New York, 1962, p. 118.
127. Cf. e.g. Bhavabhūti, *Māl.* 3, 15 +.
128. For Śiva and the moon see also *Change and continuity in Indian religion*, The Hague, 1965, p. 53 f. Compare e.g. Bāṇa, *Kād.* 126; 398; (346); and *Harṣac.* 4, p. 162; (Budhasvāmin, *Bkśs.* 20, 105).
129. Cf. e.g. Bhāravi, *Kirātārjunīya* 5, 44; Somadeva, *Kathāsaritsāgara* 74, 111 'the tasteful water of the Ganges which seemed to be impregnated with the nectar of the moon, from dwelling on Śiva's head'.
130. Bāṇa, *Harṣac.* 1, 1 (2); 1, p. 19; 24; Murāri in Ingalls, *Anthology*, 32; see also 33; 39; 42, etc.
131. Meyer, *Trilogie*, III, p. 203; the same, *Sexual life in ancient India*, London, 1930, p. 472; see Bhāravi, loc. cit.
132. *Mṛcchakaṭika*, 4, 23. That the god had to place the moon on his head to allay the burning effect of the poison which he had drunk is another story.
133. J. B. Chaudhuri and Roma Chaudhuri, *Sanskrit poetesses*, Calcutta, 1939, p. 30 f.
134. Gaurī (Umā) and Gaṅgā are 'the two goddesses dear to Śiva': Somadeva, *Kss.* 90, 3.
135. '... that river, which with the ridges of its waves seems to be making a ladder for mortals to ascend into heaven by' (Somadeva, *Kss.* 93, 77).
136. Ingalls, op. cit., nos. 30; 33; 45, etc.
137. Cf. e.g. Bāṇa, *Harṣac.* 8, p. 272; Budhasvāmin, *Bkśs.* 21, 171.
138. See *Rāmāyaṇa*, 1, s. 34 ff. For a detailed account see Zimmer, *Myths and symbols*, New York, 1946, p. 112; for the iconography of this mythical event the same, *The art of Indian Asia*, New York, 1955, I, pp. 88 ff.
139. *BrahmavP.*, *KJKh.* 34, 13 ff.
140. Compare also Ingalls, op. cit., p. 69 f.
141. Bāṇa, *Harṣac.* 5, p. 192.
142. Ingalls, op. cit., 33; 42; 65; 92; 101.
143. Bhavabhūti, *Māl.* 1, 1.
144. One might also study parallels such as 'Pearls rain from a cloud which is Brahmā, the source of wisdom; another cloud is Viṣṇu, adorned by stars, protector and vigorous; another Śiva, surrounded by circles, illuminated by aureoles, drunk with power' (Ranade, op. cit., p. 158).
145. Curiously enough Śiva is, no doubt in imitation of his rival, said to have appeared, in his Bhairava form, in the same way from a pillar which cleft asunder with a loud noise: Somadeva, *Kss.* 106, 181.
146. Bāna, *Harṣac.* 6, p. 209 (... *hara iva kṛtabhairavākāro harir iva prakaṭitanarasiṃharūpaḥ*).
147. For his 'white smile' see e.g. Bāṇa, *Kād.* 269; 289.
148. Bāṇa, *Harṣac.* 8, p. 283.
149. Bāṇa, *Kād.* 218.
150. Somadeva, *Kss.* 108, 82. Compare *Aspects of early Viṣṇuism*, p. 100.
151. Somadeva, *Kss.* 47, 46 ff. For the Mother see e.g. R. E. Enthoven, *The folklore of Bombay*, Oxford, 1924, pp. 185 ff.

152. See Lecture V, p. 106.
153. *ViṣṇuP.* 3, a. 17 and 18.
154. Budhasvāmin, *Bkśs.* 20, 328; Kṣemendra, *Samayamātṛkā* 4, 25.
155. Kāl., *Ragh.* 10, 7 ff.; Viśākhadatta, *Mudrār.* 3, 21 and see e.g. Ingalls, op. cit., p. 94.
156. Bāṇa, *Harṣac.* 7, p. 235.
157. Budhasvāmin, *Bkśs.* 4, 19; Kṛṣṇamiśra, *Prab.* 4, 30 +.
158. Kṛṣṇamiśra, *Prab.* 4, 30 +.
159. Bāṇa, *Kād.* 41; 70.
160. Bāṇa, *Kād.* 97.
161. Kāl., *Ragh.* 6, 49; 10, 10; compare also Bāṇa, *Kād.* 137; 387.
162. For instance, '(Viṣṇu) who, for the sake of the lord of the gods, seized back from Bali the goddess of wealth and splendour' (Junāgarh inscription of Skandagupta, *C.I.I.*, III, 56). For an elaborate eulogy upon five *avatāras* (boar, dwarf, Man-lion, Kṛṣṇa and tortoise) see Kṛṣṇamiśra, *Prab.* 4, 30 +.
163. See e.g. Ingalls, op. cit., pp. 94 ff.
164. Kāl., *Kum.* 3, 44; Bāṇa, *Harṣac.* 4, p. 149; Harṣa, *Ratn.* 1, 4 and see e.g. Ingalls, op. cit., p. 68.
165. Bāṇa, *Harṣac.* 4, p. 149 ('tufted with tossing side-locks of curly hair, the boy was like a reborn Kāma with his head encircled by the smoke line of the flame of Śiva's anger'); 5, p. 186.
166. Somadeva, *Kss.* 1, 1.
167. Aśvaghoṣa, *Bc.* 10, 3; Bāṇa, *Kād.* 162; 224; 259.
168. *MatsyaP.* 181, 14; 183, 8; Bhāravi, *Kir.* 5, 2.
169. Bāṇa, *Harṣac.* 144.
170. Somadeva, *Kss.* 2, 15.
171. Bāṇa, *Harṣac.* 6, p. 220.
172. Harṣa, *Ratn.* 1, 4; Bāṇa, *Harṣac.* 7, p. 241.
173. Bhaṭṭa Nārāyaṇa, *Veṇīs.* 3, 10.
174. Bāṇa, *Kād.* 247; Budhasvāmin, *Bkśs.* 25, 85, where the poison is worth praising because it touches Śiva's neck.
175. Kāl., *Kum.* 7, 36; 40; Bhāravi, *Kir.* 14, 56; 64 f.; Bāṇa, *Kād.* 113.
176. *MatsyaP.* 193, 21 ff.
177. Cf. the interpolated śloka after *Mbh.* 1, 16, 33 (1, 18, 42 B.). Compare also the Tamil references provided by Lehmann, op. cit., p. 46, and Śūdraka, *Mṛcchakaṭika* 1, 2.
178. Some examples of combined references to Śiva's characteristics, which may of course be endlessly varied, are Subandhu, *Vās.* 181 'Immediately the stars shone forth, scattered like drops of the stream of water of Jahnu's daughter (= the Ganges) wandering in the winding hollows of the mass of matted locks of Śiva, shaken by the fury of his twilight dance'; ibidem, 4 'Victorious is the god whose crescent gleams like a silvern pearl set by Umā upon his brow, when from his blazing eye she gathers the black collyrium'; in the invocation at the beginning of the *Hitopadeśa* (1, 1) Ganges and moon combine; Somadeva, *Kss.* 35, 1 'May the head of Śiva studded with the nails of Gaurī engaged in playfully pulling his hair, and so appearing rich in many moons, procure you prosperity'.
179. Bāṇa, *Harṣac.* 2, p. 89.
180. Viśvanātha, *Sāhityad.* 578.
181. Bāṇa, *Harṣac.* 1, p. 17.
182. Viśvanātha, loc. cit.
183. For which see e.g. Ingalls, op. cit., 106; 124; 146.
184. Bāṇa, *Harṣac.* 3, p. 106.
185. Bāṇa, *Harṣac.* 4, p. 131; cf. 7, p. 248.
186. Bāṇa, *Harṣac.* 4, p. 132.
187. Cf. Tawney and Penzer, op. cit., I, p. 55, n. 1.
188. Viśākhadatta, *Mudrārākṣasa*, 3, 20.
189. Bāṇa, *Harṣac.* 4, p. 135; cf. also p. 162; 6, p. 201.
190. Bāṇa, *Harṣac.* 4, p. 164. For the lotus and its 'symbolism' see e.g. Zimmer, *Myths and symbols*, passim; W. E. Ward, 'The lotus symbol', *Journal of aesthetics and art criticism*, XI (1952); M. Bénisti, *Le médaillon lotiforme*, Paris, 1952.
191. Bāṇa, *Harṣac.* 5, p. 183.

192. Bāṇa, *Harṣac.* 2, p. 68; cf. 6, p. 199; 212; Kāl., *Ragh.* 2, 35. Compare also J. Gonda, *Similes in Indian literature*, Leyden, 1949; K. Chellappan Pillai, *Similes of Kālidāsa*, Calcutta, 1945.

193. *Bhaṭṭikāvya* 8, 89.

194. Bāṇa, *Harṣac.* 3, p. 105.

195. Bāṇa, *Harṣac.* 3, p. 118 (a stream solidified to rival Viṣṇu's sword).

196. Cf. e.g. also *Mbh.* 13, a. 145.

197. See e.g. A. K. Coomaraswamy, *The aims of Indian art*, Broad Campden, 1908; S. Kramrisch, *Gründzuge der indischen Kunst*, Hellerau, 1924; H. Zimmer, *Kunstform und Yoga im indischen Kultbild*, Berlin, 1926; S. N. Dasgupta, *Fundamentals of Indian art*, Bombay, 1951.

198. Cf. e.g. Jesudasan, op. cit., p. 95.

199. Cf. Ramaswamy Sastri, op. cit., p. 32 and *BhāgP.* 3, a. 28.

200. See also G. S. Ghurye, *Gods and men*, Bombay, 1962, pp. 31 ff.

201. Somadeva, *Kss.* 114, 1.

202. Somadeva, *Kss.* 68, 2.

203. See e.g. *Mbh.* 1, 65, 18 ff. (Menakā sent by Indra to tempt Viśvāmitra 'with beauty, youth, arts, smiles and speech'); 1, 120 Jālapadī and Śaradvat; 1, 203, 20 ff. (Tilottamā), and compare H. Lüders, *Die Sage von Ṛṣyaśṛṅga*, Nachr. Göttingen, 1897, pp. 87 ff. (= *Philologica indica* (Göttingen), 1940, pp. 1ff.).

204. Neither this relation nor the aim of the ascetic practice is clearly indicated in the poem, but Umā-Pārvatī is a reincarnation of Śatī, a daughter of Dakṣa (Kāl., *Kum.* 1, 21) and Śiva had started his ascetic way of life after his conflict with the latter (cf. 1, 54).

205. Kāl., *Kum.* 3, 58; 69.

206. Some of the relevant passages of the narrative literature are worth studying. Thus Somadeva (*Kss.* 71, 127 ff.) tells us the story of the wicked Kanakamañjarī who would perform with all due rites an incantation for obtaining control over an imp of the fever-demon, who has the power of removing fever, so that she herself might be able to cure those who suffer from that disease. For that purpose she left the women's apartments, secretly and at night, by a postern-door and, sword in hand, made for a deserted temple of Śiva. There she killed a goat and anointed the liṅga with its blood, making also an offering to it of its flesh; then she threw the animal's entrails round it by way of a garland, honoured it by placing on its summit the goat's heart, fumigated it with the smoke proceeding from the goat's eyes and presented to it the animal's head by way of oblation. After having smeared the front of the sacrificial platform with blood and sandalwood she painted on it a lotus with eight leaves, and on its pericarp a representation of the demon of fever—with three feet and three mouths, and with a handful of ashes (which are believed to convey misfortune and are often used in magic rites) by way of weapon—and of his attendant imps, whom she summoned with a spell, to complete this rite with an oblation of human flesh.

207. *Mbh.* 1, 16, 39 *tato nārāyaṇo māyām āsthito mohinīm prabhuḥ | strīrūpam adbhutaṃ kṛtvā*; *ViṣṇuP.* 1, 9, 108; see also *MatsyaP.* 251, 7 f.; Somadeva, *Kss.* 74, 37; as Viṣṇu's thirteenth *avatāra* (*BhāgP.* 1, 3, 17), and compare Thomas, *Epics*, p. 91 f. and M. N. Srinivas, *Religion and society of the Coorgs*, Oxford, 1952, p. 210.

208. *VāyuP.* 25, 44 ff.

209. Cf. also *BhāgP.* 8, 8, 41 ff.

210. P. K. Maity, *Historical studies in the cult of the goddess Manasā*, Calcutta, 1966, p. 82. For Hanumat see also Ghurye, *Gods and men*, pp. 226 ff.

211. Ph. Baldaeus, *Afgoderye der Oost-Indische heydenen*, Amsterdam 1672, ed. by A. J. de Jong, Thesis, Utrecht, 1917, p. 14.

212. Śiva, here called Ixora (i.e. Īśvara), strikes off one of Brahmā's heads (cf. *LiP.* 1, 96, 49; see also *ŚivaP.* V b, 5, 42 and compare H. Meinhard, *Beiträge zur Kenntnis des Śivaismus nach den Purāṇa's*, Thesis, Bonn, 1928, p. 41), from the blood a giant is born; the day on which this happened is henceforth Poṅgal, a '*dies infestus*'; Śiva must atone for his crime and goes off as a *yogin*, collecting alms in the head which he carries in his hand (the motif of Indra's *brahmahatyā*); the alms were however, in spite of himself, reduced to ashes by the glances of his third eye; he meets the *munis* and their wives; the *munis* make attempts

to kill him, but he slays the tiger and the elephant they send and makes garments and trophies out of their skin; Viṣṇu after having changed himself into a girl, produces a child out of Śiva's seed; this child is Śiva's penance; finally he makes Śiva's third eye blind and puts an end to his state of sinfulness. So, 'the poets say', the latter has good reason to be grateful.

213. See Thomas, *Epics*, loc. cit.

214. *BhāgP.* 4, a. 12.

215. Ingalls, op. cit., p. 72.

216. See e.g. Kāl., *Kum.* 7, 48; *Ragh.* 17, 14; Bāṇa, *Harṣac.* 2, p. 82.

217. According to the *Mahābhārata* (8, a. 24) the three sons of Tāraka, after their father's defeat, obtained boons from Brahmā who refused to give them immunity from death: 'after a thousand years our three cities will become united into one; that foremost one among the gods who will, with one shaft, pierce these three cities, will be the cause of our destruction'.

218. *ŚB.* 6, 3, 3, 25; *AiB.* 2, 11.

219. Cf. *MS.* 3, 8, 1.

220. Viz. the *upasads* (see L. Renou, *Vocabulaire du rituel védique*, Paris, 1954, p. 45).

221. See *AiB.* 1, 23 ff.

222. *KB.* 8, 8; cf. 24, 10; 25, 1.

223. Cf. also *ŚB.* 3, 4, 4, 3 ff.

224. *TS.* 6, 2, 3. Compare also S. Lévi, *La doctrine du sacrifice dans les brāhmaṇas*, Paris, 1898, p. 45 f.

225. Cf. *TS.* 6, 2, 3, 3 'verily he drives away his enemies from these worlds so that they do not come back'.

226. Cf. also the interpolated passage after 7, 173, 56 ab.

227. Cf. e.g. also *BmḍP.* 2, 72, 81; *VāP.* 97, 82 etc.

228. See e.g. *MatsyaP.* 129 f.; a. 135 ff.; *BhāgP.* 7, 10, 53 ff.

229. Ingalls, op. cit., n° 67, cf. 49; Somadeva, *Kss.* 100, 48: even Gaurī contributed to the victory by worshipping Gaṇeśa.

230. Kālidāsa, *Megh.* 59; *Kum.* 7, 48.

231. *Mahimnastava*, edited and translated by W. Norman Brown, Poona, 1965, st. 18. For a passing mention e.g. Bhāravi, *Kir.* 12, 14.

232. Ingalls, op. cit., 56.

233. Viśākhadatta, *Mūdrarākṣasa* 1, 2; cf. *Bhaṭṭa Nārāyaṇa* 1, 3.

234. *MatsyaP.* 136, 5 f.

235. Mayūra, see Ingalls, op. cit., n° 61. Maṅkha's *Śrīkaṇṭhacarita* (XIIth century) describes in twenty-five cantos the destruction, by Śiva, of the demon Tripura.

236. *Mbh.* 7, 173, 57 speaks of *trīṇi sametāni antarikṣe purāṇi.*

237. It is true that in later times the place 'where Śiva flung down Tripura, the asura', is said to lie to the north of the Narmadā (H. H. Wilson and F. Hall, *The Vishṇu Purāṇa*, V, London, 1870, p. 118).

238. The Vaiṣṇavas produced many tales and legends which, in variation or continuation of the *avatāra* themes, are to account for some institution or some historical or pseudo-historical event, for instance how the land of Kashmir was rescued from the wicked demon 'Waterborn' (Ambujana). See *Nīlamata*, st. 111 ff.; cf. J. Ph. Vogel, *Indian serpent-lore*, London, 1926, pp. 235 ff. This region was indeed hallowed by Viṣṇu to such a degree that staying there could result in 'washing away' one's sins (Somadeva, *Kss.* 39, 36 f.).

239. Compare e.g. *ViṣṇuP.* 1, 9, 140 ff.

240. See e.g. *ViṣṇuP.* 1, 8, 15 ff.

241. Kāl., *Ragh.* 10, 8; Aphsad inscription of Ādityasena, *C.I.I.*, III, 42, pp. 200 ff.; Mayūra, Sūryaśataka, 92.

242. Cf. Mayura, *Sūryaśataka*, 42.

243. *ViṣṇuP.* 1, 9, 104; cf. Bāṇa, *Kād.* 195; Budhasvāmin, *Bkśs.* 19, 80. Quite consistently Sītā is in Jayadeva's drama Prasanna-Rāghava (XIIIth century ?) shown as falling in love with Rāma before he had even lifted up the bow by bending which he had to win her hand. For Śrī-Lakṣmī and the ocean from which she was born see e.g. also places such as Somadeva, *Kss.* 74, 213; 100, 15.

244. Ingalls, op. cit., n°s 108; 109; 136; 138.

245. The beloved of the boar is the earth, for she is said to have been most dear to Viṣṇu in his boar incarnation (Somadeva, *Kss.* 124, 223): the god indeed continued his amorous sports with her by appearing in this avatāra (*KālikāP.* a. 30).

246. I refer to *Aspects of early Viṣṇuism*, p. 230 f. For Viṣṇu's *gāndharva* marriage with the Ganges (Gaṅgā) see *DevīBhP.* 9, a. 14.

247. *Mbh.* 2, 42, 15 ff.; *ViṣṇuP.* 5, a. 26; (*MatsyaP.* 47, 13 ff.: Kṛṣṇa and his consorts); cf. also Māgha, *Śiśupālavadha* 2, 38; Somadeva, *Kss.* 104, 126.

248. *Harivaṃśa*, 2, a. 47 ff. = a. 104 ff.; see especially 109, 28 (= 6093).

249. *BhāgP.* 10, 52, 21 ff.

250. I refer to *Die Religionen Indiens*, I, p. 252 f.

251. Compare e.g. A. Baumgartner, *Das Rāmāyaṇa und die Rāma-Literatur der Inder*, Freiburg Br., 1894, p. 67 f. and see also L. Renou (L. Renou and J. Filliozat), *L'Inde classique*, I, Paris, 1947, p. 507 f.

252. 'In der Verwandlung Kischtna Awatarum gennant, soll er 16000 Weiber gehabt haben. Die unzüchtigen und unflätigen Dinge, die sie von ihm schreiben, sind unzehlig, und geben Ursache zu solchen Sünden, wie denn die Sünden unter ihren Göttern in eben denjenigen Figuren präsentiert werden, darinnen sie geschehen sind' (B. Ziegenbalg, *Malabarisches Heidenthum*, ed. W. Caland, Amsterdam Academy, 1926, p. 47).

253. *BrahmavP.*, *KJKh.* 124.

254. See e.g. H. Goetz und R. Ilse-Munk, *Gedichte aus der indischen Liebesmystik des Mittelalters*, Leipzig, 1925; Gonda, *Die Religionen Indiens*, II, p. 153 f. (on Jayadeva's Gītagovinda, see the bibliography, p. 153, n. 7); Aurobindo, *Songs of Vidyāpati*, Pondicherry 1956.

255. See J. C. Mathur, *Drama in rural India*, London, 1964, pp. 78 ff.

256. Compare e.g. A. Dasgupta, *The lyric in Indian poetry*, Calcutta, 1962, p. 100. The performer of a kīrtana is expected to sing a benedictory prelude in order to create a sacred and spiritual atmosphere. See also ibidem, p. 123. See also E. J. Thompson and A. M. Spencer, *Bengali religious lyrics: Vaishnava*, Calcutta, 1925; W. G. Archer, *The loves of Krishna in Indian painting and poetry*, New York, 1958; D. Bhattacharya, *Love songs of Vidyāpati*, London, 1963; M. E. Opler, *S.W. Journal of Anthropology*, XV, pp. 223 ff. for religious pageants depicting scenes from the life of Rāma.

257. *Haribhaktivilāsa*, p. 677: Sinners may attain the highest abode of Viṣṇu by singing his name. It seems worth while to quote some lines from two modern Indian authors (Bhattacharya, *Love songs of Vidyāpati*, p. 24 f.) 'In the cult of Vaiṣṇavism the romance of Kṛṣṇa and his favourite Rādhā was exalted as a means to spiritual release .... In portraying all his loves as married women, the story emphasized the supremacy of love over duty and the need of the soul to allow nothing, not even morals, to stand between itself and God' (and J. C. Ghosh, *Bengali literature*, Oxford, 1948, p. 37 f.) 'Even today there is nothing sweeter to the Indian heart than such images as Kṛṣṇa playing the flute by the waters of the Yamunā, Kṛṣṇa playing games with his friends in the fields and woods, and making love to the milkmaids in the *kadamba* groves'. In order to demonstrate the importance of the love of God as an incentive of human activity Tulsidas would, in later times, point to such examples as Bharata who, for the sake of God, left his mother, Prahlāda who left his father, the gopīs who left their husbands. See e.g. R. D. Ranade, *Pathway to God in Hindi literature*, Bombay, 1959, p. 60, etc.

258. *BhāgP. Mah.* (Introd.), 6, 76.

259. A. B. Keith, *A history of Sanskrit literature*, Oxford, 1920, p. 57. For a closely related version see *VāmanaP.* a. 51 ff.

260. Hence also similes such as Bāṇa, *Harṣac.*, 4, p. 163.

261. Bāṇa, *Kād.* 441 *sṛṣṭer gurū.*

262. She is already mentioned in the *Kena U.* 25 (3, 12).

263. *Die Religionen Indiens*, II, p. 258 f.; M. Eliade, *Patterns in comparative religion*, London and New York, 1958, p. 280; E. O. James, *The cult of the Mother-goddess*, London, 1959, pp. 103 ff. (The contention that the name Umā means 'light' is unfounded; the least improbable explication is 'Mother').

264. Kālidāsa, *Kum.* 1, 23.

265. Cf. Kālidāsa, *Kum.* 1, 31 ff.

266. Kālidāsa, *Kum.* 1, 50; 3, 16; Bāṇa, *Kād.* 441.
267. Kālidāsa, *Kum.* 1, 59 f.; 3, 17; Harṣa, *Ratn.* 1, 1; cf. also Somadeva, *Kss.* 92, 9 'Śiva, who was won by the toilsome asceticism of Gaurī'.
268. See e.g. *MatsyaP.* 1, 154, 62; *MārkP.* 52, 12 f.; Kāl., *Kum.* 1, 54 and compare H. Zimmer, *The king and the corpse*, New York, 1948, part II.
269. Cf. e.g. also *MatsyaP.* a. 154.
270. *Sāhityadarpaṇa*, 227 comm. Compare however passages such as Daṇḍin, *Dkc.* 2 where Śiva is put on a par with a number of adulterous gods for violating five thousand wives of munis.
271. Cf. also ibid., 3, 42. I cannot to my regret dwell here on the relation between these great gods and nature as seen by the Indian poets. It may suffice to draw attention to some quotations from South-Indian poets, the former paralleling the relation between the human soul and God on the one hand with the flower and the source of its life on the other: 'Like a lotus which refuses to open to any warmth other than that of the sun, his soul will not melt at any influence but Viṣṇu's' (Perumāl, *Tirumoli* 5, 6), the other illustrating the ambiguous role of nature in divine history: 'The same sea which tosses its waters as though it were shaking up a mat for Viṣṇu to sleep on lies between Viṣṇu-Rāma and his hope to recover Sītā' (cf. Jesudasan, op. cit., p. 174).
272. See e.g. Gonda, *Similes in Sanskrit literature*, p. 70 f.
273. Cf. e.g. Aśvaghoṣa, *Buddhacarita* 13, 16.
274. A very frequently recalled mythological motif; cf. e.g. Daṇḍin, *Dkc.* 5. See also S. Konow, in *Festschrift-J. Wackernagel*, Göttingen, 1923, pp. 1 ff.
275. Kālidāsa, *Kum.* 4, 42; cf. 8, 20. It is not surprising that on this occasion Kāma laughs (Ingalls, *Anthology*), 323), because his power is more than human (ibid. 326).
276. Compare e.g. Harṣa, *Priyadarśika*, 1, 1: when her marriage rites were performed Gaurī's sight was troubled by the smoke of the sacrificial fire, etc.; Kāl., *Kum.* 1, 53; canto 6 and 7.
277. Keith, op. cit., p. 89. See Kālidāsa, *Kum.*, canto 8. It is nowadays difficult to see why this beautiful passage which soon passes into a description of nature, should have given offence.
278. Kālidāsa, *Kum.* 8, 91.
279. *Mbh.* 13, 83, 40 ff. makes no mention of the love joys of the divine pair lasting so long, but *Rām.* 1, 35, 6 speaks of a long hundred years of the gods—a year for men being equal to a day for the gods (*Manu* 1, 67, etc.)—; I cannot dwell here on the anxiety of the denizens of heaven lest the fruit of so long a cohabitation of these two powerful deities will be far too mighty and terrible for the world to endure. See e.g. also Somadeva, *Kss.* 20, 73 *yadā nābhūd ratānto 'sya gateṣv abdaśateṣv api / tadā tadupamardena cakampe bhuvanatrayam.*
280. Cf. e.g. *BhaviṣyottaraP.*, a. 136.
281. Cf. e.g. Somadeva, *Kss.* 31, 32.
282. I refer to my books *The Savayajñas*, Amsterdam Academy, 1965, p. 344 f. and *Die Religionen Indiens*, II, pp. 206 f.; 212 f.
283. *BĀU.* 1, 4, 3.
284. See e.g. Meyer, *Trilogie*, III, p. 293.
285. Thus the predilection of Indian sculptors for reliefs and images depicting this divine male-female polarity is no chance occurrence. See e.g. H. Krishna Sastri, *South Indian images of gods and goddesses*, Madras, 1916, pp. 120 ff.; Banerjea, *Development of Hindu iconography*, pp. 181 f.; 552 ff., etc.
286. *SanatkumāraS.*, *Kārtt.* 4, 9 f.; cf. Meyer, op. cit., I, p. 19.
287. *LiṅgaP.* 1, 41, 11. Compare also H. Meinhard, *Beiträge zur Kenntnis des Śivaismus nach den Purāṇas*, Thesis, Bonn, 1928, p. 29.
288. Ingalls, *Anthology*, 85. Hence also Pārvatī's function as 'the fitting refuge of all women' (Somadeva, *Kss.* 80, 38).
289. He could even be disturbed on seeing the apsaras Tilottamā (ibid., 27, 66).
290. Kṛṣṇamiśra, *Prabodhacandrodaya* 3, 16; cf. 2, 35.
291. See e.g. T. G. Mainkar, *Kalidasa*, Poona, 1962, p. 65.
292. See e.g. A. K. Coomaraswamy, *The dance of Śiva*, Bombay, 1948, pp. 83 ff.; L. Frédéric, *La danse sacrée de l'Inde*, Paris, 1957.

293. The dance which he executes in the Chidambaram Temple and which forms the well-known motif of the Naṭarāja images expresses one very fundamental idea. It represents his five activities: emanation or unfolding which arises from the drum held in one of his right hands; preservation or duration, imparted by his other right hand which is uplifted in the sign of safety; destruction or, rather, re-absorption symbolized by the upper left hand which bears a tongue of flame; hiding the transcendental essence behind the garb of apparitions, and the bestowal of grace and release made visible by one foot which is held aloft, and to which the hands are made to point. The other foot, planted on the ground and on which in the well-known images the god balances himself, gives an abode to the tired souls struggling in the saṃsāra.

294. Subandhu, *Vās.* 165.

295. H. Zimmer, *The art of Indian Asia*, New York, 1955, I, pp. 88; 122 ff.

296. *Bharatīya-Nāṭyaśāstra*, 4, 2 ff.; one might consult the translation by Manomohan Ghosh, *The Nāṭyaśastra*, II, Bombay, ^{2}1967. For this tradition see e.g. S. Konow, *Das indische Drama*, Berlin-Leipzig, 1920, p. 37; F. Bowers, *Theatre in the East*, London, 1956, p. 9; Gargi, *Theatre*, p. 193 and compare Gonda, *Acta Or.* (*Lugd.*), XIX, pp. 442 ff. An evaluation of this tradition by a present-day Indian author may be found in A. Rangacharya, *Introduction to Bharata's Nāṭyaśāstra*, Bombay, 1966, p. 22 f.

297. This tradition is another confirmation of what on these pages has been suggested about the importance of these mythical themes.

298. In a very ingenious stanza (*Mālatīmādhava* 5, 23) consisting of four times 54 syllables Bhavabhūti describes Cāmuṇḍā (a form of Durgā) executing the Tāṇḍava dance while having the same appearance and paraphernalia as Śiva is associated with when making these rhythmic movements. While dancing the goddess wears an elephant hide with big nails protruding which accidentally pierce through the moon which is on her head with the result that the nectar begins to ooze out falling upon the skulls worn by the goddess; these skulls begin to live and start a loud laughter; all creatures become afraid and begin to pray the goddess for protection. The black serpents she uses as armlets are pressed, emit flames of poison so that the goddess tossing her arms comes to displace mountains. The quarters of the universe are sewn by the circular movement like that of a fire-brand caused by the whirling of her head terrible through the rays from her third eye, the flag attached to her club tossing away the stars in the firmament. The goddess dances so perfectly that all minor deities begin to applaud loudly in appreciation. 'Near the fair Umā, who beats the time, you will see Śiva dancing in a graveyard the dance of Destruction and the swift dance of Time, the same that he performed with faultless rhythm, at the request of all the gods, when an arrow of fire, guided by his will, destroyed the three flying cities of the Titans' (Ilangō Adigal, *Shilappadikaram*, translated by A. Daniélou, p. 27).

299. Viśākhadatta, *Mudrārākṣasa* 3, 30 ... *rudrasya raudraṃ rasam abhinayatas tāṇḍaveṣu smarantyā / saṃjātodagraprakampaṃ katham api dharayā dhāritaḥ pādaghātaḥ*.

300. Subandhu, *Vās.* 63.

301. For singing in honour of Śiva see e.g. Somadeva, *Kss.* 59, 81; 66, 162.

302. Thus stage-plays, e.g. all three dramas of Bhavabhūti, were brought on the stage on the occasion of a *yātrā* (a popular religious festivity including processions, a theatrical performance, etc.: see N. Chattopādhyāya, The *yātrās* or popular dramas of Bengal, London 1882); cf. also L. Kretzschmar, *Bhavabhūti*, Halle S., 1936, p. 111; N. Stchoupak, *Uttararāmacarita*, Paris, 1935, p. 3; Todar Mall, *Mahāvīra-caritam*, Oxford, 1928, p. 218.—Long ago (*Acta Or. Lugd.*, XIX, pp. 385 ff.). I drew attention to the frequent references in Sanskrit literature to girls playing at ball. In some cases the ritual significance of this entertainment is beyond doubt, for instance Daṇḍin, *Dkc.* 6 where a young girl is, at fixed dates, to play at ball in honour of Pārvatī in order to find an excellent husband. In the same work, 4 a princess goes with her girl friends to a forest in order to worship Śiva with such a game (*madanadamanārādhanāya nirgatya ... kandukenānukrīḍamānām*).

303. Somadeva, *Kss.* 99, 40.

304. 'If a *kathakali* actor is playing Śiva he does not try to act Śiva, he is Śiva' (Gargi, *Theatre*, p. 73).

305. Jesudasan, op. cit., p. 65: It is well known that this identification of the dancing worshipper with his God was also an element of the Viṣṇuite Kṛṣṇa cult; see for instance

ViP. 5, 13 'many *gopīs* imitated the different actions of Kṛṣṇa and in his absence wandered through Vṛndāvana representing his person. 'I am Kṛṣṇa', cries one, 'behold the elegance of my movements' . . . (24 ff.). For the religious significance of dances in general see W. O. E. Oesterley, *The sacred dance*, Cambridge, 1923; G. van der Leeuw, *Wegen en grenzen*, Amsterdam, ²1948, ch. I.

306. Somadeva, *Kss.* 114, 124 *nṛtyantyau saṅkarasyāgre tam eva śaraṇam śritau.*

307. See e.g. Kālidāsa, *Megh.* 38 (35).

308. Somadeva, *Kss.* 106, 11.

309. Ibid., 121, 124.

310. Public temple dancing took place also in honour of Viṣṇu.

311. For singing in a sanctuary of Viṣṇu (*keśavāyatana*) see e.g. Somadeva, *Kss.* 36, 115. For a description of Kṛṣṇa's dance with the milkmaids (*rāsalīlā* or *rāsakrīḍā*) on the first day of spring (Indra festival), the dancers claiming benedictions ('May the king and his vast empire never know famine, disease, or dissension. May we be blessed with wealth, and, when the season comes, with rains') see Ilangō Adigal's *Shilappadikaram*, op. cit., p. 19 f.; M. Singer (ed.) *Krishna*, Honolulu, 1966, Index, p. 266; Bankey Behari, *Minstrels of God, passim*; B. Kakati, *Viṣṇuite myths and legends in folklore setting*, Gauhati, 1952, pp. 41 ff. For Kṛṣṇa's elephant dance performed after upsetting the perfidious designs of king Kaṃsa, and his wrestler's dance performed after killing Bāṇa and other dances see the same work, p. 27 f. The above quotation: p. 120.

312. Bhāsa, *Dhūtaghaṭotkaca*, 1, 1.

313. See above, p. 122.

314. *Mbh.* 7, 173, 42 ff. The story is told in illustration of the statement that, when Mahādeva becomes angry, nobody, not even the gods, can have peace, wherever they might hide themselves.

315. For another version in which Dakṣa is only a figure of secondary importance see *Mbh.* 10, a. 17 f.

316. *Mbh.* 12, app. I, 28, in the crit. ed.

317. Similarly, *VāP.* a. 30. See the English translation of this episode in Wilson and Hall, op. cit., I, London 1864, pp. 120 ff. For other purāṇic particulars on Dakṣa see V. R. Ramachandra Dikshitar, *The Purāṇa index*, II, Madras, 1952, pp. 58 ff.

318. Cf. *BhāgP.* 4, a. 2 ff.

319. *Hariv.* a. 222, 44 ff. (12255 ff.).

320. Compare ṚV. 10, 95; *ŚB.* 11, 5, 1.

321. *Mbh.* 1, 70, 16; cf. also *Hariv.* 1, 10, 22 ff.

322. *ViP.* 4, 1, 6 ff. In *MatsyaP.* a. 12 the story is told otherwise: by pleasing Śiva and Pārvatī Ilā was transformed into a *kiṃnara* and came to be a male for one month and a female for another month. For some particulars see Kantawala, *Cultural history from the Matsyapurāṇa, passim*; there is no occasion to enter into a discussion with V. S. Agrawala, *Matsya Purāṇa, a study*, Benares, 1963, p. 130 f.

323. *MatsyaP.* 24, 11; cf. 119, 39; 120, 39 ff.; 61, 21 ff.

324. Kālidāsa, *Vikram.* 1, 7 +.

325. Whereas the *Mahābhārata* (3, 93, 17 ff.; 7, a. 62 Bo. etc.) connects the famous place named Gayā with a *rājarṣi* called Gaya, the son of Amūrtarayas, who was a distinguished sacrificer and received a boon from Agni (cf. also *Rām.* 2, 99, 11, etc.), the *Vāyu-Purāṇa*, a. 105 (Gayāmāhātmya, cf. D. R. Patil, *Cultural history from the Vāyu Purāṇa*, Poona, 1946, p. 5) makes mention of an *asura* of the same name who was so devout in the worship of Viṣṇu that his accumulated merit alarmed the gods. Through Viṣṇu's intervention the place covered by his body on which the gods had, on Viṣṇu's advice, sacrificed, became holy ground. See also Meinhard, op. cit., p. 26 f.

326. It would of course be necessary to study the relative tales in full detail and to determine not only the variations transforming the main theme but also such minor deviations as inserted motifs, descriptions, expatiations, changes in the choice of words and epithets, etc. etc.

327. I refer to *Aspects of early Viṣṇuism*, p. 166 and elsewhere; *Die Religionen Indiens*, I, p. 236 f.

328. Bhāsa, *Dhūtavākya* 1, 1.

329. Compare *BmḍP.* 2, 73, 81 f.; *VāyuP.* 98, 81; Hacker, *Prahlāda*, Mainz Academy, 1959, I, p. 17.

330. Notice also cases of transfer of epithets, etc.: *VāyuP.* 54, 66 Śiva is described as *vajrahasta* 'wielding the *vajra*' (an epithet originally belonging to Indra) and such changes of character as Rāvaṇas becoming a teacher of *bhakti* (*BhāgP.* 6, 11, 14 ff.).

331. See *Mbh.* 6, 91, 17; 7, 130, 30; 8, 37, 23 and compare my observations in 'A note on Indra in purāṇic literature', *Purāṇa*, IX, Benares, 1967, pp. 222 ff. (esp. p. 235 f.).

332. Kāl., *Kum.* 2, 63 f.; 3, 1 ff.; cf. also 2, 29.

333. I refer to my relative remarks in *Purāṇa*, IX, pp. 252 ff.

334. Compare W. Kirfel, *Das Purāṇa Pañcalakṣaṇa*, Bonn, 1927, pp. 6 ff.; 44 ff.

335. A. N. Jani, *A critical study of Śrīharṣa's Naiṣadhīyacaritam*, Baroda, 1957, p. 93; cf. p. 233 f.

336. Śrīharṣa, *Naiṣadhacarita*, 21, 34 ff.

337. Ibid., 18, 24. For Śiva see lecture V, p. 102.

338. Śrīharṣa, op. cit., 21, 32 ff.

339. Ibid., 12, 38: the white ocean of the fame of a king is so profound that the white Kailāsa can lie submerged in it, as if it were the crystal phallus of Śiva (cf. K. K. Handiqui, *Naiṣadhacarita of Śrīharṣa*, Poona, 1956, p. 183). Cf. also 21, 37.

340. Ibid., 12, 92.

341. *Ibid.*, 16, 16. The wreath was obtained by Śiva himself through his friendship with Kubera. Cf. e.g. *Rām.* 7, 13, 22 f.; *Samayamātṛkā* 4, 26.

342. *Elaeocarpus ganitrus.*

343. Śrīharṣa, op. cit., 21, 40.

344. Ibid., 12, 37. For Lakṣmī see also 6, 80; 20, 4: 'She shone like Lakṣmī, her eyes resembling fullblown lotus blooms'.

345. Ibid., 12, 95.

346. It may be interesting to notice that also in the version of this well-known story as represented in the *Kathāsaritsāgara* (56, 237 ff.) Śiva is mentioned in a comparison.

347. See e.g. *MārkP.* 17, 11.

348. Cf. also *MatsyaP.* 249, 82.

349. *śrīr anantaram utpannā ghṛtāt pāṇḍuravāsinī.*

350. Maity, *Historical studies in the cult of the goddess Manasā*, pp. 82 ff.

351. *Mbh.* 3, 107, 20 ff.

352. *Rām.* 1, 41, 23 ff. See also Zimmer, *Myths and symbols*, pp. 109 ff.

353. Cf. also *Mbh.* 3, App. I, 14, 4 f.

354. *VāyuP.* 42, 37.

355. *ViP.* 2, 2, 31; 2, 8, 103 (cf. 98) and compare *BhāgP.* 5, 17, 1.

356. See e.g. *KūrmaP.* 1, 2, 91 ff. (Śivaite).

357. Todar Mall, op. cit., p. XXIV.

358. *ŚivaP. Jñānasaṃhitā*, 59 ff.

359. Hacker, *Prahlāda*, II, p. 176 f.

360. *BrahmavP.*, *KKh.* 47, 50 ff.; see Zimmer, *Myths and symbols*, pp. 3 ff.; compare also such anthologies as Ranade, *Au-delà des marches.*

361. For the interpretation of similes occurring in the Bhagavadgītā see also J. M. Nallaswami Pillai, *Studies in Śaiva Siddhānta*, Madras, 1911, pp. 159 ff.

362. Mention may be made of the *Jñāneśvarī* (Bhāvārthadīpikā) by the Marāthi saint Jñāneśvara who lived towards the end of the XIIIth century (translated by V. G. Pradhan, edited by H. M. Lambert, London, 1967). This 'poem' written in a form of rhythmic prose is mainly based on the Bhagavadgītā, but purāṇas have supplied the author with a wealth of additive material with which to elaborate and illustrate his teachings, the whole work comprising roughly nine thousand stanzas.

363. *Devī-Gītā*, 9, 10. This *gītā* constitutes the chapters 31–40 of book 7 of the *Devībhāgavata-Purāṇa*. For other particulars concerning these works see U.Ch. Bhattacharjee, 'Gītā literature and its relation with Brahma-vidyā', *Indian Hist. Quarterly* II (1926) (Calcutta), pp. 537 ff.; 761 ff.; H. von Glasenapp, *Über vier puranische Nachbildungen der Bhāgavadgītā*, *Festgabe R. von Garbe*, Erlangen, 1927, pp. 139 ff.; P. E. Dumont, *L'Īśvaragītā, le chant de Śiva*, Baltimore-Paris, 1933; Parameswara Aiyar, *Imitations of the Bhagavadgītā*, *The cultural heritage of India*, published by The Ramakrishna mission, II, Calcutta, pp. 204 ff.; [2]1962,

p. 204; R. Hauschild, *Die Aṣṭāvakragītā*, Berlin Academy, 1967; K. Yoroi, *Ganeśagītā*, Thesis, Utrecht, 1968.

364. This *gītā* claims to form part of the Padma-Purāṇa; it is however not found in the Ānandāśrama edition.

365. The minor *gītās* of the Mahābhārata cannot, strictly speaking, be regarded as imitations.

366. For other instances see Bhattacharjee, op. cit., p. 763.

367. *Brahmagītā* (*SkandaP.*) 2, 37 Śiva is *vedasiddha-*.

368. *Brahmagītā* 4, 92–114; cf. *KenaU.* 3 and 4.

369. In *KenaU.* the name given to that wonderful female being is Umā Haimavatī, in later times well-known names or epithets of Śiva's spouse.

370. Cases of adoption are generally speaking far from wanting. Thus such an unmistakable reference to Rudra-Śiva as *Śvetāśvatara-Upaniṣad* 4, 10 'One should know that nature is *māyā*, and that the Great Lord is the owner of *māyā*' is in Viṣṇuite circles taken to refer to Śrī, who is the Śakti, Nature, and the cause of the attachment to the affliction caused by *māyā* and hence of the daily round of earthly existence. Cf. *Kāśyapa-S.*, ch. 35. Introducing his account of the Tāraka battle, in which Śiva's son, Skanda, is the hero, the author of *Matsya-Purāṇa* a. 172 inserted a glorification of Viṣṇu to whom the gods resorted for aid (V. S. Agrawala, *Matsya Purāṇa*, Benares, 1963, p. 270).

371. Cēramāṉ Perumāḷ, *Ādi Ula* 7, see Jesudasan, op. cit., p. 93.

372. Bhaṭṭa-Nārāyaṇa, *Stava-cintāmaṇi*, ed. Mukunda Rāma, Srinagar 1918, 86 (... *tvayi karmaphalanyāsakṛtām aiśvaryam īśa yat* cf. BhG. 12, 11; 18, 12 etc.); see e.g. also ibid. 104 *jyotiṣām api taj jyotiḥ* (BhG. 13, 17).

373. Cf. e.g. also Budhasvāmin, *Bkśs.* 18, 104; 480.

374. Bh.S. Upadhyaya, *India in Kālidāsa*, Allahabad, 1947, p. 311.

375. Kāl., *Ragh.* 3, 49.

376. Kāl., *Ragh.* 3, 49.

377. Cf. especially Kāl., *Ragh.* 10, 18; 24; 44; cf. 15, 103.

378. Kāl., *Ragh.* 10, 84. I refer to Keith, *History of Sanskrit literature*, pp. 92 ff.; 98 ff.; the same, *Classical Sanskrit literature*, London-Calcutta, 1927, p. 45; A. Hillebrandt, *Kālidāsa*, Breslau, 1921, p. 146.

379. Compare Bhavabhūti, *Māl.* 1, 1 ff.; 5, 1 f.; *Mahāv.* 2, 9 f.; 2, 11; 6, 14 f. and *Māl.* 1, 5; *Mahāv.* 1, 1; *Utt.* 5, 27 f. I also refer to Todar Mall, *Mahāvīra-caritam*, p. XXIV f.

380. Translated by D. H. H. Ingalls, *Anthology* (see above, n. 106).

381. Thus Śrīharṣa, *Naiṣadhacarita* 21, 12.

382. Priyaranjan Sen, *The story of Chandidas*, Calcutta, 1963, p. 16.

383. *KālikāP.* 5, 11 ff., translated by H. Zimmer, *The king and the corpse*, pp. 264 ff.

384. It may be true that the Indian trinity never played a prominent part in the convictions of the masses, poets often availed themselves of this doctrine in order to compose well-balanced tripartite expositions or illustrations of an idea. 'The rising of the sun ... is warmly praised (that is influenced by means of a eulogy) by Śiva because he is, as it were, afraid lest Sūrya should obscure the splendour of the moon on his head; by Brahmā, who is comfortably seated in the hollow of a newly-opened lotus; and by Kṛṣṇa-Viṣṇu, who, as it were, fears the humiliation of his own body, which is black as darkness' (Mayūra, *Sūryaśataka*, 16), or with an exhibition of artificiality (*cakrī cakrārapaṅktiṃ harir api ca harīn dhūrjaṭir dhūrdhvajāntān ... stauti*) 'Viṣṇu praises the row of wheel-spokes (of the Sun's chariot), Indra the horses, Śiva the ends of the flags on the yoke' (ibid., 71); see also ibid. 91 ff.

INDEX

Narmadā 113
Nāthamuni 77
navel, birth from 49; *see* ὀμφαλός
negated nouns as names for Viṣṇu 16; *see* Aghora 43
Nīlakaṇṭha 14
nīrājana 83
Nirṛti 36
Niṣkala 48, 78–86
nityotsava 83
nyagrodha 112
nyāsa 66, 73, 79–86, (esp. 82)

ojas 56
Oṃ 67, 71 f.
ὀμφαλός 6, 30, 51
(the) One becoming plurality 30, 34; *see* vyūhas (esp. 50, 57), Niṣkala, Sakala
(the) One God 30, 34
oneness with higher power/God 67–8, 85, 88, 108, 119; *see* aṃśa
opposition of Viṣṇu and Śiva 122 f.
order, religious 64, 67
outsider Rudra (Śiva) 10, 13, 87, 133, 135

padam 8
pairs, *see* dvandvam
palāśa 113
pañca brahmāṇi 47
Pañcabrahmas 48
pañcagavya 83 f.; *see* dung
Pāñcarātram, Pāñcarātrins 26, 49 ff., 55–61, 65 f., 76 f., 81, 93 ff., 98; *see* Sātvata-religion
pañcasaṃskāra 65
Pañcaśikha 49
pañcavaktra 35, 37, 41, 42–8, 73; *see* five
pañcavīras 51
paṅkti 46
Para-Brahman 55, 57, 59
parallelism in sentence structure 116
parallelism macrocosmos/microcosmos 46; *see* correlation
paramapadam, *see* Highest place
Paramātman 14, 59, 79, 95
Parameśvara 41, 108, 115
Pāraskara 39
Parjanya 11, 35
pārṣada 82
Pārvatī 91, 98, 108, 114, 117, 122; *see* Umā-Pārvatī
Pāśupata 13, 92 ff., 97, 106
Paśupati 10, 12, 14, 17, 38 ff., 41
paśutva 65
Patañjali 101
personal god 28, 34, 108
Pervader, pervasiveness 5, 9 f., 15, 23, 31; *see* 52, 57, 76
phallic aspect 13 f., 113; *see* liṅga
physical appearance of Rudra, Siva, Viṣṇu 3, 123
pināka 15
pipal, *see* aśvattha
Pitaraḥ 36
pity of God 117
plants 111 ff.
popular religion 62–4 (versus Skt. tradition), 67, 116 ff.
prabhu 35
pradakṣiṇa 38, 74, 80, 83
pradhāna 58
Pradyumna 49, 51 ff., 54, 56, 58 f., 82, 91, 108
Prahlāda 104–7, 136, 139
Prajāpati 11, 19 f., 28 ff., 35, 38, 40 f., 43 f., 46, 50 f., 53, 56, 59 f., 73, 102
Prājāpatya-marriage 130
prakṛti 41, 47, 49, 53, 57 f., 60, 99, 103
praṇāma 83
prāṇapratiṣṭhā 69
prāṇas 47; *see* breath
prāṇāyāma 70, 73
praṇidhi 79
prasāda 21, 48, 55, 65, 88, 119, 129
prasāda = food offered to Viṣṇu 74; *see* 68, 80 f., naivedya
pratiṣṭhā 9, 18
Pravargya 10
pūjā 23, 111; *see* temple ritual
puṇḍra 65 f., 71, 71–2, 109
purāṇas *passim*; *see* relations